T0133776

Voice Technology in Healthcare

Leveraging Voice to Enhance Patient and Provider Experiences

Voice Technology in Healthcare

Leveraging Voice to Enhance Patient and Provider Experiences

David Metcalf, PhD
Teri Fisher, MSc, MD
Sandhya Pruthi, MD
Harry P. Pappas

CRC Press
Taylor & Francis Group
Boca Raton London New York

CRC Press is an imprint of the
Taylor & Francis Group, an **informa** business
A PRODUCTIVITY PRESS BOOK

CRC Press
Taylor & Francis Group
6000 Broken Sound Parkway NW, Suite 300
Boca Raton, FL 33487-2742

Printed on acid-free paper

International Standard Book Number-13: 978-0-367-40386-7 (Hardback)

Visit the Taylor & Francis Web site at
http://www.taylorandfrancis.com

and the CRC Press Web site at
http://www.crcpress.com

About the Authors

David Metcalf, Ph D

David Metcalf has more than 20 years of experience in the design and research of Web-based and mobile technologies converging to enable learning and health care. Dr. Metcalf is Director of the Mixed Emerging Technology Integration Lab (METIL) at UCF's Institute for Simulation and Training. The team has built mHealth solutions, simulations, games, eLearning, mobile and enterprise IT systems for Google, J&J, the Veterans Administration, U.S. military, and the UCF College of Medicine among others. Recent projects include Lake Nona's Intelligent Home prototype and a Blockchain and Quantum Computing Simulator. Dr. Metcalf encourages spin-offs from the lab as part of the innovation process and has launched Moving Knowledge and several other for-profit and nonprofit ventures as examples. In addition to research and commercial investments, he supports social entrepreneurship in education and health. Dr. Metcalf continues to bridge the gap between corporate learning and simulation techniques and nonprofit and social entrepreneurship. Simulation, mobilization, mobile patient records and medical decision support systems, visualization systems, scalability models, secure mobile data communications, gaming, innovation management, and operational excellence are his current research topics. Dr. Metcalf frequently presents at industry and research events shaping business strategy and use of technology to improve learning, health, and human performance. He is the coeditor and author of Blockchain Enabled Applications (2017) (With Dhillon and Hooper), Connected Health (2017), HIMSS mHealth Innovation (2014) and the HIMSS Books bestseller mHealth: From Smartphones to Smart Systems (2012).

Teri Fisher, MSc, MD

Dr. Teri Fisher is a Sport & Exercise Physician and Clinical Assistant Professor in the Faculty of Medicine at the University of British Columbia (UBC) in Vancouver, Canada. He is an experienced TEDx and keynote speaker, educator, consultant, podcaster, and briefcaster who integrates his passions for medicine, education, voice technology, artificial intelligence, and e-health innovation. Dr. Fisher is the founder and host of "Voice First Health", the industry-leading website and podcast that highlights the rapidly expanding intersection of healthcare and voice-first technologies. Voice First Health also produces the leading educational health-related catalog of flash briefings. Dr. Fisher is also the founder of Alexa in Canada, the leading Amazon Alexa resource for Canadians, and Briefcast.FM, the premier flash briefing network. He is the host of the "Alexa in Canada" Podcast and the "Voice in Canada" Flash Briefing, the #1 rated Amazon Alexa Flash Briefing and News Skill in Canada. Through all of his shows, he helps to facilitate voice-first technology literacy and speaks on how artificial intelligence and voice-first technology are revolutionizing our lives. Dr. Fisher holds a Bachelor of Science degree from McGill University, and Bachelor of Education, Master of Science, and Medical Doctor degrees from UBC. When he's not conversing with his smart speakers, he can be found trying to keep up with his active wife and coaching his 2 children on the ice rink or baseball diamond.

Sandhya Pruthi, MD

Sandhya Pruthi, M.D., is a Professor of Medicine and a consultant in the Division of General Internal Medicine and Breast Clinic in the Department of Internal Medicine at Mayo Clinic in Rochester, Minnesota. She joined the staff of Mayo Clinic in 1994. She has worked in Global Business Solutions at Mayo Clinic for 15 years progressing in leadership responsibilities. She originally was a medical reviewer of health content and later assumed responsibilities as Chief Medical Editor. Dr. Pruthi assumed the role of Associate Medical Director for the Content Management and Delivery Ecosystem.

Dr. Pruthi earned the B.S. from the Faculty of Science at the University of Manitoba, in conjunction with her research at the Health Science Centre. She earned her M.D. at the University of Manitoba and subsequently completed a rotating internship at the University of Manitoba and a residency in family medicine at Mayo Clinic.

In her role as Associate Medical Director for the Content Management and Delivery Ecosystem Dr. Pruthi is responsible for providing clinical perspective and guidance to the development, implementation and promotion of health and wellness content products and services. Dr. Pruthi works with the vice chair of Content Management and Delivery to develop and implement strategy and tactics to deliver value to Mayo Clinic.

She frequently participates at external conference speaking on behalf of activities and/or products related to Mayo Clinic's commercialization of content. Dr. Pruthi also partners with the Senior Director Health Information in management and oversight of nearly 60 medical editors who review health information to ensure that content is medically accurate, reflective of best-available evidence, compatible with a Mayo-wide interpretation of that evidence.

Dr. Pruthi's research interests include chemoprevention of breast and biomarkers that might be useful for predicting breast cancer risk. She is the principal investigator at Mayo Clinic for several nationwide breast cancer prevention trials jointly coordinated by Mayo Clinic Cancer Center. She is the chief medical editor of the Reader's Digest Women's Health Encyclopedia, and has authored numerous articles, book chapters, audio/video materials, abstracts and letters.

Dr. Pruthi is a fellow in the American Academy of Family Physicians and received the Mayo Quality Innovation Program Award, the Mayo Clinical Practice Innovation Award and a recipient of the Center for Innovation CoDE Innovation Award. Dr. Pruthi is deeply involved in teaching and mentoring activities and developing patient and consumer health information content. Dr. Pruthi is President of the National Consortium of Breast Centers and is a member of the American Academy of Family Physicians and Alliance for Clinical Trials in Oncology.

Harry P. Pappas

Pappas is the Founder & CEO of the Intelligent Health Association, the RFID in Healthcare Consortium along with the Voice in Healthcare Alliance and the "Alexa in healthcare Consortium". Harry is also the founder and CEO of many other entities.

Harry is a successful, High Tech. Serial entrepreneur in several industries but has a strong focus on the healthcare technology sector.

A technology geek from the age of 12 years old. Pappas is a self-employed, technology centric professional with HANDS ON expertise in technologies such as: Auto-ID, Biometrics, BLE, NFC, RFID, RTLS, Robotics, Sensors, Voice and Wireless technologies as they apply to the Healthcare eco-system.

Goal: to get the healthcare community to adopt new technology, software, apps, Voice and other forms of technology that can have a dramatic impact on improving patient outcomes, patient care and patient safety while driving down the cost of Healthcare for all citizens.

Mantra: "Help Others", Do "SOCIAL GOOD" during your lifetime.

About the Technical Contributors

Art Director/ Production Editor:

Michael Eakins is the Creative Lead of the Mixed Emerging Technology Integration Lab (METIL) at the Institute for Simulation & Training and has 10+ years of production experience for simulation, training, and gaming. He received his M.F.A. in Digital Media at the University of Central Florida in 2017. Michael has produced a wide variety digital / print publications across multiple industries such as education, industry, and academia.

About the Contributing Authors

Ilana Meir, MS

Voice Design Coach, CareerFoundry

Ilana Shalowitz Meir is a Voice User Interface Designer specializing in health conversations. She has spoken extensively on the application of VUI design principles, including delivering the keynote address for the Voice of Healthcare Summit. For her contributions to the healthcare design field and voice community, Speech Technology magazine named her a "Speech Technology Luminary".

Audrey Arbeeny

Audiobrain

Owner and Emmy Award-Winning CEO/Executive Producer for Audiobrain, a globally recognized sonic branding boutique dedicated to the intentional development of music and sound to promote health and wellness. Audrey oversees Audiobrain's ongoing research in areas of psychoacoustics and biomusicology, and has created many sonic branding initiatives and research in the health and wellness industry. With over 25 years of experience, she is recognized as a pioneer in sonic branding. Audrey is currently in the process of developing a research study focusing on the positive effects of sound on patient care in their home environments via smart devices and emerging technologies.

Nathan Treloar

Orbita.ai

Nathan Treloar is President and Co-Founder of Orbita.ai, a provider of conversational AI technologies and services for healthcare organizations. He has over 25 years of experience delivering innovative products and business solutions at HBOC (now McKesson), FAST, Microsoft, RAMP, and, most recently, Ektron. Mr. Treloar is a respected expert and speaker on voice applications in healthcare, as well as on applications of search, text and data mining, and knowledge management technologies, and has advised hundreds of the world's largest companies and government agencies.

Stuart R. Patterson, BA, MBA

LifePod Solutions, Inc.

Stu is the cofounder and CEO of LifePod Solutions, a pioneer in the provision of proactive, voice-first, virtual caregiving services. He has led high-growth ventures in a variety of markets including: voice/virtual assistants, AI-based speech recognition/synthesis and NLU, mobile and online apps and services, identity management, clean-tech and digital healthcare solutions. He was recognized as one of the Top Ten Leaders in Speech from 2000 to 2003 and a World Economic Forum Technology Pioneer in 2003. He co-authored a patent for a Guided Personal Companion service originally designed to assist autistic children. Stu is also on the Foundation Board of the Dimock Center, a full-service community health center in Roxbury, MA.

David Kemp

Oaktree Products, Future Ear

David Kemp is the Manager of Business Development & Marketing at Oaktree Products and the Founder and Editor of Future Ear. In 2017, Dave launched his blog, FutureEar.co, where he writes a daily post on what's happening at the intersection of voice technology, wearables and hearing healthcare. He has been published in the Harvard Business Review, writes frequently for the prominent voice technology website, Voicebot, and has been featured on NPR's Marketplace. Dave travels the country giving talks to hearing care professionals on the technological evolution that the hearing aid is currently experiencing and the new use cases today's hearing aids are supporting.

Rupal Patel, PhD

VocaliD & Northeastern University

Rupal is the Founder and CEO of VocaliD, a voice technology company that provides AI-generated voice as a service. Rupal began her career as a speech clinician where she became fascinated with the potential of using speech technologies for assistive communication which then led to a doctorate in speech science. Her interdisciplinary research applies empirical evidence about speech motor control to develop novel communication technologies. She is currently on leave from Northeastern University where she is a tenured professor in the Khoury College of Computer Sciences and the Department of Communication Sciences and Disorders. Named one of The Top 11 Visionaries in Voice 2019 by Voicebot.ai and Fast Company's 100 Most Creative People in Business, Rupal has been featured on TED, NPR, and in major international news and technology publications.

Anne Weiler

Wellpepper

Anne Weiler is CEO and co-founder of Wellpepper, a clinically-validated and award-winning platform for interactive treatment plans that uses mobile, web, and voice interactions to improve patient outcomes and deliver over 72% patient engagement. Wellpepper is the winner of the Alexa Diabetes Challenge, to use voice skills to improve experiences for people with Type 2 diabetes. Prior to Wellpepper, Anne held global product management roles at Microsoft, in new product development and emerging markets.

Devin Nadar

Boston Children's Hospital

Devin works at the Innovation and Digital Health Accelerator at Boston Children's Hospital and focuses on identifying innovative ways that start-ups and established industry leaders can work with Boston Children's Hospital to solve clinical pain points and accelerate the adoption of their products and services in pediatrics. She cultivates partnerships that align with the strategic goals of the hospital and leverages those relationships to thoughtfully introduce new technologies to the hospital. In the past, Devin worked at athenaHealth, where she worked on product development and implemented athenaHealth's EMR and billing software in specialty clinics and large hospital systems. She also taught English to elementary students in northern France and coordinated a study abroad program in the French Alps for Tufts University. Devin received her B.A. in Economics and French from the Colorado College.

Robin Christopherson, MBE, MA Cantab

AbilityNet

Honoured to be awarded an MBE in the 2017 new year's honours list for his services to digital inclusion, Robin was also recently named in the 2019 list of the 'World's 100 Most Influential People in Digital Government' (compiled by APolitical with nominations from bodies including the UN, Harvard University and global NGOs). In 2016, he also won the Special Award at the UK 'Tech4Good' Awards in similar recognition of his services as a digital inclusion evangelist spanning two decades (previous winners include Professor Stephen Hawking). With tech in his veins, Robin has been a long user of voice-first technology - from screen reading software (Robin is blind) to voice recognition (from the very earliest days of Dragon Dictate) - and more recently a prolific podcaster; co-hosting the RNIB weekly 'Tech Talk' podcast and the daily Echo skill demo show 'Dot to Dot' (now with well over 1000 episodes).

Bruce Wallace, PhD

AGEWELL NIH SAM3 Sensors and Analytics for Monitoring Mobility and Memory, Bruyere Research Institute, Carleton University

Dr. Wallace is currently the Executive Director of the AGE-WELL National Innovation Hub on Sensors and Analytics for Monitoring Mobility and Memory (AW-NIH:SAM3); Adjunct Research Professor and Contract Instructor within the Systems and Computer Engineering Department, Carleton University and an Affiliated Researcher with the Bruyère Research

Institute. His research is focused on techniques for passive assessment of well-being for older adults that are facing cognitive and physical declines associated with illness or aging and includes extensive collaborations with industry, health sciences and medical researchers to bridge the gap between clinical/medical understanding and commercialization.

Frank Knoefel, MD

Bruyère Memory Program, Bruyère Continuing Care, Bruyère Research Institute; Faculty of Medicine, University of Ottawa

Dr. Knoefel is a Physician at the Bruyère Memory Program in Ottawa, Canada and Senior Investigator at the Bruyère Research Institute. He holds appointments in the Department of Family Medicine, University of Ottawa (Associate Professor) and Systems and Computer Engineering, Carleton University (Adjunct Research Professor). His clinical expertise is in how cognitive changes affect activities of daily living, including driving, and his research is focused on the use of technology to facilitate aging in place.

Timon LeDain

Macadamian

As Director of Macadamian's growing business in connected health and the Internet of Things (IoT), Timon is responsible for Macadamian's IP strategy, partnerships, and emerging technology development initiatives, his areas of focus include healthcare, voice experiences, and consumer products.

Steve Szoczei

Macadamian

With over 20 years of experience in visual, interaction, and product design, Steve has a wide perspective on creating meaningful experiences. As a Principal Designer, he has designed web-based, mobile, and desktop software solutions, leading the design from conception through to implementation and delivery. With a background in industrial design, Steve has always been focused on end-users needs - functionality, usability, and aesthetics - in the design of any given experience.

Geoff Parker

Macadamian

Geoff has over 20 years of experience in the software development industry and has worked in a variety of fields including medical devices, health information systems, enterprise integration, scientific modeling, speech recognition, cloud, and cluster computing. He thrives on working with clients to understand their business, identify requirements, and deliver robust, secure, creative solutions that address the regulatory requirements of today's healthcare market.

Ed Sarsfeld

Macadamian

A UX Architect with over 20 years of experience in the IT industry, Ed is a leading contributor to Macadamian's Innovation Lab's voice UX efforts. He has worked closely with a wide range of clients on multiple software platforms spanning industries from aviation to healthcare. Through his acuity of information architecture, user-centered design principles, interaction design, conversational interfaces, and visual design, he has developed client and user solutions focused directly on meeting and exceeding their expectations and goals.

Lee Engfer

Mayo Clinic

As a senior editor and content strategist, Lee has managed the development of health content for voice experiences, mobile apps, websites, wellness programs, books and newsletters. She's played a lead role in creating voice-first content, including the Mayo Clinic First Aid skill. She has a passion for meeting people's needs for trusted health information throughout their health journey.

Joyce A. Even, MBA

Mayo Clinic.

Joyce Even is a health care executive with 30+ years of in-depth understanding of healthcare management as well as content creation, management, and delivery to educate and activate individuals to effectively manage their health at any stage of life, improve outcomes, and reduce costs. She is responsible for extending Mayo Clinic's health and wellness knowledge globally via multiple formats, languages, and delivery channels, which includes innovation in voice and chat ready content.

Paula Marlow Limbeck, MA

Mayo Clinic

Paula Marlow Limbeck is a versatile content strategist and editor with 20+ years of experience in developing health content for diverse audiences and modalities. With a background in behavioral sciences, she delights in creating content that engages users and prompts health behavior change. Paula leads a staff of exceptional strategists who envision and deliver on new content initiatives in voice, video, interactive care, mobile, video and print (and whatever comes next).

Jay Maxwell

Mayo Clinic

Jay Maxwell oversees content development for Mayo Clinic's global business solutions. Jay has three decades of publishing experience in web, mobile, print, voice and broadcast channels. He has led large and diverse teams in both for-profit and nonprofit organizations. As a journalist, Jay has served on a state chapter of the Society of Professional Journalists (SPJ) and has been a recipient of SPJ's Sigma Delta Chi Award.

Jennifer Warner, MA

Mayo Clinic

Jennifer Warner is an active contributor to emerging best practices for voice-first and omnichannel content strategy and product development. At Mayo Clinic, she helped create the first comprehensive voice-enabled health information library and is responsible for advancing new voice applications for clinicians, patients and consumers. Her 25+ years of creating and delivering compelling, actionable health content also includes extensive experience in digital, print and television media for WebMD, CBSHealthWatch, ABC News, EverydayHealth.com, HealthAdvisor.com and others.

Matthew P M Cybulsky MA, MBA, MSHA, PhD

IONIA Healthcare Consulting, The Voice of Healthcare Podcast

Matt arms organizational teams with immersive consultative support addressing strategic, operational, and innovative delivery initiatives supported by behavioral science, lean management approaches, and technology applications including VoiceFirst. He's partnered with many organizations achieving positive outcomes and lasting impacts.

Heather Deixler, M. Phil., J.D.

Latham & Watkins LLP

Heather Deixler is counsel in the San Francisco office of Latham & Watkins LLP, where she counsels public and private companies operating in the healthcare and life sciences industries on transactional and regulatory matters. Ms. Deixler is a Certified Information Privacy Professional (CIPP/US and CIPP/E) with a particular focus on health information privacy and security, including compliance with the Health Insurance Portability and Accountability Act of 1996 (HIPAA), the Health Information Technology for Economic and Clinical Health Act of 2009 (HITECH), and federal and state privacy and information security laws. She works with clients to develop and implement compliance programs and respond to security breaches, advises on regulatory compliance matters related to healthcare privacy and security including online privacy policies and terms of service, and counsels on such issues in healthcare transactions.

Bianca Rose Phillips, LLB, BComm, GradDipLP, LLM, Scholarly Academic

Swinburne University of Technology, Australia

Bianca is a lawyer and officer of the Supreme Court of Victoria. Bianca lectures in law and conducts medical law research. Her current work investigates law making processes in digital health.

Harjinder Sandhu, PhD

York University, MedRemote, Nuance Healthcare, Twistle, SayKara

Dr. Sandhu has 20 years' experience in speech and machine learning in healthcare, and is the former VP and chief technologist of Nuance Healthcare R&D. He started his career as a professor of Computer Science, taught at York University for a number of years, co-founded a startup that was doing speech recognition for dictations and sold it to Nuance. He also co-founded a startup that is focused on patient engagement.

Yaa Kumah-Crystal, MD, MPH

Vanderbilt University Medical Center

Dr. Yaa Kumah-Crystal is an Assistant Professor of Biomedical Informatics and Pediatric Endocrinology at Vanderbilt University Medical Center. Dr. Kumah-Crystal's research focuses on studying communication and documentation in healthcare and developing strategies to improve workflow and patient care delivery. Dr. Kumah-Crystal works in the Innovations Portfolio at Vanderbilt HealthIT on the development of Voice Assistant Technology to improve the usability of the EHR through Natural language communication. She is the project lead for the Vanderbilt EHR Voice Assistant (V-EVA) initiative to incorporate voice user interfaces into the EHR provider workflow.

Dan Albert, MS

Vanderbilt University Medical Center

Dan helps lead the Product Development team in Vanderbilt University Medical Center's HealthIT group. Dan's team provides informatics solutions for Vanderbilt including clinical decision support and innovation projects. Dan's team is building a voice assistant to improve clinician interaction with EHR systems.

Neel C. Desai, BS, MD

St. Elizabeth Physicians & MedFlashGo, The Happy Doc

Neel Desai is a board certified family physician in northern Kentucky where he teaches first and second year medical students from the University of Cincinnati and the University of Kentucky. He is an active contributor to The Happy Doc Podcast, a podcast dedicated to physician burnout prevention. He also advocates for the Osteogenesis Imperfecta (OI) community, as OI affects his son Ethan. He enjoys spending most of his free time with his wife Debbie, Ethan, his two dogs, Daisy and Luna, and attempting to play guitar.

Taylor Brana DO

The Happy Doc Podcast, MedFlashGo, Dental Flash Go, MCAT Flash Go

Dr. Taylor Brana is a physician, entrepreneur and developer of voice-first education platforms, including MedFlashGo. As the creator of The Happy Doc Podcast, Taylor envisions a world where all individuals can be fulfilled and pursue their passions. He understands developing this vision relies on utilizing voice technology to help educate society as efficiently and as effectively as possible.

Michelle Wan

Elastic Path Software

Michelle Wan is a software developer at Elastic Path Software. During her time as a student at the British Columbia Institute of Technology, she was fascinated by voice technology and wanted to learn how to develop Alexa skills. She received the BCIT Outstanding Student Leadership Award for her work developing a Lab Simulation skill for nursing students. In her spare time, she enjoys tinkering and fixing old electronics laying around at home.

Ed Chung, MD

BioBright

Dr. Chung is Chief Medical Officer at BioBright, a Boston startup working on biomedical data analytics and voice as both a novel data source and interactive control modality. His career path has taken him through community hospitals, quaternary care medical centers, and technology firms as a clinical informaticist and physician leader. In addition to leading BioBright's healthcare-related efforts, he continues to care for patients as a pediatric hospitalist.

Jim Schwoebel

NeuroLex

Jim Schwoebel is founding CEO of NeuroLex Labs, a company that is making voice computing accessible to everyone. NeuroLex's first product, SurveyLex, allows users to create, design, and deploy voice surveys as URL links in less than a minute. Jim is also the author of Introduction to Voice Computing in Python, a book with 200+ starter scripts on GitHub to train the next-generation of voice computing experts.

Suraj Kapa, MD

Mayo Clinic College of Medicine

Suraj Kapa, M.D., is a consultant in the Division of Heart Rhythm Services and specializes in cardiac electrophysiology. Dr. Kapa also serves as director of the Virtual Reality innovations group and does extensive research in artificial intelligence and its applications to medicine. He also dedicates a lot of time in the large animal translational lab to develop new catheter, sensing and mapping technologies.

Acknowledgments

David Metcalf

I would like to thank Katy, Adam and Andrew for their patience during the extended hours and effort while putting the book together. and colleagues and students at UCF and through the NSF I-Corps program that identified the power of voice technology years ago and shared their knowledge and future strategies that inspired us to pursue this area of research early. Thank you to my coauthors and our outside collaborators and contributors, and of course to God for the wisdom, ability and grit to bring this effort to life.

Teri Fisher

I want to thank my wife, Kim, for her love and all of her encouragement and support, not just with this book, but with all of my crazy ideas. I want to thank both of my children for keeping me on my toes and always making me laugh. Thank you to the contributors of this book, without whom this project would not have been possible. A big thank you to my co-authors, David, Harry, and Sandhya, for their friendship as well as their tireless work and dedication throughout this entire process. Thank you to all of my podcast guests for their invaluable insights from whom I have learned so much. Finally, a heartfelt thank you to you, the reader, the listener, the member of the #VoiceFirstHealth Community, for your ongoing interest, ideas, questions, and discussions to help make the conversation about voice technology and healthcare louder than ever before.

Sandhya Pruthi

I want to thank my husband, Rajiv, and my sons, Shiv and Neel, for their unconditional support and inspiration to pursue my passion and dedication to healthcare education. A special thank you to my amazing coauthors, David, Teri and Harry for their patience, energy and friendship. I sincerely appreciate the invaluable insights and expertise of all of our contributors and together we have brought to fruition this incredible resource on voice first technology to enhance the patient and provider healthcare experience.

Harry P. Pappas

I wish to thank my dear wife and girlfriend of many years, Linda who has unstintingly, supported, and encouraged me with my many business interests, many careers, and adventures. I also thank my son, Mark and my daughter, Maria for their patience with me.

About This Book

Welcome to Voice Technology in Healthcare. On behalf of the editors, authors, and chapter contributors, we hope that you enjoy this unique book that combines some of the best of voice technology thought leadership, trends analysis, and evidence-based case studies. We have endeavoured to combine the best of book publishing, ebooks and our unique audio format. We hope that as you experience these versions of the book you will enjoy the healthy balance of evidence-based cases and thought pieces, along with the personal, warm and very human experience of hearing the voices of top experts in the world that appeared on the Voice First Health podcast and seeing transcripts of these conversations come to life. We have tried to strike a balance between elements of how voice technology is changing the experience inside the home, inside the clinic, and inside of the future of diagnostics and evidence-based medicine. All around us every day, voice technology is changing the way we interact with our devices, with our systems, and with other people. The long history of exploration of orality and the way that it can engage the human experience provides substantial potential as this technology grows and is used in unique ways. We hope that you enjoy this publication and our attempt to bring you the best curation of chapters that highlight topics as diverse as voice technology and genomics, voice technology and artificial intelligence, voice technology and education in healthcare, as well as an overview of the fundamentals of voice technology for improved health and well-being outcomes. We cap off the book with a chapter that serves as a roundtable discussion and lightning rod for the trends identified inside this unique book. We invite you to join the conversation and continue the exploration of voice technology by sharing with us some of your successes and opportunities through HIMSS resources, at VoiceFirstHealth.com, and on social media using the hashtag #VoiceFirstHealth. Additional bonus content includes audio tracks of the transcripts included in the book so you can literally hear the voice of our experts and experience some of the voice content first hand. Also watch for the Alexa skill version of the interactive text and the audio search interface that is a companion to the print and ebook version of the book. We hope that you enjoy this unique book experience that honors the balance between literacy and orality to advance voice technology in healthcare.

Thank you,

David Metcalf

Table of Contents

Section 1

Introduction to Voice Technology

Chapter 1:

The Opportunity for Voice in Healthcare

Teri Fisher, MSc, MD

Editor's Note

In this introductory Chapter, world expert and top podcaster, Dr Teri Fisher leads us through a brief history of voice and how it relates to health. He also sets the premise for a theme pre-sent throughout the book — Voice as the next operating system - with compelling evidence and examples from the patient, provider and future technology perspectives. He also un-packs the clever acronym of V-O-I-C-E: Versatile, Omnipresent, Innate, Contextual, Efficient - concepts that pervade the evidence-based cases presented throughout the book.

Our First Sounds

Thump, thump. A heart beat. The first sounds that we hear.

Our mother's voice. The first sounds that we identify.

In utero, we are enveloped in a cacophony of sounds emanating from our mother: heartbeats and breaths, coughs and sneezes, laughs and cries, and… her voice.

As we continue to develop, the voice of our mother becomes recognizable to each of us. Before we are consciously aware of what is happening, we develop a bond with our mother. Research shows that infants are able to identify the sound and characteristics of their mother's voice even before being born (1). More recent research shows that infants can even perceive certain characteristics of their native language while still in utero (2). We are exposed to - and begin to recognize - our 'mother tongue' even before we are born.

When we enter the world, we take our first breath and use that air and newly initiated vocal cords to communicate with our voices. There is no formal teaching, no training, no learning during these first few seconds. Using our voices - crying - is innate and instinctive, and it communicates a very critical message: "I am here." With great excitement and relief, our mothers embrace our cries, our voices, and begin speaking to us. The ability to hear sounds and use our voices to communicate with one another is deep-seated and a large part of what makes us human beings.

Our ability to communicate through the spoken word, and the relationship to technology and healthcare, is the basis for this entire book. However, before we can truly understand the implications for healthcare, we must first understand what voice technology is and why we are on the precipice of an entirely new epoch of technology.

Voice First

Since the industrial revolution, technology has evolved and our methods of interacting and communicating with technology have transformed as well. If we examine the last 40 years we can identify major disruptions in the fundamental ways computers operate and the implications this has in the context of voice technology.

I can recall coming home from school in the mid-1980's and being greeted by my excited parents. "We bought this new machine," they said. "It's the latest technology and everyone is talking about it!" I was extremely intrigued and immediately ran into our home office. There, sitting on the desk, was a square, monochrome screen perched on top of a rectangular module with a coiled cord attached to a keyboard. It was our very first personal computer. I can remember sitting down at the desk, inserting a 5 1/4 inch floppy disc, turning on the computer, and waiting with great anticipation for MS-DOS (Microsoft Disc Operating System) to load. I was eventually greeted with a text prompt and I started typing some primitive commands on the keyboard. I was fascinated by the technology and I spent many hours typing various commands and learning the skills to navigate the operating system.

Approximately 10 years later Microsoft introduced their graphical operating system, Microsoft Windows. Windows, combined with the use of a mouse to control the operating system, changed the way we interacted with computers. We now had a graphical user interface and we could use the mouse to click, drag, and drop things across a screen. You may remember one of the earliest programs that took advantage of this input method was a primitive "paint" application. I can recall opening the program and using the mouse to draw a variety of simple illustrations. It was incredible.

In the late 2000's, there was another technological breakthrough that revolutionized the way we interact with computers. In an iconic presentation, the late Steve Jobs, then CEO of Apple, stood up and introduced the first iPhone to the world. This device put an incredibly powerful computer in the palm of our hands. This magical device was a huge leap in technology. We could now control our own personal computer using just our fingers to simply pinch, tap, zoom, and swipe - all on a piece of glass.

We have witnessed the evolution of some incredible technology over the years, but nothing like what we are about to see, or more specifically, hear. What has been the underlying theme amongst the devices mentioned so far? In the case of the personal computer with MS-DOS, we used a keyboard as an input device to communicate with the computer. In the second example with MS-Windows, we used a mouse to control the cursor on a screen. In the third iPhone example, we used our fingers to interact with a touch-sensitive piece of glass. In all of these scenarios, a specific hardware device was required in order for us to interface with technology (i.e. keyboard, mouse, and touchscreen). Furthermore, in all three cases, it was necessary for us to learn or be taught how to use the device. In other words, we had to adapt the way that we communicated with computers in order for the technology to understand us.

Now, for the first time in our history, and due to advances in computing power, artificial intelligence, and natural language processing and understanding, technology has caught up to our most natural and instinctual form of communication. We no longer have to adapt to the technology; the technology is adapting to us - to our voices. We can now simply speak to computers, and computers can understand and respond intelligently to what we are saying. This is a fundamental paradigm shift. Simply put, it is worth repeating: we no longer are adapting to computers; computers are adapting to us.

This transformative development is not going unnoticed, as all of the major technology companies are investing billions of dollars into developing smart speakers (or more precisely, smart microphones and speakers) that we simply talk to (e.g. Amazon, Apple, Google, Microsoft, Samsung, and others). We have now arrived at a pivotal time when the technology can listen and speak to us using our preferred method of communication - by using our voices first.

The "voice first" era is upon us. This term, coined by Brian Roemmele, refers to the fact that we as human beings, "are voice first before we are born" (3). Additionally, our way of communicating with technology will no longer be tied to a physical device. We will now primarily use our voices. We will speak to computers first, before typing or texting for a variety of reasons that will be explored below. Voice-first and voice-enabled technologies are leading the way as the next frontier in human-computer interfaces. While voice will be the primary method of communicating with computers, there will still be roles for keyboards and touch screens for specific use cases. Furthermore, while the computers will primarily speak to us there will also continue to be excellent applications for viewing graphical and video content. Our world is very quickly embracing the voice interface and our interactions are rapidly evolving to where each of us will use our voice first to talk to a computer.

Types of Communication

There is a compelling case for why a voice interface is the future of computing. Not only is voice the future person-computer interface, but it extends much further than that. In my opinion, voice is becoming the next operating system, the "vOS". Why is voice so compelling and why are we literally on the verge of a technology revolution? To answer this question, we must first examine the various types of communication that we use today. Depending on how one defines these types of communication, the most common classification system is comprised of 4 types: written, visual, nonverbal, and verbal.

Written

If you are reading the written version of this book, I am communicating my thoughts and ideas to you through the written word. (If you are listening to the audio version, I am using verbal communication, with more on that later on.) Whether it is this book, a magazine article, a blog, or a street sign (with words), this type of transmission of messages is through words and their meanings. To be able to receive this type of communication, the recipient must have an intact sense of sight (or touch, in the case of braille) and the ability to process language once the letters on the paper, screen, or other display are processed into words and sentences. In other words, the recipient must be focused on the written word using sight (or touch) in order to visualize the words and decode the message being sent.

Visual

While we as human beings are voice first, we are also extremely visual animals. Whether we are looking at a photograph, a map, or the latest social media graphic, we are constantly processing massive amounts of information through our sense of sight. It is often said that pictures are worth a thousand words and this is indeed very true. For example, to describe in words the precise directions to a landmark on a map would take much longer than it would for us to simply glance at the landmark on a chosen GPS application. Clearly, in order to be able to take in visual forms of communication, again one has to have a sense of sight and the cognitive ability to process what one is observing.

Nonverbal

If you were to look at me and notice that I was smiling, what message would that send to you? What if you noticed that I was frowning and perhaps even trying to hold back tears? How would you interpret what you were observing? Nonerbal communication is extremely powerful. Nonverbal communication includes body language such as facial expressions, posture, eye contact, and hand movements, for example. Again, you will notice that in order to interpret these noverbal signs, the sense of sight must be intact and the recipient must be looking in the direction of the message source.

Verbal

Verbal communication refers to the use of the spoken word. This could be from another person, an audio recording, or a phone call, for example. The types of words and the complexity of sentence structures also play a role in how we convey and interpret verbal communication. One critical difference between verbal communication and the 3 other types (written, visual, and nonverbal) is that in the case of verbal communication, one does not necessarily have to be using sight to obtain the meaning of the interaction or the communicated message. If one can hear and speak, one can communicate verbally. One does not have to be looking in the direction of the source or intended target of the information. As long as one is within earshot of the sound, one can understand the message. If one can use his/her voice, a dialog is possible. This is a critical difference: written, visual, and nonverbal communication require that one observes the source of the communication, while verbal communication is not subject to the same limitation and reliance on sight. Why is this important? Let us examine the implications this has on the use of voice and why this modality of communication is unlike any other.

Why is Voice the Next Operating System?

Voice technology is rooted in the ability to understand and convey messages using verbal communication. This is a fundamental difference in the evolution of technology that makes voice so compelling as the next operating system.

There are 5 main reasons that voice will be the next operating system and I have summarized these factors in the following framework using the acronym V-O-I-C-E:

V - versatile

O - omnipresent

I - innate

C - contextual

E - efficient

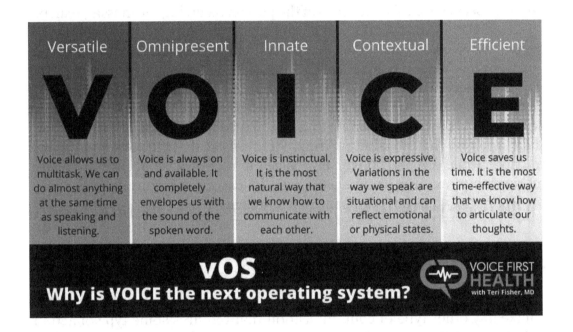

1. *Voice is Versatile*

Voice is the most versatile form of communication that we have at our disposal. With voice one can multitask, as a person's attention can be focused elsewhere and yet that person can still be speaking or be aware of what is being said. In contrast, with written communication (e.g. handwriting, typing, or texting) the process of physically recording words requires the use of multiple senses (i.e. sight and touch) and increased cognitive load. One must think about the words to say and then record those words using some type of device and the sense of touch. The intended recipient must then read (i.e. visually observe) the words in order to be aware of the message being portrayed.

Even interpreting body language (i.e. nonverbal communication) and sign language - while extremely effective for communicating thoughts and feelings - requires the receiver of the message to look at the person conveying those messages. By definition this requires the person to use sight to receive the message.

In the case of voice however, the receiver of the message does not have to be looking at the transmitter. The only requirement is that the person needs to be within earshot of the sound of the voice and possess an intact sense of hearing. Because of this, the focus of the person receiving the message can be on anything they want. One can truly multitask while speaking or listening to someone's voice. In fact, we can do just about anything while we are speaking and listening. We can hold verbal conversations with each other when we are doing a variety of activities, such as driving, cooking, or exercising. It is very difficult, or even dangerous, to attempt to do some of these activities while typing, clicking, tapping, or texting (i.e. written communication). In fact, there are laws that prohibit us from communicating with these nonverbal methods while driving; conversely, voice interactions are not only safe and efficient, but are also being encouraged by car manufacturers as they are incorporating voice assistants into their vehicles.

2. Voice is Omnipresent

Voice is always on and envelopes us with the sound of the spoken word. Unlike any other type of communication that requires some type of action to initiate a dialogue (e.g. type, text, etc), voice can be summoned with just a thought and the spoken word. This eliminates one layer of complexity when sharing thoughts and ideas. Consider even the mobile phone: you are required to lift your phone, make visual contact with it, and then do some type of maneuver to initiate the dialogue, whether that is tapping or swiping (unless you have summoned your virtual assistant by voice and in that case you are using verbal language). In the case of the written word, one clearly has to grasp a pen to begin capturing one's thoughts. In the case of typing, one has to open an app or program to begin constructing the message.

In the case of voice however, you simply speak or listen. Assuming that a microphone is somewhere in the vicinity, there is no other action required to simply start speaking one's ideas. Voice simply "works". Similarly, your ears are always "on" and any sound transmitted from a speaker can be heard. This type of communication is the most seamless and frictionless type of communication available to us at the present time. The sound of voice surrounds us. It is always available and ready to be used.

3. Voice is Innate

Voice is the most natural way that we know how to communicate. Recall the example that began this chapter. When babies are born the first thing they do is use their voices - they cry. Furthermore, even before they are born they learn their mother's voice. While there are certainly skills to learn when it comes to typing, texting, or even clicking, the ability to speak develops naturally (with some exceptions for speech challenges). Speaking to a computer requires little if any training at all. If one can talk, one can communicate with a voice-first device. We are very social members of the animal kingdom and computers are becoming participants in our social verbal interactions.

4. Voice is Contextual

While voice is innate, it is also extremely expressive. Whether you are sharing your most fond memories or describing your greatest nightmares, the emotion can be heard in your voice. The variability in a person's voice is immense: from whispering to shouting, talking to singing, each utterance out of a person's mouth carries so much more information than just the words that are spoken. Furthermore, we can naturally adjust the volume, pitch, frequency and other variables to the context and message we are conveying without consciously processing this information.

Not only does the voice reflect the context of the situation, voice also reflects the physical health of a person. When one becomes sick with laryngitis, one's voice changes - a change that is evident to those that hear the voice, not by sight but by listening with the ears. In fact, research has shown that vocal biomarkers, the characteristics of our voices beyond the words that are spoken, are a sign of our emotional states and biological processes. We are entering an era where voice is likely to become a key vital sign for healthcare providers - a vital sign that is non-invasive and can be interpreted in real time from a distance.

5. Voice is Efficient

Voice saves us time, and time is one of the most valuable commodities that we each possess. In our busy lives, anything that saves us time is critical. Consider the fact that the average typing speed is approximately 40 words per minute. Compare that to the average speaking speed of approximately 150 words per minute, and you have a mode of communication in voice that is three to four times faster than typing. Even as we grow and develop more advanced communication skills including reading, writing, typing, and texting among others, we continue to choose to use our voices as the most efficient way to communicate with each other. If given the opportunity to communicate via the method of your choice with someone standing next to you, what would you choose? Would you speak to the person or send an email or text? Why?

Rate of Adoption

Being versatile, omnipresent, innate, contextual, and efficient, voice is so compelling a method of interfacing with a computer that we are already seeing great consumer interest in this technology. Witness the rapid adoption of Amazon Alexa, Apple Siri, Google Assistant, Microsoft Cortana, Samsung Bixby and other voice assistants. In fact, voice assistants are being adopted at a rate faster than any other consumer technology in our history, including the mobile phone (4). This is creating a new paradigm of what is known as ambient computing (i.e. smart microphones and speakers in our environment) that is transforming our world as we know it to a world in which smart voice assistants are listening to us and are able to respond to us on an intelligent and personal level.

Our children are now growing up talking to computers before they know how to read, write, type or text. This is a phenomenon that we have never experienced before. In the past children would need to know how to interact with a keyboard, mouse, or touchscreen to communicate with a computer. In other words, these children had to learn a skill beyond speaking to have any type of meaningful interaction with a computer. Now, as soon as a toddler can put a few words together, he or she can talk to a computer.

At the other end of the age spectrum are the elderly who comprise one of the segments of the population that is adopting this technology at an extremely rapid rate. This is largely because there is essentially nothing new to learn. Again, as long as there is a microphone within the vicinity of the person, the person can simply speak and the device will respond. There is no hardware interface to learn. There is virtually no learning curve.

As a result, we are on the verge of something profound happening in our society. While voice first devices will eventually disrupt every sector in our world, we are already starting to witness a radical transformation in the way that we experience the entire healthcare journey. From the home to the hospital, from the ER to the OR, from the clinic to the ward, voice has applications in every aspect of medicine. Voice technology is about to revolutionize healthcare and it is precisely this fact that will be explored in greater depth throughout the remainder of this book.

The Healthcare Experience

Have you ever woken up and felt like something was off? Maybe you rolled over in bed and had a sore throat? Maybe a headache? Possibly you felt like you had been sweating all night and you soon realized that something was not right. Perhaps various thoughts started running through your head such as, "I'm going to have to call my work to let them know that I'm home in bed. I think I need to go see the doctor. I have to arrange childcare." After accomplishing these tasks, you proceed to drag yourself into your car, drive to the doctor, and wait in the waiting room while shivering. The physician eventually sees you, takes a history, examines you, and tells you that you need some antibiotics. You drag yourself back into your car, drive to the pharmacy and wait while the pharmacist gets your medication ready. You finally drive back home and climb back into bed. It can be a big ordeal, likely one that you would prefer not to have to deal with when you are feeling ill.

However, what if it did not have to be that way? What if you could get the personal care you needed without ever leaving the comfort of your own home? Due to voice first technology, I believe that we are about to witness the biggest technological shift since the introduction of the internet itself and the entire healthcare journey, not only in our homes but in all areas of healthcare, will be entirely transformed. In the near future, each of us will speak with our own personal live-in artificial intelligent (AI) healthcare teams that know our intimate medical details - chronic conditions, fitness levels, nutrition habits, medications, emotions, and much more.

Reconsider the previous scenario but this time imagine it taking place in the not-so-distant future. Perhaps it might go something like this:

You wake up and feel that something is off. You roll over in bed and become aware of your very painful throat. You realize you had been sweating all night and that something is not quite right. Before thoughts start racing through your head about how your day will be disrupted due to your illness, your voice assistant (VA) hears that you are up and says, "Good morning". You reply, "I don't feel so well," and you cough. Already, the assistant is doing some analysis of your voice and cough, and already it has an idea of what the diagnosis could be. Your voice assistant responds with, "I'm sorry to hear that. Would you like me to help?" You reply "Yes please," and your VA proceeds to ask you some pertinent medical questions: "Do you have a runny nose? Do you have a sore throat? Do you have a fever?" You answer the questions and the VA responds with "I think you might have strep throat. Would you like me to order a Strep test and have it delivered right now?" You gratefully say you would. The VA says "And while I'm at it, you obviously can't go into work today. Would you like me to make a phone call to work for you and let them know that you are sick at home today?" Within a few minutes a drone drops off a rapid Strep test at your house and you take the test. Your VA walks you through how to do it, analyses it (through bluetooth or similar connected technology), and confirms that you do indeed have Strep throat. The VA knows your medical history and that you are allergic to certain antibiotics and says, "Would you like me to have a prescription delivered to you in the next hour?" You answer affirmatively. The medication gets delivered, you take it, and the VA reminds you when each dose is due and then monitors your recovery, listening for any signs of possible complications or problems that would alert you to go see your doctor. You have just obtained your entire medical care, care that is efficient and personalized, from the comfort of your own home. This scenario is not that far off in the future and some elements of this scenario are already in place today.

How does this pivotal time in our history relate not only to healthcare at a personal level, but also at a health care systems level? As a Canadian and North American physician, I am incredibly proud of the quality of healthcare that we are able to provide to our population. We are very fortunate to have excellent training programs that produce compassionate and competent healthcare providers. However, as with any healthcare system, there certainly are challenges (financial, accessibility, and bureaucratic to name just a few). Attempts have been made to address these issues but despite these efforts, many of these challenges persist today. I believe that is about to change.

Healthcare is ripe for change, voice technology is poised to make that change, and I am extremely optimistic that with voice technology we can finally take unique and innovative action to completely redefine what healthcare looks like... and sounds like. So, what does that mean? To redefine healthcare using voice technology, we must first define what makes an effective healthcare system. There is a lot of debate about what makes the optimal health care system and the concept of "the right health care at the right time at the right place" is one leading framework for the solution. This is precisely where voice-first technology has the ability to completely disrupt and transform health care. Let's tackle each of these elements in turn.

The Right Health Care

To tackle the concept of "the right health care at the right time at the right place", we must first define "the right health care." One definition is that the right health care is the most cost-effective medical advice or intervention that can be obtained under the particular circumstances that results in improved health outcomes. That may mean seeing a doctor, being prompted to take one's medication, or seeing a therapist. Alternatively, it could mean having the appropriate post-op care plan or chronic disease plan in place to know what to do and when to do it. However, herein lies an inherent problem with the current North American medical system – how does a lay person know definitively what is, or even how to obtain, "the right care" without asking a knowledgeable person first?

Imagine however, if there was an artificial-intelligent (AI), voice-first personal assistant in your home - a "health assistant" that you could access anytime you wanted to, who could help find relevant health information and services, or connect you to certain health care professionals to obtain the right care? What if you could simply speak to your personal health assistant, one that knows who you are, what your medications and allergies are, what your chronic health conditions are, and who your personal health care providers are? What if your assistant could ask you a few questions about your current condition and then tell you how or where to obtain the right health care for your situation? Maybe it could provide the "right health care."

Perhaps the assistant could ask you questions about your current runny nose and listen to your cough in order to help you determine that you probably have a common cold and that the "right care" is to get into bed with some soup and get some rest (and not clog-up healthcare facilities). This could potentially eliminate the need for unnecessary visits to the doctor or emergency room.

Some safeguards would undoubtedly have to be in place to deal with emergencies and perhaps getting the right care is actually having the assistant automatically call 911. But just imagine if every person had a health assistant that truly helped the individual get the "right care" for their particular situation?

The Right Time

The "right time" to obtain care for a particular health care concern is also of utmost importance. If a relatively routine, non-urgent issue is treated as an emergency, this can tie up healthcare resources and be wasteful on the system. If an emergency situation is treated as routine, the consequences can be even more dire. The question arises then of how does the average lay person know when they should obtain medical care for a particular problem or concern? How could voice first technology help with this? Consider the personal voice assistant again. Based on your personal history and your particular health concern, the assistant could advise you to make an appointment with your family doctor for that day or the following week, or to go to the emergency department, or even directly connect you with emergency services. We would effectively have a triage "nurse" in every home that could determine the urgency of the situation and help to direct the health care resources of the population on an individual basis. Perhaps the AI assistant could then triage the appointment and schedule the appointment in a seamless and efficient manner. Imagine the value of such a device, keeping in mind we have not even touched on the fact that incredible amounts of data could be collected through this system in real time. This data could power research projects to give us insight into the health care systems and drive predictive and personalized artificial intelligent healthcare like never before. This data could then be used to further optimize our medical systems. While there are significant privacy issues around this, they will be discussed later on in this book in an entire chapter devoted to privacy and security.

The Right Place

It is not unusual for a patient to access medical care in a location that is not ideal for the particular problem. For example, a patient might end up in an emergency room, not because the situation is an emergency but because the person did not know the appropriate place to get timely care for the particular issue. Clearly, the emergency department is not "the right place" for a common cold. How could a voice-first assistant help in this case? First, as discussed previously, a personal voice first assistant could help to triage and then direct patients to the right place. If this practise were to become the standard of care, one would expect that appropriate medical problems would be directed towards the right places which would ultimately help to increase the efficiency of our medical systems.

Consider the elderly aging parent that wants to remain in their own home instead of moving to a care home. What is the right place for this person? Maybe if this citizen had the support of a personal AI voice-first health assistant who could provide guidance about when to take their medications and to make sure that they were eating a healthy diet, this senior could remain in their own home that much longer. In the eyes of the senior, home is certainly "the right place." The chapter on proactive voice technology will provide further discussion in this regard.

Another example is the patient who is unsure if they require vaccinations prior to going on a vacation. Where is the right place to obtain this advice and the vaccines – a doctor's office, a community health clinic, a travel clinic, or somewhere else? The patient could discuss this with their VA who could first confirm which, if any, vaccinations are due, suggest "the right place", and then book an appointment to obtain the vaccines in a timely manner.

The Voice First Healthcare Experience

Voice first technology will undoubtedly impact all aspects of health care. This includes benefits to the patients and the providers of our healthcare systems. There are already multiple use cases in existence today and below is a small sampling of ways healthcare has and will be impacted. These too will be covered in greater detail throughout the rest of the book.

The Patient Experience

Imagine you are in your kitchen and you are slicing a fresh carrot for a salad. Unfortunately, you slip and cut your finger. Often at this point, a person in this position would look for some first aid information. Clearly, this is more of a challenge when one is bleeding, especially when it comes to trying to flip through a first aid manual, find the right page, read the instructions, locate a first aid kit, and perform the first aid. However, imagine if you could just speak to a voice assistant and it could instruct you on what to do for your particular situation. There would be no need to go hunting for a first aid manual or trying to balance the booklet while attempting to carry out the First Aid procedures on yourself. Using voice first technology in the case of first aid is clearly more efficient and it is already in use today.

As another example, let us consider again the aging parent who wants to maintain their independence and continue to live at home, but is becoming forgetful and experiencing a sense of loneliness and isolation. One of the incredible benefits of voice technology is that it is seamless and requires essentially no learning whatsoever. What if the parent simply woke up in the morning, said "good morning," and the voice assistant then initiated the care. Perhaps the voice assistant would ask, "How did you sleep?" and then record that information for the family or health care provider. The voice assistant would then remind the person to take the appropriate medications. The voice assistant literally would be acting as a care aide, be a link to family members and health care providers, and be a source of companionship. Research has shown that having a VA device in the home lowers the sense of loneliness and isolation (5). Imagine if having this device could allow someone to remain in their home longer. This too is no longer fantasy - it is already happening today.

What about the management of chronic diseases such as diabetes, or the monitoring of post-operative care plans? While these are illnesses or situations that people experience 24 hours/day, people generally only see their doctors for a fraction of that time. Imagine instead if you had a device that was a surrogate for your doctor, "someone" who you could have constant communication with and helped to optimize your care. You could have your questions answered, get advice, obtain guidance on the management of your illness or injury, or even communicate with your healthcare team when necessary. Moreover, as you began to interact with these devices, the smart assistant would start to notice when things were not going right and when you, your family, or your caregiver needed to be notified. Imagine a device being proactive and telling you to obtain the appropriate care before you ran into serious problems.

Finally, what if the sound of our voices could actually provide a glimpse into our physical health? Could it be used as a diagnostic tool? Consider the analogy of digital photography: whenever one takes a digital photo, one also collects what is known as metadata - the data that is captured in addition to the actual photograph, such as the camera model, shutter speed, aperture setting, GPS location, and other data points. Similarly metadata, or vocal biomarkers, can be collected from our voices beyond the words that are uttered. When my son comes home from school and I ask him, "How was school?" he could respond exuberantly with "IT WAS GREAT!!". However, if asked the same question on a different day, he could respond hesitantly and in a subdued tone, "It... was... great..." While both responses are made up of exactly the same words, they have completely different meanings, based on the intonation and inferences made from the tone of voice. If you can describe the differences in the way these statements are said - and you can based on pitch, prosody, and other variables - then you can use artificial intelligence to identify patterns in a person's voice. This brings a whole new meaning to the phrase, "I can hear it in your voice." These smart assistants can identify changes in mood, watch out for depression, and detect cognitive decline such as Alzheimers and Parkinsons. One can obtain real-time emotional insights and one can even detect certain diseases. In fact, research has already shown a statistically significant correlation between the way someone speaks and the risk of coronary artery disease (6).

Currently, health care providers use parameters such as blood pressure, heart rate, respiratory rate, and temperature as key vital signs. I believe that our voices are going to be one of the most powerful vital signs that we have - a vital sign that is full of data, can be obtained from a distance, and is entirely non-invasive.

Consider also those living with disabilities or in group homes - how could voice assistants help with their daily lives? Could preventative health programs be administered through voice-first assistants in each home? What about guidance for physiotherapy or speech language pathology exercises? The possibilities in a voice-first word are endless and these scenarios are just the tip of the iceberg. Section 2 of this book is dedicated entirely to these and many more use-cases on how voice technology will impact patients.

The Provider Experience

While voice technology will impact patients in a variety of ways, they are not the only segment of the healthcare system that will be transformed. Providers are constantly searching for ways to make their work more rewarding, impactful, efficient, and to ultimately improve the health of their patients. The arrival of smart digital assistants will transform the work of healthcare workers in profound ways that we are only beginning to imagine. Almost any scenario where it would be more efficient to speak with a computer than it would be to enter data will likely be impacted. Here are a few selected use cases to illustrate the potential of the voice-first world from the perspective of the providers.

Voice assistants, powered by artificial intelligence (AI) and natural language understanding (NLU), are new editions to healthcare, but voice recognition (i.e. transcription) itself is not new. Many medical professionals have been using voice transcription software to transcribe clinical notes for a long time. This however is not a smart (AI) system - it simply copies the words it hears. In fact, medical documentation is a tremendous burden for healthcare providers and physicians in particular. This laborious task of maintaining medical records is often quoted as one of the largest inefficiencies in the healthcare system and one of the most important contributing factors to physician burnout (6). Imagine how voice-first technology could transform medical record keeping and electronic medical records (EMRs).

Under the current system, physicians typically either type clinic notes on a computer while with a patient, or write or dictate their notes after seeing a patient. The result is that physicians spend many hours completing paperwork after clinical duties are complete. There are now a number of companies tackling this issue, what I consider to be the "holy grail" of medical documentation. These companies are developing voice assistants to function as AI scribes for physician-patient encounters to document the clinical notes automatically and in real-time. This ultimately relieves the physicians of the required paperwork and allows them to focus on the patient instead. Imagine what this would do for the increasing number of burned out physicians? This is discussed in much more detail in the chapter on medical transcription.

The other aspect of the medical documentation burden is the level of inefficiency in current electronic health record systems (EHRs). EHRs have not yielded the results that physicians had hoped for. It takes time to navigate an EHR and often this can get in the way of the patient interaction which affects physician-patient rapport. With voice technology, the control of the EHR system becomes more intuitive with simple commands. For more information on this, see the in-depth discussion in the chapter on electronic health records.

How could a voice assistant help with the actual care provided by a physician? What if a voice assistant could capture some of the more routine and mundane medical history for the physician? This could include important information about the patient that the physician should be aware of, yet is not necessarily the focus of a clinical encounter. This would have the potential to increase the efficiency of the encounter and allow the doctor to focus on elements of the encounter that are most important.

The physician's office is only one location where voice first technology will have an impact on the healthcare systems. Consider the various use cases in a hospital setting. A perfect place for the use of voice assistants is in the operating room where the surgical team is scrubbed in, sterile, and unable to touch the equipment in the room. Being able to talk to various medical devices would not only be more efficient, but would also reduce the risk of infection during procedures. Imagine being able to control the entire surgical suite and functions of the room by voice. The results could be both increased efficiency and better health outcomes. Refer to the chapter on voice technology in medical devices for further discussion on this topic.

What about the hospital bed? Imagine a burn patient lying in a bed, experiencing difficulty moving due to pain. Perhaps this patient could control his or her environment, including the bed itself, the entertainment system, and access to healthcare providers, all through the sound of their voice. This has clear benefits for the patient, but is also more efficient for the healthcare system. Nurses would no longer be summoned to the rooms of these patients to simply turn on or off the TV. They could focus on tasks that are more appropriate for their skills.

Health care professionals could also use voice assistants in pre-op and post-op care to check-in with patients or to answer frequently asked questions in the hospital and at home. What about the nurse that needs to record every single pill that is administered during a shift in a hospital? What if the nurse could just talk to the voice assistant? Or what about the use of voice assistants in teaching medical students and residents in simulated situations? The possibilities for applications of this technology are limited only by our imaginations. Section 3 of this book will dive into some of the many use cases and the ways voice technology will transform how health care providers do their jobs.

The Future of Voice Technology and Healthcare

With new technology comes new challenges. As we gradually turn the control of our patient and provider experiences over to a voice assistant, questions will naturally arise around privacy, security, reliability, logistics, data ownership, and protection of personal health information. Ethical use of artificial intelligence in healthcare is also a critical issue. In this book we have dedicated chapters to voice technology in healthcare in the context of law, data ownership, privacy, security, and other key topics that must be considered at this early stage of the technology. The hope is that these chapters will be a starting point to generate critically important discussions among stakeholders in this area.

Since the origin of time we have been using our voices. Our human existence has been built around communicating with each other. From sitting around a crackling campfire sharing stories to attending a concert to hear your favourite singers perform their latest song; from being a shoulder to cry on for your son or daughter, to singing happy birthday to your mother or father; to discussing your intimate thoughts and fears with your doctor to being inspired by hearing creative ideas at the latest conference, we have all been using our voices to share ideas, entertain, educate, care for each other, and make contributions to society. While computers have become increasingly more powerful to help us do so, they have been playing catch up with our unique ability to speak to each other. Now, we are on the precipice of an entirely new existence - one where our innate ability to speak is merging with the evolution of technology. We have never experienced this before. The voice era has arrived. Voice, our most powerful possession, is the new operating system of our lives.

In the following chapters, it gives me great pleasure to introduce you to the contributing authors of this book - a group of world-renowned thought leaders, practitioners, technologists, influencers, and those that are on the cutting edge of the intersection of voice technology and healthcare. I encourage you to explore this book, listen to the words with your ears wide open, and hear the sounds of healthcare in the very near future. Finally, feel free to join the discussions online using the hashtag #VoiceFirstHealth.

1. Queen's University. "Fetus Heart Races When Mom Reads Poetry; New Findings Reveal Fetuses Recognize Mother's Voice In-utero." ScienceDaily. ScienceDaily, 13 May 2003. www.sciencedaily.com/releases/2003/05/030513080440.htm

2. Moon, Christine & Lagercrantz, Hugo & Kuhl, Patricia. (2012). Language experienced in utero affects vowel perception after birth: A two-country study. Acta paediatrica (Oslo, Norway : 1992). 102. 10.1111/apa.12098.

3. "Voice First Revolution with Brian Roemmele." Alexa in Canada Podcast.

27 November 2018. https://alexaincanada.ca/voice-first-revolution-with-brian-roemmele/

4. Activate Tech & Media Outlook 2018. Consumer Adoption. 16 October 2017   https://www.slideshare.net/ActivateInc/activate-tech-media-outlook-2018

5. Reducing Social Isolation in Affordable Senior Housing using Voice Assistant   Technology.   https://leadingage.org/sites/default/files/AARP%20Foundation.pdf.

6. Maor, Sara, Orbelo, Lerman, Levanon, and Lerman. Voice Signal Characteristics Are Independently Associated With Coronary Artery Disease. July 2018Volume 93, Issue 7, Pages 840–847. https://doi.org/10.1016/j.mayocp.2017.12.025

7. Sinsky et al. Allocation of Physician Time in Ambulatory Practice: A Time and Motion Study in 4 Specialties. Ann Intern Med. 2016;165(11):753-760.

Chapter 2:

Increasing the Effectiveness of Voice Interactions through Design

Ilana Meir, MS

Editor's Note

As discussed in the previous chapter, voice is the most natural method of communication that we use. However, just because we have the ability to use our voices, this does not mean that we are all equally proficient as communicators. In fact, health care providers take formal training to learn how to communicate effectively, demonstrate empathy, and develop rapport with patients. As voice technology takes on an increasingly more important role in healthcare, designing voice applications should take into account these same principles and more. It is not sufficient to simply throw some words together and hope for the best. This chapter, written by Ilana Meir, an authority on healthcare voice user interface (VUI) design, discusses these critically important concepts that one must consider in the development of any healthcare voice application. With this in mind, this chapter forms a foundation for the rest of this book and will provide you with invaluable insights into how the most effective voice applications are being built today.

An acquaintance once asked me for fashion advice. I said sure, but you should know I'm not that kind of designer. I'm a Voice User Interface designer.

Whatever the application, design is the last-mile logistics that delivers a solution to one or more problems. Designers take the literal and symbolic meanings of the elements of their area—fashion, VUI, interior, service or graphical design— and combine them to create something that takes on its own meaning. Think of your favorite cafe. Is it full of plush fabrics and rounded edges encouraging you to sink in and drift off in thought? Or is it full of cool metal and warm wood encouraging you to stay alert? Everything from the appearance and positioning of tables and chairs, to the colors, to the location of the waiting-line reflect design choices. If the cafe is well-designed, it will convey a single, cohesive look that will influence your impression of the place and your behavior in it.

Beyond the overall feeling created in the interaction, good design satisfies the needs of both the creator and the user, in this case the cafe owner and the cafe-goers in the community. Design makes interaction pleasant and useful so all parties continue to engage in the relationship. In other words, design supports the health of a business by creating products that keep customers coming back for more.

It may come as a surprise that working with Voice User Interfaces, the interface widely-cited as the most natural interface, warrants a specialized approach. Do we really need to go through the labor of thinking through all the elements of conversation? After all, aren't we all well-practiced at the simple act of conversing? Yet, we also know that there is an "art" to conversation: each of us can think of times we misinterpreted what someone was trying to say or didn't know quite what to say ourselves. Surely someone could have done better.

Conversations have a host of elements that we take for granted when we use them in everyday interactions: the words, the tone, the sequence of questions. That is, we take it all for granted until we have to communicate strategically. Then we think carefully about how to tailor the conversation to the audience. We raise the topic at just the right moment with the right words coupled with the right tone and emphasis so there can be no mistake about what we mean to say and with hopes the outcome of the conversation will be in our favor.

When we mimic natural person-to-person conversation through a VUI, be it a voice assistant, avatar, or robot, every conversation is necessarily a strategic one: if the message communicated by the system is not useful and pleasant, the person has no reason to further engage with the system over time. Even simple commands like "Set an alarm for 7" can benefit from a designer carefully planning the system's architecture and responses: should it sound in the AM or PM; is it recurring or a one-time event; if recurring, on which days of the week; when shut off, does it sound again in case the user fell asleep? More complex and robust interactions introduce more points of interaction and a greater need for clever design work to satisfy all stakeholders. The strategic, specialized approach of VUI Design is especially warranted in healthcare where there's a great need for brand differentiation, the audience is diverse, and the stakes are high.

This chapter will examine how the components of voice design come together to help healthcare organizations achieve their goals. While the principles can be applied to any application of voice technology across different types of healthcare organizations, the focus will be on how provider and payer organizations can use voice technology to effectively communicate with patients and members. For simplicity and clarity, voice technology systems, be they virtual assistants, avatars, robots, or other automated conversations representing the healthcare organization will be referred to as "systems" and the people interacting with the voice technology systems will be called "patients".

Preparing for VUI Design

Needs Identification: The Benefits of Understanding Stakeholders

Before sitting down to write and diagram, a VUI designer will seek to understand the needs of all stakeholders to ensure the voice interaction achieves the aims of the healthcare organization. Often, an organization will think about what they want their patients to do without consideration for what their patients want. Or they may want to help patients solve a problem without thinking about how it aligns with the organization's strategic goals. These lopsided approaches result in one side talking at the other instead of having a conversation. If the conversation's design is rooted in a deep understanding of all stakeholders, everyone benefits and the interaction becomes a partnership, with each helping the other. As in other design disciplines, a voice designer stands at the center of the stakeholders and pulls in all their needs and points of view into one elegant interaction.

Needs discovery for voice design requires systemic inquiry using such techniques as interviews, surveys, in-person and online "netnography" observations, and literature reviews. Since there are already wonderful, existing resources available for conducting this research, including design tools and expert agencies specializing in healthcare, I won't detail these methodologies. I will mention, though, that to completely understand the patient experience, one must also look at the community of people around them affecting their care, including family, caregivers and organizations advocating on their behalf. Although speaking directly to patients and their support system is ideal, they can be difficult to recruit. In cases when speaking to patients would require too many resources, a second-best option is speaking with staff members who spend most of their time with them, for example, case managers and care coordinators, physicians, nurses and therapists. Online community boards also provide troves of information: The Epilepsy Foundation has tens of thousands of comments on just one of its discussion threads.

To fully understand the needs of the healthcare organization side, it's essential that designers gather information not only from providers and staff, but also those involved with formulating higher-level competitive strategy. In fact, I always advise clients and students to talk to their marketing department when they start using voice technology in their organization. I send them there because the marketing department can provide a whole host of information, such as the organization's competitive positioning, the look and feel of the organization's brand, demographics of its service area, and possible previous market research. Through this process, one must note that while voice interactions are not a marketing communication, they convey elements of the brand that should be consistent across touchpoints to give shape to the organization's characteristics that set it apart from its competitors. I will later detail the specific elements that communicate brand and culture through voice.

No doubt, needs identification takes time, but there is a stark difference between conversations a designer crafts to incorporate stakeholder understanding and those that do not. Below are examples of how a conversation may unfold without and then with stakeholder insights.

Scenario: Increasing Medication Adherence Meets Financial Planning

A health insurance company ("payer") wants to increase asthma medication adherence. While it has pharmacy records of which medications were picked up in the last month, there is a data lag between the pickup and the insurance claim of two weeks. In other words, a patient may have received their medication 12 days ago, but the data says it hasn't been picked up yet. At the same time, research uncovered that some patients only need their inhalers in the spring and fall; because it's expensive, they wait to pick it up until they urgently need it. Studies also show that some patients have duplicate medications at multiple pharmacies which the payer data is unable to reflect. A voice designer will account for all of these patient scenarios, building in language to anticipate the patient perspective while prompting action to pick up the inhaler.

Let's imagine a patient receives notification on their phone that their insurance company would like to speak with them about a medication via their voice assistant.

Conversation Example 1:
No Research or Design Incorporated

Voice Assistant: Our records show you haven't pick up your asthma medication yet. It is important to have it on you at all times. Get to the pharmacy...

Patient: I don't need it.

Voice Assistant: Sorry, I didn't understand that. Our records show your asthma medication is ready to be picked up. Get to the pharmacy as soon...

Patient: I said I don't need it right now!

In this example, the system does not acknowledge the shortcomings of its data and ends up frustrating the patient by not accounting for their experience. As a result, the conversation devolves, and with it the patient's trust in and relationship with the payer.

Let's try the conversation again, taking into account the knowledge we gathered from research.

Conversation Example 2: Designed with Stakeholder Knowledge

Voice Assistant: Our records show your asthma medication is ready for pickup at the pharmacy on 4th Street. It *does* take a couple weeks for our records to update, though. Did you already pick up your asthma medication at the pharmacy on 4th Street?

Patient: No, I don't need it.

Voice Assistant: OK, I'd like to make a note here so we don't ask you about it again. Could you tell me why you don't need it?

Patient: I only use my inhaler when the seasons change.

Voice Assistant: Got it: you use your inhaler seasonally. OK. If you want, I can remind you a couple weeks before the season changes so you have the medication ready to use when you need it. Do you want me to send you a notification before the season starts to pick up your medication?

Patient: Yes! That'd be great. Thank you.

In this example, the system started out by using data to identify which of potentially multiple pharmacies had a medication for the member and then prompted the patient to provide information so the system could then in turn provide a relevant response. By accounting for all stakeholders' needs, a pleasant interaction unfolds, turning the whole conversation into a welcome service for the member. You can imagine that the member would welcome another interaction with the system and thinks more highly of the payer for providing such a great service that supports them in taking care of their asthma. With thoughtful design, the payer has opened up the line of communication and strengthened its relationship with members while increasing medication adherence. Only an understanding of the needs of the different stakeholders could yield such a seemingly-personalized and beneficial conversation.

Determining the Place of Voice

In addition to needs identification, a VUI designer seeks to understand how voice will fit within the overall patient care and communication strategy. To do so, designers must map out how the organization currently addresses the issue at hand and identify opportunities particularly well-suited for the voice modality. Consider an organization that has the goal of helping newly-diagnosed cancer patients understand their condition to prepare them for upcoming treatments. A natural impulse would be to design a conversation for the days immediately following the cancer diagnosis. However, in cases the provider would like a patient in treatment as soon as possible, an analysis of touchpoints will reveal in the days after diagnosis a cancer patient is on the phone setting up scans, attending appointments, talking with and writing their employer and loved ones to prepare them for what's to come, all while trying to process everything themselves. Patients are already busy with interactions. They may not have time or brain space to make room for one more conversation. An organization may choose to streamline the process for cancer patients and include a voice interaction as a main component, or it may choose a quieter time to engage the patient in a voice interaction.

The place of voice as it fits in with related communications in a patient's experience should also be considered before starting to build a conversation. For example, studies show that mailing patients fecal immunochemical tests (an at-home colon cancer screening kit) significantly increases completion rates of all colon cancer screenings. The completion rate rises if clinics send patients a reminder letter after they receive the kit. What if this reminder were delivered by a voice system instead? Providing an avenue for dialogue may increase completion rates, but to maximize the conversation's efficacy, it would have to acknowledge the context and frame the information correctly. Instead of opening the conversation with a "Let's talk all about colon cancer and how to get screened", a designer would start the conversation by continuing the patient's experience: "In the past few days, your doctor mailed you a screening kit you can do right at home...". This approach continues the line of communication from one touchpoint to the next, creating an additive effect.

Whether considering voice as part of all communications or as a part of all the touchpoints within a single experience, ensuring the voice interaction works in conjunction with current communications will increase the usage of the voice interaction and enhance patients' experience with the organization overall.

Assessing the Voice Modality

Part of assessing how a voice interaction can work with other communications is assessing if it is appropriate in the given setting. The first question is: Is the conversation or information exchange more effective by voice or another modality? Using voice, I've tried explaining to people with diabetes how to check their feet for cuts or sores; the details are cumbersome to explain, tiresome for the patient to hear, and overall it's difficult to retain the information. What I found to be a much better experience is using a voice user interface to explain the importance of foot checks and consequences of infection while employing visual aids to explain how to perform the inspection. Each modality plays to its strengths and communicates the information efficiently and effectively.

Voice is a promising modality for answering common questions related to procedures, but first a base level of literacy must be established, often using visuals. Simple explanations, such as "the doctor will look in your ear," can be communicated easily via voice, but we can quickly encounter health literacy difficulties when describing processes of body parts that are not commonly referenced or in view. For example, a patient undergoing a Whipple procedure (pancreaticoduodenectomy) will need to understand where the affected organs lie. A visual aid is much more effective at communicating this type of information than voice. If resources permit, an interactive experience with a graphical user interface that integrates voice and images may be the most immersive experience, but a bit of creativity with a "low tech" solution can also engage patients. Imagine a sheet of paper with color-coded pathways through the relevant anatomy. A voice experience can lead the patient through the pathways:

Patient: Where is my pancreas?

System: Let's look at the blue pathway. Starting at the mouth, follow it down to the stomach. Do you see the part labeled "stomach"?

Patient: Yea, I see it.

System: Oh good. A lot of people hold their *whole belly* when they're full or hungry, but really food goes right there, a little to the left of center...

Once again, the patient receives information with more ease when voice stands as the conversation guide and other pieces of the interaction are assigned to other modalities.

Content Choice as Branding

Determining what content to pursue is as strategic a decision as where to allocate funds across the organization. Which content is developed affects the patients' perceptions of the overall feeling of the organization and its expertise, and thus should remain consistent with the overall brand. Brand characteristics should stay constant across all touchpoints, including how staff are trained, and should be central to the voice persona as well. That way, there's a consistent, particular look, feel, and sound to interacting with your organization that cannot be mistaken-or replaced- by another organization. Sometimes it's an easy choice: Mayo Clinic has long been a source of easy-to-understand medical information on its website, so it feels like a natural and strategic move to provide first-aid information in a voice-searchable format using voice assistants. A payer may decide to make a voice interaction describing insurance benefits. While both of these cases are educational, the branding message they communicate is different: Mayo builds on its position as "knowledge leader" while the insurance company reinforces "transparency" as a brand attribute.

Healthcare organizations often already contain the expertise to inform VUI design work, so it becomes a matter of identifying who holds the knowledge a designer requires to prepare for the design. Again, consulting with marketing is essential for a designer to decide on content. (Note that sometimes that decision comes from the design department and sometimes from another department.) The marketing department can provide the organization's brand identity documents that can serve as guidelines for content and the overall voice experience.[1] Usually marketing departments will test different styles of messaging to determine what goes over well with patients and also differentiates their brand from the competition. To illustrate the point, we can read the positioning of three health systems: NorthShore University HealthSystem uses the tagline "Healthcare for What's Next", Cleveland Clinic Trademarked "Every Life Deserves World Class Care", and Kaiser Permanente associates itself with "Thrive". A designer will collaborate with other departments in the healthcare organization to develop voice content that satisfies stakeholder needs while following through on the brand's differentiating characteristics.

Although there is a lot of preparation to be done before designing a voice user interface, it gets easier (and quicker) with time. The scope of the VUI application also factors into the depth of the preparation. If the application is an interactive FAQ, there's likely no need for a series of interviews: simple web analytics may yield the answers to the questions patients ask most frequently, and the writer of the web content has already done the work to frame the answers. The designer then can proceed to adapt the writing to a conversational format.

Designers also develop a knowledge-base and an intuition that speeds up the preparation process. For example, I have designed many conversations about mammograms so I am very familiar with the variety of patient attitudes and beliefs relating to the screening, the needs of healthcare organizations to increase scheduling and attendance, and requirements needed to report quality measures. Also, certain common features among projects allow for an accelerated design process. For example, uncomfortable side effects cause some patients to stop taking many different medications. A designer can become well-versed in talking about side effects in general and can deftly address such common problems as dry mouth or dizziness. No matter the timeline and scope of the VUI project, a designer will consider the needs of all stakeholders, consider the place of a voice interaction within an organization's portfolio of communications, and play to the strengths of the modality of voice interaction in order to facilitate mutually-beneficial relationships between patients and healthcare organizations through the voice user interface interaction.

---

[1]In cases that the marketing department does not have these documents, or perhaps the company is in its early stages, the designer can develop the voice experience based on clues from materials exhibiting the characteristics of the organization. Some ideas of where to find these clues include: advertising, brand colors, employee welcome packet and guidelines, and the mission statement.

Designing for Voice User Interfaces in Healthcare

Once a content plan has been formulated based on an understanding of stakeholders, a designer will refine the characteristics of its delivery. The delivery of content will affect patients' perceptions of an organization's brand and culture, as well as their overall relationship with the organization. They'll start by developing a persona. Wally Brill, Head of Conversation Design Advocacy and Education at Google, describes, "The persona of any system is the consistent character. It's not just a voice: It's a combination of voice, interaction design, and dialog. It's the impression a system gives of 'who' you are interacting with."

Who will be speaking with your patients? If the system is a role within the organization, there would be careful thought put into who to hire. In the same way, designers give careful consideration to building the persona. Everything from the sound of the voice, to word choice and sentence prosody, to how the conversations unfold over time represent the organization's brand, communicate its culture, and establish a certain relationship dynamic.

Choosing the components of a persona in healthcare can be a more nuanced endeavor than in other industries because health is one of the most personal and sensitive topics in our culture. The next section will examine the components of persona and how they can be used to effectively convey brand, culture, and build relationships with patients.

How do we think of the type of relationship between a system and a patient?

Before getting into the particular characteristics of a persona, it's worth stopping to consider what type of relationship would ideally form between the voice system and patients. Just as patients have different sorts of relationships with their friends and family and an organization's staff in the nursing, customer service, and billing departments, they'll form a specific type of relationship with the system. What type of relationship best models how patients should interact with the system? We can look to brands in other industries as examples: One passenger of Alaska Airlines said her experience with the brand is like a "friendly aunt". In their article entitled

Building Brand as a Relationship, marketers Mark Bonchek and Cara France note the shift between the driver/passenger relationship of taxi drivers and their customers to an intended friend/friend relationship between rideshare drivers and their customers. A healthcare organization will want to aim for a relationship that matches the aims of the voice interaction. For example, if an interaction intends to pass along medical information to patients and encourage them to ask questions, the inclination would be to emulate a doctor/patient relationship. After all, doctors are knowledgeable and authoritative.

However, there is also commonly a feeling of power imbalance and, increasingly mistrust, which creates a barrier in the doctor/patient relationship and results in a fear of asking questions. Aiming for a relationship that maintains that knowledgeable and authoritative stance while also communicating trust, say a mentor/protege relationship, is better-suited for the knowledge transfer and inspires patients to turn to the VUI with questions.

Usually an organization will have more than one type of voice interaction with more than one aim. Even if the platform changes, the content changes, or the voice changes for a certain topic, the relationship type of the system to the patient should remain constant. The choice of relationship reflects on the brand and the interaction with the VUI touchpoint. As with other communications, the choice can have a halo effect that evokes positive associations with the entire organization.

Of course saying a certain relationship exists doesn't make it so: the system must act in a way that conveys its identity and suggests the desired relationship dynamic.

How does the choice of voice reflect on the brand and affect communication?

The voice of the persona that speaks the message conveys the brand characteristics. Two examples of distinct voices that align well with the overall brand come from the auto insurance industry. Allstate chose Dennis Dexter Haysbert as the deep, resonant voice for its commercials; he communicates authority, sturdiness, and dependability, all desirable characteristics for an insurance provider. Geico Insurance chose a cheeky gecko with a smart-sounding British accent because, in the gecko's words, he "...can be trusted.

I ask you if you want to save hundreds on car insurance. And you're like yes, thank you, mind babysitting my kids?".

As well as these brands did translating their brand's persona to their spokesperson's voice, in healthcare it is often not that straightforward. Advertising giant Bill Bernbach relayed the wisdom, "If you stand for something, you will always find some people for you and some against you. If you stand for nothing, you will find nobody against you, and nobody for you." It follows then that in advertising you should take a stance that will appeal to some and alienate others. Every single person is a consumer of healthcare, so you want to be as inclusive as possible. How do you accomplish that inclusiveness for healthcare? Is there one voice that embodies a gender, age, race, culture, education, and class that will appeal to all? In the future there may be a scalable way to let consumers choose the voice with which to interact for any given topic, or even (with more caution) predict with whom a consumer might like to speak; but for now, the short answer is "no". However, by questioning what your voice represents, you can appeal to the widest audience possible and use other design tools to create a connection between the system and the patient.

Let's look more closely at one of the most basic considerations in choosing a persona's voice: gender. Although your brand might be distinctly "male" (e.g., Allstate and Geico) or "female" (e.g., Progressive Insurance, Panera Bread) you may choose a different voice to suit the audience and the topic. For example, in my work, men usually prefer a man to talk to them about prostate health. Similarly, many women may prefer to speak with a woman about breast health. Of course these assumptions are generalizations, and not everyone prefers to speak with a member of the same sex about health or even has a preference. Other considerations when choosing a persona's voice include age, accent, and the speed of delivery. One may deviate from the brand's main characteristics in favor of choosing the voice patients will most readily accept.

That said, it's best to limit the total number of voices used by a single organization and keep the voice consistent across interactions intended for a particular patient group. For example, during a care transition (e.g., a patient going home from the hospital after surgery) the organization may want to use a voice system to check in on a patient multiple times and answer questions a patient has at any time. The voice reaching out to the patient and the voice responding to questions around that care transition should be the same. This strategy creates a unified experience for the patient to always talk to the same "person" and also creates the impression that they have the full attention of a single person dedicated to this aspect of their care. Regardless of the topic set, key to finding the right voice is realizing that while the voice will convey the core brand characteristics, the voice is an interpretation of those characteristics.

What style of language is best for voice in a healthcare setting?

Beyond the voice of the persona, the language the persona uses affect patients' perception of the organization. In other applications of voice, the persona's language use can be a differentiator. When using voice in healthcare, though, especially when conversing with patients, there are certain principles that should be applied no matter the persona. Above all, patients should feel comfortable interacting with the system, easily follow the conversation, and retain the necessary information.

Along the same lines as interpreting the voice for the voice modality, it is beneficial for an organization to deviate from the language style guide used by other departments. Once, after I gave a talk on elements of conversation design in healthcare, an audience-member from a large payer organization told me that the conversational tone of my projects—despite their success—would not meet the requirements of their brand's style guide which took a much more formal tone. Sometimes, formal tone is equated with a professional tone. However, a conversational tone can be just as professional and is often more approachable. Consider these two ways of asking the same, simple question:

Formal: For whom would you like to schedule the appointment?

Conversational: Who is the appointment for?

Both examples convey the same meaning. The formal version imposes on the listener a high level of standard English that may be confusing, jarring, or alienating to some patients. Although the conversational example ends in a preposition, which is grammatically incorrect, it reflects how people speak with each other day-to-day and is more linguistically inclusive and therefore accessible. In addition, because the conversational example is shorter and linguistically less complex, it requires less mental effort (also known as cognitive load) to understand. Keeping sentences short, simple, and reflective of everyday conversation makes for a comfortable voice interaction for the most people and is thus preferable to the more formal style an organization may use for other modes of communication. Again, if a brand is like a person, it would naturally reinterpret its communication style for the new voice modality to create a pleasing interaction for the greatest number of people.

To reach the most people, it is also important that the system uses language around medical concepts and terminology to match the lowest common denominator of patients' health literacy level. As in the above case of formal vs. conversational language, simpler language about health issues is easier to process than complex terminology.

According to the U.S. Department of Health and Human Services' most recent study of health literacy in 2003, 35% of those surveyed had only basic or below basic level of health literacy. The highest rates of low literacy were among the elderly and those on Medicare, Medicaid and Uninsured. In other words, designing conversations at a low level of health literacy makes the information accessible to the most vulnerable populations.

The Agency for Healthcare Research and Quality (AHRQ) offers a health literacy toolkit that outlines strategies for clearly communicating health information. These strategies translate well to the conversation modality. Below are the AHRQ's guidelines and how I interpret them for VUIs in healthcare.

AHRQ Guideline	Voice Design Guideline
Greet patients warmly: Receive everyone with a welcoming smile, and maintain a friendly attitude throughout the visit.	Open interactions with a friendly greeting.
Make eye contact: Make appropriate eye contact throughout the interaction. Refer to Tool 10: Consider Culture, Customs and Beliefs for further guidance on eye contact and culture.	Depending on the type of VUI, the system can indicate the patient has its undivided attention in different ways: Avatar/Robot: Make eye contact (Conventions for when to make eye contact may differ across cultures) Smart Device: Use a sound effect to let the patient know the system is listening and let the patient know it's their turn to speak. Light rings and other light effects and be illuminated throughout the listening period or lightly pulsed.
Listen carefully: Try not to interrupt patients when they are talking. Pay attention, and be responsive to the issues they raise and questions they ask.	- Adjust time before system errors to accommodate the time it takes a patient to think. Some questions might take longer to process (e.g., answering ""How old are you?"" vs. ""When did you last talk to your doctor about that?"") or it might take some patients longer than other to process (e.g., a person with average cognitive function vs. impaired cognitive function). - Develop system recognition of patient utterances to include all which ways patients ask the same question - Be prepared with answers to common questions"
Use plain, non-medical language: Don't use medical words. Use common words that you would use to explain medical information to your friends or family, such as stomach or belly instead of abdomen.	Same applies to writing voice content.

Use the patient's words: Take note of what words the patient uses to describe his or her illness and use them in your conversation.	It can be difficult using today's speech technology to repeat back a patient's exact words. Before responding to a question, a system can repeat back the theme it registers which will often be close to what the patient used. A designer can also organize information using lower literacy categories so when they are repeated back, it meets the most patients at their level of literacy. **Example 1** 　Patient: "My stomach hurts" 　System: "When your stomach hurts…" **Example 2** 　Patient: "My stomach's in pain" 　System: "When your stomach hurts…" This implicit confirmation has the added benefit of building patients' confidence and trust in the competence of the system.
Slow down: Speak clearly and at a moderate pace.	Same applies to writing voice content. Note that some regions of the U.S. speak more slowly than others and people with hearing impairment may need information slowed down even further.
Limit and repeat content: Prioritize what needs to be discussed, and limit information to 3-5 key points and repeat them.	These limits reduce cognitive load and apply as standards in the field of voice design - Limit the number of items relayed in a list. The fewer the items in a list, the greater proportion can be remembered. - Repeating information is fairly standard for voice user interfaces. Patients should be able to request repetition with the caveat that the information may be worded slightly different the second time around.
Be specific and concrete: Don't use vague and subjective terms that can be interpreted in different ways.	Same applies to writing voice content **Vague:** "Get exercise" **Specific and Concrete:** "Take a walk every day. Start by walking around the block…"
Show graphics: Draw pictures, use illustrations, or demonstrate with 3-D models. All pictures and models should be simple, designed to demonstrate only the important concepts, without detailed anatomy.	When the interaction takes place on a mobile phone, app, or smart display, it is preferable to use visual aids in conjunction with conversation. If the interaction is voice-only, consider sending visual aids to the patient's phone or other graphical user interface.
Demonstrate how it's done: Whether doing exercises or taking medicine, a demonstration of how to do something may be clearer than a verbal explanation.	

Invite patient participation: Encourage patients to ask questions and be involved in the conversation during visits and to be proactive in their health care.	After the system answers a question, don't end the interaction there; ask patients if they have any further questions. Or move the conversation along by suggesting adjacent topics.
Encourage questions	
Apply teach-back: Confirm patients understand what they need to know and do by asking them to teach back important information, such as directions.	This one is difficult to achieve with present technology, however there are many <u>educational robots</u> in development and it is likely a skill they will acquire in the not-too-distant future

You may have noticed that there is some overlap between the effect of word choices and interaction design choices (e.g., time before error-out) on the literacy level of the conversation. We'll cover interaction design choices next, but first consider some other wording principles that will increase understanding at all levels of health literacy. Here I take general voice design guidelines and apply them to the healthcare setting.

Voice Design Guideline	Healthcare Application
Provide instructions sequentially When instructions are given sequentially, the cognitive load to understand those instructions lessens. It becomes especially important when speaking with impaired cognitive ability, such a people with dementia.	Example: Directions for mixing medication *Non-sequential:* "Add water after opening the cap to mix the medicine" vs *Sequential:* "To mix the medicine, first open the cap, then add water"
Use <u>Conversation Markers</u> (e.g., Ok, First, Next, Finally) Conversation makers make the speech sound more natural and orient the listener. They also help organize topics into cohesive blocks which makes them easier to comprehend.	Example: **Patient:** Can you tell me how to mix this medication? **System:** Sure! "To mix the medicine, first open the cap, then add water. Finally, give it a shake"
Limit lists <u>Experts suggest </u>people with average mental capability can remember a maximum of 4-9 items in a list. According to the widely-accepted <u>serial-position effect</u>, people tend to best remember the first and last items in a list. Still, people with even <u>mild Alzheimer's </u>have trouble recalling the first two items in a list.	- Lists should be kept to a minimum of around three items especially when designing for populations with possible mental impairment. - If there are more than three items in a list, offer the patient time to write them down, and ask the patient if they're ready to hear more items before continuing.
Direct the user's focus through <u>word order and stress</u> Putting new information last lessens the cognitive load because the listener does not have to keep track of information through to the end.	Example: **Patient:** When will the doctor come in to check on me? **System:** The doctor will come by tomorrow at 7am.
Use <u>silence and breath</u> to demarcate changes in content and increase comprehension Pauses indicate a change in topics and allow listeners to process what they've heard before the system introduces a new topic.	Example: **Patient:** Where is the closest Urgent Care? **System:** The closest Urgent Care is on 222 Bewell Lane. [Pause] Would you like me to navigate you there?

When a healthcare organization uses these principles, their diverse patient types have equal access to the information; therefore, the organization cannot only reach its entire patient population but also give the impression to each individual that the organization is "for them".

Interaction Design as an Opportunity to Convey Brand and Culture

Use of certain elements of voice interaction design that convey culture should also be standard practice. In his canonical work The Social Transformation of American Medicine, Paul Starr describes the cultural shifts over the past few centuries that led to a concentration of power and authority among medical professionals. In the past couple of decades, there has been recognition that a patient-centered approach to care increases value. One example of this recognition is the Centers for Medicare and Medicaid Services implementation of HCAHPS (Hospital Consumer Assessment of Healthcare Providers and Systems) scores as a method of quality assessment. HCAHPS scores will also determine hospital bonuses or penalties. Another example is the establishment of the Society for Participatory Medicine, which arose from this new approach to medicine, describing its mission:

- To guide patients and caregivers to be actively engaged in their health and health care experiences.

- To guide health professional practices where patient experience and contribution is an integral goal of excellence.

- To encourage mutual collaboration among patients, health professionals, caregivers and others allowing them to partner in determining care.

So how does one convey this collaborative approach to medicine in a voice system?

The answer partially lies in topics we have already covered: demystifying medical jargon through use of plain language and using the health literacy guidelines. Also, content can cover the pros and cons of different course of treatment plans so patients can make better-informed decisions about their care. Below are other voice design techniques that are more patient-

friendly, giving them more power in the interaction.

The Difference Between Information vs. Conversation

First, design a conversation. It can be tempting to take an FAQ and put the entire block of text in a lump for the VUI to animate. No doubt it's efficient, but it also violates a core VUI design principle by placing an undue cognitive load on the patient. This method also removes the back and forth between patients and the system which allows give and take of power. The text turns into a wall of speech that conveys a center of power with the system. To balance the power dynamic for a more participatory care approach, the design should take on the form of a conversation, using any of the methods below.

Be Brief, Be Relevant:

If a patient asks about a topic, keep a tight focus when answering the question. James Giangola, Lead of Conversation & Persona Design at Google describes, "Listening is often considered a 'passive' skill in contrast to speaking, which is thought to be more 'active' and 'productive.' In reality, listening involves a lot of work. So it's important for your VUI to give the listener a break from listening and let them have their turn, too." Narrowing the scope of the answer also reduces the risk of the system sounding like it has an agenda to push. Consider these two possibilities:

Scenario: Stroke Education

Approach #1: Long with an Agenda

Patient: What is a stroke?

System: Sure, strokes: Usually, blood gives oxygen to the brain, but sometimes it gets blocked from getting there. A stroke happens when the brain doesn't get the oxygen it needs, so it stops working normally. To help you stay healthy, doctors recommend quitting smoking, losing weight, and cutting down on drinking. Exercising can also help fight against the high blood pressure that often leads to a stroke. Would you like to hear more about strokes?

Patient: No.

Approach #2: Brief and Relevant

Patient: What is a stroke?

System: Sure, strokes: Usually, blood gives oxygen to the brain, but sometimes it gets blocked from getting there. A stroke happens when the brain doesn't get the oxygen it needs, so the brain stops working normally. Would you like to hear more about strokes?

Patient: Yes, please.

The first example weighs down the patient cognitively while touching on sensitive topics the patient did not expect the system to broach. By contrast, the brief and relevant example puts the patient in control of the course of the conversation as it responds directly to the request.

Ask a Question:

The system representing a healthcare provider is the expert, but patients also come to the interaction with their own knowledge. Asking a question creates a dynamic where the system (and therefore the healthcare organization) acknowledges the patient before them, thereby creating a feeling of mutual respect. Even if ultimately the content is the same, asking a question immediately redistributes power.

Scenario: Colon Cancer Screening

Example 1: "Yes" Answer	Example 2: "No" Answer
Patient: How can I tell if I have colon cancer?	**Patient:** How can I tell if I have colon cancer?
System: The best way to find out if you have colon cancer is by talking to your doctor about getting a screening called a colonoscopy. Have you heard of a colonoscopy before?	**System:** The best way to find out if you have colon cancer is by talking to your doctor about getting a screening called a colonoscopy. Have you heard of a colonoscopy before?
Patient: Yea, I have.	**Patient:** No.
System: OK. Would you like to hear more about them?	**System:** Oh OK. If you want, I can tell you all about them. Would you like to hear about colonoscopies?
Patient: Yes, please.	**Patient:** Yes, please.
System: Great. As you may know…	**System:** Great. The first thing to know…

While it's not the most efficient way to convey information, slowing down the conversation with the extra question is a particularly useful tactic to open a dialogue about a topic patients usually approach with trepidation.

Moving the Conversation Along While Sharing Control

One of the basic principles of VUI Design is that the system should move the conversation forward. In VUI design for healthcare, there should be a conscious effort for the system to suggest and the patient to lead. For example, the system brings up the option of setting a reminder for that earlier scenario of a patient who needs an inhaler when the seasons change. Because the system offered to provide a service to the patient, it was servile and therefore the power was in the patient's hands.

In instances where the system must convey information, say if a surgeon seeks to gain informed consent from a patient before a procedure, then either asking a patient which topic they'd like to cover first, or asking permission to continue with a line of thought realigns the interaction with a culture of participatory care. Here are examples of both methods:

Scenario: A surgeon must gain informed consent from the patient before a total hip replacement surgery

Conversation 1: Patient Chooses the Order of Topics

System: Your doctor would like to go over a few topics before your procedure so you know what to expect. Before I get started, do you have any questions about your procedure?

Patient: How long will it take me to recover?

System: Sure, let's talk about your recovery. Usually it takes people three to six weeks to fully recover from the surgery. The good news is, most people can walk the same day they have the replacement put in! Would you like to know more about the recovery?

Patient: No, thanks.

System: Ok, I'd like to tell you about what happens during the surgery and some risks. Which would you like to hear about first?

Patient: Risks.

Just like a patient-centered interaction with a physician, the system is designed so the patient can go through the necessary information in the order that is most pressing to them. This approach places the patient's mindset at the center of the conversation.

Conversation 2: System Asks Permission

System: Your doctor would like to go over a few topics before your procedure so you know what to expect. First things first, I'd like to talk about how to get ready for the surgery. Can I continue?

Patient: Sure.

System: Thanks!

Mimicking a care provider asking for permission before examining a patient, the second conversation leaves it to the patient to consent to hearing about a topic before the system delves into it, returning control back to the patient even in this more deterministic interaction.

How Can Design Make the Most of Technology Restrictions

Some conversations are more deterministic because of restrictions imposed by the content, and other conversations may seem constrained because of restrictions imposed by technology. VUI design can work creatively with information architecture to mold an interaction that is seemingly personalized from even a stiff voice technology platform.

Let's say we have three patients with questions about the social side of living with a condition: A patient on a low-carb diet preparing for a PET scan wants to know: What should she say to a new client about why she won't be ordering the pasta specialty at a restaurant? A patient with heart failure avoiding salt wants to cook for his friends: How can he possibly make something that doesn't taste bland? And a patient with IBD is looking at the upcoming Thanksgiving dinner wondering: How can she indulge in the treats of Grandma's cooking while avoiding a flare? Or not indulge and avoid an interrogation?

These questions are highly individualized, but together they reveal a pattern: navigating social situations with food restrictions. Given the spectrum of conditions and scenarios where social interaction and food intersect, there are probably enough questions to keep healthcare staff occupied for days (if patients reach out at all). A voice designer will bring together these two perspectives and create a hierarchy of information that is as specific or widely-applicable as the system allows. Each conversation will answer patients' questions, putting them on the path to healthy behaviors while saving the healthcare organization's staff time.

Below are a few ways a designer might organize and apply the findings from research to the structure and design of a conversation with varying levels of system flexibility.

Scenario: Patient and System are engaged in a conversation about health. System knows the patient has a diet with food restrictions, but does not have more information.

System Flexibility: Cannot Differentiate Between Different Diets

System: I noticed you're on a special diet. Would you like me to make some suggestions for how to talk to family and friends about your diet?

Patient: Yes, please.

System: OK, first: do you feel comfortable telling them about your medical information?

> *[System is ambiguous about gender and number to make question generalizable to most situations. It is also uses a general term, "medical information" that could be applied to PET scans, heart failure, and IBD equally]*

Patient: Not really. No.

System: All right. You don't have to share any medical information with anyone. If it comes up, you can try saying you "don't *feel like* eating" that dish tonight. Sometimes people do insist, you can say something firmer like "I really don't want to right now". Occasionally, people will ask again. Feel free to change the subject to anything: the weather, sports, decoration in the room. They'll get the hint that the subject is not up for discussion and move on. I've just sent those tips to you if you want to go over them or just ask me again!

Patient: Thanks!

System Flexibility: Diets Organized by Condition (PET scan, heart failure, IBD)

System: I noticed you're on a special diet. Would you like me to make some suggestions for how to talk to family and friends about your diet?

Patient: Yes, please.

System: OK, first: to give you the best information, could you tell me what diet you're on?

User: I have a PET scan.

System: OK. Just one more question: do you feel comfortable telling your friends and family about your medical information?

User: No, not really.

System: All right. Even a nibble of bread can affect the results of a PET scan, so I'm glad we're talking about this. You know, a lot of people nowadays follow a low-carb diet. You can say something like "I'm trying out the low-carb thing". If they ask for details, can you say "I don't want to get into it". Feel free to change the subject to anything: the weather, sports, decoration in the room. They'll get the hint that the subject is not up for discussion and move on. I've just sent those tips to you if you want to go over them or just ask me again!

System Flexibility: Diets Organized by Diet Type (Low-Carb, Low-Salt, Highly-Individualized)

System: I noticed you're on a special diet. Would you like me to make some suggestions for how to talk to family and friends about your diet?

Patient: Yes, please.

System: OK, first: to give you the best information, could you tell me what diet you're on?

User: I have a PET scan.

System: Sorry, I don't know much about that. Did your doctor tell you the name of the diet? For example, low-salt.

Patient: No carbs.

System: Oh, OK. I know about the low-carb diet. Just one more question: do you feel comfortable telling your family and friends about your medical information?

Patient: Not really, no.

System: All right. You know, a lot of people nowadays follow a low-carb diet. You can say something like "I'm trying out the low-carb thing". If they ask for details, can you say "I don't want to get into it". Feel free to change the subject to anything: the weather, sports, decoration in the room. They'll get the hint that the subject is not up for discussion and move on. I've just sent those tips to you if you want to go over them or just ask me again!

We can see the conversation morphs depending on what the technology allows. Every scenario, though, shares practical advice with the patient to navigate the social setting. System constraints can be daunting, but usually there is room for design to work around the limitations to achieve the aims of the dialogue.

Concluding VUI Design

There is no real end to design work. While a perfect interaction cannot be achieved, VUI designers continually pursue an improved product through an iterative process that tries to predict and respond to an increasing number of scenarios. One way they'll improve interactions is to test the effectiveness of different messaging.

Prudence should be at the forefront of these tests, as every VUI interaction between a system and patient should be considered a health intervention. After all, if the VUI uses language to prompt a patient to take action, it is akin to a provider doing the same. When engaging in such testing in healthcare, a VUI designer should use the same pathways as other testing in the healthcare field, including assessment by the organization's (or local) Institutional Review Board and registration with clinicaltrials.gov. That way, the test can be administered to protect its human subjects according to the ethical standards of their organization and the wider healthcare community.

Opportunities abound for applications of voice technology in healthcare and there is much eagerness to get started. VUI design is the essential approach for successful voice interactions. Patients have already begun to expect seamless digital experiences: 41% report they would switch providers over a poor digital experience, and that number is even higher 61% among those aged 18-24, with 29% reporting they have already switched providers due to a poor digital experience. A well-designed voice experience is the next competitive advantage that will soon become an imperative. There is more at stake than patient loyalty, though. Good voice design has the power to forge stronger relationships between healthcare organizations and their patients, providing for the platform for the two groups to come together to achieve what we all want: improved health for ourselves and our communities.

Works Cited

"About Us." Society for Participatory Medicine, 5 Oct. 2019, participatorymedicine.org/about/.

"Alexa Design Guide." Amazon Alexa, Amazon, developer.amazon.com/docs/alexa-design/relatable.html.

"America's Health Literacy: Why We Need Accessible Health Information." Office of Disease Prevention and Health Promotion Health Communication Activities, U.S. Department of Health & Human Services, 2014, health.gov/communication/literacy/issuebrief/.

Bayley, Peter J., et al. "Comparison of the Serial Position Effect in Very Mild Alzheimer's Disease, Mild Alzheimer's Disease, and Amnesia Associated with Electroconvulsive Therapy." Journal of the International Neuropsychological Society, vol. 6, no. 3, Mar. 2000, pp. 290–298., doi:10.1017/s1355617700633040.

Blendon, Robert J., et al. "Public Trust in Physicians — U.S. Medicine in International Perspective." New England Journal of Medicine, vol. 371, no. 17, 2014, pp. 1570–1572., doi:10.1056/nejmp1407373.

Bonchek, Mark, and Cara France. "Building Brand as a Relationship." Harvard Business Review, 9 May 2016, hbr.org/2016/05/build-your-brand-as-a-relationship.

Brill, Wally. "Are Friends Electric? ." Ubiquitous Voice: Essays from the Field, Edited by Lisa Falkson, Independently Published, 2018, p. 63.

Center for Drug Evaluation and Research. "(IRBs) and Protection of Human Subjects." U.S. Food and Drug Administration, FDA, 11 Sept. 2019, www.fda.gov/about-fda/center-drug-evaluation-and-research-cder/institutional-review-boards-irbs-and-protection-human-subjects-clinical-trials.

Community Forum. The Epilepsy Foundation, www.epilepsy.com/forum-topics.

Coronado, Gloria D., et al. "Effectiveness of a Mailed Colorectal Cancer Screening Outreach Program in Community Health Clinics." JAMA Internal Medicine, vol. 178, no. 9, 2018, p. 1174., doi:10.1001/jamainternmed.2018.3629.

"Deductible Rewards | Allstate Insurance." Deductible Rewards | Allstate Insurance, Allstate, 2 Apr. 2019, www.youtube.com/watch?v=gO6wHlWyJ2E.

Epstein, R. M., and R. L. Street. "The Values and Value of Patient-Centered Care." The Annals of Family Medicine, vol. 9, no. 2, 2011, pp. 100–103., doi:10.1370/afm.1239.

EVERY LIFE DESERVES WORLD CLASS CARE Trademark of Cleveland Clinic Foundation - Registration Number 2643638 - Serial Number 75978454 :: Justia Trademarks. Justia, trademarks.justia.com/759/78/every-life-deserves-world-class-care-75978454.html.

"Gecko Interview - GEICO Insurance." Gecko Interview - GEICO Insurance, Geico Insurance, 17 Dec. 2018, www.youtube.com/watch?time_continue=30&v=d4Gi7BxriuE.

Giangola, James, and Philippe Cao. "Conversation Design: Speaking the Same Language - Library." Google Design, design.google/library/conversation-design-speaking-same-language/.

Gobet, Fernand, and Gary Clarkson. "Chunks in Expert Memory: Evidence for the Magical Number Four ... or Is It Two?" Memory, vol. 12, no. 6, 2004, pp. 732–747., doi:10.1080/09658210344000530.

Greene, Lane. "The Importance of Pauses in Conversation." Johnson, The Economist Newspaper, 14 Dec. 2017, www.economist.com/books-and-arts/2017/12/14/the-importance-of-pauses-in-conversation.

"Health Literacy Universal Precautions Toolkit, 2nd Edition." Agency for Healthcare Research and Quality, U.S. Department of Health & Human Services, Feb. 2015, www.ahrq.gov/health-literacy/quality-resources/tools/literacy-toolkit/healthlittoolkit2-tool4.html.

Healthcare for What's Next. NorthShore University Healthsystem, www.northshore.org/whatsnext/.

HIMSS Analytics. "Why Are HCAHPS Scores Important?" HIMSS Analytics - North America, HIMSS, 29 July 2019, www.himssanalytics.org/news/why-are-hcahps-scores-important.

Krupnick, Matt. "Virgin America Fans Ask If Alaska Airlines Takeover Will Mean Loss of Cool." The New York Times, 11 Apr. 2016, www.nytimes.com/2016/04/12/business/virgin-america-fansaskif-alaska-airlines-takeover-will-mean-loss-ofcool.html.

Mcleod, Saul. Serial Position Effect. Simply Psychology, 2008, www.simplypsychology.org/primacy-recency.html.

Nimmon, Laura, and Terese Stenfors-Hayes. "The 'Handling' of Power in the Physician-Patient Encounter: Perceptions from Experienced Physicians." BMC Medical Education, vol. 16, no. 1, 2016, doi:10.1186/s12909-016-0634-0.

Petit, Zachary. "Legends in Advertising: Bill Bernbach, the Original Don Draper." Print , 12 Mar. 2014, www.printmag.com/featured/legends-in-advertising-bill-bernbach/.

"Quality Health Care Provider: Kaiser Permanente." Thrive, Kaiser Permanente, thrive.kaiserpermanente.org/.

Skills from Mayo Clinic. Mayo Foundation for Medical Education and Research, www.mayoclinic.org/voice/apps.

Starr, Paul. The Social Transformation of American Medicine: the Rise of a Sovereign Profession and the Making of a Vast Industry. Basic Books, 2017.

"Study Finds U.S. Healthcare Consumers Will Switch Providers Over Poor Digital Experiences." Cedar, 9 Oct. 2019, www.cedar.com/2019/10/09/study-finds-u-s-healthcare-consumers-will-switch-providers-over-poor-digital-experiences/.

Temming, Maria. "Robots Are Becoming Classroom Tutors. But Will They Make the Grade?" Science News, 19 Aug. 2019, www.sciencenews.org/article/robots-are-becoming-classroom-tutors-will-they-make-grade.

Chapter 3:

The Science Behind Sonic Branding: How Audio Can Create Better Patient, Caregiver, and Healthcare Provider Outcomes

Audrey Arbeeny

Editor's Note

As discussed in the previous chapter, there is an art and science to producing effective voice dialogs for healthcare applications. However, voice is only one component of an overall sonic experience. In addition to voice, audio interactions also include anything that a user may hear, including sounds and music. Consider the field of music therapy and one can find many examples of how these factors can have a significant impact on health and wellness. In this chapter, Audrey Arbeeny, a world leader on sonic branding, discusses the importance of designing a comprehensive sonic identity to create superior healthcare experiences, where literally every sound that a user hears has a specific purpose. To create truly exceptional voice experiences for patients and healthcare providers, sonic branding must be part of the overall voice strategy. This chapter provides insight and guidance to those looking to understand this critical component of voice first technologies.

Have you ever remembered every word to a song you haven't heard in years? Been comforted by that familiar voice of a loved one when you needed to hear it most? Picked up on the nuance of someone's tone of voice that reflected a different emotion than the words they were saying?

Voice is a powerful emotional communicator. In recent years, there's been a tremendous rise in interest in voice-first and sonic branding, this new, revolutionary, valuable communication tool that is a "Brand Imperative" today for enhancing your message and customer experience. For me, it's surprising that it's taken this long to see intense levels of interest in creating audio assets for sonic storytelling, because it's actually not new. What is new is the numerous new needs, and new ways to harness and leverage your audio assets. This, I believe, is what has driven what seems like a sudden and necessary interest in sonic branding.

Voice and sound are rapidly at the forefront of today's technologies, from smart homes and assistants to AI. Our technological advancements have brought the voice into our home, our car, and our workplace. Many of our interactions are now through voice. We have podcasts, chatbots, virtual assistants, smart-enabled vehicles, even insurance companies and manufacturers providing Alexa-enabled perks for use of their products and services. And it is widely embraced and ingrained in our lives. I've seen a two-year-old swiping through pictures on a smart phone and pushing the FaceTime app icon. We have skills, flash briefings, you name it, and it's talking!

All this has sparked both a growing need and new opportunities for developing sonic branding within the healthcare industry, as the technological advancements in this industry are moving at lightning speed, rivaling other industries that have been engaged in the discipline for many more years. Healthcare is an industry that is long overdue for embracing the advantages of sonic branding, because the benefits and effects of music and sound to promote health and healing are well documented and proven, as I will explain below.

For a long time, not many were listening to what their brands sounded like, and what the customer needed from that sound, certainly not with the zeal and saturation they are embracing voice-first and sound-first now. Sonic branding has arrived in a very big way, and this should really matter to you, because the future will not only be voice and sound driven, but the coupling of that with the emotional and holistic benefits of music and sound will create better, unparalleled, health--inducing outcomes for products, patients, healthcare providers, and caregivers alike.

So What Exactly is Sonic Branding?

Sonic branding is the art and science that surrounds the strategic development and deployment of a consistent, authentic sound experience of a brand. A sonic identity is the strategic and creative alignment of this experience, to create a narrative that delivers unified, memorable, and differentiating communications. It is more than a jingle, and more than a sound logo.

My work is focused on sonic branding, which includes voice, but also music, sound, and vibration. I've been doing this for over 25 years, at a global level for some of the top brands in the world. And it's one of the most powerful, underutilized disciplines that has the ability to make any experience richer, instantly recognizable, uniquely identifiable, informational, more intuitive, and most importantly, simply feel better.

I am fortunate to have built a company where I can blend all of my passions and skills: music, psychology, psychoacoustics, biomusicology, interactive branding, and technical expertise, and we have created hundreds of initiatives that are changing the world. For us, whether we are sonically branding the Xbox 360, IBM, Major League Soccer, Toshiba, or a very recent surgical robotics project, all of these disciplines were employed, and our mission statement has always been the same:

Audiobrain embraces and advocates for the power of music and sound to promote well-being.

In today's digital world, consumers can access almost anything very quickly. Because often there is little or no human-to-human interaction, they increasingly crave emotional experiences that engage them on a deeper level. Through sonic branding, there's a great opportunity to fulfill this need. The right sound, when crafted intentionally, strategically, and consistently, can instantly bridge the emotional experience and help articulate a brand's personality.

Sonic Branding Then and Now

Audiobrain has always been at the forefront of technology, and we have been asked to work on some of the world's largest initiatives involving music, sound, and voice branding over the past two decades. From our sonic branding projects and product sonifications like the Xbox 360, to voice branding and UI/UX design for hearables like Logitech's Ultimate Ears and Jaybird products, we have created many of the world's most iconic sounds, and have developed, prototyped, and implemented them into emerging technologies that are now forever changing the landscape of how we think, act, and respond to our interactions. We've been fortunate to collaborate with brands such as Google, Holland America Line, NBC Olympics, and many more.

To understand what's involved, a well-documented example of quality sonic branding is our work for Microsoft's Xbox 360. When Audiobrain created the sonic branding initiative for the Xbox 360, its crafting was deliberate, well researched, collaborative, strategic, creative, and ultimately empathetic and authentic to the Xbox 360 experience. Our goal was to bring the brand to life as a living breathing entertainment system.

After developing the sonic strategy, we then created the system boot up, sonic logo, product sounds, events, broadcasting, and many other Xbox 360 touchpoints, all carefully crafted through its unique sonic lens. Everything flowed from that central narrative.

We also created the sonic fingerprint, that Xbox 360 "breath," that in a split second can communicate the brand personality, embed in your memory, and immediately make you feel the experience the second you hear it. To this day, the Xbox 360 sonic branding is often referred to as iconic; it is highly recognizable and immediately creates that emotional connection when heard.

Many other projects have followed throughout the years as we honed our craft, built methodologies in an industry that had no roadmap, conducted our research and testing, and kept pushing the bar on the technology side. True to our Mission Statement, whether the sounds were for entertainment, information, navigation, a theme, or a voice, we crafted them through the brand's lens and ensured that every sound was important to the brand.

We built a process that ensured that every sound had a meaning and would be significant to the end user. In 2005, we created a sonic branding initiative that included an interactive voice response (IVR) system for Colt, a UK based technology services company. When created as a sonic branding initiative, all of the voices in the various languages shared the same expressions as the other branding elements, such as the brand theme or the brand on-hold music, and the similarities in the cadence, pitch, and personality across the different languages was consistent and authentic to the brand. This was our first full voice branding initiative, where we saw an intentional development of many branded global voices developed from a singular brand filter.

Others, such as IBM, also paid a great deal of attention to their sonic branding. For example, we used the same voices in IBM tutorials that the consumer heard in their advertising. We leveraged their sonic branding globally, by creating consistency with events, and we built a sonic toolbox of event sounds to use globally. We were invited to be on the IBM Sense Layering Team and Illustrated Sensory Branding in 2006 at IBM's Merlin Center, an experiential environment created to effectively demonstrate the future of high technology banking to bank executives. The experience starts in a living-room like environment featuring warm biscotti and coffee. It gradually transitions into an experience that has been described as a virtual theme park for banking executives.

IBM was the first brand for whom we created executive walk on music, in 2005. In the past, their executives walked onto a stage accompanied by arbitrary music chosen by the venue's AV person. In one case, it was a comical, inappropriate song, and the audience laughed. After their executive spoke, he asked us to create on-brand walk-ons, so no one would be embarrassed by the music played for their entry like he was. Now, nearly all the brands we work with request executive walk-ons. We also created sonic branding guidelines, so globally the brand would have a consistent tone and feel.

Along with our commercial success with many brands, we stayed technically advanced, and continued to conduct research on the power of music and sound, and the science behind it, and actively sought projects that were in health and wellness. While there are many brands in healthcare, the projects in this industry were few and far between. There were many reasons for this; the primary ones, I believe, were concerns about potential government regulations, compliance required for sounds (frequencies, durations), potential harmful effects, its influence on patients, and many other constraints.

In the early 1990s and 2000s, there were a handful of healthcare companies, such as Bayer Healthcare, Merck, and GlaxoSmithKline that understood the value of a consistent, authentic sonic brand experience. For Bayer Healthcare, we created a multi-tiered Proof of Concept and other educational materials to illustrate with sound and imagery, what sonic branding could do for them. For Merck, we created sounds and initiatives that enhanced the customer experience.

For GSK, we created many initiatives for brands such as Tums and Polident. But their Panadol brand was the first to fully create a consistent, unified, global sonic branding initiative that included a multitude of touchpoints, a global launch, education for both their team members and their global agencies, as well as sonic branding guidelines. Everything was unified, yet with flexibility to be culturally specific. We had a VP of Global Innovation as a champion, and we even created a "sonic experience indicators" project: 100 sounds to show what various emotions could sound like through the GSK lens. This was all pre- 2010, and very ahead of its time.

To this day, I would say that IBM and GSK were perhaps the most forward-thinking brands we worked with in that time period when it came to the intentional use of music, sound, and voice. Sonic branding was not very well embraced, or even well known, at that time.

Despite the many commercial initiatives we had underway, we could not penetrate the healthcare industry very well. To me, this seemed ironic since health and well-being are very personal things that consumers are often emotional about. But it was an uphill climb.

The Research Study That Did Not Happen

We have donated pro bono sonic branding from day one for causes in health and well-being. In 2003, in a case that we were particularly passionate about, we tried to create an in-facility research study that would substantiate our understanding that appropriate music and sound would yield better patient outcomes. We came very close, after I met a well-known surgeon who was building a new state-of-the-art, illness-specific testing facility. Here is an excerpt from his letter to me:

"Dear Audrey:

It was a pleasure speaking with you the other day. I have always been amazed how important music is to the overall mental and physical state of a patient. As you know, we are currently building one of the finest, state of the art testing facilitates at (hospital). Our Architects have spent much time and attention to detail. Besides being aesthetically beautiful, the medical institutional look has been camouflaged with art, woodwork and unusual decorative materials. However, music may prove to be the most important humanistic component to this center.

I have been having a difficult time convincing the medical community of the importance of music in patient care. Patients are always anxious about medical procedures. Besides the thought of having a procedure, patients are concerned about what may be discovered. Often, patients may need to wait in a holding or procedure room before a doctor arrives. Although this wait may be brief, the 5 minutes a patient is lying on a stretcher staring into the ceiling may seem like forever. I have noticed that if gentle music is playing, this wait does not seem to produce the same anxiety. I have also noted that patient sedation is easier during the procedure if the patient quietly relaxes while listening to pleasing music.

My observations have much scientific basis. A patient of mine has provided me with 16 references of published studies discussing the effects of music on the human physiology. However, despite this literature, music is still viewed as a luxury and not a part of conventional patient care.

This is where I believe that you can help. Our new (facility) will be a model for all institutions. With its state-of-the-art equipment, attention to patient comfort, and humanistic care, I believe that adding music will make this unit a truly unique and compassionate place. If you could work with a company to provide equipment, and your music, we can assure inclusion in any research we perform investigating the effect of music on patient care. Thank you for your help. I look forward to your response."

This letter was written almost 17 years ago. This surgeon is clearly validating the power of music and better patient outcomes. After spending almost two years drowning in paperwork for permission to do this research, pro bono, we sadly, realized it was not going to be approved to move forward. Still, we continued on our mission, and are entering an entirely different world now: one ripe with opportunities to create the kind of experience outlined above, with the technologies that are undoubtedly creating healthy outcomes that were unfathomable 15, 10, even 5 years ago. There is no doubt that carefully crafted music, sound, and voice experiences will elevate the benefits and the experiences new healthcare technologies are delivering. Health organizations and caregivers are creating thoughtful communications, leading to better understanding, and patients are receiving significantly better outcomes, care, comfort and yes, even empowerment.

Sound Science: Audio Can Create Healthier Outcomes

There is substantial research that has for many years validated the connection between music, emotion, and memory (Jäncke). Music and sound are emotional triggers, connecting with us on a visceral level, and their effects are immediately felt. This is because music and sound reach the limbic system, the deep, emotional center of our brain, embedding memories, and creating emotional responses (Psychology of Sound - The Impact of Sound on the Brain).

In a study by The Montreal Neurological Institute and Hospital – The Neuron at McGill University on the neuroscience of music and its association to pleasurable experiences, scientists found that the pleasurable experience of listening to music releases dopamine, a neurotransmitter in the brain ("Musical Chills"). Dopamine is known to play a pivotal role in establishing and maintaining behavior that is biologically necessary. This is a fascinating study and one of many that scientifically prove the positive effects of music on the brain.

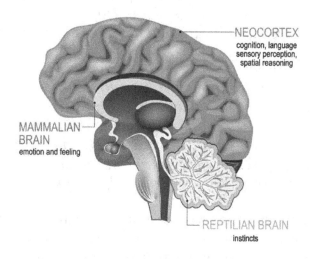

Brain evolution

NEOCORTEX
cognition, language
sensory perception,
spatial reasoning

MAMMALIAN BRAIN
emotion and feeling

REPTILIAN BRAIN
instincts

From primal screams to rousing choirs to crowd chants in sports stadiums, music and sound resonate on a deep level, and we are naturally wired sound receptors. Even before our birth, our mother's body is a system of sound, rhythms, and vibration. From as early as 18 weeks, a fetus can begin to sense sound and vibration.

Many studies have been done and the results prove that sound has a profound impact on health and well-being. There is so much science and research supporting its benefits that it can be overwhelming in its depth. Below, I'll outline some key findings and facts that summarize why this is so important to the healthcare industry.

Because of where and how music is housed in the brain, its holistic benefits are substantial. There are many studies that examine:

- The biological effects on humans when we listen to appropriate sound

- The disturbances that harsh or inappropriate sound can have on patients

- The communal benefits of music and sound

- The healing effects of music and sound

- The new research being focused on elder care

- The benefits for those with autism, cancer, depression, anxiety, loneliness, and many others.

In numerous studies, the results are favorable and indicative of the profound effect appropriate music, sound, and voice can provide, such as:

- The study "The Benefits of Music in Hospital Waiting Rooms" concluded that stress levels were significantly decreased; results indicated that music reduced self-reported stress levels, and that visitor stress levels were inversely related to perceptions of customer service (Routhieaux and Tansik).

- "Reducing Noise Pollution in the Hospital Setting by Establishing a Department of Sound: A Survey of Recent Research on the Effects of Noise and Music in Health Care" looks at the effects of noise on health, the problems of noise pollution in the health care setting, and the benefits of replacing noise with music to reduce heart rate, blood pressure, breathing rate, emotional anxiety, and pain. By combining these areas of research, the authors propose the establishment of a department assigned to (1) control the amount of noise in a hospital and (2) provide a center of music therapy for all individuals in the hospital setting, including in-patients, out-patients, doctors, and staff. Due to the large specificity of these areas, a unifying source, or "Department of Sound," is suggested to aid in thoroughly addressing and combining these two concepts most effectively (Cabrera and Lee).

- "The Benefits of Music on Health and Athletic Performance" examines the effect of music during warm-up on athletes' short-term maximal performances, and it found significant ergogenic effects. The music motivational effects have been linked to increases in individual perception of self-esteem and sense of confidence, enhanced arousal, as well as facilitating motor coordination. Moreover, this auditory stimulus can be used as a tool to "psych up" in preparation for performance, shift intentional focus, boost self-efficacy, and encourage psychological skills usage (Chtourou).

- In "The Science of Vibration: How Different Frequencies Affect Our Brain Waves," different frequencies are examined as well as their effect on the brain. This overview looks at the study of brainwaves and incorporating these frequencies in music to stimulate and parallel the brain (The Science of Vibration).

In NPR's "The Power of Music," the author reports that scientists have found that music stimulates more parts of the brain than any other human function (Mannes). That's why she sees so much potential in music's power to change the brain and affect the way it works.

There are numerous other sources. One of my favorite organizations is The Monday Life, an amazing organization that brings the best healing environments to hospitalized children. They provide summaries of research studies on the benefits of music therapy on mental and physical health.

Here you can find studies validating that (Mechanic and Burns):

- Music has proven therapeutic effectiveness in psychiatry, obstetrics, and pediatrics, promoting well-being, controlling pain, and neutralizing negative emotions. Music can reduce pain and anxiety as much as 50%.

- Engaging hospitalized children with interactive music therapy allows for emotional and physical comfort.

- Music reduces the burden of pharmacotherapy, such as narcotics, on pediatric patients.

A New Technological Landscape Means Big Opportunities in Healthcare

The tech landscape has changed dramatically in the past six years, and monumentally in the past three. Currently our initiatives in the health and wellness space have risen about 45% in the past two years.

In the past two years alone, we created the sonic branding, user experience design, and product sonification for surgical robotics, and we created and tested the sonic landscape and UX design for a heart health device. In addition, we created the sonic branding, music, sounds, and voice branding for dozens of educational videos and interactive pieces that help communicate and educate on both illness and wellness. We created the sonic landscape and implementation for a virtual reality tour of a cancer research facility. All of these initiatives demonstrate new ways of thinking and working, in a community that is primed, and challenged, to use technologies and sound to promote healthier outcomes through their efficiency, efficacy, and empathy.

For our surgical robotics sonic branding, the initiative was originally a prototype to test the feasibility of intentional audio, as the physician's eyes are often engaged on a computer screen. For those in the operating room, critical information needs to be conveyed quickly, yet it is also sometimes a very noisy environment.

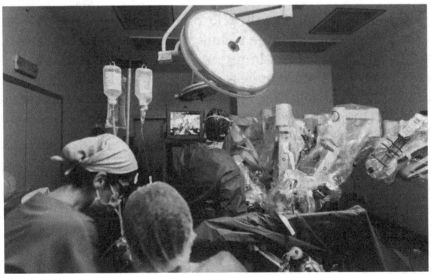

This global firm came to us to help them build a sonic branding prototype initiative. While they wanted the sounds to provide the healthcare team with valuable information, they also envisioned many more surgical robotic products in the near future. To develop sounds that need to convey critical information, engage the end user, and also differentiate the firm making the product, we posed the following questions:

- Was there an opportunity to brand the surgical robot with a "marquee sound" so this and future offerings would be recognizable as their products?

- Could the sounds be crafted with more intuition?

- What were the hierarchy of the sounds? Which were the most important, what various states needed to be addressed? Was there a critical warning state? Successful completion state? In progress state?

Very quickly into the project, it became apparent that this was quite a complex undertaking. There were compliances for certain critical alerts. There were too many sounds. While the original vision had what seemed to be the most appropriate placements of sounds, the testing showed that there were some that were more intrusive in the actual operating room. When not in a real-time setting, the sounds seemed to flow, but when tested with real surgeons, they found they preferred the set to be more limited to the core, key interactions where they truly needed sound. We knew this would be the case, as the ask seemed numerous, but this often happens on projects, and clients are often very ambitious at the start as to the number of sounds they want to create, only to soon find out the number they really need is less.

We tested with recordings of the OR to hear the machinery that a normal setting would have. We received technical specs in advance to have the right parameters for the speakers in use. We tested our sounds and added the ambience of the OR to further hear what they would sound like when there was other uncontrollable noise that our sound would be competing with. We wanted to make sure we were choosing the best pitch, frequencies, and length to help our sounds be heard better.

We also found three points where we would create the core "marquee moment," branded sounds that could represent a sound logo/ identity for broader use:

- the startup sound

- the power down sound

- the overarching unique, consistent sounds crafted for the robotics device

Our project evolved and garnered interest from many more team members, and soon others were weighing in, impacting the work that was initially designed to be an illustrative Proof-of-Concept as to how intentional audio might work for surgical robotics. Because of significant efforts and the excitement around the initiative, combined with the quality of the sounds and enrichment to the experience, these sounds are now actually being implemented, and we've completed our first surgical robotics initiative. It was complex, challenging, and rewarding. There were many other parts of this initiative that we evolved and refined, and we are very excited that in the end, we created sounds that are functional, intuitive, branded, appropriate to the interaction, and will help produce a healthier outcome for the healthcare team, the patient, their caregivers, and the brand. That is very rewarding and powerful sonic branding.

Counterpace: A New Wearable for Heart Health

The Counterpace system consists of two elements: a dual heart and movement sensor worn on the user's chest, and a connected app that guides a user to coordinate step timing with their heart pump cycle while running or walking, based on detected heart and step events. This device is grounded in existing technology and research. There have been incredible benefits shown from aligning the timing of rhythmic muscle contraction and blood vessel compression with the relaxation phase of the heart, and medical pumps have already been used to achieve this effect, reducing the effects of heart disease, high blood pressure, diabetes, and other illnesses. These same benefits can be gained by utilizing the natural compression of blood vessels that occurs during walking and running. The key is to align each footstep precisely between heartbeats, which is something that elite athletes manage to do intuitively, but the majority of us need guidance to reach. With Counterpace, users are assisted in reaching a satisfying and efficient rhythm of running in time with the beat of their own heart, which improves heart health and maximizes circulation and oxygen delivery throughout the body.

Audiobrain was tasked with creating sounds that achieve multiple goals: they had to uniquely and memorably express the identity of Counterpace as a brand, and be the guiding indicator that the user would run to. Having an audio cue to guide users' running pace was a key aspect of the functionality; it would be impractical, even unsafe, to use a visual cue and require a runner to look at their phone for the entire session. When the product was brought to us, the development team was working with generic sounds that were adequate indicators, but not branded or pleasant.

We began by developing a range of concepts in collaboration with the Counterpace team, and eventually pursued a select few to provide users with a range of audio prompts to choose from. These concepts were used to create a branded splash screen that plays when the app is opened; rhythmic elements and sound beds that indicate whether the user is "in the zone" (i.e. step and heart rate are aligned) as well as the audible element used to indicate the adaptive step timing target. The app also features voice cues that express some of the more complex or variable information which supplements the UI sounds.

After the splash screen and setup, the first sound a user will hear at the beginning of their Counterpace experience is a sound indicating that their heart rate is not yet adequately matched to their step rate. This sound is inspired by the blip of sonar, invoking the idea that the device is searching for something that is not quite locked onto yet. There is an additional voice prompt that clarifies this information. Users can also run to tempo-mapped music that adaptively syncs to the target step rate, to guide the runner with a sound that both informs their movement and enhances the overall experience.

A study performed by Dr. Bleich and others and published in ASCM's flagship journal Medicine & Science in Sports & Exercise confirmed that "synchronizing foot strikes when running to the diastolic portion of the cardiac cycle [when heart muscles are relaxing] results in a significantly reduced HR and minute ventilation compared with stepping during systole [when heart muscles are contracting]" (Constantini et al.). Users report experiencing not only the measurable health benefits, but also that the product makes exercise more interesting and fun. The sound design and musical elements are key to this. Other studies have shown that music can enhance exercise experience, performance, and endurance (Ford). There are also well researched cognitive and brain benefits to rhythmic or coordinative exercise. In a study called "The Effects of Physical Exercise with Music on Cognitive Function of Elderly People: Mihama-Kiho Project," researchers found that "Physical exercise combined with music produced more positive effects on cognitive function in elderly people than exercise alone" (Satoh et al.).

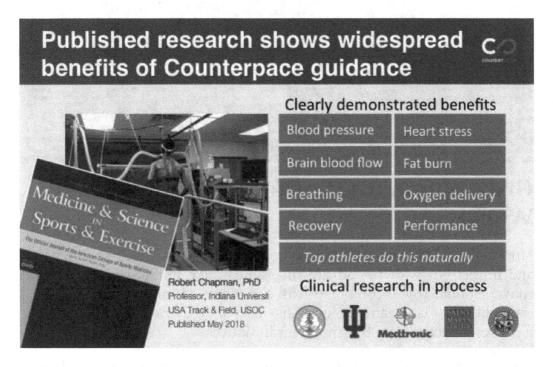

For Cycle for Survival, we created many sonic branding initiatives, pro bono, because we believe they are doing amazing work in awareness and fundraising for rare cancers; and that funding has created some breakthrough research. One project in particular is a virtual reality tour of the research center at Memorial Sloan Kettering, and it provides an empathetic look at and education in exactly how much goes into this kind of research. Our music and sound, combined with the physician's voice, draw you in for a keen understanding of their work. We are extremely proud that we've been able to collaborate and bring our expertise to enhance the patient, caregiver, and healthcare provider experience, and provide insight into what this organization does.

Great Opportunities for a Sound Science World

Most of the health care industry has not fully utilized strategic sound, voice, and music, but with the advent of products like home devices, AI, and conversational voice, combined with the many interactive and high tech capabilities we now can employ, it has become imperative, and beneficial, for them to incorporate this into their initiatives.

Medical devices are making tremendous advancements to help people stay well, interact with their physicians and caregivers, and send results back for analysis in real-time. There are companies like VocaliD that are creating synthetic voices that are tremendously helpful to so many people, or Canary Speech, that uses voice to identify conditions sooner.

I recently was privileged to speak at the Voice of Healthcare at Harvard Medical School this summer. I will forever be grateful to Bradley Metrock, CEO of Score Publishing, Founder of VoiceFirst.Community, host of "This Week in Voice," and the creator of this event. I was both inspired and astounded by the quality and quantity of work being done in the healthcare industry revolving around voice and sound. For me, it affirmed everything I believed about sound and health, and provided a wealth of information on technologies and the state of voice and sound in the healthcare industry. One of the many notable people in attendance was Dr. Teri Fisher, a physician who also hosts the "Voice First Health" podcast, develops flash briefings, has spoken at TEDx, and is one of the brightest advocates in this space. He has since had me as a guest on his podcast. I find those in voice, and particularly voice in healthcare, to be very communal, supportive, open to sharing, and passionate about what each of us is contributing to this new technological landscape. The work that is emerging is astounding.

One area that is having significant technological growth in utilizing voice and sound is in caring for the elderly. People are living much longer. We have many caregivers (myself included) looking after family members who have more medications, more conditions that need monitoring, and more information that needs to be conveyed to their healthcare providers.

There are now products like Lifepod, a proactive voice platform and caregiver portal, that provide two-way voice service for older adults aging in place and chronically ill patients as well as their caregivers, right in their homes. But unlike traditional voice assistants, LifePod can be controlled remotely by a caregiver, using an easy, online portal to configure and schedule proactive voice check-ins, reminders, and other services.

We also have products like Dexcom G6, FDA approved, with a sensor and an app that can read diabetes blood sugar levels without blood. If you check your levels several times a day, this means no pricking, and this is life-changing for those with Diabetes.

At Harvard, the Keynote was given by Heidi Culbertson, CEO and Founder of Marvee, which is pioneering voice technologies in caring for aging populations. She told her personal story for her passion in this field. Heidi's mother, Marvee, at the age of 90, began to lose her vision due to macular degeneration, a common eye disease among the aging. Heidi saw a profound impact on the quality of her mother's life with the advent in 2014 of Amazon Alexa, which she could control with her voice. Since then, Marvee has become a recognized leader in voice-first strategy and conversation design, and they specialize in creating voice experiences to engage older adults. They are a strategic voice design consultancy focused on the aging population.

It seems many in this community, like me, have personal stories that have ignited a passion, a desire to promote healthier outcome with voice, sound, and music. The work Marvee is doing creates healthier lives for so many.

Many industry experts predict that nearly every application will integrate voice technology in some way in the next 5 years (Cahill). My own elderly father now has four at-home devices that enable him to stay home and not have to make another trip to the physician's office. He had one device last year. Now, he no longer has to travel to get his Coumadin levels checked. His pacemaker is remotely monitored, and his apnea machine sends the data to both his physician and to me, as I receive it on an app.

Another area of technological advancement is in helping people with disabilities. Gartner, Inc, a global leader in research, predicts that by 2023, the number of people with disabilities who are employed will triple ("Gartner Unveils Top Predictions for IT Organizations and Users in 2020 and Beyond"), due to AI and emerging technologies that reduce barriers to access. This was discussed at their Gartner IT Symposium by Daryl Plummer, VP, Distinguished Analyst, Chief of Research, and Chief Gartner Fellow who said:

> *"People with disabilities constitute an untapped pool of critically skilled talent. Artificial Intelligence (AI), augmented reality (AR), virtual reality (VR) and other emerging technologies have made work more accessible for employees with disabilities. For example, select restaurants are starting to pilot AI robotics technology that enables paralyzed employees to control robotic waiters remotely. Organizations that actively employ people with disabilities will not only cultivate goodwill from their communities, but also see 89% higher retention rates, a 72% increase in employee productivity, and a 29% increase in profitability"* ("Gartner Unveils").

Technologies are advancing every day. Our ability to create voices in many different languages is both significant and yet still challenging as there are so many different dialects. At Audiobrain, we are about to collaborate with a synthetic voice development company, as well as three others in this field.

My Personal Story and Journey in Sonic Branding: My North Star

My journey into sonic branding began before I was even born. My mother was a highly musical person. She was born in Manhattan and her family had limited financial means, but an abundance of love and an appreciation of the arts. An elderly woman who lived below gave her piano lessons, and my mother practiced on a cardboard keyboard, as she did not have a piano. Music and sound were everything to her. She sang and played every single day from childhood. So of course, when I was born, she wanted to give me all the love and joy of music and playing instruments that she wanted in her life. I started taking piano lessons when I was around three or four.

I think it was more for the discipline at that age, but I really enjoyed it. It made me feel good and I too loved music and sound from a very young age. I would feel things when I would play or hear music, even at six or seven years old. I could physically feel it throughout my body; I knew something was connecting with me emotionally. My dreams had soundtracks. Music could move me to cry even at a young age.

I started flute around age eight, had started a rock band in my teens with my brother, and studied voice at Carnegie Hall a few years later. My parents were very supportive on the condition that we study non-musical academics to have a fall-back career. So I studied accounting only because I was good in math (direct correlation between math and music) as well as psychology, and I developed a keen passion for "the science of sound." It is something I continue to have to this day; it is a part of my being.

I then thought that maybe I wanted to be a music therapist, and I worked on a summer program that would prove to be a very important turning point in my professional and personal life. Applying my own proposed study, I used music therapy with children that were deaf and blind, as well as developmentally disabled. This was at a state institution; the kids were wards of the state, and the conditions at that time were less than favorable. In their classroom, I would put their little feet on speakers, I would let them feel the vibration of the music, and I would give them something to tap like a tambourine or anything they could shake or tap. And they would respond. When they returned to the ward that evening, I tracked their behavior. Would they be less harmful to themselves? Many had behavioral issues that I believed came from being institutionalized at that time, decades ago. Some would hit themselves or bang their heads. After doing my music sessions with vibration, this behavior decreased tremendously, even if just for one day. And they would stay calm and sit still long enough so I could teach them to feed themselves with a plate guard, so they wouldn't have to be part of an assembly line of hospital workers with many other children to feed. Their lives were made just a little bit brighter through music and sound. All of this substantiated my belief that music and sound was scientifically important, and this is where my real truth journey into psychoacoustics and biomusicology began.

As for my band, after a period of time I began to realize that I liked being in the studio much more than performing in front of an audience. Being in the studio gave me a sense of having a vision, starting something, being able to shape and complete it, and I liked that process.

I then got a job at a music production company. At the time they did predominantly music for advertising and I was tasked with heading up the special projects group with one of the owners. We called this "Identity Work," which is now what we all know as sonic branding. This owner was very interested in branding as it was the hot topic at the time, and he believed sound would one day be equal to the visual branding process. We went to many branding conferences, and there I formally learned the discipline of branding. We created initiatives that were far more immersive than advertising scores. We followed the branding process, looked at competitors' user interaction, and brought a process to sound development that did not exist before, as this was all quite new. We had no blueprint to follow. And we worked with many global brands. That was where my sonic branding expertise, in a formalized way, began. But in practice, it was something I already knew, believed in, and had the understanding to help bring successful outcomes to our projects.

That company gave me tremendous opportunities and learning experiences, but at the same time I had my own vision that was far more research driven, grounded in science, and that would be 100% dedicated to sonic branding. So in 2003 I started Audiobrain with my colleague Michael Sweet. I wanted to focus all that I knew and was passionate about -- music and its ability to heal and create wellness -- and combine it in a business sense, to be able to make a living while at the same time never letting go of my passion for using music and sound to enrich people's lives. Because my own background was not in music for advertising, I had a vision for a more formalized, science and strategy driven process.

And so I focused on Audiobrain as a business, creating music and sound that was intentional, carefully crafted, scientifically researched, and validated through strategy and testing. At the same time, we do pro bono work for those less fortunate who may not have the finances to fund quality audio or better holistic outcomes. For many years, this is how I balanced my passion for the science and psychology of sound with my need to make a living and create meaningful sound across all brands. This is my North Star, because I know firsthand how extraordinary music and sound is with its power to heal, help, and support health and wellness.

The Future Will Bring A Healthier Outcome for All

Rising technologies have enabled us to move from robotic-sounding voice feedback to conversations with real or real sounding voices, from buzzers and alarms to more holistic and meaningful signals. We now are beginning to have a real mindfulness about the sounds we are hearing, and the experiences our end users are having. So particularly for the healthcare industry, this is a triple benefit.

By combining the holistic benefits of music and sound with new technologies, we have the ability to create more complete experiences, as well as to advance those technologies, and create an identity for the products and brands behind them. This could range from voice branding to wearables, from Artificial Intelligence to machine learning, and includes hearing aid advancements, synthetic voices, navigation sounds in medical devices, as well as overall holistic care, wellness and healing programs, and any services that could utilize music and sound.

But we are not there yet. As an example: with my dad's four devices, the technology is astounding. However, only one gives sound feedback. And while I receive the readings in the app, I don't know what they mean. I have no auditory signal if the mask fit is incorrect. So in an industry that is growing at rapid speed, with technology and voice on the rise, we now see an increased need for sonic feedback, sounds that communicate how to navigate, give feedback when something is complete, or an error or emergency is detected.

These products also need to create empathy and bring a humanness that is so expected in today's general business product interactions. So the brands working in this industry are not only tasked with creating medical devices, informational systems, and wellness, at the same time they are businesses with their own personality and messages to communicate in a very clear and meaningful way. And this is where the landscape is changing. When a team can share information or speak to a patient in real-time, that's very significant. When we can monitor physiological changes in real time, that's very significant. I remember being at the FUSE conference about eight years ago and the world-renown physicist Michio Kaku was speaking. He said, and I paraphrase: "You're probably wondering why a physicist is here at a design conference but you will be designing products that will enable us to detect diseases 10, 15, 20 years in advance before they manifest." At the time it did not sound realistic, and that reality is here, now.

While we create the most amazing technology, devices, programs, and advancements in the healthcare industry using music, sound, voice, and vibration, we must balance our technology with the appropriate sonic branding because its ability to impact the experience for patients, caregivers, and professionals is profound. We cannot leave empathetic audio experiences out of the holistic health care experience. If we embrace and align the sound with the information, and the experience with care and empathy, we will improve the world, and create significant, better, healthier outcomes for all.

If we can create our technologies with voice and sound that is appropriate to the experience, provides meaningful feedback, and creates a healthier sounding environment, and if we balance high tech with empathy, we will truly see increased, more holistic outcomes that exceed any expectations. The future will indeed be one filled with health and wellness.

Audrey Arbeeny is the Founder/CEO and Executive Producer of Audiobrain, recognized as global leaders in sonic branding. She teaches and lectures on sonic branding at Pratt Institute and is a visiting lecturer and mentor at the Masters in Branding Program at School of Visual Arts. Audrey recently completed two terms on the Board of Governors of the National Academy of Television Arts and Sciences New York Chapter and has been Music Supervisor for nine Olympic Broadcasts with NBC, for which she has received 2 Emmy Awards. Audiobrain creates sonic branding work throughout the world for Holland America Line, IBM, KIA Motors Corp, Microsoft, Toshiba, and many others.

References

1. Cabrera, Izumi Nomura, and Mathew H. M. Lee. "Reducing Noise Pollution in the Hospital Setting by Establishing a Department of Sound: A Survey of Recent Research on the Effects of Noise and Music in Health Care." Preventive Medicine, vol. 30, no. 4, Apr. 2000, pp. 339–45. ScienceDirect, doi:10.1006/pmed.2000.0638.

2. Cahill, Peter. Your Mobile Strategy Needs To Include Voice. 29 Sept. 2017, https://www.forbes.com/sites/groupthink/2017/09/29/your-mobile-strategy-needs-to-include-voice/#4aa30a0d5ce8.

3. Chtourou, Hamdi. EBSCOhost | 93708110 | BENEFITS OF MUSIC ON HEALTH AND ATHLETIC PERFORMANCE. 2013, https://web.b.ebscohost.com/

4. Constantini, Keren, et al. "Synchronizing Gait with Cardiac Cycle Phase Alters Heart Rate Response during Running." Medicine & Science in Sports & Exercise, vol. 50, no. 5, May 2018, p. 1046. journals.lww.com, doi:10.1249/MSS.0000000000001515.

5. Constantini, Keren, et al. "Synchronizing Gait with Cardiac Cycle Phase Alters Heart Rate Response during Running." Medicine & Science in Sports & Exercise, vol. 50, no. 5, May 2018, p. 1046. journals.lww.com, doi:10.1249/MSS.0000000000001515.

6. Ford, Steve. "Upbeat Music Boosts Exercise Time during Cardiac Stress Testing." Nursing Times, 7 Mar. 2018, https://www.nursingtimes.net/news/research-and-innovation/upbeat-music-boosts-exercise-time-during-cardiac-stress-testing-07-03-2018/.

7. "Gartner Unveils Top Predictions for IT Organizations and Users in 2020 and Beyond." Gartner, https://www.gartner.com/en/newsroom/press-releases/2019-22-10-gartner-unveils-top-predictions-for-it-organizations-and-users-in-2020-and-beyond. Accessed 24 Oct. 2019.

8. Jäncke, Lutz. "Music, Memory and Emotion." Journal of Biology, vol. 7, no. 6, Aug. 2008, p. 21. PubMed Central, doi:10.1186/jbiol82.

9. Mannes, Elena. "'The Power Of Music' To Affect The Brain." NPR.Org, 1 June 2011, https://www.npr.org/2011/06/01/136859090/the-power-of-music-to-affect-the-brain.

10. Mechanic, Oren J., and Marley E. Burns. "Music Therapy- Helping Hospitalized Children Non-Profit." The Monday Life, 13 Jan. 2012, http://www.themondaylife.org/music-therapy.

11. "Musical Chills: Why They Give Us Thrills." Newsroom, 10JAN2011, https://www.mcgill.ca/newsroom/channels/news/musical-chills-why-they-give-us-thrills-170538.

12. Routhieaux, R. L., and D. A. Tansik. "The Benefits of Music in Hospital Waiting Rooms." The Health Care Supervisor, vol. 16, no. 2, Dec. 1997, pp. 31–40. europepmc.org, http://europepmc.org/abstract/med/10174442.

13. Satoh, Masayuki, et al. "The Effects of Physical Exercise with Music on Cognitive Function of Elderly People: Mihama-Kiho Project." PLoS ONE, vol. 9, no. 4, Apr. 2014. PubMed Central, doi:10.1371/journal.pone.0095230.

14. The Science of Vibration: How Different Frequencies Affect Our Brain Waves | Spirit Science. 15 Dec. 2015, http://thespiritscience.net/2015/12/25/the-science-of-vibration-how-different-frequencies-affect-our-brain-waves/.

Chapter 4:

Secure Voice

Nathan Treloar

Editor's Note

As we begin to embrace voice as the new operating system and we design incredibly effective and engaging voice applications (as described in the previous two chapters) that serve to enhance the healthcare of our patients, questions naturally arise about the security and privacy of the data that is collected. With new technology comes some apprehension about these issues and it is with a clear plan that we must proactively address these concerns. This chapter, by Nathan Treloar, an industry-leading expert in this field, provides a comprehensive overview of the issues and strategies involved in protecting our voice interactions. He covers everything from securing voice applications to regulatory considerations to HIPAA compliance. He completes the chapter with a look to the future and how these critical issues will impact and be impacted by voice first technology.

Introduction

Since Amazon introduced Alexa in November 2014, connected speakers have become one of the fastest-growing innovations in the consumer tech industry. In January 2019, Amazon announced that more than 100 million Alexa enabled devices had been sold globally.[1] In January 2019, Google boasted that more than 1 billion devices, including Android phones, have Google Assistant built-in.[2]

Consumer interest in voice for healthcare applications has trailed general adoption of voice assistant technology but is on the rise. A report published by Voicebot.ai[3] on consumer adoption of voice assistants in healthcare found that only one in thirteen U.S. consumers have used voice assistants like Amazon Alexa or Google Assistant for healthcare purposes (as of September 2019), while one in two **would like to use** voice assistants for healthcare uses in the future.

For many good reasons described in this book, the healthcare industry has also begun to accept that voice assistants are an important new frontier for digital healthcare. The potential benefits of voice as a tool to improve patient engagement, increasing clinical efficiency, and deliver better outcomes is readily apparent. Voice assistants are being used for a variety of healthcare applications ranging from answering questions, managing medications, sending messages between patients and care givers, capturing healthcare data, scheduling appointments, and more.

But along with all the enthusiasm about voice assistants in healthcare comes an appropriate and sobering amount of concern about privacy and security of healthcare data. General wariness of technology related to cybersecurity is real and growing — especially in the wake of high-profile data breaches.

In a survey published by Microsoft in April 2019, 41% of voice-powered virtual assistant users said they had concerns about privacy and security.[4] The fact is, most voice assistant solutions transfer data over the internet and are therefore potentially subject to the all-to-familiar "hacks" for which that medium is infamous. While this is not a new concern in digital healthcare – smartphone apps for healthcare ("mHealth" apps) are also subject to this risk – voice assistants introduce yet another digital communication channel to consider, and one with its own set of unique security concerns.

In healthcare, these privacy concerns are amplified by the inherent sensitivity of personal health data, which may include medical diagnoses, lab reports, vital data measurements, drug prescriptions, and more. This data, when it can be attributed to an individual, is called Protected Health Information or PHI and is defined in the U.S. under the rules set forth in the Health Information Portability and Accountability Act of 1996, or just HIPAA. According to HIPAA[5], PHI is "individually identifiable health information" that may be stored or transmitted by a 3rd party on behalf of an individual.[6]

We'll discuss HIPAA and other regulations directed toward ensuring privacy and security of healthcare data later in this chapter, but let's start by exploring the nature of the privacy concerns specific to voice assistants.

Privacy Concerns of Voice

We've been here before. With the introduction of any new technology, there are always concerns that someone will abuse any access to PHI that technology might provide.

When the telephone was introduced, people worried about who was listening on the line when they talked to their doctor. When the internet came, the idea of patient portals where information about their personal health might be exposed caused waves of concern. Mobile devices and the mobile healthcare applications ("mHealth" apps) that came with them also brought about new concerns about privacy – among them, the fact that their inherent portability meant they could be left behind by mistake for anyone to pick up.

Every advance in technology introduces new challenges and new risks that need to be mitigated. We are in a nascent stage with voice and privacy. Unfortunately, the companies that sell voice-powered virtual assistants have been more reactive than proactive when it comes to personal data privacy, leading to public relations challenges. Case in point, it was revealed in 2019 that Amazon, Google and Apple regularly record and review what is spoken over their smart speakers and other devices. The reasons given by these businesses – to use this anonymized information to improve their services – may be technically accurate but did little to placate those concerned about the possibility of sensitive personal healthcare data getting into the wrong hands.[7]

---

[1]The actual definition of PHI under HIPAA includes a more precise definition of the 3rd-parties in-volved in storing and transmitting PHI. They may be "covered entities" or "business associates". A covered entity under HIPAA is a healthcare provider, payer, or healthcare data clearinghouse, while a business associate is any organization providing services to a covered entity that involves holding or transmitting PHI.

The fact that audio commands issued to voice assistants like Amazon Alexa and Apple Siri were being reviewed by humans caused enough concern, but the nature of an always-on, always-listening voice assistant created further challenges. When it was observed that those same voice assistants can be accidentally invoked to possibly record personal conversations, the flames of concern were fanned even more.[8] Amazon responded quickly and introduced in July of 2019 the option for customers to opt out of having their voice recordings added to a pool for manual review.[9] Apple and Google made similar changes, but the damage was done.

Major voice assistant platform providers are working to restore trust among skeptical consumers, but they have work to do. The VoiceBot.ai survey cited earlier shows that in September 2019 30% of consumers are "very concerned" about privacy in voice assistants. This is up from about 26% in January 2019.

While work to address the real and perceived data privacy issues continues among the major voice platform providers, there are specific measures that can be taken by voice application developers to ensure data privacy and security in voice applications. We'll explore these next.

Securing Voice Applications

The safeguards that must be in place in any digital healthcare application to properly protect personal healthcare data are a pantheon of technical, physical, and administrative approaches. They include things like making sure all data passed through the application is properly encrypted, locking down physical access to the device on which the application is running (e.g. a PC or smartphone), and ensuring a centrally-controlled unique username and password for each user.

Detailing all of the possible safeguards for digital healthcare applications is beyond the scope of this chapter. Instead, we'll take a look at specific considerations and best practices to ensure the security of voice assistant applications for digital healthcare.

Authentication

Voice applications over smart speakers and other voice-enabled devices require special approaches for establishing the identity of the user. For example, anyone can wake up an Alexa device that is owned by another person by simply saying, "Alexa" or whatever the "wake word" is used for the device. Unless specific measures are taken, that individual is now inside the user's device and has access to all the voice applications or skills the user has enabled. It's a bit like finding someone's unlocked smartphone. This simple fact introduces one of the complexities of securing voice in healthcare – authentication.

There are several approaches to authenticating users of voice applications.

1. Device ID. Assign a user to a specific voice device on the assumption that the device is only physically accessible to that user.

2. Spoken Password or Passphrase: Require a user to say a password, personal identification number (PIN) or passphrase.

3. Spoken Password or Passphrase with Confirmation: Require a user to say a password, PIN or passphrase that triggers a separate temporary PIN sent via a text message, in-app message, or email message for a secondary confirmation. Sometimes called two-factor authentication or just "2FA". This approach is the most common among modern digital applications. It requires another piece of information be on file with the application service provider in order to trigger the confirmation: an email address or phone number. Typically, this two-factor authentication is not required each time the user attempts to engage the voice assistant, but it can be.

4. Voice Profile. When the user speaks, the voice assistant recognizes them by the audio characteristics of their voice. If you have an Alexa device, you can say, "Alexa, who am I?". Alexa will attempt to recognize the user's voice. If she doesn't recognize you, you will be offered an option to train Alexa to know your voice. By itself, this doesn't equal complete authentication, but can be used as a "factor" for identification in the next approach.

Third-party conversational platforms can remove the complexities associated with enabling one-time passwords, PINs, and passphrases by offering pre-configured templates that can be used to ensure the person engaging with the voice assistant is who they say they are; an imperative when dealing with sensitive health information.

Authorization and Account Linking

A voice assistant application needs to not only identify the user (authentication) but establish that the user has the rights to access the services of the application (authorization). User authorization allows the voice application to be personalized to the needs and data of the user. For example, a care management voice application for diabetes may only allow the user access to content and services specific to their type of diabetes and their care plan.

The usual method of authorization for voice assistant applications is called Account Linking. Account Linking grants voice applications powered by Amazon Alexa, Google Assistant, and other voice assistant platforms the right to access data and services in another system, such as electronic medical records systems. Account linking uses OAuth[10], an industry standard protocol allowing or authorizing one application to connect with a backend application without having to share credentials.

Account Linking is handled when a user first sets up the voice assistant applications. In the Amazon Alexa parlance, this is when the voice skill is first enabled in the user's Amazon Alexa account. During account linking, the user is presented with a username/password challenge. Once the user successfully provides their credentials, the voice platform generates a user authentication token. This token is then used by the voice assistant application to prove that it has been granted permission to access the information on behalf of the user.

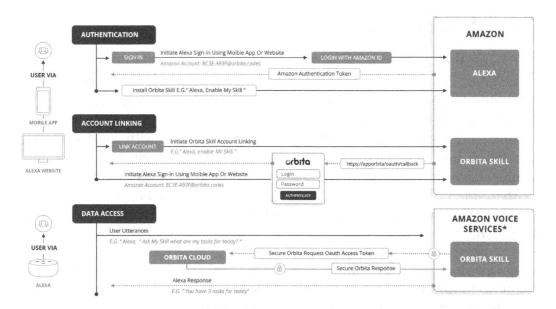

Consider this example of a voice assistant application that retrieves medication information for a patient. The patient may simply say, "What are my medications this morning?", which will trigger a request containing a packet of information that includes:

- The Intent matching the user's request. E.g. GetMedications

- Any slot values. (Slots are basically variables in utterances. E.g. time of day = "morning")

- Various metadata values, including time of day, session ID, etc.

The voice application uses the information in the packet to determine how to satisfy the request. In this example, the application would securely retrieve a list of the medications from the patient's records using the user authentication token established during Account Linking.

Developing a voice-powered virtual assistant that requires account linking is not a trivial endeavor. Modern voice platforms simplify this process by offering an out-of-the-box OAuth provider that is easy to set up and configure.

De-Identification

Removing the identifying information associated with healthcare data is an established approach to reducing security risks in digital health applications. This "de-identification" approach can be applied to voice assistants, as well, as a way to ensure that the voice assistant platform, whether Amazon Alexa or Google Assistant, has no ability to correlate the data with an identifiable user. This best practice leverages anonymous user accounts created and managed within a secure system separate from the voice assistant platform. With de-identification, only a unique token is passed to the virtual assistant platform (e.g. Amazon Alexa) and no identifying user account information is shared.

Consider this scenario. John Smith is a patient using an Amazon Echo at home to monitor and improve adherence to an experimental prescription drug he's taking as part of a clinical trial. The Echo device allows him to use an Alexa voice assistant to indicate when he's taken medication (e.g. "Alexa, I've taken my 9 AM medication") as well as hear a report on his overall medication adherence.

Even though John is using an Amazon Echo to provide information to the Alexa-powered voice assistant, Amazon has neither the ability to identify John nor the ability to directly access any of John's PHI stored securely within the linked system (see Authorization and Account Linking).

Limiting or Disabling Voice Cards

Some voice assistants include visual elements that may be displayed during the voice interaction. For example, content can be written to the Amazon Alexa voice cards made visible on Alexa powered devices with screens. Limiting the sensitive information written to these screens is one way to reduce the privacy and security risks of the application.

Limiting or Disabling Voice Analytics

Like voice cards, it may be desirable or necessary to disable and/or limit the patient specific information sent to the analytics and reporting services. Some voice platforms offer a feature to disable analytics down to a specific voice intent.

Employee Training

People assume it's the end users and the applications themselves that are the weakest link when it comes to risks associated with data breaches. However, employees of organizations creating and maintaining digital healthcare applications are more likely to be the source of compromised PHI security.

Shred-It, a leading information security company, found that hackers are actually less of a threat than employees.[11] According to the study, which surveyed more than 1,000 business owners and executives in the United States, 47 percent of business leaders say human errors – such as accidental loss of a device or document – have led to data breaches within their organizations.

If your organization is developing a voice assistant application, know that the most effective method for preventing data breaches is employee training. The right time to train employees on cybersecurity policies is when you onboard them. In doing so, you set clear expectations and provide a baseline of knowledge they will need to adhere to the required policies. After that, regular training should also be provided to keep employees up to date on all relevant cybersecurity topics.

The Shred-It study also showed that 86 percent of C-suite executives and 60 percent of small business owners agree that the risk of data breach is higher when employees work remotely. Make sure you have policies in place for how employees use company devices, access company information, communicate, and share data.

---

[2]OAuth (Open Authorization) is an open standard for token-based authentication and authoriza-tion on the internet. OAuth allows an end user's account information to be used by third-party services, such as Facebook, without exposing the user's password.

Usage Context

There are factors to consider for securing voice assistants that that are outside the control of the technology itself. For example, when placing a smart speaker in a hospital room, it may not be possible to tell if what patient is intended for the "ears" of the device. Nor is it possible to know the sensitivity of information the patient is going to share, or whether they are going to stay in that one skill that is deemed HIPAA-compliant. Only common sense can prevent someone from speaking aloud sensitive information into a voice device in a crowded room. It is important to consider the type of data being collected, the context of the user, and the modalities available (voice, chat, touch screens, buttons, etc.).

One approach is to issue a notice at the start of the conversation or within the dialogue to warn the user about sharing sensitive information. "Now I'm going to ask you for information that you might not want others to hear. So please be concerned with X, Y, and Z."

Strategies for a crowded area may include physical barriers like a small cubicles or walls, a dividing line or box that keeps the next person in line at a distance or use of "beam focused" microphones instead of omnidirectional. Another approach is to detect whether the user has headphones and only then triggering a voice response.

Limiting PHI

The surest way to prevent PHI from being compromised is to design a voice experience that prevents access to PHI data in the first place. A voice assistant that asks the patient the right question in the right context is extremely important. With the wrong cue, a patient could start talking about all their medical issues when all you really wanted was their name.

Not all health applications require PHI. For example, a voice assistant application for post-discharge education need not require PHI to be useful. Consider which data is required for the voice assistant to function. Which requests can be fulfilled without a second authentication? Can this data be provided without validation? With some analysis, it's possible to discover that none of the information passed through the voice assistant needs to identify a patient or risk compromising their privacy.

When you're designing how the data will be collected, have a mechanism in the voice assistant that is explicit about the data you do and do not want to collect. Consider stating at the beginning of the conversation that we would like to avoid collecting specific information. "I just need your first name."

Sometimes the voice-powered virtual assistant will take the conversation offline. If the voice assistant detects that the conversation is reaching a point where personal information may be required, the voice assistant may say send a link via email or text to verify the user, followed by a continuation of the conversation on a more secure channel – web chat, mobile chat, or phone call, as examples.

Transparency of Data Use

Use of behavioral data to inform the user experience is a sensitive topic not unique to voice assistant applications and one that needs to be administered more carefully in healthcare world. Past gaffes in use of user behavioral data by industry leaders—Amazon, Facebook, Apple, Google, and others— has borne out that transparency is the best approach.

- Be upfront in your applications Terms and Conditions and Privacy Policy about how data is collected. Explain what data you might collect and why.

- Give users control over their data. When you give people control, they understand that they have a say in the information that's being used, and it gives them insight into how and why it's being collected.

- Give users a choice to opt out. Be clear that users have the power to switch the data flow off – and also be clear about what the trade-offs are, including poorer user experience.

Some of these ideas are best practices recommendations, but some are required by established laws and regulations. We turn to those next.

Regulatory Considerations

The two largest regulatory frameworks that protect privacy and security of healthcare data are the Health Insurance Portability and Accountability Act of 1996 (HIPAA) in the United States, and the EU's General Data Protection Regulation (GDPR). These two frameworks operate in different geographic locations with different intentions but share some basic similarities and requirements.

HIPAA defines how PHI is classified and handled but differs from GDPR in terms of breach reporting, consent management and permission processes. GDPR focuses on protecting a wider array of identifiers, including voice and medical records, but also addresses many other types of protected information not covered by the HIPAA.

Both regulations share some basic foundational principles requiring safeguards to be in place to protect data. Such safeguards include access controls to ensure data reaches only those with necessary access rights, protection of data during transmission and at rest, and onward transfer of data protection responsibilities to suppliers and vendors that handle the data.

A voice assistant solution should be designed from the ground up with data privacy and security safeguards in place to ensure compliance. Importantly, beyond the technical considerations, voice application developers must also maintain the organizational roles, policies, procedures and infrastructure that comply with the latest HIPAA and/or GDPR rules.

HIPAA

HIPAA is a set of U.S. regulations designed to protect patient medical records and PHI handled by health insurance providers, health care providers, doctors, and hospitals or their third-party service providers. Any voice assistant solution designed for the U.S. market that may store or transmit PHI is a likely subject to the regulations of HIPAA. This may include voice applications use for clinical trials, call center operations, remote patient monitoring, in-facility operations, or any of a variety of other scenarios.

There are a couple of key considerations regarding voice and HIPAA. One is the fact that your actual voice, or voice signature, is considered personal identifiable information (PII). In other words, voice recognition, like facial recognition, can identify an individual and potentially be used to attach an identity to healthcare data, thereby creating Protected Health Information or PHI. The second is that device ID is also considered an identifier. If you have a computer, smartphone, or smart speaker with a unique ID, that's PII. Even your car, equipped with a smart speaker interface, may be considered a device in this context.

HIPAA regulations that pertain to voice applications are generally contained in two HIPAA rules: the Privacy Rule and the Security Rule.[12]

The **HIPAA Privacy Rule** includes regulations to limit the use and disclosure of PHI in healthcare treatment, payment transactions, and other operations by covered entities. It requires doctors to provide patients with an account of each entity to which they disclose their PHI, while still allowing relevant health information to be used within the proper context and authorized channels. It also gives patients the right to access their health information.

The **HIPAA Security Rule** establishes standards to protect ePHI (electronic PHI) created, received, processed, or maintained by, or on behalf of a covered entity. The Security Rule requires appropriate administrative, physical and technical safeguards to ensure the confidentiality, integrity, and security of ePHI.

HIPAA also requires that a Business Associates Agreement (BAA) be in place with any third-party suppliers that handle or may handle ePHI.[13] A Business Associate is any organization or person working in association with or providing services to a covered entity who handles or discloses PHI. A BAA is a legal contract between the organization providing the service, such as Amazon or Google, and the organization using it, such as a healthcare system or healthcare insurance provider.

Any organization that develops and maintains a voice assistant that stores and transmits PHI on behalf of a covered entity is a business associate and must be equipped to execute a BAA if required. The business associate does the backend work to ensure compliance with HIPAA by maintaining the policies and procedures that allow it to meet the obligation of the BAA. This includes having an established information security management program (ISMP) that addresses the administrative safeguards that HIPAA requires of business associates.

With the understanding that security risks continue to change, the business associate must constantly be assessing and monitoring all relevant activities to ensure that controls are effective and meeting objectives. The business associate's suppliers and vendors need to be vetted, as well, to determine their access needs and mitigate any risks they bring to the protection of ePHI. Pending each supplier review, appropriate agreements are executed, including a BAA for those suppliers who are, themselves, considered business associates.

HIPAA Safeguards

HIPAA requires safeguards in these areas: Administrative, Physical, and Technical.

- Administrative safeguards are broken down into security management, workforce security, information access management, security awareness and training, business associate contracts.

- Physical Safeguards include cloud-based platforms, physical access to ePHI throughout facilities, equipment, and other durable resources. Relevant training is required for all new hires and for all employees when changes are made to any systems that affect PHI.

- Technical safeguards apply to the systems, operations, and staff required to ensure protection of ePHI. They include:

  - Access control of all information systems handling ePHI and ensure that system activity can be traced to a specific user.

  - Audit controls for hardware, software, services, and procedures that record and examine activity in information systems containing or using ePHI.

  - Integrity protection of ePHI from improper alteration or destruction.

  - Transmission security where covered entities have effective protection of ePHI data transmission. Encryption must be used when ePHI is transmitted electronically.

To many IT departments at healthcare organizations, completely securing a voice application may need to go well beyond HIPAA. There is no formal certification process for HIPAA, and it applies only to the U.S. healthcare market. If an organization works in other regions, as many increasingly do, HIPAA does not apply.

GDPR and Other Regulations
General Data Protection Regulation (GDPR)

GDPR, introduced by the European Union in 2018, requires companies to comply with data privacy guidelines to protect personal data for citizens of the EU.[14] It also addresses the transfer of personal data outside the EU, so it impacts non-EU business and organizations that handle personal data of EU citizens.

Voice recording can continue under GDPR but can only take place if the data subject gives their consent.

For any developer of voice assistant applications to be compliant with GDPR, at least one of the following criteria for voice recording must be met to obtain consent:

- Recording is required to comply with a contract

- Recording is required to satisfy legal requirements

- Recording is required to protect the interests of one or more participants

- Recording of calls is necessary for safety or is in the public interest

- Recording is in the legitimate interests of the recorder, provided those interests are not overwritten by the interests of the participants in the calls.

Other requirements include:

- Recording must be stored securely, and appropriate controls applied to prevent data from being accessed by unauthorized individuals.

- Data can only be retained for the length of time that it is required to fulfill its purpose.

- Data subjects have the right to access their personal data (GDPR Article 15) within 30 days of request.

- Data subjects have the right to be forgotten, where personal data of an EU subject must be deleted if a request is made, provided the deletion does not violate state or federal laws and the data are no longer necessary for its purpose.

Even though it is only applicable to the EU, at the rate at which data privacy is becoming a widespread concern, it's likely the U.S. will implement similar regulations in the not-so-distant future.

Privacy Shield

Privacy Shield is the U.S.-based commitment to the same six principles of GDPR.[15] Because United States is not a member of the EU, there's no other real commerce regulation between the two in the way of data privacy. The EU-U.S. and Swiss-U.S. Privacy Shield Framework were designed by the U.S. Department of Commerce, and the European Commission and Swiss Administration, respectively. They provide both sides of the Atlantic with a mechanism to comply with data protection requirements.

California Consumer Privacy Act

The California Consumer Privacy Act (CCPA), enacted in 2018, is another relevant privacy law to consider that has even more rigorous requirements than GDPR.[16] It will start being fully enforced July 1, 2020. The law requires businesses over a certain user and/or revenue threshold to disclose what personal data they collect, the purposes they intend to use the data for, and any third parties it will be shared with. It should also require that they provide a discrimination-free opt-out to personal data being sold or shared. Businesses must also comply with consumer requests for their data to be deleted. This act will be important for companies that do business in California.

Other non-regulatory organizations that are influencing security in the voice industry include:

The National Institute of Standards and Technology (NIST)

The National Institute of Standards and Technology (NIST) is a non-regulatory agency of the United States Department of Commerce that is working on standards to secure voice technology based on consensus within the industry as well as from practical use.[17]

Cloud Security Alliance (CSA)

Cloud Security Alliance (CSA) is a nonprofit organization that focuses on best practices of cloud security through agreements from big name vendors: Google, Microsoft, Amazon, Apple, etc.[18] They take into account HIPAA, Information Security Management System ISO 27,001, NIST, and HiTrust.

Corporate Security Programs

Many established healthcare organizations already use standards from other industries or have their own standards for data privacy and security. Issues like user authentication, data privacy in shared spaces, network and device hacking, secure system integration (e.g. with an EHR), are universal concerns that healthcare organizations are working on.

Given that voice is so new, companies who are on the cusp of how voice evolves may be better equipped to anticipate problems and take measures that benefit both consumers and health organizations. They know that enterprise-grade considerations are critical from a planning perspective, not just for regulatory compliance.

Amazon Alexa and HIPAA

In April 2019, Amazon announced that a version of their voice-powered virtual assistant, Alexa, will now be HIPAA-eligible.[19] This means it is now available for applications that involve PHI and require HIPAA compliance.[20] Importantly, Amazon is now also able to execute BAAs with HIPAA covered entities, like hospitals, as well as other business associates, to guarantee protection of data in compliance with HIPAA guidelines.

Amazon is being selective and moving forward carefully with the roll-out of HIPAA-eligible Alexa environments. The environments are currently available to a limited number of developers by invitation only and limited to the Alexa Skills Kit, so they apply only to consumer-facing Alexa skills used at home.

Amazon's announcement was important news for the healthcare industry as it opened up the possibility of a many new types of voice assistant applications. Very generally, any voice application that involved a personalized healthcare experience is now possible to implement using the Alexa Skills Kit.

To be clear, the Amazon announcement refers to the availability of a HIPAA "eligible" version of the Alexa Skills Kit (ASK)— not HIPAA-compliance. The distinction is that Amazon is providing enabling technologies and services, not a complete voice assistant. It is the responsibility of the voice application developer to make sure that the entire solution complies with the rules of HIPAA. This includes making sure that the data captured through Alexa is securely stored and transmitted among services *outside* of Alexa.

For example, a weight management voice assistant needs to know the identity of the user reporting their current weight. This weight data becomes a form of PHI. The assistant may also manage medication schedules, blood pressure readings, or blood sugar levels if the user has diabetes. While this data may pass through Alexa, it is not solely stored or acted upon by Alexa. That is also done in the voice assistant's application code. Therefore, the responsibility for securely handling that data lies significantly with the application developer.

---

[3]Google has not made any claims of HIPAA-compliance for their Google Assistant voice platform but does offer other HIPAA-eligible cloud services that can be used for creating voice-powered virtual assistants that operate outside the Google Assistant framework.

Use Cases

When announced in April 2019, there were six voice assistant applications in the HIPAA-eligible Alexa program:

- Express Scripts: Check status of home delivery prescriptions.[21]

- Cigna Health Today: Manage health goals.[22]

- My Children's Enhanced Recovery After Surgery (ERAS): Provide post-surgery progress updates to care team.[23] (See case study later in this chapter.)

- Swedish Health Connect: Find locations and schedule appointments.[24]

- Atrium Health: Find locations and schedule appointments.[25]

- Livongo: Members query lab results and receive personalized health insights.[26]

The variety of use cases even across just these first six voice applications highlights the potential for HIPAA-eligible Alexa. Other possible applications for healthcare that bridge consumer and clinical gaps include:

1. <u>Remote Patient Monitoring/Population Health</u>

   Applications that track patient health between clinical visits are key to providing both the patient and their care providers visibility into wellness and ensuring more timely and informed interventions. Early pilots of voice-powered remote patient monitoring (RPM) solutions have shown promising results with respect to patient engagement and quality of care. Solutions that deliver care plans generated by real-time voice-driven responses are on the horizon.

2. Clinical Trial Optimization

For most drug and device development, the FDA requires pharmaceutical and biotech companies to collect data from the clinical trial participants. Accuracy and timeliness of these data are critical to the success of any trial. Hands-free, voice-powered experiences through which trial participants can easily receive reminders and respond to regular, requisite assessment surveys improve engagement and, correspondingly data quality. Drop off rates – a nemesis of trial timeliness – are reduced. Drugs come to market more quickly and more cost-effectively. Both healthcare providers and pharmaceutical manufacturers are exploring the use of voice-powered virtual assistants in these types of applications.

3. Medication Adherence

Patients who understand and are educated about their conditions, know everything they need to know about the use of their prescribed drugs, and are supported in their care journeys, are more likely to adhere to treatment and medication. Major pharmaceutical brands are developing beyond-the-pill voice assistant experiences that improve post-prescription patient engagement and adherence. Lack of medication adherence is one of the costliest burdens to the healthcare system. Real-world savings are realized.

Beyond HIPAA

As indicated, there's much more to achieving HIPAA-compliance than simply adopting a HIPAA-eligible platform. The approaches described earlier in this chapter provide some insights into what goes into achieving real security of a voice assistant – whether developed on Amazon Alexa or another voice platform.

Providers, payers, pharmaceutical firms, and healthcare solution vendors that carry responsibility for patient experience are all impacted by this news from Amazon's news of a HIPAA-eligible Alexa environment. Still, the news does not remove the requirement for voice assistant application developers to implement the necessary policies and procedures that will result in a full HIPAA-compliant Alexa skill. If a developer is a service provider to a covered entity, they are themselves a business associate in the HIPAA "chain" and must agree to BAA's with Amazon and, potentially, with their clients.

Healthcare will see continued deployment of consumer-facing skills that do not require HIPAA's rigor, but with the option for HIPAA-compliant Alexa skills will come demand for more clinical use cases requiring HIPAA-compliance. Clinicians and patients alike have been using hands-free, voice interfaces in their homes and have been demanding the same usability for clinical care applications, so it is inevitable that voice-powered virtual assistants are headed in this direction.

The Future

There are a number of technological advances that have the potential to further improve how voice assistants can be secured.

Voice profiling, for one, shows great potential as a method for authenticating users. Software can now pick up signals in audio voice that reveal telling details about the speaker well beyond just the semantics of the spoken words. By analyzing tone, inflection, and other "extra-semantic" properties of voice audio, AI-based systems are able to extract information that can be used to identify the individual with great precision. Combined with other identification factors, these vocal "bio-markers" can be used as a highly reliable authentication test.[27]

Facial profiling, another type of bio-marker, is already well-established. Users of the latest Apple iPhone have the option of using facial recognition to unlock their phones. The same feature is available on other voice-enabled consumer devices and offers another option for authentication to developers of voice assistant applications. The Nest Cam IQ Indoor is another device with built-in facial recognition—Face Match— that's triggered when a face comes into in front of the camera's field of view.[28] It works with both the Google Assistant speaker and Amazon Alexa. By just looking at the camera, the user can be authenticated. Facial profiling is also available on some smart speakers.

The advantages of these bio-marker approaches for authentication are clear. People who have difficulties remembering passwords have a much easier time accessing their voice assistant with voice profiling and/or facial recognition as an authentication tool. These methods will become more common as the functionality evolves and devices get smarter.

Ironically, these emerging authentication methods come with their own privacy concerns. The Nest camera, for example, is an always-on, always-watching device in your home. Google's policy states that the camera sends video footage to Google "...only if you or someone in your home has explicitly turned the camera on...". While you can always turn the camera off, just like you can turn off the microphone on your smart speaker, you have to remember to do so to prevent Google from getting your footage.

Another approach that voice developers are working on to improve the security of voice applications is being able to automatically recognize when PHI shows up, or is about to show up, in a voice assistant conversation. By automatically recognizing when PHI is being shared, the voice assistant can be programmed to pre-empt the exchange, direct the user to a more secure channel, or add warnings or restrictions if it senses that something private is impending.

Use Case: Boston Children's Hospital

About Boston Children's Hospital

Boston Children's Hospital is a world-renowned pediatric hospital (top-ranked by U.S. News & World Report), home to the world's largest pediatric research enterprise, and the primary pediatric teaching hospital for Harvard Medical School. Beyond its many accolades and research firsts, Boston Children's is also an early innovator in voice-powered applications for healthcare. In early 2016, Boston Children's launched one of the first Amazon Alexa skills for healthcare, KidsMD, which allows Alexa users to seek general information about common pediatric ailments and medication dosing. More recently, Boston Children's was one of the first six healthcare organizations invited by Amazon to develop a voice skill for Amazon's HIPAA-eligible environment for Alexa.

The Solution

First announced in April of 2019, the HIPAA-eligible environment for Amazon Alexa was designed to enable creation of Alexa skills that can transmit protected health information, or PHI, in compliance with the regulations of HIPAA. Boston Children's voice skill for the HIPAA-eligible version of Alexa is called "My Children's Enhanced Recovery After Surgery (ERAS)" and is a pilot extension of the hospital's larger ERAS Cardiac Surgery program designed to ensure that parents and caregivers of children recovering from heart surgery are supported with regular check-ins and other services to improve recovery.

The My Children's ERAS skill allows parents and caregivers to conduct remote check-ins through a voice interface available on any Alexa-powered smart speaker. By simply saying, "Alexa, open My Children's" to get started, parents and caregivers are able to provide the clinical care team with updates on their child's recovery progress, including information about activity level, appetite, and pain. The Alexa skill can also be used to access information about the child's upcoming post-op appointments.

HIPAA-Compliance

Because HIPAA defines PHI as any healthcare information that can be attributed to an identified individual, and because the My Children's ERAS Alexa skill captures and transmits this identifiable PHI electronically, it falls squarely into the compliance territory of HIPAA.

Beyond the specific functional and technical measures taken to ensure the privacy and security of PHI, HIPAA requires contractual vehicles be in place that document the obligations of the parties involved in the transmission of PHI. Amazon and the six healthcare partners building on this new HIPAA-eligible Alexa service, including Boston Children's, needed to agree to specific terms and conditions under which those obligations would be met. In the HIPAA parlance, the healthcare organizations are the "covered entities", and Amazon, as the service provider to those entities, is the "business associate". The agreement is called a Business Associates Agreement or BAA. While the details of the agreements are between Amazon and the healthcare partners developing the Alexa skills, the terms of those BAAs must adhere to the minimum requirements provided by HIPAA's governing body.

Lastly, Boston Children's, like any Alexa skill developer, must also provide terms and conditions of use, plus a privacy policy, that users of the ERAS Alexa skill are required to acknowledge and accept. These are spelled out on the Alexa skills store page for the ERAS skill and must be accepted by the end user before the skill is enabled.

Security Beyond HIPAA

Creating the ERAS Alexa skill would not have been possible without a HIPAA-eligible version of Alexa, but it also required other approaches to ensure privacy and security of the overall application.

To start, Boston Children's needed to ensure that users of the ERAS Alexa skill were both <u>authenticated</u> (confirmed to be who they claim to be) and <u>authorized</u> (confirmed to have the rights to use the application) – two concepts that are not specifically called out by HIPAA or addressed by Amazon HIPAA-eligible Alexa development tools, but necessary for any digital application, voice or otherwise, dealing with personal data.

To support authentication and authorization, potential users of the ERAS Alexa skill are first provisioned an account in the Boston Children's clinical system and granted privileges to access this account using the Boston Children's application – the My Children's ERAS Alexa skill, in this case. At the same time, they are provided a secure means to acquire a Personal Identification Number or PIN that will be used for identifying themselves to the Alexa skill.

To authorize access to the Boston Children's ERAS Alexa skill, the user must first enable it in their Amazon Alexa account using the standard method, at which point they are prompted to enter the account information (a username and password), provided to them by Boston Children's, that will allow the skill to connect with the necessary clinical system. Once this information is provided, the Alexa skill is securely linked to that clinical system using the OAuth-based Account Linking feature of Amazon Alexa. This ultimately serves to both ensure that the user is authorized to access the system, and to enable data to be stored and retrieved from that system by the Alexa voice skill. In practice, it allows a user to report a pain level through the Alexa skill that can be recorded in their clinical record. Likewise, it enables requests for information about an upcoming appointment to be securely and correctly retrieved.

This leaves authentication. To confirm users' identities, they are prompted to provide a unique PIN each time the ERAS Alexa skill is invoked. This PIN is provided verbally when the skill is launched and, combined with the account linking performed when the skill is enabled, serves to complete the connection between the voice skill and the backend clinical system.

Solution Benefits

Ensuring privacy and security of data for an application like Boston Children's My Children's ERAS Alexa skill is an imperative for both the hospital and the patients and families it serves. But for both healthcare providers and consumers, voice-powered clinical support applications like the ERAS Alexa skill show great promise as a new way to engage patients for post-acute care.

Patients and their families benefit from the ERAS skills intuitive, hands-free interface and the 24/7 self-service reporting and appointment management it offers. The novelty of a voice-powered interface reduces barriers to adoption and improves patient satisfaction. A key metric for any healthcare provider.

The hospital sees operational benefits, as well. Dr. John Brownstein, Chief Innovation Officer at Boston Children's, said of the ERAS pilot, "We're in a renaissance of voice technology and voice assistants in health care," said Brownstein. "It's so appealing as there's very little training, it's low cost and convenient." The ERAS skill frees up hospital staff who would otherwise be required to proactively check-in on these patients. Add to this the benefits of more timely and complete data reported through the voice skill and the overall benefits of the solution are clear.

About the Author

Nathan Treloar is President and Co-Founder of Orbita.ai, a provider of conversational AI technologies and services for healthcare organizations. He has over 25 years of experience delivering innovative products and business solutions at HBOC (now McKesson), FAST, Microsoft, RAMP, and, most recently, Ektron. Mr. Treloar is a respected expert and speaker on voice applications in healthcare, as well as on applications of search, text and data mining, and knowledge management technologies, and has advised hundreds of the world's largest companies and government agencies.

References

1. Dieter Bohn. "Amazon Says 100 Million Alexa Devices Have Been Sold—What's Next?" The Verge, website, January 4, 2019, www.theverge.com/2019/1/4/18168565/amazon-alexa-devices-how-many-sold-number-100-million-dave-limp.

2. Dieter Bohn. "Google Assistant will soon be on a billion devices, and feature phones are next." The Verge, website, January 7, 2019, www.theverge.com/2019/1/7/18169939/google-assistant-billion-devices-feature-phones-ces-2019.

3. VoiceBot.ai. Voice Assistant Consumer Adoption Report for Healthcare 2019, https://voicebot.ai/voice-assistant-consumer-adoption-report-for-healthcare-2019/

4. Mehta, Tushar. "Survey: 41% of users have privacy concerns with Google Assistant, Amazon Alexa, and other voice assistants." XDA-Developers, website, April 19, 2019, www.xda-developers.com/microsoft-survey-voice-assistant-privacy-concern/.

5. U.S. Department of Health and Human Services, Health Information Privacy under HIPAA https://www.hhs.gov/hipaa/for-professionals/privacy/special-topics/de-identification/index.html#protected

6. Gartenberg, Chaim. "Apple's hired contractors are listening to your recorded Siri conversations, too—Just like Alexa and Google Assistant." The Verge, website, Jul 26, 2019, www.theverge.com/2019/7/26/8932064/apple-siri-private-conversation-recording-explanation-alexa-google-assistant.

7. New York Times, "Is Alexa Listening? Amazon Echo Sent Out Recording of Couple's Conversation", May 25, 2018 https://www.nytimes.com/2018/05/25/business/amazon-alexa-conversation-shared-echo.html

8. Rubin, Ben Fox. "Amazon now lets you stop human review of your Alexa record-ings." CNet, website, August 2, 2019, www.cnet.com/news/amazon-now-lets-you-stop-human-review-of-your-alexa-recordings/.

9. Shred-It. "Shred-it Study Exposes Employee Negligence as Top Information Securi-ty Risk to U.S. Businesses." Ipsos, website, June 20, 2018, www.shredit.com/en-us/about/press-room/press-releases/shred-it-study-exposes-employee-negligence.

10. U.S. Department of Health and Human Services (HHS). "HIPAA for Professionals." HHS, website, June 16, 2017, www.hhs.gov/hipaa/for-professionals/index.html.

11. U.S. Department of Health and Human Services (HHS). "Covered Entities and Business Associates." HHS, website, June 16, 2017, www. hhs.gov/hipaa/for-professionals/covered-entities/index.html.

12. European Union. "General Data Protection Regulation." Intersoft Consulting, web-site, May 25, 2019, gdpr-info.eu.

13. U.S. Department of Commerce and International Trade Administration. "Privacy Shield Framework." EU-U.S. & Swiss-U.S. Privacy Shield, website, July 12, 2016, www.privacyshield.gov/welcome.

14. State of California. "California Consumer Privacy Act." State of California Depart-ment of Justice, website, 2018, https://oag.ca.gov/system/files/initiatives/pdfs/19-0019%20%28Consumer%20Privacy%20-%20Version%202%29.pdf.

15. U.S. Department of Commerce. "National Institute of Standards of Technology." Website, www.nist.gov.

16. Reavis, Jim. "Cloud Security Alliance." Cloud Security Alliance, Co-founder and Chief Executive Officer, website, 2009-2019, cloudsecurityalliance.org.

17. Amazon Web Services, Inc. (AWS). "HIPAA Overview." AWS, website, 2019, aws.amazon.com/compliance/hipaa-compliance/.

18. Express Scripts. "Express Scripts." Amazon Business, website, 2019, www. amazon.com/gp/product/B07QB7P6Y2?&sc_category=Owned&sc_channel=BG&sc_campaign=hipaa&sc_content_category=Health&sc_funnel=&sc_country=WW&sc_segment=

19. Cigna. "Cigna Health Today." Amazon Business, website, 2019, https://www.amazon.com/gp/product/B07QB7NMPG?.&sc_category=Owned&sc_channel=BG&sc_campaign=hipaa&sc_content_category=Health&sc_funnel=&sc_country=WW&sc_segment=.

20. Boston Children's Hospital. "My Children's Enhanced Recovery After Surgery (ERAS)." Amazon Business, website, 2019, www. amazon.com/gp/product/B07QB7PQYW?&sc_category=Owned&sc_channel=BG&sc_campaign=hipaa&sc_content_category=Health&sc_

funnel=&sc_country=WW&sc_segment=.

21. DIT/ET Providence St. Joseph Health. "Swedish Health Connect." Amazon Busi-ness, website, 2019, www.amazon.com/gp/product/B07PGJYYF6?&sc_category=Owned&sc_channel=BG&sc_campaign=hipaa&sc_content_category=Health&sc_funnel=&sc_country=WW&sc_segment=.

22. Carolinas Healthcare. "Atrium Health." Amazon Business, website, 2019, www.amazon.com/gp/product/B07H1T46DC?&sc_category=Owned&sc_channel=BG&sc_campaign=hipaa&sc_content_category=Health&sc_funnel=&sc_country=WW&sc_segment=.

23. Livongo Health. "Livongo Blood Sugar Lookup." Amazon Business, website, 2019, www.amazon.com/gp/product/B07QHF76RN?&sc_category=Owned&sc_channel=BG&sc_campaign=hipaa&sc_content_category=Health&sc_funnel=&sc_country=WW&sc_segment=.

24. Alsever, Jennifer. "Forget Face ID. The Future of Secure Authentication Is Your Voice." Fortune, website, January 6, 2018, fortune.com/2018/01/06/artificial-intelligence-voice-profiling/.

25. Wollerton, Megan. "The best facial recognition cameras of 2019." CNet, website, October 16, 2019, www.cnet.com/news/top-facial-recognition-home-security-cameras-for-2019-google-nest/.

Section 2

Voice Technology and the
Patient Experience

Chapter 5:

Automated, Virtual Caregiving using Voice-First Services: Proactive, Personalized, Wholistic, 24x7 and Affordable

Stuart R. Patterson, BA, MBA

Editor's Note

In this chapter, Stuart R. Patterson outlines a unique approach to serving the needs of our aging population by leveraging the use of voice assistants. The author explains the advantages of using voice technologies for seniors and other persons of all ages who may need care around the clock, whether they are in their own home, aging in place, or at a managed health and wellness facility, such as an assisted living facility. The author compares the use of two different voice assistant models as a function of the patient's needs: a combination of proactive models versus a reactive approach to needed health services. The section on the history and the rapid adoption of Voice technologies over the last 20 years is a welcome addition. Finally, LifePod's Case study with the Commonwealth Care Alliance (CCA) is an excellent example of the power of this technology.

Introduction and Overview

The appeal of voice-first interfaces in the online-service world is obvious – the user can "Just talk to them!" Now, with the advent and adoption of virtual assistants such as Siri and Alexa, we can imagine talking to all sorts of online services via smart speakers, or eventually ambient microphones and speakers in the wall, in our home. The past 50 years of local or online services using automated voice processing and natural language understanding, however, have all used a "reactive" or self-service model – that is: the end-user initiates all voice-first interactions with the virtual assistant, whether it be an online search for information (e.g., the weather), a command to do a task (e.g., set a timer) or an attempt to complete transaction (e.g., an online purchase).

To care for someone is to be proactive

Human caregiving, on the other hand, is and must be proactive – to care for someone, we must take the initiative and act! Telling a care recipient, as many online services do today, to remember to (a) log-in to the online service or portal, or (b) ask a virtual caregiver what the care recipient should do for themselves, is simply not the same as proactively caring for someone. It is, instead, training and reminding the care recipient to take the initiative and query an online portal or smart speaker app that operates solely in "reactive" mode.

A human caregiver speaking to their relative or patient in person would never say: "Ask me what you should do to care for yourself." But that's essentially what online service providers do when they send text and email reminders imploring those in need of care to access their reactive-only online, mobile or voice-first services.

When it's done well, of course, human caregiving has many other laudable attributes. It is, after all: personalized (i.e., it's adapted to the needs of each individual care recipient), wholistic (i.e., it takes into account physical, emotional, social and spiritual health or wellbeing), and it's often capable of learning over time (i.e., it doesn't continue doing something "to help" that the care recipient says isn't helping). At young ages, and for some care recipients with special needs, care must also often be around-the-clock or 24x7.

Can we automate human caregiving?

This chapter, therefore, examines the promise of two-way voice interfaces – i.e., both reactive and proactive voice-first services – in the new world of connected, digitally-enabled care of individuals, be they family members or institutional healthcare or managed care clients, in their homes. Can automated caregiving be configured to deliver the essential features of human caregiving enumerated above? Can the care recipient's interface to virtual or online caregiving services be fully supported by today's voice technologies? If so, how?

How will an automated, online caregiving service "know" if and when to initiate a voice dialog with the care recipient? How does an online caregiving service also know what physical, mental or social challenges the care recipient needs help with ... today, tomorrow or a week from now? And can the voice-first online service be configured to record and report what the care recipient is saying? How will the two-way voice service know when to alert the caregiving team that something is wrong or, just as important, that everything's alright?

Several new, voice-first services have recently been announced or launched that are capable of varying levels of caregiver-configured proactivity. The chapter includes, therefore, a brief overview of these services and concludes with a case study of 50 care recipient–caregiver pairs who have been using one such service, LifePod, successfully for nearly a year.[1]

A brief history of automated voice processing and reactive-only virtual assistants

Reactive-voice services first started over 50 years ago when programmers demonstrated that users speaking into a microphone connected to a local computer could be recognized, eventually transcribed, with reasonable accuracy by that computer. It took another 10-20 years before network-based speech recognition was capable of replacing or supplementing automated, touch-tone interfaces to customer service centers that many callers referred to simply as "touch-tone hell".

To make the leap from PC-based recognizers that could train on a single user's voice (e.g., Dragon), however, to automated speech recognition (ASR) algorithms that could recognize a variety of speakers' voices, the "domain" or subject that the speaker could speak about had to be limited. Dedicated 800- numbers ensured that the callers would be calling about a limited number of domains, and companies like SpeechWorks and Nuance deployed, along with their partners, hundreds of conversational, ASR-driven call center services from the late 1990s onward.

Thousands of similar services are now being deployed and accessed via online or mobile screen UIs to complement the visual and tactile UIs that online services have used for 25+ years. In all of these services, the voice-activated service or avatar knows what domain/subject you want to talk about, meaning none of them tried to recognize, until recently, just about anything you might say or to offer a virtual, voice-activated app store that could conceivably carry on a conversation about each and every app's domain!

Virtual assistants are not new

The first "virtual assistant", however, tried to do exactly that – it tried to create a friendly, voice-activated persona that could provide a bundle of personal-productivity services that a user could talk to instead of reading and typing on a mobile screen. It may come as a surprise to many readers, but this virtual assistant, named Wildfire, was launched by Bill Warner and his team in 1994! It is hard to believe that Wildfire was famous for its natural-sounding voice interface, its human-like persona and its self-service utility nearly 15 years before Apple launched Siri on the iPhone in 2011.

Only three years after Siri, of course, Amazon launched the first smart-speaker with a built-in virtual assistant named "Alexa". Amazon's innovation, actually, was not as much in its powerful voice-first assistant that could answer random questions and complete digital tasks or stream music for the user, as it was in the far-field microphone arrays that could reliably recognize a "wake-word", even with ambient or background noise, from 10-15 feet away. Amazon's Alexa, and the Echo/Dot/Show devices that support it, have since been imitated by Google (Google Assistant), Apple (Siri) and Samsung (Bixby) and others, who have rolled out smart speakers and networks to support in-home, and now mobile or desktop, use of their virtual assistants.

The self-service, reactive-only model is all we've known

If we are to understand the potential for voice user interfaces (aka "VUIs") to serve in the noble task of caregiving, we must appreciate that <u>all virtual assistants to date have used a single-user, "self-service" model, meaning that the user speaks and the voice-capable assistant reacts</u>. On a smart speaker, a virtual assistant will only react or "wake-up" when it hears the wake-word (or, in some cases, the user presses a certain button). The smart speaker will then attempt to understand the words spoken by the user after the wake word, then try to decipher what the user's words actually mean (aka, the user's "intent"), and finally attempt to do what it has understood the user to want it to do. In other words, these virtual assistants operate exclusively in "reactive mode", and none can speak on their own, proactively, unless they've first been summoned by the user.

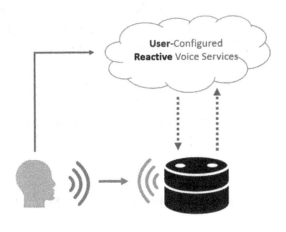

Virtual Assistants
Siri, Alexa, Google Ass't., Bixby

Given that proactivity is an essential component of human caregiving, where does this leave caregivers who wish to harness the naturalness of "just talking" to care for others using automated online services? Simply put, it means that caregivers must be given the ability to configure – generally based on input from the care recipient – proactive, voice-first dialogs that smart speakers will initiate (i.e., they'll start talking without first hearing a wake word) according to a schedule and about certain things that are important for the care recipient's health and wellbeing. In fact, the closer a virtual assistant's proactive prompts and dialogs are to what a real person would actually say, were they to be keeping the care recipient company in-person around-the-clock, the better!

A brief history of proactive, automated communication technologies

So, if caregiving requires proactivity at its core, then human caregivers must be able to setup, configure or program a "virtual online caregiver" in order to communicate proactively with their care recipients at appropriate times – i.e., based on a pre-set schedule or based on a data-driven trigger (such as the readings from a continuous glucose monitor or "CGM").

As described herein, virtual caregiving devices and services capable of some level of automated proactivity have been tested and are now being made available to institutional and family buyers/subscribers. But what proactive communications modalities went before ... and why haven't they been sufficient to provide proactive, automated care?

Real-time, proactive communications started with plain old, landline, analog telephone calls.[2] The first real-time phone calls involved, of course, one person calling another and talking to them only if the line was not busy and the other person answered.

Store-and-forward benefits ... and limitations

Before long, however, answering machines and network-based voice mail provided an additional feature – the caller could "leave a message" which the recipient would hear as soon as they checked their machine or voice mailbox. For proactive caregiving, however, the difference between reaching someone when you call them and speak to them in real-time, versus leaving them a message that they need to retrieve and listen to, is critical. For example, if I call my mother to remind her to go to the doctor's office for an important appointment or pre-op test, but don't get her and have to leave a message, then my proactive call is for naught unless she listens to the message in time. On the other hand, if my mother answers the call and I speak to her, then my proactive reminder is communicated right then, on time.

From analog to digital communications and networks

This difference between real-time or near real-time caregiver communications and store-and-forward communications with some sort of "message waiting" indicator can also be found in written, digital communications – i.e., in email vs. text messages – which exploded in popularity once the internet was created and opened up to consumers. Few people read most, let alone all, of their emails as soon as they appear in their mailbox; which explains, in part, why the digital world was so excited by the advent of short message services (SMS) or text messaging. When it started, senders of texts could be confident that the intended recipient would see and read their message as soon as or very shortly after it arrived on their cell phone (even when it meant being rude!). Over time, however, the sheer volume of text messages has made it impractical for most people to read/respond to them all in real-time, as they arrive. This makes text messages too unreliable for proactive, time-sensitive messaging from a human caregiver to their elder parent or chronically-ill patient.

Device- or UI-dependent accessibility challenges ... and opportunities

In the caregiving context, there is also the very real issue that many care recipients simply will not or cannot use or operate a cell phone, no matter how the screen UI is rendered (e.g., because they are visually or cognitively impaired). And there's no way, without voice, for the text message recipient to tell whether one message is more important (e.g., from their physician) or less important (e.g., from their cell carrier) without reading it, because the cell phone will make the same simple "beep" tone when either message arrives.

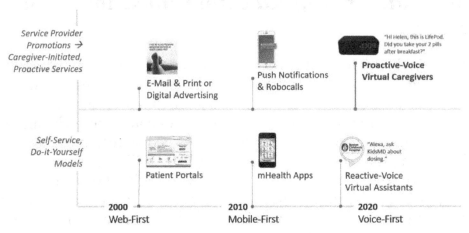

Per the diagram above, push notifications and outbound robocalls have complemented the self-service mobile apps and patient portals in healthcare. Similarly, tens if not hundreds of healthcare institutions have piloted reactive-voice virtual assistants as the next step in automated, online caregiving. After all, can't care recipients "just talk to" a virtual assistant at any time?

Most, though not all, care recipients can, in theory, "just talk to" a voice-first online service but, again, the difference between initiating a real-time, automated dialog and sending or leaving a voice message is fundamental. In fact, all Alexa-based, virtual caregiving services to date have relied on either "dropping-in", which is a real-time communication modality, or on sending/leaving a voice message or "notification", which lights a colored message-waiting light.

As with text messages, the problem is that the intended recipient might not notice the light or might decide to check it later or might not even remember what the light means or how to retrieve the message. As of late 2019, mainstream virtual assistants simply cannot be programmed or configured to speak to a care-recipient user or patient in their home without first being spoken to – making all of their VUIs "reactive-only".

If VUIs are so powerful, why must the user be trained how to talk to them?

One of the biggest ironies of services that are capable of "natural language voice recognition and understanding" is that users must be told or taught how to use or speak to them! Indeed, the first-time buyer of a smart speaker is guided through, with online/mobile/packaging instructions and help, the setup and connection process which becomes ever more complicated as the number and diversity of available apps and smart home, IoT connections grow. Once an account is connected and "talking" normally, the user must then learn and remember, at a minimum: (1) to speak closely enough to the device, (2) to say the correct wake word/phrase (e.g., "Alexa!" or "Ok Google!"), and (3) to say something after the wake word that the virtual assistant can understand.

As amazing as these systems and services have become, every speech recognition event is and always has been based on <u>probabilistic, AI-driven</u> algorithms or digital decision-making and pattern matching which are based on massive data sets. In other words, if a user departs from the syntax or word order options and the vocabularies that the reactive-voice service has been programmed to expect at any moment or "turn" in the dialog, then the service will fail to recognize what the user said or intended and will not respond appropriately, if at all. While the internals of speech recognition and NLP are beyond the scope of this chapter, these challenges of reactive-only voice recognition and dialog management merit a more detailed examination.

Learning to talk to, and therefore to use, voice-activated services

After any user utters an appropriate wake-word, a voice service like Alexa will listen to, analyze and try to process and respond to what the user says immediately thereafter. Although the virtual assistant's understanding capabilities continue to improve at an amazing rate, the phrases that can be understood must fit into a limited number of categories, including:

1. A request/command to play, speak or stream content such as music, news, weather, time, etc.;

2. A random question, which the virtual assistant tries to answer by

transcribing the phrase/string and searching the web for an answer that can be spoken back to the user using text-to-speech;

3. An invocation phrase of a first-party (1P) or third-party (3P) skill.[3]

4. A request/command to perform some action in their home via smart-home IoT devices such as "Alexa, turn the lights off!"

This is an incomplete list, but it serves to underscore the basic point that Alexa users must learn "how to talk to" this very advanced virtual assistant if they're going to get it to do what they want, or to answer their questions, or to access 3P skills using solely a reactive-voice model.

Turning the telescope around

With a proactive-voice model, on the other hand, the service appears to know what to say to the user and when. For example, the proactive-voice dialog could be a morning check-in such as "How did you sleep last night?", or an evening medication reminder such as "Don't forget to take your two evening pills before going to bed!". The care-recipient user only needs to be able to answer the intuitive question (e.g., "I didn't sleep well at all.") or acknowledge, if they're so inclined, the helpful reminder (e.g., "Ok, thanks.") which obviously requires no training or practice whatsoever.

Therefore, by "turning the telescope around", most if not all of the problems experienced daily by users of self-service, automated VUIs are resolved for a care recipient because their caregiver has set up the dialogs or routines they need, and they can truly "just talk to or answer them" without any training. Over time, in fact, Beta users report that LifePod's proactive, voice-first service becomes a virtual companion that they rely on and look forward to talking to – a friendly representative of their human caregiving team – an average of 8-10 times per day!

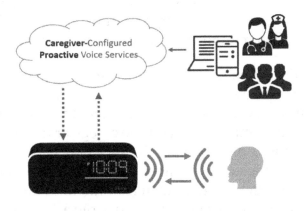

Virtual Caregivers
Virtual Assistants & LifePod

Person-centered, Personalized Care: Knowing What to Say and When

Once we construct either a stand-alone device or a device connected to a network that is capable of proactive-voice or two-way interactions with a care recipient, then the next critical question is: How will the proactive-voice persona know what to say and when?

Over the past decade, as voice has moved to an always-on, ambient interface in the home, innovative entrepreneurs have created a variety of devices and user interfaces that are capable of proactively speaking to a care-recipient user and have used three basic approaches to this essential question of "personalization": (1) local device control and configuration; (2) local voice commands, on-screen menus and connected mobile apps; and (3) cloud-based portals accessible by desktop or mobile browsers.

Local, on-device personalization

Several products rely on local device configuration.[4] One of these, Reminder Rosie, is configured as a clock radio in which up to 25 voice reminders can be stored in the voice of a caregiver such as the care recipient's son or daughter. These voice recordings are then played according to the schedule that is also entered by the caregiver locally on the device. Both the schedule and the voice prompts can thus be personalized to needs of the care recipient.

The fact that the device and configuration settings are not accessible via the internet, however, means that the caregiver must be present in person to set it up or modify it when reminders need to be added or changed.

In addition, the device being off-network means that there is no way for the device to alert caregivers if and when the care recipient indicates that they are not complying with the medication reminders, for example. It also means that there's no simple option for the caregiver to configure a periodic "check in" (e.g., "How are you feeling?") that can trigger an alert if the care recipient reports feeling poorly or needing assistance. Also, being device-based, the voice recognition and language understanding capabilities are relatively limited, especially when compared to the ASR and NLP capabilities in today's reactive-only, virtual assistants.

Local personalization options and mobile apps for connected caregivers

Several companies have built humanoid robots, capable of limited motion and often with "faces" intended to express feelings or emotions, that are also capable of reactive- and proactive-voice dialog management.[5] These robots are generally configured, and personalized, using some combination of voice commands, menus accessed on the robot screen and a mobile, or companion, app. Pillo's mobile app, for example, allows caregivers to dynamically choose from a set of 10 preconfigured "check-ins" and "reminders" that can be scheduled to play proactively. While the words of each check-in or reminder cannot be edited online by the caregiving team to personalize the automated dialogs for every care recipient, the schedule can be and text messages can be configured to be sent to caregivers when it appears that care recipients have not taken their medication, for example.

Cloud-based personalization and dialog management capabilities

Our company, LifePod Solutions, has developed a platform and service that support extensive, ongoing personalization, by the caregiving team, of the voice-enabled interactions that a LifePod-powered smart speaker can initiate, with a care recipient, thanks to a cloud-based portal and dialog management system for caregivers.[6] As shown on the left in the diagram below, caregivers can access the portal through their web or mobile phone browser to setup or modify proactive-voice routines and the times when they will play or "talk to" the care recipient.

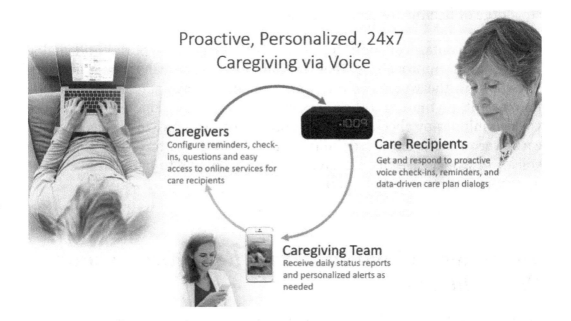

The caregiver portal provides preconfigured, voice templates for various versions of three basic types of dialogs or routines: check-ins; reminders; and prompted access to streaming content. An illustrative example of each is provided in the table below:

Check-In	"Good morning, Carol, how did you sleep last night?
Reminder	"Hello Carol, just a reminder that you have a doctor's appointment today at 2 PM.
Access to Streaming Content	Good evening, Carol, it's 6 o'clock and time for dinner. Would you like to listen to some Frank Sinatra music while you eat?

Family and professional models: Many-to-many or many-to-one or one-to-many

For starters, the cloud-based approach allows for a "many-to-many model" as well as a "many-to-one" or a "one-to-many" model. That is, many caregivers can share responsibility for many patients or care recipients at home; e.g., health professionals working for single caregiving institution and caring for hundreds or thousands of patients in their homes. Or, a large family can configure proactive dialogs for one, older relative or parent. Or, in the one-to-many case, a single professional caregiver can manage the proactive routines intended to monitor and support 10 or more care recipients, for example, which might be well-suited to an in-home care/ concierge or healthcare service provider.

Another advantage of the internet-accessible caregiver portal and dialog management approach is that human caregivers can access it from anywhere in the world – either via their online browser or their mobile phone – at anytime. In other personalization models, one element of the voice-reminder or check-in setup process, for example, might require the caregiver to be in close proximity to the device (e.g., to record their own voice), in which case the caregiver may only be able to help with setup or updates when they're there in person.

The power of words ... and the ability to choose the right ones

Perhaps the biggest advantage of the online, caregiver-controlled portal approach is the ability of the caregiver or caregiving team to edit the actual words that the LifePod speaker will speak whenever necessary. This allows a caregiver to compose personalized prompts or phases which can be evocative and enjoyable for the care recipient to hear, even when they're being reminded to do something that's good for them! Using "trigger words" that only the family or professional caregivers know, means not only that they are apt to be understood by the care recipient but also that they will be appreciated!

One straightforward example of this important feature is the "Hydration Reminder" dialog or routine. Dehydration is <u>a leading cause of older adults going to the ER</u>. As such, LifePod caregiving teams often put in multiple daily reminders for their care recipients to "hydrate". The pre-configured words in the hydration-reminder template (shown below), however, might encourage a care recipient to "have some water", but the care recipient might be like Lee Ann who said: "Can you change it to say: 'black tea'? I don't like plain water, but I drink lots of black tea!"

Pre-Configured Template: Hydration Reminder

☑ **Add Wellness Check-In**   ×

Wellness Check-In Templates◀	**Description** ⓘ	Hydration
Daily Exercises		
Hydration	**Date & Time**	10/20/2019 📅 at 11 ▼ 10 ▼ am ▼
Medication		↺ Repeat Never Daily Weekly Monthly Yearly
Morning Check-In		
	Voice Prompts	Initial question ⓘ
		Just wanted to see if you're staying hydrated throughout the day. Have you had some water today? ▶
		Reply if answer is yes or positive ⓘ
		Great! Staying hydrated is important. ▶
		Reply if answer is no or negative ⓘ
💡 **TIP**		Okay. It might be a good time to get a drink of water now. ▶
You can receive text alerts when replies are positive, negative, not understood, no response or for all.	**Text Alert**	☑ Alert me via text when the response is: Positive ▼
		Save Routine Cancel

As if to underscore the importance of personalization, Lee Ann once asked if we could add the name of her professional caregiver, "Brianne", before various healthy-habits reminders saying: "Could you get LifePod to say 'Brianne wants you to' before that prompt" because, as Lee Ann was quick to explain, "I love Brianne and I'll do anything she tells me is good for me!" This example illustrates that having a virtual assistant proactively "speak" the same words that the care recipient's closest human caregiver would use is likely to engage the care recipient and help motivate them to do what the virtual assistant suggests!

Supporting Wholistic Health via Proactive Voice

Another important element of virtual caregiving via an automated, voice-first UI is what types of care are needed – should the service focus be on physical, emotional, social or spiritual health or wellbeing? In the healthcare world, the term "person-centered care" is often cited as an important approach to: improve healthcare safety, quality, and coordination, as well as quality of life, [especially in] caring for older adults with multiple chronic conditions and/or functional limitations.[7] In other words, an efficacious, automated service should focus on whatever the individual care recipient needs to be healthy on multiple levels or wholistically.

This idea that one's health is not only physiological or biological but also emotional and/or social is, of course, not new. Similarly, many healthcare professionals stress the importance of "the social determinants of health" as one of the most important components that influence someone's overall sense of wellbeing. Here is a list of the "determinants of health" compiled by the Centers for Disease Control and Prevention:

- Biology and genetics. Examples: sex and age.

- Individual behavior. Examples: alcohol use, injection drug use (needles), unprotected sex, and smoking.

- Social environment. Examples: discrimination, income, and gender.

- Physical environment. Examples: where a person lives and crowding conditions.

- Health services.

The CDC goes on to define the social determinants of health as: "The complex, integrated, and overlapping social structures and economic systems that are responsible for most health inequities. These social structures and economic systems include the social environment, physical environment, health services, and structural and societal factors. Social determinants of health are shaped by the distribution of money, power, and resources throughout local communities, nations, and the world."[8]

Suffice it to say that physicians and social or care workers of all types agreed long ago that person-centered or personalized care should address all of the determinants of health – be they "social" or otherwise – not just one or two.

Just a spoonful of sugar helps the medicine go down …

Over 50 years ago, technology leaders such as IBM began to experiment with machines that could "remind" patients to take their pills or do their exercises ... but that was essentially all they could do. The setup or technology involved is not as important as the breadth, or lack thereof, of the use cases or reminders that these prototype devices could deliver. While many such trials seemed to work early on, their efficacy seemed to fade quickly with time, because the focus on a single purpose – e.g., urging the user to adhere to their health plan or medication protocol – caused these stand-alone, disconnected devices to be perceived as "medical nags". As a result, volunteers who agreed to be supported by these automated assistants soon tired of the repetitive reminders that rarely, if ever, changed ... and turned them off or put them in the closet! To be successful then, proactive reminders served up by an automated service must also include dialogs that are social or intended to entertain.

The power, and flexibility, of online caregiver control

With a connection to the world of online-accessible content, the internet, and the additional ability to speak proactively, according to a schedule of routines configured with and by a caregiver, it becomes easy to add proactive routines or dialogs that not only <u>monitor</u> how a care recipient feels about non-biological or non-health related elements of their life, but also to <u>support</u> them, proactively, by reminding them of social or entertainment-related activities that will often help them to be happier or to feel less isolated. A few examples of such routines should illustrate this exciting benefit of a proactive, voice-first caregiving service:

- "Good morning, Carol, ...

"... would you like to hear the weather?"

"... would you like to listen to the news?"

"... it's your grandson's birthday today. Would you like to call him?"

"... your favorite show, Jeopardy, starts in 5 minutes on channel 50!"

"... today's Tuesday, which means you meet with your knitting group at 10 am!"

- "Good evening, Carol, ...

"... it's time for dinner, would you like to listen to some of your favorite music while you eat?" or

"... how was your day?" ... and, if she says "Lousy!" then the virtual assistant can say "Oh, I'm so sorry to hear that ... I'll let your daughter know right away."

Social isolation and loneliness – a new pandemic?

With many millions of people living alone in the U.S. and around the world, it is worth singling out the potential beneficial impact of regular, proactive-voice interactions on feelings of social isolation and/or loneliness. A recent study concluded that living alone and being socially isolated for an extended time could cause the same or similar damage to one's overall health as smoking 15 cigarettes a day.[9] Another study tried to quantify the cost of loneliness in the US and found that among Americans aged 65 or older, social isolation costs the US government nearly $7 billion in additional health care costs per year.

Remarkably, tests with 50 clients of Commonwealth Care Alliance (CCA) who have been using the LifePod proactive-voice, caregiver-controlled service, suggest that talking to the automated-voice assistant or service can help to mitigate the feelings of social isolation which so many people suffer. As Dr. John Loughnane, head of Acute Care Services and CIO of CCA, wrote after their Beta tests had been running for four months: "[LifePod] supports important behavior modifications that improve patient engagement in medication regimens, exercise and diet" and "is an antidote to loneliness, a social determinant of health."

Caregiving Data Leads to Caregiver Learning Leads to Machine Learning

Perhaps the most important requirement of a human caregiver is that they be sensitive to the feelings and sensitivities – be they physical, emotional or social etc. – of the person(s) they are caring for. As patients, we are familiar with the physician's practice of asking us to write-up our health "history", and the best professionals will start nearly every, in-person visit or exam with a real-time verbal confirmation such as: "How are you feeling now?"

or "What seems to be bothering you?" And we rarely "feel" exactly the same for long, especially as we get older or as we deal with one or more chronic diseases.

As such, a good, human caregiver is constantly: (a) checking-in to see how their patient or loved one is feeling, and (b) tracking the care recipient's progress over time, especially as they prescribe and provide various therapies or activities or even verbal support to help their care recipient feel better!

Two-way voice for data collection and monitoring

In the digital, connected world, of course, many of the biological or physical factors that can cause a chronic condition to worsen can now be tracked automatically, around-the-clock – e.g., diabetes patients can now wear a CGM and the data from the CGM can be sent to caregivers' cell phones via the cloud. But a medical sensor or device may not transmit 24x7 for a number of reasons. Many such devices, in fact, are not "wearables" and require the care recipient to take some action to enter/transmit the data online – e.g., a connected scale cannot upload your weight each day unless and until you step on it.

Here again, personalized proactivity dramatically expands the utility of a typical voice-first service designed for automated, virtual caregiving by: (a) supporting daily check-ins and alerts triggered by their responses; and (b) providing a new, proactive communications channel and interface to not only remind a care recipient to measure something or submit time-sensitive data online, but even to collect the data verbally by voice input.

Voice-first, daily check-ins can take the form of proactive-voice questions that are phrased naturally – just as the human caregiver would ask were they there in person. A morning check-in, for example, could be configured as:

- "Good morning, Carol, ...

    - "... did you have a good night's sleep?" or

    - "... how are you feeling this morning?"

And an evening check-in could be phrased in a similarly natural fashion:

- "Good evening, Carol, …

  - "… did you have a good day today?" or

  - "… how are you feeling this evening after your procedure this morning?"

Proactive-voice as a complement to connected, sensor-based data collection

With IoT devices and sensors becoming more powerful yet easy-to-use every day, they are being used in more and more connected healthcare-in-the-home scenarios to facilitate the constant transmission of vitals data (e.g., the CGM example) or the daily input of a bodily metric or measure. Many of these devices, however, require the client to remember to use them one or more times per day in order to ensure that there are not gaps in the data.

Cardiologists and heart-care specialists, for example, may wish they could monitor multiple vital signs while also encouraging their CHF patients to exercise regularly and eat healthy foods, but when asked, most will agree that the most important single measure to track is the patient's weight. As such, patients at risk of a heart event who need to be monitored by their healthcare provider are often given a connected, digital scale to use once a day.

What happens, however, if the client forgets to step on the scale one day? With a proactive-voice, connected service, the caregiver can program a trigger to play an automated reminder saying, for example, "Please remember to step on the scale before you go to bed!" Over time, voice input may prove to be reliable and secure enough for the scale to be disconnected and the reminder could be "Please step on the scale and tell me your weight today."

In other words, two-way VUIs can not only help ensure that online-connected devices are used as needed to collect health-monitoring data, but they can also serve as an important, new channel for caregivers to collect quantitative and qualitative data from those they care for on a regular, even daily, basis.

Mining voice data

Just as a human healthcare professional might ask a patient a series of questions to assess their overall wellbeing and record the answers, it should be clear by now that a two-way, voice-first service that can be controlled and configured by a human caregiver, or triggered by a programmatic interface, can do the same. These questions can be practical and physical (e.g., "Your doctor would like to know how you're feeling today after starting the new medication?"); or they can be more behavioral (e.g., "Did you go for a walk today?"); or even social (e.g., "Would you like your daughter to call you today?"). By asking these types of questions via a virtual caregiving service once, twice or seven times per week, a caregiving team essentially has a new and easily configurable source of longitudinal data on nearly any topic of choice. Indeed, a major insurance provider approached the inventor of LifePod[10] and asked if the proactive-voice prototype might be configured to ask the same three questions several times a week as a straightforward way of tracking the progress of a care recipient's memory loss or dementia!

Data-driven adaptation of care over time

Those in need of frequent, in-person care have often emerged from in-patient acute care or a serious operation or treatment, and they must carefully follow prescribed protocols, of medicines and of behaviors, if they want to recover as quickly as possible. The good human caregiver will quickly learn what helps or irritates their care recipient post-op, whether it's a certain motion or a position in bed or even a previous, treasured activity (e.g., certain events or friendly visitors). This type of learning is data-driven only the data is the feedback or responses of the patient (e.g., their complaints of pain). Moreover, even small data sets are useful: If you tell a caregiver once, for example, that you cannot raise your arm over your head without experiencing severe pain, then they will normally suggest you do gentle exercises that don't require lifting your arm over your head.

Automated voice data also comes in the form of care recipients' utterances or responses to questions posed by the proactive-voice service such as: "How does your repaired knee feel today?" or "How much did that exercise hurt on a scale of 1 to 10?" or open-ended questions like "How are you feeling today?" As noted above, these types of questions can easily be configured by the human caregiver using LifePod's caregiver portal and dialog management system ... and they can be dynamically updated or modified as needed based on the care recipient's recovery journey.

Voice data is somewhat more complex than other, more traditional forms of data as it can clearly be used to collect the equivalent of survey or questionnaire responses directly from patients under care, but it may also provide clues – in the vocal patterns or the voice signal itself – that will help in the diagnosis or risk of patients developing certain diseases or conditions. Other chapters in this book are sure to delve deeper into this exciting new area of research.[11]

Trend spotting and pattern matching

Since caregivers are given daily summaries of each care recipient's responses to LifePod's proactive questions, it is straightforward for them to add proactive check-ins to ask ever more specific questions about a particular pain or ailment and to review the daily reports to evaluate how an illness or injury is trending. As noted above, they may also update or modify the words in the proactive prompt such that it explicitly reminds the care recipient not to push an exercise too hard or raise their arm too high.

In some areas, of course, the computer can do an even better job, based on pattern-matching and machine-learning (ML), of realizing when something's not quite right or of detecting issues that might merit more attention or analysis. Two simple examples should suffice here: the first around frequency of and reasons for "no response" by the care recipient, and the second around daily usage patterns that emerge for certain proactive questions.

No input/response detected: If the LifePod service is configured to ask if the care recipient would like to take some action (e.g., have some coffee, go for a walk, or listen to the news in the morning) at the same time each morning and the care recipient doesn't answer for 1-2 weeks in a row, the caregiver may or may not pick up on the pattern when they review the daily reports. If they do notice a string of no responses, they can just ask their care recipient as we did once only to learn that the care recipient doesn't talk to anyone before they've had their second cup of coffee!

If, on the other hand, the caregivers don't notice such meaningful usage patterns, it's a simple matter to program an algorithm that will ... and, in the future, that algorithm could be configured to automatically ask the care recipient whether LifePod's schedule or questions should be changed in order to elicit a response. For example, if LifePod were configured to ask an older adult if they'd like to listen to "Frank Sinatra music with dinner", and they say "No, thank you" for two or three weeks in a row, the routine could be configured to offer that same adult Ella Fitzgerald instead of Frank Sinatra, or it could simply do what a human caregiver might do – ask if the care recipient would prefer not to be offered any music with dinner.

Computers don't mind 12-hour days ... and don't sleep either

Though an automated, two-way voice platform and UI that is easily configurable by human caregivers may support remarkably effective levels of proactivity and personalization as described herein, it is difficult to argue that voice-enabled virtual care will ever be equal to in-person, human care. In one or two areas, however, digital and connected care may actually exceed what we can reasonably expect of human caregivers: in persistence or coverage-over-time and in cost.

Much has been written about "caregiver burnout" – the toll that in-person human caregiving takes on the caregiver. For doctors, this issue is increasingly common, but is primarily experienced in an institutional setting (i.e., the doctor's office, home or hospital), not a result of doctors visiting patients or spending too much time caring for patients in their homes. For in-home care professionals or for unpaid, family caregivers, however, the challenges of caregiving can be serious. Putting someone else's needs above one's own can be exhausting, particularly if those needs stem from serious physical, medical or emotional illnesses. This is even more true if the medical condition of the in-home patient is chronic and can't be cured or if deteriorations in the sick person's condition can and do occur at unpredictable times, day or night. Type 1 diabetes patients, for example, can die in their sleep if someone does not detect a sudden plunge in their blood sugar level in time, which explains why CGM technology and monitoring has been such an important breakthrough.

The AI-powered, connected caregiver is in

Indeed, over the past 50+ years, the development of always-on, digital monitoring and treatment systems has clearly revolutionized healthcare delivery and efficacy. In a similar vein, virtual assistants will not get fatigued or fail to repeat what they've been configured to do as long as they're plugged in or battery-powered and connected to the network. And the computer-generated, text-to-speech (TTS) voice and persona won't become irritated when it's asked the same question 10 times in the same day.

Furthermore, subscriptions for these services will generally be based on "a fixed price per period" just as subscription services for other networked services (e.g., phone calling, internet access, etc.) have been. Indeed, the ability to automate proactive, personalized, wholistic care has the potential to reduce the cost of healthcare in the home dramatically.

For these reasons, a platform-as-a-service such as LifePod, infused with the emotional intelligence of the caregiver and capable of managing proactive, voice-first interactions, will be able to provide 24x7 monitoring and support at a relatively low, fixed cost when compared to the alternative of having 24x7 in-person care, whether it is paid or unpaid. Over time, as the two-way voice UI is integrated with motion/presence detectors and biophysical sensors (e.g., detecting heartbeats while the care recipient is sleeping or sitting), then more and more issues can and will be detected and alerted – to the care recipient or the caregiving team or both – automatically.

Moving from Configurable Care to Flexible Response

While it is beyond the scope of this chapter to discuss all that's coming thanks to the discovery and development of two-way voice UIs and connected voice networks to leverage them, there is one, well-established service and industry space that is worth special mention: the Personal Emergency Response Systems or PERS market. According to the National Council on Aging: "Every 11 seconds, an older adult is treated in the emergency room for a fall; [and] every 19 minutes, an older adult dies from a fall."

Clearly, the industry known for "push-button calls for help" has room for innovation that could serve to decrease the number or frequency of injurious falls as well as the number of cries for help that go undetected because the older adult does not have a PERS button within reach for whatever reason.

Many entrepreneurial ventures are working with integrated monitoring technology and motion detectors to optimize solutions to improve our ability to predict if someone is likely to fall in the near future or even to detect automatically, using ML and AI, that they may have fallen when it happens. But what if a person who falls in their home or apartment could "wake up" their virtual assistant by say something natural like "LifePod, I've fallen, I need help now"?

This first use case would start with a reactive-voice cry for help and any VUI designed to respond to such a plea must be carefully developed by professional VUI designers, linguistics experts and experienced dialog management specialists. In fact, it is important to note that, as of this writing, it would be difficult if not impossible for a third-party to create such a VUI using one of the more popular, voice-first development options such as Alexa Skills, Google Assistant Actions or Bixby Capsules. No matter how it's developed, the automated dialog that engages upon detecting that a user has cried for help must first determine whether it's a true emergency by asking questions that resemble those asked by PERS call center reps today, and the virtual assistant's voice network and dialog management server will need to be tightly integrated with an existing PERS network and call center to be effective.

Assuming that "voice-enabled fall detection" is soon possible, the PERS space would also benefit from a voice-first UI designed to handle so-called "false positives" – that is, where the user's cry for help does not require an emergency response. Here again, there is a future opportunity to determine – using natural, automated-voice dialogs – why the user has actually asked for help and what type of help they need in cases where it is not an emergency that requires an immediate response from a health professional. In fact, using state-of-the-art voice UIs, automated dialogs will soon be able to reliably determine:

- Why did the user cry for help or push their PERS button?

- How urgent is the need for assistance?

    or

- Who would be best placed to provide the assistance?

And it is worth repeating that initiating any such dialog via a virtual assistant on an in-home smart speaker, upon detecting the push of a PERS button (as in #1 above), will require two-way voice capabilities, i.e., networked reactive- and proactive-voice dialog management.

Another future enhancement of today's PERS services that becomes possible with proactive-voice capabilities, under programmatic/API or human control, is extending so-called "passive fall detection" systems with, for example, a well-designed proactive prompt saying something like: "Hello Carol, it appears that you may have fallen – are you okay?" Finally, as the two-way voice UI migrates to wearable devices such as watches, wristbands and bracelets, the opportunities to use voice-first UIs to extend both the detection of falls and the efficacy or appropriateness of the response expand even further.

Caregiving Conclusions

This chapter on virtual, voice-enabled caregiving began by suggesting that nearly all voice-activated services to date have been reactive-only, meaning that the user must activate them or "wake them up" by speaking a special phrase and then say a command or ask a question that the voice-first service or device is capable of reacting or responding to appropriately. It has further been suggested that, despite the obvious differences between voice and any other online interface modality – i.e., we can "just talk to it" – voice-first UIs have not changed the fact that all online services to date have operated according to this reactive-only mode. This chapter also contends that making it easy for humans to converse with machines in a meaningful way about a particular subject or action will always require some level of user setup and training as long as the VUI operates exclusively in this reactive, self-service mode.

Assuming these assertions prove to be valid, then the biggest breakthrough of voice will not be in providing yet another type of UI/UX or application for users of reactive-only online services – it will be in the advent of a truly proactive user interface to online services that can be configured and controlled by a third-party such that an online service can finally help "care for" or serve another user.

Caregiving of any sort is proactive. While the online tools available for self-service healthcare (e.g., online portals and mobile/connected apps) continue to evolve and improve, they can only be used by the patient and this self-service-only model requires that the patient be both able and willing. Proactive, voice-first technologies, on the other hand, offer the ability for an automated online service to initiate a conversation that cannot be ignored … in the same way that a care recipient would typically not ignore a dialog that's started, in-person, by their human caregiver.

The advent of proactive voice and, by implication, two-way voice interfaces means that automated, intelligent, online services can finally be used by caregiving organizations – be they a widespread yet tight knit family or a major managed care provider serving a single state – to monitor and care for patients in their home. As shown in this chapter, these services will be powered by and infused with the emotional intelligence of the human caregiver, and they also have the potential to be personalized, wholistic and data-driven, and to operate 24x7 at a fraction of the cost of an in-person, human caregiver.

If most or all of these claims are true, then two-way, voice-first interfaces represent an exceptional opportunity for the global healthcare industry and millions of family caregivers to use connected devices and online services to care for those in need.

Case Study: Commonwealth Care Alliance (CCA) Beta Trial

Excerpts from the Executive Summary Report

Overview

LifePod and CCA collaborated on a Beta trial to evaluate the use and impact of the proactive-voice LifePod service by CCA Members (i.e., care recipients) and Care Partners (i.e., paid caregivers/providers). From the end of 2018 till this writing, there have been 50 participating CCA Members who have been using the LifePod Beta service.

The success of the Beta trial was assessed based on in-person surveys with Members and Care Partners as well as through detailed analysis of CCA call and visit (or "encounter") data. These tools provided quantitative and qualitative measures of the following metrics:

1. Care Member and Care Partner satisfaction with the LifePod service

2. Improved Member health and wellness outcomes

3. Streamlining of Care Partner workload

4. Enhanced Care Partner engagement with Members

Results of the Beta Program demonstrated remarkable success across all measures as described in this report summary.

LifePod Service Overview

LifePod's Virtual Caregiver Beta service expands the capabilities of Amazon's smart speakers and the voice-activated assistant that controls them (i.e., Alexa) with patented innovations that make LifePod an easy-to-use, proactive-voice service for CCA clients living at home. LifePod's "proactive voice" capability enables the LifePod service to speak to a CCA Member <u>without</u> first being "woken" by them. Using the Caregiver Portal shown at right, CCA Care Partners are able to set up and schedule proactive voice dialogs to check-in on and support their Members throughout the day. In addition, Care Partners receive daily email reports listing their Members' responses to LifePod-initiated questions and dialogs.

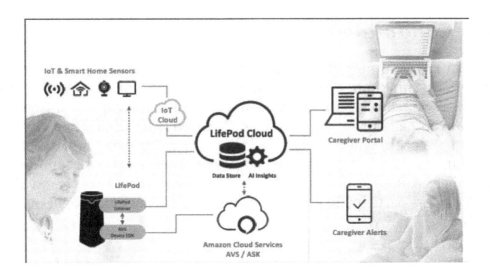

CCA Goals for Beta

For its Members, CCA's overarching goal for the LifePod Beta has been to improve health and wellness outcomes by providing a proactive, voice-first platform with the aim of increasing CCA Care Partner-Member engagement, promoting improved care plan adherence and achieving patient-defined health and quality-of-life goals. The CCA model has proven that increased engagement enhances outcomes for patients. LifePod's ability to proactively interact or "speak" with patients about wellness activities, increased social engagement, and medical care reminders may play a vital role in achieving the goals of improved quality, clinical and financial outcomes and patient and provider satisfaction.

For its Care Partners, CCA's primary goal for the LifePod Beta has been to augment the role of the Care Partner by increasing the frequency of Member "touches" without having to be there in person or engage by phone. With LifePod, the Care Partner is able to monitor and influence a Member's health and wellness status multiple times a day without having to take any actions. This may increase Care Partners' insight and enhance their ability to intervene with patients earlier when medical or social issues are just beginning to affect their lives. Ultimately, CCA hoped to determine whether the use of a personalized, proactive-voice service would allow for a managed care model to also be "proactive" and engage earlier and more frequently to slow the cycle of worsening disease trajectory and improve patient outcomes.

Beta Candidate Selection

The Beta Program targeted at least 50 CCA Members who would use the service for a minimum of four months. CCA staff helped to identify CCA Members who showed a high call and visit volume, or a rising trend in volume over the prior six-month period. The frequency of calls and visits by the Beta Members typically exceeded the average for the CCA population. Candidates were selected and LifePod devices were installed beginning in September 2018, with all 50 installed by December 31st. (As of this writing, CCA Members participating in the Beta have been using LifePod for over 10 months.)

Onboarding

During installation, CCA and LifePod staff gathered details of the Member's daily routines related to their care plan, wellness and social activities. Customized routines were created for each Member consisting of reminders, check-ins and content services that were scheduled at appropriate times of day according to the Member's needs. On average, nine routines were created for each member. As appropriate for each Member's level of acuity and ability to speak clearly, Members were introduced to reactive Alexa functionality which is also available on the LifePod Beta device. The service was demonstrated to the Members, and they were given a brief training on how to "wake-up" and speak to Alexa as well as how to most easily respond to LifePod's proactive prompts. Care Partners were also trained to use the Portal and modify their Members' routines. All trainings were accomplished in 1-2 hour sessions.

Success Criteria

Originally, CCA established two success criteria for Members using LifePod:

- 5% fewer inbound calls from Members to CCA staff; and

- 5% fewer face-to-face visits between Members and CCA staff.

During the data collection and analysis phase, CCA added a third success target:

- An effective reduction in CCA support costs of $30 per Member per month or more

Assessment Methodology

To assess achievement of the success criteria, data was collected from CCA's Business Intelligence Team to compare encounter trends for Members for the six months before LifePod installs began (March – August 2018) to the then-most recent three months of LifePod use (March – May 2019). Data was collected for Members not using LifePod over this same period as a control. The following metrics were evaluated:

- Inbound calls from Members to CCA staff

- Face-to-face, in-person visits

- Outbound calls from CCA staff to Members

- Care Partner encounters (a subset of outbound calls and face-to-face visits)

Note that the last two metrics were not assigned with target success criteria, however they were analyzed for their relevance to the CCA Beta Program.

To assess satisfaction with the LifePod service, in-person surveys were conducted with both the Members (i.e., care recipients) and the Care Partners (i.e., caregivers).

Results of CCA's 50-Member Beta Program

Quantitative Results:

For both LifePod and non-LifePod Members, a significant drop in encounters other than face-to-face visits was observed during the period January-May 2019 (i.e., in the months following the installation of LifePod Beta devices). A possible explanation for this drop is that LifePod installations coincided with the introduction of the new Guiding Care patient care management platform, and fewer encounters were recorded in the new system across the entire Member population. As a result, it would be inappropriate to attribute the significant drop in LifePod Member encounter frequency for Beta participants directly to the introduction of LifePod's personalized, proactive voice-first routines. In order to eliminate the influence of this system-wide change on the LifePod data, the analysis team therefore quantified the relative change in encounters between LifePod Members and non-LifePod Members during this period.

The data show that the average monthly rate of inbound and outbound calls and Care Partner encounters dropped more significantly over the evaluation period for LifePod members than for non-LifePod members. Specifically:

- Inbound calls for the LifePod Members decreased 12.5% more than the control group, exceeding CCA's 5% success criteria threshold for this metric.

- Outbound calls for the LifePod Members decreased 3.85% more than the control group.

- Care Partner encounters decreased 27% more than the control group.

- Curiously, face-to-face visits for both cohorts rose during the evaluation period. However, for LifePod Members, average monthly visits rose by only 10% compared to 20% for the control group, i.e., the rate of increase was half that of the non-LifePod members. The fact that average visits per month grew 50% more slowly for LifePod Members than for the control group could represent a significant cost savings.

To calculate the potential monetary impact of these improvements, hourly rates for CCA staff and estimated call and visit durations were applied to the reduced encounter rates. As shown in the table below, the resulting total estimated monthly cost savings is $63.52 per Member per month. This estimated savings from the use of LifePod exceeds CCA's success criteria of approximately $30 cost savings per Member per month.

	Non-LifePod Members	LifePod Members	LifePod Improvement over Non-LifePod	Estimated Cost Improvement
Inbound Calls	(72%)	(81%)	12.50%	$4.83
Outbound Calls	(78%)	(81%)	3.85%	$2.89
Face-to-Face Visits	20%	10%	50%	$56.25
Total Estimated Cost Savings/Avoidance				$63.52

Table 1: Percent Change in Average Monthly Encounters Attributed to LifePod from 6 Months before LifePod Install to Last 3 Months of LifePod Use and Estimated Cost Savings

Note: The decline in Care Partner Encounters (a subset of the other encounter types discussed) saves an estimated $31.50 per Member per month. While these numbers are already reflected in the savings above, it is noteworthy because Care Partners are often the main touchpoint between Members and CCA.

Qualitative Results:

Surveys were conducted with 49 Members and 16 Care Partners to assess the level of satisfaction with different aspects of the LifePod service and features. Member feedback on user satisfaction questions related to features and the service showed an 88% or higher favorable response. In addition, 96% of Members would recommend LifePod to other Members, 98% are satisfied overall with LifePod routines, and 100% felt supported throughout their day by LifePod.

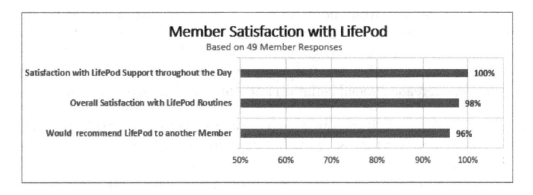

Survey results for Care Partners showed that 60% or more were 'satisfied' or 'very satisfied' with seven key benefits from using LifePod. 100% of Care Partners would recommend LifePod to others, and 93% said they are satisfied with LifePod supporting them throughout their day in their role as caregiver. Care Partners noted that LifePod appeared to assist with important health outcomes for their Members by keeping them on track with their care plans and medical appointments, and providing social companionship. One Care Partner, for example, stated: "For members who don't have anyone, I think it's good - it's some form of communication, so they feel like they're in touch with the world. " And another said: "It helps my Member stay on track with diet, fluid intake, exercise and stretching."

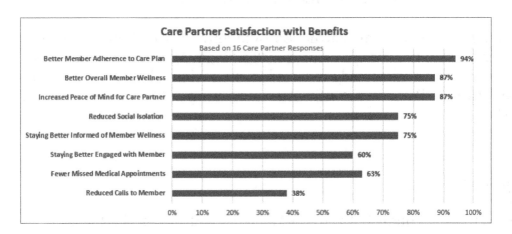

Care Partner Satisfaction with Benefits
Based on 16 Care Partner Responses

Benefit	Percentage
Better Member Adherence to Care Plan	94%
Better Overall Member Wellness	87%
Increased Peace of Mind for Care Partner	87%
Reduced Social Isolation	75%
Staying Better Informed of Member Wellness	75%
Staying Better Engaged with Member	60%
Fewer Missed Medical Appointments	63%
Reduced Calls to Member	38%

CCA Beta Case Study: Take-Aways

The LifePod Beta Program with CCA's 50 Care Members and 16 Care Partners showed highly-favorable quantitative results and positive qualitative feedback from both Members and Caregivers regarding the LifePod service, features and benefits. Together these results indicate that operational efficiencies were gained while Members and Care Partners reaped the benefits of more frequent engagement, improved care plan adherence, decreased social isolation and enhanced wellness outcomes.

The quantitative results show a reduction in average monthly inbound calls of 81%, a result that is 12.5% better than the 72% reduction for non-LifePod Members, which exceeds CCA's 5% success criteria threshold for this metric. A decline in average monthly outbound calls of 81% for LifePod Members represents an improvement of 3.85% over the 78% reduction for non-LifePod Members. While face-to-face, in-person visits rose across the entire CCA population over the evaluation period, average monthly visits rose by only 10% for LifePod Members as compared to 20% for non-LifePod members. This 50% better performance far exceeds CCA's 5% success criteria. Together, these results represented an estimated $63.52 savings per Member per month which exceeds CCA's success criteria of $30 savings per Member per month.

The qualitative feedback shows the 49 Member survey respondents were overwhelmingly satisfied with the LifePod service, with a full 88% responding favorably to user satisfaction questions, and 96% saying they would recommend it to other Members. Care Partners had similarly strong, positive feedback. Out of 16 respondents, 100% said they would recommend it to others, and 60%-94% were 'satisfied' or 'very satisfied' with key features and benefits of the service.

Both Care Partners and Members indicated that LifePod contributes to health and well-being outcomes, which accomplishes an important part of CCA's goals for the LifePod Beta. As one CCA Member said: "I love this LifePod! It keeps me less isolated." This sentiment is a clear example of potential behavior benefits. A relative of another Member stated: "LifePod really helps Eric daily ... with his medication reminders and appointments." This is an example of how LifePod promotes care plan adherence. This feedback demonstrates that while encounters may be reduced in number or frequency, the quality of encounters and the care provided can be enhanced through the use of LifePod resulting in both cost savings and improved patient outcomes.

In addition, industry research suggests that more frequent "touches" or communications of any sort between caregivers and their care recipients can be beneficial (e.g., by reducing stress, increasing care plan adherence, supporting desired changes in behavior, etc.) and consequently may lead to improved health outcomes. Both family and institutional caregivers, however, have many competing priorities and are very time-constrained, such that in-person or real-time touches are often limited in number and frequency (i.e., to once or twice per month).

In the CCA Beta program, the LifePod service augmented the engagement of the CCA Partners, by delivering an <u>average of 9 touches per day</u>, without requiring any additional action on the part of the Care Partners such as in-person visits or calls. LifePod's ability to increase the number and frequency of Care Partner-Member touches supports the widely-held belief that personalized patient engagement will promote enhanced health outcomes and is likely a major reason why the Beta program achieved its quantitative and qualitative goals.

The CCA Beta test results exceed the criteria established for declaring the CCA Beta Program a success, and warranted moving to the planned next phase of expanding the deployment of LifePod to 500 CCA Members.

References

1. In the interest of readability and in order to have to avoid listing/ describing more than one virtual assistant every time they're mentioned, Alexa-based examples have been used to explain the possibilities and limitations of today's mainstream, virtual assistant architectures and services. Most of today's major virtual assistant services share the same basic architecture and operate in the same way, especially as they all use a "reactive-only" user paradigm. That said, there are innumerable, substantive differences in the capabilities that each ecosystem provider (e.g., Amazon, Google, Apple, Samsung ...) offers to app developers and those differences certainly impact the user experience in ways that are simply too numerous to cover in this chapter.

2. It's worth noting that these were called "POTS", as in plain old telephone service, by many professionals in the space for roughly 50 years!

3. Alexa provides the most often used, 1P skills like music, setting timers and shopping in their online store. As such, users can make requests of 1P skills without first saying a unique "invocation phrase"; users also benefit from Amazon's natural language processing that is generally not accessible or active in a 3P skill. On the other hand, with over 50,000 3P skills on Alexa, the user needs to know what specific words will "invoke" the one they want ahead of time ... or they may never find it.

4. While this chapter is not intended as a product or service review, two relatively well-known examples of this style of voice-enabled, caregiving device are Onkol and Reminder Rosie.

5. Of note in this category are two relatively new robot-like caregiving devices, Elli-Q from Intuition Robotics and Pria developed by Pillo Health, which come on the heels of Jibo, an ambitious innovation meant to be the "world's first social family robot" that ran out of funding shortly after its launch in 2018.

6. As this chapter summarizes the important findings of nearly two years of LifePod testing prior to commercial launch, it includes a high-level

overview of how LifePod works from the caregiver's and the care recipient's perspective.

7. J Am Geriatr Soc. 2016 Jan;64(1):15-8. doi: 10.1111/jgs.13866. Epub 2015 Dec 2. Person-Centered Care: A Definition and Essential Elements.

8. Commission on Social Determinants of Health (CSDH), Closing the gap in a generation: health equity through action on the social determinants of health. Final report of the Commission on Social Determinants of Health. 2008, World Health Organization: Geneva.

9. Loneliness: A disease? Indian J Psychiatry. 2013 Oct-Dec; 55(4): 320–322. doi: 10.4103/0019-5545.120536

10. An experienced, serial inventor named Dennis Fountaine.

11. An overview of some of the work being done in this area can be found here.

Chapter 6:

Voice and Wearables

David Kemp

Editor's Note

David Kemp, the author of this chapter, focuses on the integration of voice technologies with wearables and hearables to address not only today's healthcare issues, but tomorrow's needs as the global population ages. David leads us on an educational journey on how the growth of hearables has taken place in the past five years, with the use of new Bluetooth technologies and the adoption of Apple's AirPods by the masses. This technology has allowed earphone users to connect their hearing abilities to their smartphones, and from there to voice devices, the internet and the cloud. These devices give users hands-free capabilities and new abilities. David also discusses the growth of biometric medical sensors for vital body functions in hearables and their effects on our well being. This chapter follows the growth of wearables and voice technologies as they converge for improved hearables and better hearing aid technology for our seniors.

The Voice Assistant and Wearable Computing Combination in the Medical Setting

Voice technology represents one of the most fascinating and exciting areas of innovation in recent memory due to the transformational effect it can have on a wide variety of industry sectors. We've seen voice assistants proliferate into homes at unprecedented rates relative to other consumer technology products as consumers continue to outfit their homes with smart speakers and smart displays to serve as hubs for their voice assistants.

Now, as voice assistants begin to migrate outside of the home and the phone and into new environments, the tech companies that enable this technology have set their sights on new avenues for their assistants to begin infiltrating. The connected car, the smart office, classroom, hotel room and other analog settings being converted into smart areas are becoming primed for our assistants to move into. Two of the most exciting environments that Alexa, Siri, Bixby, Google and all the other not-so-prominent voice assistants seem to be headed next, however, are our wearable devices and the healthcare setting.

Consumer trends indicate that the demand for one's voice assistant is rising as smart speaker and display owners are increasingly outfitting their homes with more devices, allowing for more access points to the assistant.[1] Based on the growing demand for more access to the assistant, it would seem that wearable technology is poised to serve as one of the next logical homes for consumers' assistants, providing an always-available access point to the consumer. The logic is that the more that consumers grow dependent on their voice assistants, the more likely they'll be to want their assistants with them on-demand.

The medical setting, on the other hand, represents an industrial complex that is in desperate need of efficiencies that can be derived from the power of the frictionless computing interface that voice assistants offer. The voice user interface allows for a hands-free method of communicating with one's technology, which is critical for a professional who is often preoccupied with their hands. In addition, voice computing has the potential to offload much of the clerical work that plagues the healthcare professional, to the voice assistant, allowing for the professional to devote more of their time and attention back to the patient.

While the other chapters in this book focus on the various inefficiencies and opportunities that voice technology can take advantage of and be used to solve, this chapter will explore the marriage of wearable computing and voice technology and consider the impact of said marriage to the healthcare setting. In order to understand the effect of this combination, it's important to first focus on how the stage was set to enable this fusion by shedding a light on the years of innovation surrounding wearable technology leading up to this point.

This chapter will examine how we got to the point we're at now with the technology and the types of exciting new opportunities that this melting pot of innovation will give way to. Once we've established a solid foundational understanding of the type of technology and feature-set that's been implemented into wearables, we'll then move onto how voice assistants can be overlaid on top of this existing innovation. Finally, this chapter will conclude by highlighting the types of people that will benefit most from this technology initially.

Wearables and Hearables as a Home for Voice Assistants

Wearable technology can be defined as body-worn computers. The first mass-market products of wearable technology were step-tracking, fitness devices, followed by progressively more capable body-worn computers. As the component sets inside the devices became more sophisticated, new form factors started to become available, allowing for consumer's to augment more body parts with miniature computers. One notable example would be ear-worn computers, which were coined as "hearables" by WiFore wireless analyst, Nick Hunn, in 2014. Nick believed these devices were a natural extension of wrist-worn wearables, providing for more robust features and capabilities given the unique position in the device rests on the body.

In order to really understand why wearable technology, and more specifically hearable technology, stands to be the one of the next logical homes for voice assistants, let's start by taking a look at how hearable technology has progressed to the point where the devices are capable of housing voice assistants. The first major breakthrough that began this domino effect was the mass adoption of Bluetooth wireless hearing devices. Bluetooth is a critical aspect to making hearables a hub for voice assistants, as it ultimately extends the smartphone and all its capabilities directly to the ear-worn device. In essence, Bluetooth allowed for users to connect their ears to the smartphone, the internet and the cloud (all environments that play host to voice assistants), wirelessly and seamlessly.

2016 marked an important year for Bluetooth adoption, as it was the first year when Bluetooth headphone sales surpassed non-Bluetooth sales.[2] Apple accelerated this trend with the introduction of the iPhone 7 in September of 2016, which was one of the first smartphones to forego the headphone jack as Apple opted for more space for its processors, forcing the consumer to decide between using a dongle with their wired headphones, or instead, go the Bluetooth route.[3] Flash-forward to today and you'll see that the vast majority of new smartphones entering the market do not include a headphone jack, as many followed in Apple's footsteps by deciding to omit the wired headphone outlet as well.

In December of 2016, Apple added fuel to the Bluetooth adoption curve fire, by launching AirPods, which would go on to be one of the most successful consumer product hits since the iPhone. Apple analyst, Neil Cybart, wrote in a February update of his publication, Above Avalon, that AirPods' Google search traffic interest rose 500% year-over-year in the 2018 holiday season compared to the holiday season in 2017.[4]

Although Apple does not break out the specific unit sales of AirPods, and instead lumps the product together with its other wearables (Apple Watch and the Beats line of hearables) and a slew of other products, such as Apple TV, some analysts have reverse engineered Apple's financials to discern that the company will likely sell upwards of 55 million AirPods in 2019 alone.[5] Research firm IDC later estimated that Apple sold 15.9 units of AirPods in the second quarter of 2019, representing a year-over-year increase of 218% and setting a new estimate of 60+ million units sold annually.[6]

To put this into perspective, relative to Apple's other popular wearables, on a cumulative sales basis, AirPods are outpacing Apple Watch by 40% at the same point after launch.[7] IDC also estimates that hearables now comprise 50% of all wearable sales, up from 25% last year, and AirPods represent nearly 50% of all hearables sales. In other words, as of September 2019, AirPods represent 25% of all wearable device sales globally.[8]

AirPods successfully ushered in the hearables era, but it was not the first company to attempt to do so. A variety of ambitious startups attempted to shape the hearables market years before Apple entered with AirPods, such as the companies Bragi and Doppler Labs. Both companies failed to gain traction in the way that Apple ultimately did and went bankrupt, which begs the question, why were AirPods such a hit when previous attempts at a mass-market hearable hit were unsuccessful? To answer that question, we need to look at what's been transpiring *inside* the devices.

If you look back at Doppler Labs' Here One hearable, or Bragi's Dash Pro hearable, what you'd find are two very compelling visions. Both companies' first products were meant to be the initial iteration of a broad scope of innovations, ultimately leading to the point where the consumer would have a full-blown computer residing in their ears, complete with an operating system and all. However, no matter how grandiose the vision might have been, there were two giant obstacles that obstructed the path to this vision that no one had yet figured out how to solve: battery life and rock solid pairing to a smartphone. These two roadblocks ultimately served as fatal flaws to both sets of products, dashing the dreams of the company's founders who were aiming to usher in an era of ear-worn computing.

When Apple's AirPods rolled around, they were not initially met with much enthusiasm because they were positioned as truly wireless headphones, and lacked the bold vision that the market had been accustomed to by the high aspirations instilled in the market by companies like Bragi and Doppler. Quietly included in the AirPods rollout was the fact that Apple's proprietary chipset, the W1 chip, would be powering the devices. Apple had first implemented this chipset into its Apple Watch series, and then later for AirPods. While AirPods might not have been the most splashy product, the W1 chip solved the existing obstacles of battery life and pairing.

One of the most distinguishable features of AirPods is its ability to *instantly* pair with the user's iOS device. As soon as you pop the AirPods into your ears, the sensors built on top of the W1 chip will sense that you're wearing the devices, which will then emit a Bluetooth signal to the receiver on the iPhone's antenna to pair the device. While AirPods work with Android devices, they don't work as seamlessly as they do with Apple devices, since the Bluetooth protocol being used between devices is Apple's own 2.4 Ghz Bluetooth low-energy protocol. This protocol is used by all of Apple's mobile devices, allowing for them to pair together quickly and seamlessly. This is the type of feature that's only feasible for a manufacturer to implement that's manufacturing both the smartphone and the Bluetooth device it's being paired with, which in this example, is AirPods.

By using Apple's own ultra-low power Bluetooth protocol, it also allows for AirPods to last about 4-5 hours prior to needing a charge. Another one of the aspects that makes AirPods so clever is the companion charging case. This tic-tac sized case quickly charges the devices back to full power, which really helps to render the battery dilemma obsolete. While batteries represent one component that have not been innovated on a whole lot, the ways in which the power from the battery is extracted, used and recharged has seen quite a lot of innovation. Apple's ultra-low power Bluetooth protocol allowed for much better power conservation, while the companion carrying case that quickly charged both pods allowed for fast power recharging.

Therefore, the reason that AirPods were such a hit and the previous attempts at hearables were not, was largely because Apple focused primarily on solving the battery life and connectivity roadblocks that had been the death of AirPod's predecessors. Now that Apple has established the blueprint for a successful hearable, Apple's competitors are setting their sights on bringing their voice assistants to the ear as well, as the voice assistant war moves from the far-field to the near-field. Before jumping to this new war front however, let's examine what other component innovation is transpiring right now that our voice assistants will ultimately get to take advantage of with regard to the healthcare applications on the horizon.

Biometric Sensors and The Peace Dividends of the Smartphone Wars

Chris Anderson, CEO of 3D Robotics, published a now famous essay in the magazine, Foreign Policy, in which he <u>described</u> the state of consumer technology in the 2010's as, "The Peace Dividends of the Smartphone Wars.[9]" Chris describes this as follows:

"The peace dividend of the smartphone wars, which is to say that the components in a smartphone — the sensors, the GPS, the camera, the ARM core processors, the wireless, the memory, the battery — all that stuff, which is being driven by the incredible economies of scale and innovation machines at Apple, Google, and others, is available for a few dollars. They were essentially 'unobtainium' 10 years ago. This is stuff that used to be military industrial technology; you can buy it at RadioShack now. I've never seen technology move faster than it's moving right now, and that's because of the supercomputer in your pocket."

So, as Chris points out, what we're really seeing happen right now with consumer technology is the windfall from the massive proliferation of smartphones. All the components involved in the smartphone supply chain have become dramatically cheaper and more accessible across the past decade due to the sheer economies of scale. Therefore, we're starting to see all kinds of exciting new components or components that had previously been limited in their accessibility, make their way to more and more consumer devices.

For hearables in particular, digital signal processing chips have become increasingly cheaper over the years, which allows for much more customization at the chip-level, opening the door for other computer chip manufacturers to mimic what Apple proved successful with its W-series chip. While Apple was first to prove how to engineer a mass market hearable, its competitors now know the blueprint to success from an engineering-perspective, and thanks to the smartphone supply chain, the components are considerably cheaper and more accessible.

Some of the most exciting, "peace dividends," within the smartphone supply chain that are beginning to make their way to ear-worn devices are a variety of body-worn sensors. The first iteration of sensor implementation into wearable devices were the inertial sensors, namely gyroscopes and accelerometers, which allow for use cases such as step-tracking. These inertial sensors can detect the orientation and movement of the device, and thus that of the user. It was inertial sensors embedded in products like Fitbit that first popularized the inclusion of these type of sensors into wearable devices.

Inertial sensors have been migrating up to the ear, becoming embedded in hearables as well. Many hearables on the market support some type of fitness monitoring features with data derived from the inertial sensors. Fitness-oriented hearables largely rely on inertial sensors to populate step-count data, as well as the frequency of which the user stands and moves quickly relative to their other movements, which is inferred as exercise. Some hearing aids on the market have even begun to purpose the inertial sensors to detect falls. This is good news, as the national council of aging reports that every 11 seconds, an older adult (65+ years old) is treated in the emergency room for a fall and every 19 minutes, an older adult dies from a fall.[10]

The next phase of sensor implementation into wearable devices was that of optical, photoplethysmogram (PPG) sensors. These types of sensors use LED lasers to illuminate the skin and measures the changes in the light absorption to detect blood volume changes. In other words, these sensors measure a variety of one's vitals by measuring the intervals between each heartbeat by scanning the flow of blood.

In a phone interview I conducted with Ryan Kraudel, VP of Marketing at Valencell, a biometric sensor manufacturer, the blood flow characteristics that can now be measured include heart rate, heart rate variability, cardiac efficiency, respiration rate, and pulse pressure. In addition, biometric sensors like PPGs can complement the inertial sensors' data to more accurately measure movement-based metrics like step count, energy expenditure, and overall activity levels.

According to Kraudel, these metrics can then enable a broad range of use cases, ranging from fitness to the health and medical settings, and also allowing for telemedicine applications like remote patient monitoring. One example of this would be the metric heart rate variability (HRV), which is the time between each beat of the heart. For athletes, HRV provides insight to assess whether they're overtraining or undertraining. It can be used in the medical setting, and has been validated in many clinical studies, to identify atrial fibrillation & other arrhythmias.

PPG sensors have been around for decades, as hospitals all around the world use them every day with pulse oximeters that are placed over the finger to measure the various metrics mentioned above. What's changed recently is the size of the sensors. Now, thanks to Moore's Law, the sensors have become miniature enough to fit and embed into the tiniest of devices, such as a receiver-in-the-canal hearing aid. These sensors are now only a few millimeters square, making them invisible and feasible to place virtually anywhere.

What really makes the ear compelling from a biometrics standpoint is the unique physiology and the location on the body that it provides. The method in which PPG sensors gather and measure data (LED light emittance) is very sensitive to light scatter from bone, muscle and other tissue. Since the ear is primarily cartilage and blood vessels, it allows for a much more accurate data collection and reading. The other common issue with PPG sensors is that body movement can distort the readouts as well. Fortunately, there is little local motion within the ear, even if the body is in motion, serving as another positive to record data at the ear-level.

Another big positive with using the ear as the data collection point is that it straddles the inside and outside of the body, yielding unique benefits. For example, there are metrics that can be collected inside the ear, such as body temperature that radiates from the tympanic membrane. Wrist-worn wearables are unable to obtain that type of metric. Since the sensors can rest at the opening of the ear canal, you could also gather readouts of what's happening in the outside environment, such as detecting harmful pathogens in the air, in addition to all the body readouts being recorded from additional sensors located on the portion of the device that rests inside the ear.

Another exciting trend pertaining to the world of wearables and biometric sensors is the consumerization of medical-grade sensors, such as electrocardiogram monitors (ECG). ECGs are a recording of the electrical activity and function of the heart to identify if the heart is healthy or potentially exposed to any coronary threats. ECG monitors have long been limited to FDA class 1 or 2 medical devices, but with the introduction of the Apple Watch Series 4 and its embedded ECG monitor, we're starting to see mass-market consumer electronic devices include medical grade sensors.

The Apple Watch is able to use a combination of the ECG monitor and PPG sensors to detect rapid or skipped heartbeats, which might be symptoms of life-threatening conditions such as atrial fibrillation. Currently these sensors are limited to wrist-worn wearables given the size, but are trending toward being miniature enough to fit onto ear-worn devices.

So, what's on the horizon with biometric sensors and why does this matter to voice technology? We'll get to how this will impact voice technology, and trust me it will greatly impact it, but let's stay focused on biometrics for just a bit longer. When we're looking ahead at what's to come with sensors, the next metric sitting in the crosshairs of the bio sensor manufacturer's target-lock is blood pressure.

Companies like Valencell have developed the ability to measure blood pressure at the ear within the ISO standard for accuracy of a blood pressure cuff. Rather than having to implement a bunch of new technology, what's actually needed is data collection and data science at scale. In other words, it's more about what you do with the data than enabling new data to be collected. As PPG sensors become more ubiquitous in mass-market consumer wearables, broad swaths of the population's data will be fed into large data sets, allowing for scientists to uncover new insights via machine learning. For example, data at scale might indicate insights around blood patterns and blood flow characteristics that haven't been analyzed at scale before. Blood pressure is a perfect example of what we might be able to better understand as more data is collected, pooled and assessed through increasingly more intelligent machine learning algorithms.

The holy grail for biometric sensors, however, would be the ability to monitor glucose levels, non-invasively. To this day, there's yet to be a sound solution that's implementable with wearables to non-invasively detect glucose levels, however, it hasn't stopped a number of aspirational sensor-based companies from seeking a solution that would be a huge boon to the millions of people suffering from diabetes that must prick their fingers multiple times per day to display their glucose readings.

The inclusion of biometric sensors into wearable computers, starting with the wrist and then migrating to the ear, help to illustrate the various tools that voice assistants will ultimately have at their disposal to assess what's happening with our health data. Now that we've established how hearables have matured to the point where they're capable of supporting voice assistants and examined the arsenal of new components that the assistants can access, it's time to take a look at ways that voice assistants can begin to take advantage of this new setting.

An Always Available Assistant

According to a survey conducted by Voicebot.ai in March of 2019, 66.4 million American adults own a smart speaker, representing 26.2% of the US adult population.[11] This was a 40% increase year-over-year, and Voicebot estimates that there are about 133 million global users. but most surprising was that the average number. One of the most surprising findings that came out of Voicebot's survey was that the average number of devices per owner rose from one device to two, with 40% of smart speaker owners indicating that they own multiple devices, up from 34% a year ago.

As mentioned earlier in this chapter, Voicebot's survey data indicates that there is a rising demand for more access points to our voice assistants. As this demand increases and users continue to offload many of the tasks that they currently rely on their smartphones for, the logical progression will be for an always-available voice assistant that is accessible on-demand. Therefore, hearables represent a suitable option for an always-available assistant, readily available whenever the user needs to access the assistant.

The innovation transpiring at the component level inside the devices will continue to yield more capable wearables, such as longer battery life. The capacity to support an always-available assistant from a hardware standpoint is progressing incrementally, and meanwhile, the consumer's behavioral shift toward wanting to wear an all-day hearable to serve as a home for an access point to an on-demand assistant is underway too.

So, we can start to operate under the pretense that consumers are moving into an era where they're wearing voice-assistant enabled hearables for long periods of time during the day. Therefore, on top of serving as an access point to one's smart assistants, hearables become a viable option to double as biometric data collection devices, especially as they continually get outfitted with more sophisticated sensors as outlined above. So then, where does that data go and what do we do with all that data? Let's start with breaking down where the data is headed: the smartphone.

Apple and the healthcare data ecosystem that it has incrementally been putting into place since the introduction of the Health App and Health Kit in 2014, puts Apple in a position to provide each iPhone user their own individual, secure health data repository. Apple opening its Health app to feed its own first-party wearable data into the health app, as well as some third party wearable devices has evidenced this. Android's ecosystem could potentially facilitate a similar offering, but Apple has a head start in this regard.

If you start to combine the data generated from Apple wearable and iPhone users in conjunction with other insights like medical health records (which Apple is seeking to add) Apple's bigger healthcare aspirations start to come into focus. Apple is aiming to be the master of health data, allowing its users to manage, store and share their data, all in one place. In essence, Apple wants to be the king of health data facilitation.

At Apple's September product launch event, the company announced a new Apple app, called Research, which will allow users to opt into research studies by sharing data being collected from sensors on Apple's phones and wearables. Initially, the Research app will be "seeded" with three different research studies that users can opt into: a hearing study, a women's health study, and a heart and movement study. It's conceivable that Apple will add more and more research projects to this app, creating an "app store" of sorts for users to choose what studies they want to contribute to. Researchers love this as Apple solves the issue of signing up participants for them quickly and at scale.

While there's a tremendous amount of data that's becoming available via the biometric sensors to collect, the challenge still remains of what then to do with all that data being collected. A lay person cannot be expected to look at a chunk of heart rate data and know what they're looking at or for. Nor can we expect that this data would simply be sent to one's MD to be reviewed by the doctor. They're busy enough as is, which presents the opportunity for the smart assistant providers to repurpose their assistants toward becoming biometric data assessors.

Let's use Apple as an example to illustrate the concept. Imagine a scenario where someone owns an iPhone, wears AirPods that have the battery capacity to last for 8 hours and are outfitted with a host of miniaturized biometric sensors. Imagine too that the user is controlling many of the apps on her iPhone via Siri. Apple has been touting its wearables as, "guardians of health," and so, who better to serve as a guardian of one's health than Apple's assistant living inside the wearable, Siri? Think of this version of Siri almost as a, "Nurse Siri."

In this scenario, Nurse Siri, through pattern recognition and trained machine learning algorithms, would be responsible for detecting a wide range of abnormalities within the user's data. Rather than expect someone to assess their own data, Nurse Siri notifies the user of what's happening through alerts and notifications being triggered by what it is identifying in the data. It's not far-fetched to think that Siri, or any other smart assistant repurposed to analyze the type of biometric data that's being generated by the users' wearables, will be able to facilitate advanced notifications and preventive health alerts based on what it's learning.

For example, the ECG and PPG data being collected might be indicating a blood clot forming, only to be caught by the assistant, leading to a notification for the user of what's happening, and potentially even a timeframe as to when to expect something as severe as a stroke or heart attack. So on one hand, the voice assistant starts to become a true guardian of one's health, reading the users health data to identify any potential risks, in ways that are completely non-feasible for the user to do on their own.

The goal of the assistant in this scenario is not to replace one's doctor or other healthcare professional, but to more intelligently inform the healthcare professional of what's happening. Therefore, another role the voice assistant seems poised to fill is the data facilitator. Once a curious data set has been captured, assessed and deemed worth sending to the medical professional, the voice assistant can be directed to send the data off to be reviewed by the professional.

It's possible that the professional in this scenario would be overwhelmed by the amount of inbound data, and therefore, it might be more likely that the data will actually be received by the professional's assistant, which would have its own method of distilling the data into more digestible insights for the professional before determining if the patient needs to come and see them. It's plausible that the user would be presented with the data in question by Siri, Google, Alexa, or whichever assistant, at which point the user can determine if they want to send the data on to the medical professional that's been logged in their settings as the designated recipient of these type of data transfers.

One of the existing limitations that would pertain to this type of capability would undoubtedly be HIPAA-compliance. To date, only a select few Alexa skills have been registered by the Department of Health and Human Services as HIPAA-compliant, but Amazon has assured its developers and users that widespread HIPAA-compliance is on its agenda moving into the future. Just as we should see Apple's competitors bring to market their own wearable devices to compete with the Apple Watch and Apple's hearables, so too should we see other major smart assistant providers aim for HIPAA-compliance, especially as healthcare seems to be a destination so many of the giant tech companies are seeking to enter. Apple's focus on privacy and encrypted data should dovetail nicely into its efforts to make choice portions of its devices, software and data collection process HIPAA-compliant.

So, when we start to imagine these future scenarios where a smart assistant is playing the role of nurse, it's important to note the underlying technological progress that has persisted across the past decade to make these hypothetical scenarios possible. The devices are now capable enough to support the assistant, either directly on the device, or through a solid Bluetooth connection. In addition, all kinds of exciting new hardware has become available via the, "peace dividends of the smartphone war," allowing for much more advanced applications. Now, let's take a look at some of the earliest cohorts to really benefit from all this innovation.

A More Compelling Hearing Aid

As voice assistants continue to proliferate into more and more devices, the number of cohorts that can benefit from the power of this technology will expand as well. One profession that seems to be in dire need for voice assistant augmentation is that of the caregiver. According to Paul Osterman, professor at MIT's Sloan School of Management and author of the book, "Who Will Care for Us: Long-term Care and the Long-Term Workforce?" there's a giant crisis looming on the horizon that pertains to caregivers.

In his book, Paul <u>finds</u> that in 2030 there will be a national shortage of 151,000 paid direct care workers and 3.8 million unpaid family caregivers.[12] By 2040, the shortage will swell to 355,000 paid workers, and the family and friends shortfall will be a whopping 11 million. One of the ways to possibly help alleviate some of this rising demand is to port the voice assistant into the most highly demanded wearable for our older adults - the hearing aid.

Ten thousand Baby Boomers turn 65 years old each day in the U.S. according to Pew Research.[13] This number of Boomers crossing 65 has been consistent since January 1, 2011, and will continue until 2030. Pew's population projections estimate that Baby Boomers will comprise 18% of the total US population by 2030.[14] In addition, the US life expectancy currently sits around 78-79 years old, which the World Health Organization projects to continually rise into the 2030s.[15] In essence, there is a significant portion of Americans entering into their retirement age and are projecting to live longer than previous generations.

Our population also becomes more susceptible to hearing loss as it ages. According to a 2017 JAMA Otolaryngology study, age tends to be the leading predictor of hearing loss.[16] The sense of hearing depreciates due to a wide variety of factors, as we get older, such as long-term exposure to unhealthy sound levels and the degeneration of sensory cells.

The World Health Organization conducted a study in 2012 to measure the magnitude of "disabling hearing loss" (defined as a loss of 40dB) and found that a third of the world's population aged 65 and older have a disabling hearing loss.[17] In high-income countries, such as the U.S., that number is closer to about 18%. Couple age-related hearing loss with the rise of rock and roll and other loud forms of music that the Baby Boomer generation (and all subsequent generations) exposed them to, and it's not surprising that hearing loss is as widespread as it is.

Given that such a large percentage of the global and national population suffers from hearing loss, one might expect that the penetration rate of an amplification solution such as hearing aids would be higher than 30%. Unfortunately, hearing aid market penetration rates have historically never crossed 30% in the U.S. among adults aged 70 or older, according to research from the National Institute of Deafness and other Communication Disorders.[18]

To compound the issue, co-morbidities linked to hearing loss continue to surface.[19] These co-morbidities include, but are not limited to, increases in cognitive decline, dementia, diabetes, cardiovascular disease, depression, and hospitalization. To date, there is no research that explicitly states that hearing loss causes the aforementioned co-morbidities, but rather, the research found that hearing loss is correlated with the spikes in each co-morbidity.

So, as a population, our largest generation is crossing past the age of 65, we're living longer, and research indicates that the leading cause of hearing loss is aging. Not only are more people becoming prone to hearing loss, but also, adoption rates are staying relatively flat. This fact, coupled with the increasing amount of co-morbidities linked to hearing loss, spell trouble for the future as hearing loss becomes a growing issue if folks suffering from it do not actively begin treating it.

Fortunately, hearing aids have experienced a renaissance of late, as they're being converted into Bluetooth devices and are on the forefront of hearable technology. Back in 2014, Danish hearing aid manufacturer, Resound, introduced the first set of Bluetooth hearing aids, using Apple's proprietary, 2.4GHz ultra-low power Bluetooth protocol. These, "made for iPhone," hearing aids have since been adopted by all six of the major hearing aid manufacturers and comprise the vast majority of the hearing aids that have been entering into the market across the past four and a half years.

In 2019, Google introduced an open-source ultra low-power Bluetooth protocol available for Android, Audio Streaming for Hearing Aids (ASHA), which will serve as the basis to provide seamless connectivity between any Bluetooth hearing aid and Android smartphone.[20] Therefore, we're near the point of having universal connectivity between hearing aids and smartphones as the two main smartphone OS, iOS and Android, have hearing-aid specific Bluetooth protocols available to hearing aid manufacturers.

After the introduction of the "made for iPhone" hearing aids, hearing aid manufacturers were then enabled to create companion apps to along with their hearing aids. Companion apps allowed for hearing aid manufacturers to begin harnessing the power of the app economy and the processing power of the smartphone. Initially, these apps provided basic functions, such as fine tuning or controlling aspects of the hearing aid directly from the phone's app. As time has gone on and the apps have become more sophisticated, so too have the use cases stemming from the apps become more robust and compelling.

Some of the apps now contain features such as remote access to a hearing care professional (tele-audiology), heart rate sensor data, fall detection alerts that can be fed to family members smartphones or even a healthcare provider, and automatic program toggling based on machine learning applications.

One of the most exciting new use cases, however, is smart assistant access. Hearing aids such as Starkey's Livio AI, allow for a tap on the device to access Starkey's own Thrive assistant. The Thrive assistant will field any local queries that pertain to the hearing aids, such as, "what is my battery life?" or, "what program setting am I on?" For general queries, such as, "what is the weather," the query will be sent to the cloud and fielded by Google Assistant.

With the introduction of Google's own hearing aid Bluetooth protocol, the ability to access Google Assistant via one's hearing aids will only become more widely. We're already seeing hearing aid manufacturers adopt this protocol and make their apps available in the Google Play store. This is important as it opens the door for Android users to easily communicate with Google Assistant right in their hearing aids, either through a wake-word picked up by the phones' microphones, or for some hearing aids such as Phonak's Marvels, through the hearing aid's microphones.

It should be noted how well received voice assistants and their affiliated hardware has been among older adults. According to market research conducted by NPR and Edison Research, adults aged 55+ comprised 33% of the first adopters, which is defined as owning a speaker for more than one year, and 19% of the early mainstream, which is defined as owning a speaker for less than one year.[21] No other product in the history consumer technology has seen older adults comprise such a large portion of the early adopters and mainstream.

This makes sense. The current user interface we predominately rely on to communicate with our technology, mobile, can be limiting and restrictive to individuals who struggle to operate a smartphone due to age-related ailments such as deteriorating eyesight, mobility or dexterity. Previous generations of computing included an on-ramp period of learning that usually hindered the growth initially among older adults as the technology was deemed too technical and abstract.

That's the beauty of voice technology. When presented with the ability to communicate with technology through natural speech, our aging population might find that this is a more conducive user interface to interact with their technology compared to the incumbent method of tapping, typing and swiping on a small glass box. Voice assistants span the whole age spectrum, enabling young children all the way to our oldest adults to enjoy the benefits of the technology.

Based on the knowledge that our aging population is finding value in voice assistants today, which we know will only get better in time, and the fact that a rising number of older adults could and probably should wear hearing aids, the solution to the low adoption numbers might be to leverage voice technology to dramatically increase the capabilities of the device. While cost and stigma tend to be the most often cited culprits of the low penetration rate of hearing aids, and there is definitely some truth to that, the other way to look at the stagnant market penetration is that the value proposition is just not strong enough. Voice-assistant enabled hearing aids on the other hand, represent a good opportunity to get more people to take action on their hearing loss.

In addition to older adults finding value in being able to communicate with their voice assistants via their hearing aids, it also empowers them and reduces the burden on the caregiver. There are currently multiple smart home solutions that can be paired to a voice assistant and controlled through the hearing aid, which can accomplish a portion of the work that the caregiver is currently relied upon. Adjusting one's blinds, television, thermostat, and lights are just a few examples of aspects to one's environment that could all be controlled directly through the voice assistant residing in one's hearing aid.

As class-one FDA registered medical devices, hearing aids are at the edge of implementation of the type of biometric sensors described previously in this chapter. You can imagine the "nurse Siri" scenario applying squarely to the older adult cohort as the medical professional community might find it much easier to discern what's going on with their patient from data being collected from a device worn consistently for long periods of time each day, rather than a first hand account from the patient herself.

Much of the data captured from a hearing aid with sensors such as PPG sensors would be fed either to Apple health, or the hearing aid companion app. Once the data is there, it can then either be transferred in some capacity to the medical professional or the caregiver to keep those caring for the user abreast on her condition based on what the assistant is ascertaining from the data.

So, there's a convergence of needs from multiple angles coming together that might mutually and collectively work in conjunction on each side's behalf. We know that the demand for caregivers is rising, but that demand might be able to be satisfied from a voice assistant. We also know that a growing number of our aging population has some level of hearing loss, making them great candidates for hearing aids, which have historically not penetrated the market at the levels they should. So by empowering our aging population with voice-assistant enabled hearing aids, we might ultimately see the caregiver demand offset and the penetration rates rise as it all equates to a more compelling hearing aid and stronger value proposition.

Conclusion

Wearables, and more notably hearables, combined with voice technology will yield lots of exciting new use cases pertaining to the medical setting. Much of what's possible today stems from the innovation that's been transpiring on the hardware side of the hearables, and the foundational technologies that voice technology is built on, such as natural language processing. We're entering into an era where this combination is made increasingly more feasible.

Google, Apple, Amazon and Samsung will largely fuel the proliferation and innovation on the hardware side in the US, as they're financially and com-petitively motivated to do so, to ensure that each company's assistant gets preferential treatment or exclusive access to the user. Other, more niche entrants, as well as dark horse candidates to enter into the hardware side in a meaningful way, will have opportunities to either specialize and cater to specifically use cases. All of this bodes well for more applications to surface that pertain to the healthcare setting.

While the voice assistant providers' primary goal with their wearables will be to more extensively proliferate their assistant and provide always-avail-able access, there will be plenty of innovation brought forward by third party companies building around the component innovation that sets each voice assistant providers' wearables apart. New sensors, new types of chip designs and architectures, new ways to store and extract power, new apps to house data, new methods in which said data is transferred, and so forth. The foundational building blocks powering and enabling voice assis-tants to increasingly make a greater impact in the medical setting.

Our aging population is ripe to reap the benefits of this impending tsunami of features and functionality in a way that will empower older adults like never before. Not only will our aging population benefit, but so too can the caregivers who can lean on voice assistants to help offload the burden placed on them. This will manifest itself in the medical setting as well, as the caregiver and medical professional designated to each patient will be much more informed on what's occurring with the patient via the droves of data that will be easily accessible and available via the patient's wear-ables, most likely in the form of smart hearing aids.

Wearables and voice technology are bound to converge together to mix into a powerful combination that should give way to a number of exciting applications. One of the most pronounced settings that will see the by-products of this technological fusion will most likely be the medical setting. The stage is set, the two are rapidly converging and the use cases of the two are becoming more and more clear.

References

1. https://voicebot.ai/smart-speaker-consumer-adoption-report-2019/

2. http://www.nickhunn.com/wp-content/uploads/downloads/2016/11/The-Market-for-Hearable-Devices-2016-2020.pdf

3. https://www.apple.com/newsroom/2016/09/apple-introduces-iphone-7-iphone-7-plus/

4. https://www.aboveavalon.com/notes/2019/2/11/airpods-have-gone-viral

5. https://www.digitaltrends.com/mobile/airpods-upgrade-2019-all-new-design-2020/

6. https://www.idc.com/getdoc.jsp?containerId=prUS45488019

7. https://www.aboveavalon.com/notes/2019/2/11/airpods-have-gone-viral

8. https://www.idc.com/getdoc.jsp?containerId=prUS45488019

9. https://foreignpolicy.com/2013/04/29/epiphanies-from-chris-anderson/

10. https://www.aging.com/falls-fact-sheet/

11. https://voicebot.ai/2019/03/07/u-s-smart-speaker-ownership-rises-40-in-2018-to-66-4-million-and-amazon-echo-maintains-market-share-lead-says-new-report-from-voicebot/

12. https://www.russellsage.org/publications/who-will-care-us-0

13. https://www.pewresearch.org/fact-tank/2010/12/29/baby-boomers-retire/

14. https://www.pewresearch.org/fact-tank/2010/12/29/baby-boomers-retire/

15. https://www.bbc.com/news/health-39040146

16. https://jamanetwork.com/journals/jamaotolaryngology/article-abstract/2592954

17. https://www.who.int/pbd/deafness/news/GE_65years.pdf

18. https://www.nidcd.nih.gov/health/statistics/use-hearing-aids-adults-hearing-loss

19. http://www.hearingreview.com/2017/11/hearing-loss-associated-comorbidities-know/

20. https://source.android.com/devices/bluetooth/asha

21. https://www.nationalpublicmedia.com/smart-audio-report/latest-report/

Chapter 7:

Synthetic Voices for Healthcare Applications

Rupal Patel, PhD

Editor's Note

Dr. Rupal Patel, a world expert in synthetic speech, outlines the origin of this technology and its many applications within healthcare for patient, families, and clinicians. Dr. Patel's creation of the Human Voicebank Initiative has led to unique ways of using voice assistants for voice-impaired individuals. The author further outlines how the use of AI is helping improve synthetic speech to assist patients with dementia and their caregivers. Dr. Patel also offers a cautionary note about the use of synthetic speech and voice assistants that could create some ethical issues in the future. There are two sides to the use of AI generated synthetic speech, one providing tremendous benefits to the users, but also raising the possibility for the technology to be misused. This chapter contains cutting-edge information and is an example of the ways that voice technology is transforming our healthcare systems.

A Historical Overview of Synthetic Speech Technology

Spoken communication is arguably the primary capability that sets humans apart from other species and that truly connects us to one another. Thus, it isn't surprising that scientists and artists have been fascinated by the capability of building a machine that can emulate human speech for centuries. The earliest speaking machines, dating back to the late 1700s, were human operated mechanical models that manipulated objects such as bellows, a reed and rubber tubes to mimic the role of the lungs, vocal folds and vocal tract, respectively. These contraptions became more and more sophisticated over time with the addition of structures that could emulate the moving parts of the speech apparatus, the tongue and the lips. Joseph Faber's 1846 speaking machine, "Euphonia" was an example that is becoming commonly known given Google's namesake project.

In recent decades, with the transformation of analog to digital technology, speech synthesis has become a more prolific capability throughout a variety of applications from interactive voice response, speaking kiosks, announcement systems, and now to smart speakers and other conversational applications. Today, there are a variety of speech synthesis techniques that are commonly deployed and others which are still under development. In all cases, the goal is to convert text to understandable and natural sounding speech. The advent of electricity in the 1900's, led to acoustic models (formant synthesis) many of which were developed at Bell labs and Haskins Laboratories. These efforts were fundamental in that they advanced the fields of speech science and signal processing.

As computation became more accessible, concatenative systems gained popularity. Concatenative synthesis is ubiquitous today – the voice of Siri, Alexa, Cortana, and most commercially deployed spoken interaction systems. As the name implies, concatenative speech synthesis entails searching a database of pre-recorded speech which has been segmented into variable size units that can be rearranged and glued together to generate speech from novel text input. Given that the elemental components are high quality recordings of a human voice talent, the result is natural sounding and highly intelligible. The process is also time and labor intensive for both the voice talent and the team producing the voice. Audible glitches at the join points are a particular shortcoming even for novice listeners. Memory requirements can also be extensive given the need to store the audio segment database. Susan Bennett, the voice talent behind the Siri voice, recorded 40-50 hours of speech which was then analyzed, tagged and manipulated by teams of linguists, audio engineers and developers to produce her synthetic voice. The cost of this project is estimated to be in the order of undisclosed millions of dollars.

To address these shortcomings and to capitalize on advances in machine learning, there has been a resurgence of research activity with the focus on stochastic methods that can learn to simulate speech from smaller datasets with improved naturalness and expressivity. What used to take months to produce with the weeks of recording time, additional months of manual adjustment, annotation, and model building can now be completed in a few days. This efficiency opens up new markets and applications (Kinsella & Mutchler, 2019, Knudson, 2019). In particular, it allows small and medium sized companies to showcase a unique brand voice and even individuals to have access to a personalized digital voice for assistive communication. What was once an either, or proposition – either human talent or generic synthetic voice, is less relevant as hybrid solutions are common and the key issue is now a matter of voice choice.

Why Voice in Healthcare Now?

Over the past few decades mainstream technologies have begun to penetrate the healthcare setting. From voice recognition technologies to assist doctors in dictation, mobile apps with volumes of medical reference materials and visualizations, to sensor driven simulation labs, AI has sparked the interest of clinicians and health systems. Most recent is the adoption of smart speakers in hospital settings and the surge of startups dedicated to robots that do everything from dispense medication to assist patients in the home. The rate of market adoption of smart speakers is 3 times faster than any communication technology we have known (Kinsella & Mutchler, 2019). This means that we have entered the era of voice.

When there were only a few things that talked and their function was merely to transmit information, a handful of generic voices was sufficient. In fact, we needed to know that the sources of information were trustworthy and official. But now, as more and more applications are gaining the skill of speech, we need to differentiate what is talking, decipher the spoken intentions and the listen between the lines. We know that human speech is not transactional. In fact, infants vary their vocalizations long before they can use words to communicate. There are subtle cues that convey their intent to listeners. Similarly, a healthcare robot that is tasked with helping a patient adhere to an exercise regime cannot just bark commands at the patient. The dialogue structure, the words and the tone must all be carefully choreographed to elicit the right response. Furthermore, if the voice of the exercise robot is the same as the remote control, or the smart speaker, it is not only hard to localize what is talking but also difficult to feel truly "connected" to the robot. And that is a significant shortcoming.

Studies have shown that voice is the ultimate connector. Reeves and Nass (1996)'s seminal work on the way that humans interact with synthetic speech is key to understanding how this technology can be applied in healthcare. They found that humans treat media as a new social actor. In other words, they apply what they know to be true about humans to computers that emulate human-like skills (Nass & Gong, 2000). Moreover, gender stereotypes in the physical world are perpetuated in the virtual dimension (Mullennix, 2003; Nass, et al 1997). For example, fFemale computer voices were perceived to be more knowledgeable about love and relationships in comparison to male computer voices which were thought to be more knowledgeable about technical issues (Reeves & Nass, 1996). The likeableness of the computer voice interacted with judgements of naturalness and understandability (Carli, et al, 1995).

Nass and Gong (2000) posited four principles which are central to the argument that speech technology (both speech recognition and synthesis) is particularly suited for healthcare applications. The first principle states that the goal of speaking is to be understood. That means the words must be understood as should the intents. Feeling understood is more than just being able to follow commands. The listener needs to be able to trust the speaker, whether it is a live provider or a robotic/virtual assistant.

Second, humans use speech when the interlocutor is physically close. Presumably to build the social closeness and relationship. Physical closeness is also when one is most vulnerable and thus spoken interactions are more polite and amicable. Perhaps speaking devices should vary their voice accordingly. Nass and Gong's third principle references the fact that humans distinguish voices by gender. I would add accent and age and a number of other sociocultural factors to this list. This is important because Voice Interface Designers need to pay attention to these biases and tendencies when developing the dialogue flow and conversational interaction.

Today's voice user interfaces are speaking to a very small segment of society. There is so much value in better understanding adoption and adherence with voice-based applications by analyzing the voice output. Does it sound like the target listener in age, gender, socioeconomic group, accent, etc.? Is the rate of speech too fast for non-native listeners? Is the voice loud enough for mature users with typical age-related hearing loss? Software developers and product teams are far too focused on the complexity and power of the technology stack but not the final end point of the voice which is the interface between the technology and the customer. Nass and Gong's fourth and final principle is that humans have a broad definition of speech and that they apply this to computer speech. This means the bar is high but also the opportunities are vast.

Synthetic Speech Applications within Healthcare

The human voice is multidimensional signal that conveys one's age, gender, physical size, personality and even our daily usage patterns and habits (cf. Bachorowski & Owren, 1999; Collins, 2000; Feinberg et al., 2005; Fitch & Giedd, 1999; Hartman & Danhauer, 1976; Lass, Ruscello & Lakawicz, 1988; Linville, 1998; Munson et al., 2006; Smyth et al., 2003; Walton & Orlikoff, 1994; Zuckerman & Miyake, 1993). Words such as "deep," "rich," "high," "low," "breathy," "hoarse," "sultry," "smooth" or "loud" are used to describe the diversity of the human voice. Not only is voice intricately tied to our personal identity, it is also a rich biomarker that has been largely untapped. Given the fine motor movements involved in the production of voice and speech, subtle impairments of these skills are some of the earliest signs of underlying neuromotor conditions. Moreover, the perception of speech and voice may also be altered in conditions such as Parkinson Disease, dementia and autism (REF). These complex interactions will require careful consideration when designing voice based interfaces for health care. Just as product designers strategize about the logo, color palate, font and other graphical user traits, the addition of voice cannot be selected from a stock library. Voice branding and alignment with end users will play a critical role in the voice first era of healthcare. The use case below explore some key areas in which computer generated speech plays a role today as well as more nascent applications that are only now evolving due to improvements in synthesis quality, speed, and affordability.

Synthetic Speech for Assistive Communication

Personalized speech synthesis is a particularly compelling advance for individuals with severe speech impairment who rely on synthetic speech technology. Until recently, millions of individuals with neuromotor speech impairments who use augmentative and alternative communication (AAC) devices have relied on mass-produced, generic-sounding synthetic voices as their primary means of communication. In fact, it is not uncommon to find several students in a classroom or adults in an office or residential facility using the exact same digital voice. Not only does this impact social acceptance and self-esteem (Peschke et al. 2012, Adank et al. 2013), it causes confusion, hinders safety (Light & McNaughton, 2014) and further isolates individuals (Ridley, 2012). A classic example was the voice used by the late, Professor Stephen Hawking. Despite being British, he used an American accented voice and that same voice is also the voice of thousands of individuals – men, women and children who rely on synthetic speech for assisted communication. We wouldn't dream of fitting a young girl with a prosthetic limb of a grown man - so why use the same prosthetic voice?

As a speech clinician and scientist, I was troubled by this, so I sought to address the need for personalization by harnessing identity-bearing acoustic cues in the vocalizations produced by those in need of voice prostheses. Previous research had shown that individuals with severe neuromotor speech disorders were still able to modulate vocal prosody (Patel, 2002a, 2002b, 2003, 2004; Patel & Salata, 2006; Patel & Watkins, 2007). In other words, despite lacking fine control of the speech articulators required to produce consonants and vowels, they had relatively preserved ability to vary pitch, loudness, duration, timbre and rhythm, collectively referred to as prosody.

The breakthrough was in considering our empirical findings within the framework of the source-filter theory of speech production (Chiba & Kajiyama, 1941; Fant, 1960). The theory posits that human speech can be divided into a source component (the vocal folds) and a filter component (the rest of the vocal tract) that are largely independent. That is, source features for voiced speech such as the rate of vocal fold vibration, glottal wave shape, and periodicity, are largely separable from supra-glottal vocal tract features such as its length, shape, and cross-sectional area (Fant, 1960; Stevens, 1998). While filter characteristics are conventionally thought to be more salient for speaker identification (c.f. Fellows et al., 1997; Nolan, 1983; Nygaard et al., 1994; Remez et al., 1997; Remez & Rubin, 1993), recent work suggests that source characteristics can be highly informative especially in cases were filter cues are distorted or disordered (e.g. Jreige, Patel, & Bunnell, 2009; Matsumoto et al., 1973; Mills, Bunnell, Patel, 2014; Plumpe, et al., 1999). Given that speakers with severe speech impairment have impoverished articulation, my students and I designed a comprehensive yet succinct set of vocalization tasks that mined for speaker identity cues. We found that even a single sustained vowel contained enough vocal DNA to seed the voice personalization process. What was required was a corpus of clearly articulated speech from a matching speech donor who was capable of producing all the sounds and sound combination in the language. Once the vocalizations of the recipient and recording corpus of the surrogate speaker were obtained, both could be inverse filtered to separate source and filter characteristics of each party, respectively and then recombined digitally. The result is a BeSpoke Voice that sounds like the recipient in age, personality and vocal identity yet is as understandable as the matched speaker.

After several years of research, we had developed a method to build unique synthetic voices within the laboratory (Jriege, Patel & Bunnell, 2013). In 2014, I founded **VocaliD** to make this innovation available to the millions of users who rely on text to speech applications. The company's first product was the **Human Voicebank Initiative** – a crowdsourced effort to gather and store donor voices of all ages and backgrounds from around the world in order to create custom crafted affordable voices for all those in need. We envisioned personalized voices that were powered by a new form of biological donation - speech recordings. Recorded using everyday technology such as a home computer, encrypted to protect confidentiality, stored on the cloud, typed for a match and blended to create a unique vocal persona. Today, over 27000 speakers ranging in age from 6-91, from 120 countries have collectively contributed over 14M sentences to help those living with speechlessness. BeSpoke voices are created by combining the source characteristic of the recipient with the filter characteristics of matched voice donor from the Voicebank.

With increased awareness about the Human Voicebank and the ability to share one's voice, interest in using the platform to bank one's voice proactively also grew. Individuals who were facing an imminent laryngectomy or glossectomy or those coping with progressive voice loss from neurodegenerative disorders, were interested in banking their voice for future use. Although the concept of voicebanking for oneself was not novel, The Human Voicebank was an intuitive user interface that had been tried and tested by thousands of everyday users and thus was easily accessible even for patient groups and those with limited technological experience. In scenarios where the recipient's recordings are used to train the voice model, we call the resulting voice their **Vocal Legacy**.

One of the most powerful cases was that of a gentleman in Texas who learned about our technology 20 hours before his total laryngectomy and partial glossectomy. With guidance and encouragement from our team, he was able to bank approximately 1300 sentences. As one may imagine his determination to preserve such an important aspect of his identity was palpable. His emotions ranged from fear to hope and everything in between. He also recorded some messages for his loved ones in his own voice. Another gentleman is the United Kingdom with tongue cancer learned of VocaliD, a couple weeks prior to surgery. For him, we were able to gather his recording and build his Vocal Legacy voice prior to the surgery. Thus, he was able to communicate using the MyVocaliD app running his voice while in the hospital. He also continued to use his Vocal Legacy during speech therapy to generate an auditory model to target. In fact, within 3 months, his speech had improved considerably.

A recent pilot study shed light on the psychosocial and quality of life impact of Vocal Legacy voices amongst those coping with the aftermath of Head and/or Neck cancer (Fischman, Patel & Jalisi, 2019). Key findings suggest that the process of voicebanking was in and of itself, healing. In other words, it gave individuals a sense of control over a devastating diagnosis and hope at a time when they felt their world was collapsing. Patients also felt empowered while voicebanking because they knew that even if they didn't need the digital voice, others less fortunate could benefit. This point is critical for clinicians to understand because many are reluctant to inform patients about voicebanking for fear that patients may feel less confident about their medical care if asked to voicebank. Just as people bank blood, stem cells, and sperm as insurance for future health issues, voicebanking needs to be promoted. In terms of adoption and use of the Vocal Legacy, those surveyed were highly positive about the impact on quality of life, self-esteem and independence. Caregivers and family members have also indicated that having a Vocal Legacy has been instrumental to coping and maintaining the social connection that they assumed they would have lost forever.

Synthesized Speech for Patient Engagement

Historically, synthesized speech was commonly heard in public settings – announcements on transportation systems, automated kiosks at banks and parking garages, alerts and notifications in factories and buildings. Places where the voice was an information utility. The confluence of the internet of things and the fastest market adoption of any communication system known to man, the smart speaker (Kinsella & Mutchler, 2019), synthetic speech has entered our daily lives - in the car, in our homes, at the grocery store, at work and everywhere around us. The proliferation of voice-based interactions offers a unique opportunity to serve a broader and more diverse range of the population. When information access was restricted to text, only those who could read had access. Voice, makes information accessible by children, those with low literacy skills, those who speak other languages and individuals with disabilities. But to truly tap into the power of voice, we need more voice choice. There is a sizeable volume of literature that documents the tendency for individuals to trust, enjoy and prefer voices that sound like them in personality (Blood, Mahan & Hyman, 1979; Feinberg et al, 2006; Pipitone & Gallup, 2008; Nass & Lee, 2001), accent (Lass et al, 1980), and gender (Smyth, Jacobs & Rogers, 2003; Perry, Ohde & Ashmead, 2001). Marketing teams and brand designers have capitalized on this for decades. Voice casting and production are well tested and carefully crafted user experiences when it comes to deploying human voice talent. While still in its infancy, we are starting to see the technology giants recognizing the need for greater voice choice, which they are addressing largely through celebrity voices at the moment (e.g. Google's John Legend and Amazon's Samuel L. Jackson voice).

Spoken interfaces for coping with loneliness. Loneliness is a growing problem especially amongst the elderly as many are living longer and independently. With the rise of the nuclear family and greater career mobility, the comfort and company offered by extended families and communities with long term roots has dwindled. A recent US Census bureau report shows that only 37% of Americans have lived in their home for over a decade. There has also been a rise in families where couples work in separate cities and way from their aging parents. But it is not just that people are lonely when they are physically alone. In fact, some sociologists are referring to loneliness as an epidemic that requires a wholistic solution. John Cacioppo, a University of Chicago neuroscientist, has raised awareness about the pervasive effects of loneliness. Not only is loneliness a sense of isolation or social rejection, but Cacioppo's research demonstrates that it disrupts cognitive abilities, determination and the immune system (Cacioppo &

Patrick, 2009; Perissinotto, Cenzer & Covinsky, 2012). That's what makes loneliness a public health issue. In 2018, Great Britain appointed a Minister of Loneliness and a number of senior care insurance plans have made it a key priority of services (e.g. CareMore Health; Blue Cross Blue Shield, Cigna).

How can conversational devices play a role in combating loneliness? Teams within technology companies like Amazon and Google as well as new initiatives such as Longevity Explorers (Caro, 2018) are beginning to study how interactions with AI can help reduce social isolation. There has been considerable media on interactions between older adults and Alexa. Not only do older adults ask Alexa for information, there is reportedly a higher proportion of older adults who engage with Alexa on topics that are more personal, sharing feelings, stories and memories. Perhaps her voice makes them feel at ease and knowing that she is not a real person, reduces inhibition. Its unclear why older adults are engaging with smart speakers, nor is it clear if these findings are common across socioeconomic and cultural groups. How do users of different sociocultural backgrounds personify Alexa or Siri? Do they think of "her" as a person or a machine that sounds like a person? Understanding these factors may help answer how, and for whom, spoken AI could be most effective in combating loneliness.

The second way in which conversational interfaces could tackle isolation is by facilitating deeper human to human interactions. This is an area that has yet to be thoroughly explored. Part of the reason, I believe is because the technology still feels like an "other", a third wheel. The voice user interface is "foreign" to the humans that it may help connect. If it sounded more like a member of their family, group or community would that help? If the AI's memory and speech patterns weren't flawless, would that make it more believable? Would that be a good thing or would it be perceived as deceptive? Google's initial duplex demonstration came under considerable criticism because the human interlocutors didn't know they were interacting with an AI. The demo seemed particularly believable because of its naturalness - a combination of the colloquial style, hesitations and unconventional grammar. This paradox of the march of technology that continues to advance the quality and naturalness of synthetic speech and the sociological factors that make us uncomfortable with machines that too eerily mimic us, is a significant challenge for voice designers. Should the product remind, warn and otherwise announce that it is artificially generated? But if we do that, how do we truly create engagement? When we play video games, we know we have entered the virtual world, when we watch TV and movies, we are aware that we are being entertained. When we interact with more and more realistic and ubiquitous AI, how will we separate our virtual and physical worlds?

Engaging those with compromised memory and cognitive capacity. Analogous to loneliness, the incidence of dementia is rapidly increasing as people are living longer (Corrada et al., 2010). The World Health Organization estimates that 50 million people have dementia worldwide with 10 million new cases each year. The global social and economic impact was estimated to be $818B US in 2015 with families and caregivers bearing additional financial, health and legal burdens in their daily lives.

Caregivers often describe feeling overwhelmed by the need to be available at the beck and call of loved ones suffering from dementia. Conversational AI may play an important role in such cases to serve as the first line of care. Perhaps responses to frequent queries can be triaged to the AI. Family members may pre-record responses or craft messages to ease their loved one's worries. In fact, if the digital voice was familiar sounding, it may be better understood and have the added benefit of being comforting in times of distress (Holmes, 2018; Northwestern University, 2015; Rover 2018). Additionally, the tone of the AI would need to be carefully designed so as not to sound demeaning or disrespectful.

Computer generated voices offer an avenue for continual and frequently adaptable storytelling and narration of family pictures which those suffering from dementia often find comforting. Keeping patients informed about current day events and perhaps even tying them back to memories in the past could also be valuable. Many such applications have yet to be explored but hold promise for those with dementia and other disabilities.

Synthesized speech for improving patient – provider success. Today, synthetic speech plays a very narrow function in the patient-provider relationship. Pharmacies use synthetic or concatenated prompt systems for medication status calls. Dental and medical practices use the technology for appointment reminders. Most patient education and engagement platforms use a combination of synthetic and pre-recorded human voice. Despite recent advances in the quality of AI generated synthetic speech compared to concatenative methods, there is a common misperception that synthetic will be robotic while human voice is the only option for natural voice. In fact, for large volume, frequently changing content, today's AI generated voices can rival human talent in quality and deliver spoken audio within seconds rather than hours.

Synthetic speech can be a force multiplier for providing continuity and personalization of care. Today, following any surgery or procedure, you are given discharge paperwork and instructions for follow up care. What if those instructions could also be uploaded to an app or speaking device so that you can receive at home care at the right time and in the context of your daily routines? Perhaps frequently asked questions could also be answered to avoid calls to the doctor's office or delays. In terms of medication reminders, rather than each notice sounding the same and becoming a variant of spam, providers could add a little humor by changing the message and/or the tone of the voice. There are numerous ways in which AI generated voice can enhance the patient provider relationship for improved health and wellbeing. The first step is to consider synthetic speech as an option for more than merely sterile information exchange.

The Future of Synthetic Speech

The next wave of the AI revolution will need to address the demand for more convincing and expressive speech synthesis. While generating an acoustic representation of the orthographic transcript may have been sufficient for information transmission applications of the past, we are now witnessing the use of synthetic speech in numerous human-machine collaborations from digital assistants for health and wellness coaching, patient management, to clinical training and health education. These newer arenas require not only clear and intelligible speech, but also the warmth and naturalness of the human voice. Speech is more than just the words; how those words are said conveys meaning as well.

And as artificially generated voices become more and more human-like, there will be new social and ethical challenges. It is already foreseeable that modern day AI generated synthetic speech has the potential to be misused. Earlier this year, VocaliD and Modulate, a speech-to-speech conversion company recently launched an effort called AITHOS (for AI ethos). Our goal is to form a coalilation with other like minded synthetic media companies and domain experts to proactively engage in ways to counteract intentional misuse through technical and social channels.

As healthcare becomes increasingly personalized and moves out of institutional care into homes and places of work, we have an opportunity to redesign care around wellness as well as physical and mental health. The voice user interface will play a key role in adoption and engagement. When mobile phones first came out, they had limited functionality. Now, smartphones are a major platform for health and wellness applications. Similarly, smart speaker and other speaking interfaces, have the potential to revolutionize the way we experience healthcare; not just for conveying information or monitoring compliance, but for forging trust and engagement throughout the lifespan. As Nass concluded, computer are social actors, but to optimize our interactions with them, designers and developers will need to tap into human psychology and emotion.

References

1. Adank, P., Stewart, AJ., Connell, I., &; Wood, J. (2013). Accent imitation positively affects language attitudes. Frontiers of Psychology, 4, 280.

2. Apicella, C. L., Feinberg, D. R., &; Marlowe, F. W. (2007). Voice pitch predicts reproductive success in male hunter-gatherers. Biology Letters, 3(6), 682–684. doi:10.1098/rsbl.2007.0410

3. Bachorowski, J., &; Owren, M. (1999). Acoustic correlates of talker sex and individual talker identity are present in a short vowel segment produced in running speech. Journal of the Acoustical Society of America 106, 1054–1063.

4. Blood, G. W., Mahan, B. W., &; Hyman, M. (1979). Judging personality and appearance from voice disorders. Journal of Communication Disorders, 12(1), 63–67. doi:10.1016/0021-9924(79)90022-4

5. Cacioppo, J., &; Patrick, W. (2009). Loneliness: Human nature and the need for social connection. WW. Norton &; Company.

6. Carli, L.L. (1990). Gender, Language and influence. Journal of Personality and Social Psychology, 59, 941-951.

7. Caro, R. "Can Alexa Help Fight Isolation and Loneliness" April 10, 2019.<https://www.techenhancedlife.com/articles/can-alexa-help-fight-isolation-and-loneliness>

8. Chiba, T., &; Kajiyama, J. (1941). The vowel: Its nature and structure. Tokyo, Japan: Tokyo-Kaiseikan.

9. Collins, S. (2000). Men's voices and women's choices. Animal Behavior 60, 773–780.

10. Corrada, M., Brookmeyer, R., Paganini-Hill, A., Berlau, D., &; Kawas, C. (2010). Dementia Incidence Continues to Increase with Age in the Oldest Old The 90+ Study. Annals of Neurology, 67(1): 114-121.

11. Fant, G. (1960). Acoustic Theory of Speech Production. Mouton, The Hague.

12. Feinberg, D. R., Jones, B. C., Little, A. C., Burt, D. M., &; Perrett, D. I. (2005). Manipulations of fundamental and formant frequencies influence the attractiveness of human male voices. Animal Behavior 69, 561–568.

13. Fellows, J.M., Remez, R.E., &; Rubin, P.E. (1997). Perceiving the sex and identity of a talker without natural vocal timbre. Perception and Psychophysics, 59(6), 839-849.

14. Fischman, V., Patel, R., &; Jalisi, S. (2019). "Can You Hear Me Now? Personalization of Voice Using Artificial Intelligence in Aphonic Patients". Otolaryngology - Head and Neck Surgery, September 3, 2019. <https://journals.sagepub.com/doi/full/10.1177/01945998198581141d>

15. Fitch, W. T., &; Giedd, J. (1999). Morphology and development of the human vocal tract: A study using magnetic resonance imaging. Journal of the Acoustical Society of America, 1511-1522.

16. Hartman, D. E., &; Danhauer, J. L. (1976). Perceptual features of speech for males in four perceived age decades. Journal of the Acoustical Society of America, 713-715.

17. Holmes, E. (2018). Familiar voices are easier to understand, even if we don't recognize them. Psychological Science.

18. Hughes, S. M., Dispenza, F., &; Gallup, G. G. (2004). Ratings of voice attractiveness predict sexual behavior and body configuration. Evolution and Human Behavior, 25(5), 295–304.

19. Jriege, C., Patel, R. &; Bunnell, T. (2009). VocaliD: Personalizing Text-to-Speech Synthesis for Individuals with Severe Speech Impairment. Association for Computing Machinery, SIGACCESS Conference on Computers &; Accessibility, Pittsburgh, PA, 259-260.

20. Kinsella, B., &; Mutchler, A. Smart speaker consumer adoption report. March 2019. <https://voicebot.ai/wp-content/uploads/2019/03/smart_speaker_consumer_adoption_report_2019.pdf>

21. Knudson, J. The state of artificial intelligence. Speech Technology Magazine, Winter 2019. March 18, 2019. <https://www.speechtechmag.com/Articles/Editorial/Features/The-State-of--Artificial-

Intelligence-129813.aspx>

22. Lass, N., Ruscello, D., &; Lakawicz, J. (1988). Listeners' perceptions of nonspeech characteristics of normal and dysarthric children. Journal of Communication Disorder, 385-391.

23. Light J.C. &; McNaughton D. (2014) Communicative competence for individuals who require augmentative and alternative communication: A new definition for a new era of communication? Augmentative and Alternative Communication

24. Linville, S. (1998). Acoustic correlates of perceived versus actual sexual orientation in men's speech. Pholia Phoniatrica et Logopaedica, 35-48.

25. Matsumoto, H., Hiki, S., Sone, T., &; Nimura, T. (1973). Multidimensional representation of personal quality of vowels and acoustical correlates. IEEE transactions on audio and electroacoustics, 21, 428-436.

26. Mills, T., Bunnell, T.H., &; Patel, R. (2014) Towards Personalized Speech Synthesis for Assistive

27. Communication. Augmentative and Alternative Communication. 30(3), 226-236.

28. Mullennix, J.W., Stern, S.E., Wilson, S.J., and Dyson, C.L. (2003). Social perception of male and female computer synthesized speech. Computer in Human Behavior, 19, 407-424.

29. Munson, B., McDonald, E., DeBoe, N., &; White, A. (2006). The acoustic and perceptual bases of judgments of women and men's sexual orientation from read speech. Journal of Phonetics, 202-240.

30. Nass, C., &; Lee, K. M. (2001). Does computer-synthesized speech manifest personality? Experimental tests of recognition, similarity-attraction, and consistency attraction. Journal of Experimental Psychology: Applied 7, 171-181.

31. Nass, C., Moon, Y., and Green, N. (1997). Are machines gender neutral? Gender Stereotypic responses to computers with voices. Journal of Applied Social Psychology, 27, 864-876.

32. Nass, C., and Gong, L. (2000). Speech interfaces – from an evolutionary perspective. Communications of the ACM, 43(9), 36-43.

33. Northwestern University. "Family voices, stories speed coma recovery." ScienceDaily, 22 January 2015. <www.sciencedaily.com/releases/2015/01/150122133213.htm>

34. Patel, R. (2002a). Phonatory control in adults with cerebral palsy and severe dysarthria. Augmentative and Alternative Communication 18(1), 2-10.

35. Patel, R. (2002b). Prosodic Control in Severe Dysarthria: Preserved Ability to Mark the Question-Statement Contrast. Journal of Speech, Language, and Hearing Research 45(5), 858–870.

36. Patel, R. (2003). Acoustic Characteristics of the Question-Statement Contrast in Severe Dysarthria Due to Cerebral Palsy. Journal of Speech, Language, and Hearing Research 46(6), 1401–1415.

37. Patel, R. (2004). The acoustics of contrastive prosody in adults with cerebral palsy. Journal of Medical Speech-Language Pathology 12(4), 189–193.

38. Patel, R., &; Salata, A. (2006). Using computer games to mediate caregiver-child communication for children with severe dysarthria. Journal of Medical Speech-Language Pathology 14 (4), 279–284.

39. Patel, R., &; Watkins, C. (2007). Stress identification in speakers with dysarthria due to cerebral palsy: An initial report. Journal of Medical Speech-Language Pathology 15 (2), 149–159.

40. Perissinotto, C., Stijacic Cenzer, I., &; Covinsky, K. (2012). Loneliness in Older Persons A

41. Predictor of Functional Decline and Death. 172(14): 1078-83.

42. Peschke, C., Ziegler, W., Eisenberger, J., &; Baumbaertner, A. (2012). Phonological manipulation between speech perception and production activated a parieto-frontal circuit. Neuroimage, 59, 788-799.

43. Pipitone, R. N., &; Gallup, G. G. (2008). Women's voice attractiveness varies across the menstrual cycle. Evolution and Human Behavior, 29, 268–274. doi:10.1016/j.evolhumbehav.2008.02.001

44. Plumpe, M.D., Quatieri, T.F., &; Reynolds, D.A. (1999). Modeling of the glottal flow derivative waveform with application to speaker identification. IEEE transactions on speech and audio processing, 7(5),

569-586.

45. Reeves, B., and Nass, C. (1996). The Media Equation: How people treat computer, and new media like real people and places. New York: Cambridge University Press.

46. Remez, R.E. &; Rubin, P.E. (1993). On the intonation of sinusoidal sentences: Contour and pitch height. Journal of the Acoustical Society of America, 94, 1983-1988.

47. Remez, R. E., Fellowes, J. M., &; Rubin, P. E. (1997). Talker identification based on phonetic information, J. Exp. Psychol. Hum. Percept. Perform, 23, 651–666.

48. Ridley, L. (2012). Voice by choice. http://www.youtube.com/watch?v=CMm_XL3Ipbo

49. Rover, E. Tech solutions that make life easier for dementia care. AARP. June 25, 2018. <https://www.aarp.org/health/dementia/info-2018/technology-caregiving-dementia-patients.html>

50. Smyth, R., Jacobs, G., &; Rogers, H. (2003). Male voices and perceived sexual orientation: An experiment and theoretical approach. Language and Society 32, 329-350.

51. Stevens, K. N. (1998). Acoustic phonetics. Cambridge, MA: MIT Press.

52. Walton, J., &; Orlikoff, R. (1994). Speaker race identification from acoustic cues in the vocal signal. Journal of Speech Language and Hearing Research, 738-745.

53. Zuckerman, M., &; Miyake, K. (1993). The attractive voice: What makes it so? Journal of Nonverbal Behavior, 119-135.

Chapter 8:

Voice First Health Interview: A Diabetes Care Plan

Anne Weiler

Teri Fisher, MSc, MD

Editor's Note

This is an educational and informative voice interview between Dr. Fisher and Anne Weiler, the CEO of Wellpepper, on the use of voice technology to help guide patients through their diabetes care plans. As discussed in the chapter, Wellpepper was the winner of the Merck sponsored Alexa Diabetes Challenge, a very prestigious competition. Wellpepper focused on the use of voice to effectively communicate with diabetes patients. The interviewee discusses how voice can provide patients with more empathy, convenience, and a more natural method to communicate than smartphones. Anne Weiner is a leader in this field and this chapter certainly highlights her thought leadership.

Hear the complete podcast interview with Anne Weiler at:
https://voicefirsthealth.com/6

Teri Fisher:

Anne Weiler is the CEO and cofounder of Wellpepper and creator of the product, Sugarpod. Their company was the winner of the Alexa diabetes challenge sponsored by Merck. She comes to us with a wealth of knowledge about using technologies for patient care. Anne, would you please tell us a little bit about your background?

Anne Weiler:

Sure. I'm really a technologist by background. I've spent my whole career in the tech industry, including 10 years at Microsoft after Microsoft acquired the Canadian company Ncompass labs. We made web content management software and Microsoft acquired that company in 2001. And then I spent 10 years at Microsoft doing various things in product management, bringing products to market and finding new opportunities and I actually got into healthcare in particular through personal experience when my mom was diagnosed with a rare autoimmune disease and spent six months in the hospital and then there a lack of continuity of care when she was discharged. So my cofounder and I, who had been at that same Canadian company, founded Wellpepper to really look at how we support patients outside the clinic. And at the time when we started, we were doing that through mobile apps. And we were mobile first because we felt that people had an emotional connection to their mobile devices. But recently we started incorporating voice because we're seeing that the emotional connection that people have with voice devices is actually even stronger than mobile devices. And for certain scenarios, especially those in the home, voice can be really powerful.

Teri Fisher:

Can you comment a little bit more about the emotional connection people have with their mobile devices versus voice technology?

Anne Weiler:

Sure. I think that some of the differences are that voice is often a home interface because, if you're in the office, maybe you don't want to be talking to Alexa or talking to another device. With the mobile device in your pocket, it's always with you and it notifies you or pings you, and you react. But at the same time, people are starting to think about whether we should we be looking at the screen all the time. But what happens with voice interactions? You're in the kitchen, you're in the living room, and then you can ask Alexa something and have an immediate engagement. Amazon and Google have worked very hard on the types of interactions and the human voice is such a natural interaction, especially in healthcare, but I think people also feel more connected and we've seen that as well in testing voice with people. It feels like Alexa cares and it's because there's this ongoing communication and question and answer format.

The example I used to use for mobile engagement was the first time my iPhone popped up and said, "You have a very busy day tomorrow, your first meeting is at seven, and your last meeting is at six." I thought, "Wow, I do have a busy day tomorrow. Thank you for noticing." So mobile can also deliver empathy, which we always strive for at Wellpepper with our patient interactive care plans: to deliver that empathy through mobile. But we've found that doing a little interviewing and the kind of back and forth that you can do with voice can be even more powerful.

Teri Fisher:

Can you expand on that a little bit? Why do you feel that voice can be more powerful for healthcare?

Anne Weiler:

The benefits for voice interfaces in healthcare are broad reaching.

Convenience - It's often much easier to ask or tell Google Home or Alexa something than it is to open an app and key something in

Empathy - Voice interactions just seem friendlier. In our testing of diabetes type 2 care plans people told us that the voice assistant seemed like she cared. While app interactions can also deliver empathy, the bond with voice seems stronger.

Natural - Most healthcare experiences are based on a conversation, especially between patient and provider. Voice avoids the barriers to communication that screens may introduce.

Cost-effective - These devices deliver great experiences backed by artificial intelligence to make sense of the content that's being delivered and are less than half the price of most smartphones, making them cost effective for large deployments or lower income populations.

Ubiquitous and unobtrusive - Amazon reports selling over 100 million voice devices.1 Voice devices are small and they don't interfere with other activities either in a patient room or at home.

Teri Fisher:

Now, let's go back to Wellpepper. Could you please introduce the listeners to what you do and what the company is all about?

Anne Weiler:

Yes. We have the capability or platform for interactive patient facing care plans. And I know that that sounds complicated, but it's as basic as replacing all of the paper instructions that you get when you've had a doctor's visit or a hospital stay or when you're trying to manage a disease with a digital interaction. And we deliver those interactions in different ways. We might send you an SMS reminder for something. We might send you an email, we may have you download a mobile app. And we may have you interact with a skill, like an Alexa skill or interact through Google Home. And so it's really about those reminders: Did you take your medication? If you didn't take it, why didn't you? How are you feeling today? What are you eating? We cover things you might be doing for something like preparing for surgery, recovering from surgery or managing a chronic disease like diabetes. And we're always thinking about what is the best way to deliver these experiences based on what someone needs to do and where they are. Oh and I should also mention that we're then connecting them back to the care team because we don't believe that, just sending stuff off to patients and having them do it is enough. We need to be able to close the loop and connect them with the care team when they need additional help.

Teri Fisher:

So, this type of communication would be initiated by the healthcare team and then provided to the patient. Then the patient would use this as a tool to do whatever actions they need to take care of themselves, but also then have a report sent back to the healthcare team. Is that correct in the way I summarized that?

Anne Weiler:

Yes, what we really focus on is that patients can and will self-manage if you give them the right tools. And then we need to connect them to the healthcare team and let the healthcare team know when people need additional help. And so it's not so much remote monitoring, as much as empowering patients, giving them actionable tasks and things that they can do, and then noticing when there are challenges so patients can proactively reach out and message their provider. But we're also looking for problems. One of the things that we found, (this is text messaging, but there's absolutely no reason why this couldn't be voice-based messaging), is that 70% of the messages that patients are sending through the system don't actually need a response, but 2% of them are urgent. And those are the ones we want to notify the care team that somebody might need additional help.

When you add voice into the equation, there are some tasks that are better suited for different types of interactions. Is it a quick hit? Is the user asking a question or issuing a command, or is it a guided interaction. We're accustomed to voice surveys in healthcare, but you've got to do better than a phone tree or robocall. How do you react and adapt to the information the person wants to tell you or wants to learn? How do you make a delightful and also useful experience?

Teri Fisher:

Speaking of voice technology, you were a part of a really exciting project - the Alexa Diabetes Challenge. I was wondering if you could tell us a little bit about that whole experience?

Anne Weiler:

Yes. It was an amazing experience. We actually first started prototyping with voice back in 2017 and at HIMSS, which is the big healthcare IT event. We had been shown someone interacting with a total joint replacement care plan using Alexa and doing some of the surveys and some of the check-ins that the person had to do as part of the total joint care plan. And then someone told us about the Merck-sponsored Alexa Diabetes Challenge. The challenge was to help someone newly diagnosed with type two diabetes manage their care using voice. What we developed for this was a comprehensive care plan including voice, mobile, and devices.

We think that voice is an amazing experience and an amazing interface at certain times, but you do need other interfaces. So what we actually built was a care plan, and a physical device, which was a voice-powered scale and foot scanner, Sugarpod. We also built the mobile care plan because we know that people who are diagnosed with type two diabetes are most likely in the workforce and they have to continue to take their care plans with them and then can experience a voice interaction in the home at the end of the day. One of the things that we learned from this was really around how you integrate with the fabric of someone's daily life.

In the morning a person gets on the voice powered scale: it does one of the tasks in their care plan, which is to check their weight. But it also takes a picture of their feet and puts that through a machine-learned image classifier to look for diabetic foot ulcers, which are the leading cause of amputation hospitalizations and in the US a $9 billion cost per year to the health system. And of course, the biggest issue is that the quality of life that happens if you have an amputation. The device looks for early signs of foot ulcers, but at the same time while someone is getting their foot scan, they're actually checking off a few tasks in their care plan as well, like saying that they took their medication. Then they can take their care plan on the mobile device to work with them, fill out some more things and then also check in, in the evening through Alexa and do additional tasks there.

We thought voice was a great interface for the scale because if you have trouble seeing at all, being able to look down at a scale interface, having the scale actually talk to you is really, really helpful. But then we also had the full care plan available via mobile as well. And we tested this with real patients in a diabetes foot and wound clinic. That's where we really got the feedback from patients saying that it really felt like the voice assistant (Alexa in this case) really cared. They really were having a natural conversation with her. We had one gentleman respond when the scale prompted "step on the scale and tell me when you're ready". And he said, "ready when you are," which is exactly the kind of conversation you expect to have with a human, not necessarily with a voice device.

Teri Fisher:

So the patients step on the scale and they get pictures taken of their feet. Have you come across anybody else that has approached diabetic foot ulcers in that way?

Anne Weiler:

No, not with voice and not with pictures, but there are definitely others who are trying to tackle this problem because it's a big problem. There's a company in Alberta, Canada, doing sensor insoles. And then there's a company that's won an MIT challenge with a sensor mat. In testing the images we were talking to a physician assistant who said, generally when these people are coming in, he'll take a picture of the bottom of their feet and show it to them and they are shocked at what they see. And that's because of the neuropathy. Voice, it just makes it so much easier to explain to the person, why are we doing this and what are we doing and when are we ready to do it? Like those voice cues, it just makes perfect sense.

Teri Fisher:

This kind of goes back to what you were saying initially that the voice interface is allowing the person to create an emotional connection with this machine that is helping them to take care of themselves. So as a result of this project, share with us the outcome of the Alexa diabetes challenge.

Anne Weiler:

Well, we were the winners of the challenge. Although, there were five finalists and I feel like everyone of the five finalists was a winner because the program was really great. I think they had a hundred entries and they had reviewers from all kinds of universities and health systems and a venture capitalist as well. And they narrowed it down to five finalists. And then the five finalists attended a two day bootcamp at Amazon in Seattle. And then we all presented in September. It was actually almost a year ago now. We all presented at a demo day that was held in New York. And then we were named the grand prize winners.

We invented a new device that used voice for the Challenge, but also we had thought about the care plan very comprehensively. It's not just about what pill do you need to take or what activities do you need to do or what devices do you need to interact with? Whether that's, you know, a glucometer or a voice powered scale. But being able to wrap that all up in a consistent experience and move through the different modalities I think is key. When we were thinking about the interactions, we were thinking about, "okay, what would be the voice equivalent of this mobile experience and when is voice a better experience?"

For example, for the scale, voice is a better experience. But you know, at the end of the day, the person comes home and finds out that there's a message waiting from their clinician. And so there's a notification on the device and it says, "you have a new message, would you like to hear it?" And, and she (the voice assistant) provides the message. That's pretty natural and I think that's kind of an interesting thing: some of the things that we're doing in voice were things that we were doing previously but much more expensively through, automated phone systems and things like that. So I think there's much more opportunity to do voice interactions more cost effectively, but also with AI behind them. Because previously, with IVR (interactive voice response) type responses, people weren't really doing the analysis of what was happening. And that's partly why people would get so frustrated when they call in somewhere and get a phone tree. So that's the part where the voice integrated experiences become very interesting.

Teri Fisher:

What stage are you at now with Sugarpod? Where are you at in terms of development? What's the future looking like for Sugarpod?

Anne Weiler:

We are continuing to work with Merck on this and it looks like we will be doing some more clinical testing. I can't tell you exactly what that is yet. During the challenge we saw the device as something that would go into someone's home. But when we tested it, we tested it at Kaiser Permanente foot and wound clinic here in Seattle. We found that there was actually a nice clinical scenario as well in that oftentimes the foot exam is not happening: people are rushed for time. But if you think about what happens first when you go to the doctor, what's the first thing they do? They take your weight. So if we can actually do another task at the same time as taking their weight, it can actually make the appointment more efficient. I think we saw this at the Voice Conference that the voice capabilities are beneficial to people at home, but there are a lot of really interesting ones in the clinic as well.

Teri Fisher:

The big elephant in the room is is HIPAA compliance. What's your take on that right now in terms of how patients deal with that?

Anne Weiler:

There are definitely a lot of health skills out there. I think the question is where is the information going and how do you as a patient feel about this information. You can't actually email protected health information either, however it is up to the patient how they share their data. But I think health systems are generally a little more conservative. So while there is a lot of interest in voice in healthcare, I think that one of the challenges is going to be when we can secure it. But in the meantime, one way communication of health information can definitely happen. So I think people will continue to test things. And if you can get a patient to agree that they're okay sending information through this device, then you can actually do it. The question is which health systems are going to agree to that.

Teri Fisher:

Can you comment on where Sugarpod sits in the overall framework of Wellpepper?

Anne Weiler:

It's a great question because we are actually a software company and so it is something that we are working on. We're actually more interested in the algorithm than the physical device. It may not end up in the form that we prototyped for the challenge, but certainly being able to collect patient generated data and being able to derive insight from that and start to basically automate care is the key insight. That's our core. We see Sugarpod as a great collection device for both voice experiences as well as for these images.

Teri Fisher:

Thanks so much for taking some time out of your day to come and chat with us. I really appreciate that.

References

https://techcrunch.com/2019/01/04/more-than-100-million-alexa-devices-have-been-sold/

Chapter 9:

Voice First Health Interview: Alexa Skills for Pediatrics

Devin Nadar

Teri Fisher, MSc, MD

Editor's Note

In this chapter Devin Nadar discussed the very successful Amazon Alexa skill, KidsMD, and what led to the creation of this skill that enables Boston's Children Hospital (BCH) to reach children in their homes for more effective outreach and treatment through voice. BCH does an effective job of leveraging its expertise and delivering it through Alexa skills to its community of children. Nadar then goes on to relate the development of the Flu Doctor Skill with the collaboration of Seattle's Children Hospital. Leading by example, this chapter contains an informative and educational outline of how two hospitals have leveraged their expertise to reach their young patients with voice technologies.

Hear the complete podcast interview with Devin Nadar at:
https://voicefirsthealth.com/12

Teri Fisher:

Today we have Devin Nadar on the podcast. She works for the Innovation and Digital Health Accelerator at Boston Children's Hospital. Devin, could you please take a few moments and introduce yourself and what you do with Boston Children's Hospital?

Devin Nadar:

Absolutely. So my name is Devin Nadar and I'm the Partnership Manager here at the Innovation and Digital Health Accelerator at Boston Children's Hospital. And we do an incredible amount of different things here, but my role in particular is focusing on cultivating partnerships with industry, with startups, with exciting innovators in the field of healthcare to solve clinical pain points that we see in and out of the hospital every day, as well as have a pulse check on what's going on in health care technology today so that we're continuing to be at the cutting edge of technology and offering the best experience to both our patients and our providers here at Boston Children's.

Teri Fisher:

How did you personally get into this area?

Devin Nadar:

I actually started out working at Athena Health here in Boston, an electronic medical record and billing company. That's when I really started to get into the R and D aspect of healthcare technology. Thinking about how technology can solve pain points and how innovative companies are really tackling some of these challenges that unfortunately healthcare's kind of behind on. I found an incredible opportunity here at Boston children's hospital to really be a more integral part of the innovative ecosystem that we have. We take innovators here at the hospital and surround their projects with a mini startup team. And for me one of the most compelling things that led me here is the ability to see an idea from its infancy and from its creation all the way through product development launch and potentially even spinning out startups from our group. So that's why I made the switch to Boston children's hospital as well as just it's an incredible organization and being a part of the number one pediatric hospital in the United States. There is really not a better place to be.

Teri Fisher:

Boston has become a real hub for voice technology and innovation. So you're definitely in the right place there. Let's talk a little bit about what Boston Children's Hospital is doing in this voice first and healthcare space. How did Boston Children's Hospital get involved in it and what has progressed from there?

Devin Nadar:

So I would be remiss if I didn't start by acknowledging the incredibly supportive leadership that we have here at Boston Children's Hospital who let us explore new technologies and support us as we go on these endeavors to test out new technologies such as voice in the healthcare setting. They're really letting us push the boundaries of what technology can do again for the hospital and for our patients. So we really saw an opportunity with voice from the beginning. We thought that this was an exciting new medium to reach, first of all, families at home. One of the things that we have here at Boston Children's Hospital is just an incredible amount of expertise and knowledge around how to make your kid feel better.

And for a lot of parents, there's a number of moments where their kid may be throwing up, their child might have a really high fever, and they don't know what to do and they don't know the appropriate care to seek. And that's what we really wanted to do with KidsMD. We wanted to provide trusted content from pediatric experts. So we wanted to take the Boston Children's Hospital expertise and make it available to our patients. And voice represents an interesting opportunity there because you can really reach patients in their home. Smartphones were the first step to reaching patients where they were. And voice technology represents our ability to step inside the home and be anywhere that patients need us to an even greater degree.

Teri Fisher:

So tell us a little more about KidsMD. Is this your flagship skill on Alexa?

Devin Nadar:

Yeah. It was our first skill that we launched over two years ago and we really did want it to be a basic source of pediatric information. We wanted parents to be able to ask about common symptoms. So if your kid is sneezing or as your kid is throwing up - how long have they been doing that? And go through almost your basic kind of symptom checker checklist. But we also wanted to make it a little bit more robust in terms of what information you could put into this skill and what you could get out of it. And that's why we actually integrated with a smart thermometer (Raiing) and Thermia. What you can do is actually hook up a smart thermometer and take your child's temperature that will be put into the skill. And based on that, as well as your child's age and weight, you can get dosing recommendations for common medications that you would be able to safely give your child. These are things that you might have available if you Google online. But what we did was put it in one convenient skill so that you could diagnose your child with a little bit of help from Boston Children's Hospital at home and understand what the best next steps were to take. If that was you, you could give your child a dose of children's Tylenol at home and make sure that you were providing them with the correct dose.

Teri Fisher:

I was not aware of the the integration with thermometer. How do you get around the issues of liability when you're providing medical advice?

Devin Nadar:

You will hear lots of disclaimers. I guess that's kind of the easy way to put it - we are providing this as a reference tool, but at the end of the day it doesn't replace bringing your child to see their pediatrician or consulting with a doctor. It's supposed to be your first step when you're at home and you need the kind of immediate advice that's not just the swirling thoughts that are in your head as a parent, as to how serious this is or is this a high fever. It's meant to start you on the journey of seeking the best care and it's not meant to replace seeing your doctors. So you will hear the disclaimers in the skill. And we don't want parents to not bring their children to the doctor if that's appropriate. We're hoping that our skill helps you do a little bit of triage on that front.

Teri Fisher:

And when you collect information like the age and the weight, what happens with that information?

Devin Nadar:

That's only used for dosing calculation. It's not stored or associated with the user or in any other way.

Teri Fisher:

Right. I was getting at personal health information. A lot of people know that currently, for example, Alexa is not HIPAA compliant [except for a select few organizations at this time]. But from what you're saying, it sounds like that's not an issue for this particular skill.

Devin Nadar:

Correct. For this particular skill there's no healthcare information that is collected. We do have some internal skills that we've done at Boston Children's Hospital and we've found some interesting ways to get around the HIPAA compliance piece so that we can make skills that are helpful to our clinicians. But until there is a commercially available smart speaker that is HIPAA compliant, our hands are a little bit tied and we feel as though we can't have the impact that we want, especially in the clinical setting, until we're able to use that information.

Teri Fisher:

And that's a common running theme. I think once the HIPAA compliance does come online we will see some incredible advances. And I'm sure Boston Children's is right there waiting for that day.

Devin Nadar:

We are, we're definitely waiting for the announcement as I think everyone else is.

Teri Fisher:

Now, you have just recently announced another skill. Can you tell us about that?

Devin Nadar:

Yes, I would love to. In collaboration with the Seattle Children's Hospital, we have created the Flu Doctor skill. So what this will do is provide answers to your common questions around the flu vaccine. And we think, along the Seattle Children's Hospital, that making this information available to everyone is incredibly important to help you better understand what the flu vaccine is, when you should get it, and who should get it. And also it just answers some common questions that a lot of people have around the flu vaccine.

Teri Fisher:

Can you give us a sense of how that actually works with somebody who will enable the skill? What happens?

Devin Nadar:

Yes. It's called Flu Doctor and we, along with Mama Doc from Seattle Children's Hospital, have created a number of different videos as well as audio recordings that Mama Doc did to help answer your common questions. The skill actually prompts you on different things you can ask. So it does provide suggestions such as who should get the flu vaccine, or you can ask it where you can get the flu vaccines. And to that point, we've done a cool integration with vaccine finder, which is one of the websites that we have here at Boston Children's Hospital out of our group. You can give your zip code and it will find you the closest location where you can get the flu vaccine.

Teri Fisher:

This is bringing the healthcare advice and information and guidance into the home in a number of different ways. And I imagine it's really just a matter of time until each little topic in medicine has a skill that somebody can access to bring the healthcare into the home.

Devin Nadar:

Absolutely. And I think one of the opportunities we saw in this space is that right now if you ask Alexa a healthcare question, you often get some pretty basic advice, either from Wikipedia or there's some that are on there from WebMD and they're making advances with the Mayo Clinic. But in the pediatric space, we want to be the "go to" in terms of trusted pediatric information. And we really want to put skills out there that are going to help parents get the answers to their questions. And again, it's from a reliable source and you know that it's coming from Boston Children's Hospital. And we think that the Flu Doctor's skill in particular is just a great example of two incredible children's hospitals that are collaborating together to give parents information. It's about empowering our parents and about empowering our patients. And that's will lead to much healthier kids.

Teri Fisher:

One of the things that comes to mind for me when I'm hearing you speak about this is on the one hand this is fantastic - we've got all this great information that's being developed. On the other hand, we're getting multiple skills, and has your team given any thought to the discoverability of the skills and how that will play out for the average consumer when they have to remember the different skills to invoke?

Devin Nadar:

This is something that we've been talking to Amazon about. We've been pushing the industry because I think this is a question that everyone who is looking at voice is thinking about. You don't have the cue that says "you invoked this skill yesterday - why don't you think about invoking this skill? Because it seems to match all of the information that you've put into this voice device in the past." And I think that is a challenge and we have been trying to think about ways to get our skills discovered by users. So a lot of it is talking about what we're doing, making people aware of what we're doing. We're putting some thought into what we name our skills, of course. But I think it's an ongoing discussion and something that we need to be thoughtful about and we also need to push the big players like Amazon to do more automated matching.

Teri Fisher:

And that's certainly not only for health care. With this discoverability issue, it's going to be interesting to see how that plays out over the next year or two in terms of what Amazon and other big players do.

Devin Nadar:

I think it's across the board, kind of like you were saying. When you see this information or these kinds of survey results come out about how people use their voice devices, people tend to get into ruts and they use it for music and they use it for timers and we really want people to be a little bit more broad in their continued use and we want sticky users, as everyone does across technology.

Teri Fisher:

And speaking of that, what are the stats for the KidsMD skill, which has been out for a while now? How are users finding it? What's your feedback?

Devin Nadar:

One of the things that we're most excited about is that we continue to have new users. So we usually have about 200 unique users per week, even though this skill has been released for over two years. So people continue to find our skill and use it. We've also had over 100,000 interactions in that two year period. We think that we're out there and people are accessing the skill, but we know that we need to have a more robust V2 out there that keeps up with the new Amazon Show and the advances that the technology has made. We are in the process of releasing our V2 for KidsMD, so that should be coming in the next couple of months as well.

Teri Fisher:

You obviously have a great team at Boston Children's Hospital. Now with the partnership with Seattle, how long does it take to produce a skill such as Flu Doctor?

Devin Nadar:

So the brains behind our voice skills development is my colleague Nitin and he's pretty adept at building these skills. And so with content, we've been able to turn around skills in two months that we think are very robust.

Teri Fisher:

I'm sure this just scratches the surface of what you are doing with Boston Children's Hospital. What's your take on the future of voice in healthcare over the next couple of years?

Devin Nadar:

I think that there's so much interest, there are so many of these little projects that are bubbling up. I think it's gonna continue to just be a hot topic and I think it is going to take off. We're all waiting on the HIPAA compliance piece, but once that's solved and also once people are more familiar with voice, I think that there's going to be a lot more interest in it in the clinical space specifically because of the hands free appeal. That's one of the things I've heard across the board, that for a lot of the clinicians that we work with, that's the driving force - anything that allows them to free up their hands, find information faster, and particularly dig through the electronic medical record. If you can have a voice assistant doing that, you're going to have an incredible amount of value added.

Teri Fisher:

That's a big pain point for physicians, myself included. I'm waiting for that day when I can talk to my voice assistant and it just takes care of everything for me. That would be ideal.

Devin Nadar:

I'm very optimistic, but you know, we're not there yet, but I think that there's enough people, enough really smart people who are working on this and think that voice has a role in healthcare. So I think we're going to get there.

Teri Fisher:

Devin, thanks so much for sharing some of the insights of what's going on at Boston Children's and now the partnership with Seattle and the new skill.

Devin Nadar:

Thank you, Teri, for having me on this podcast.

Chapter 10:

The Rapid Rise of Voice Technology - And Its Awesome Power to Empower

Robin Christopherson,
MBE, MA Cantab

Editor's Note

Robin Christopherson, a world authority on technology and inclusion, takes us through the development of voice technology in the UK and beyond, as today's smart speakers are used for healthcare issues across the globe. As part of this journey, the author takes a step back and starts with the development of voice recognition and voice response technologies via our phones at home, and continues up to today's smart devices with their AI capabilities and their impact on our daily lives. He also discusses the journey from pre-PC days to the PC of 1984 to the tablet and smartphone of today, and observes the transformation of healthcare with these technologies. A large component of this chapter also describes the impact voice technology is having on those with accessibility challenges. As described, today's AI enriched voice technologies are certainly allowing all of us to have better, safer, healthier lifestyles through voice empowerment.

It's amazing how far and fast we've come with voice recognition. For text, tasks and even controlling the physical world, voice is virtually unstoppable. In this chapter we'll explore the recent rapid rise of voice technology and how one group of grateful users in particular are benefiting from it's awe-inspiring ability to empower us all.

Finding our voice

Let's consider how far and fast voice recognition technology has progressed over recent years. Even though it's been around for several decades, it wasn't until the advent of the smartphone that it really became an everyday element of our digital lives – a space-age technology that's essentially taken for granted.

Of course, it's not perfect (yet) and may not be everyone's go-to option for a quick text or reminder on the go, but it's worth beginning by appreciating just how far voice tech has come and where it's going.

The ability to talk to your computer and have it recognise what you're saying used to be a bit of a chore. You needed several specific things to get anywhere approximating the level of accuracy we take for granted today; a powerful computer, often a specially-chosen soundcard with the extra 'oomph' needed for such a task, some pretty expensive software (Dragon Naturally Speaking is the obvious outstanding example), a carefully chosen and positioned headset, quiet surroundings, the right dictation technique and lots and lots of training. This training was two-fold; for you as the user who needed to know the right commands to properly dictate and format text and, if desired, verbally control your computer, and training for the software itself to gradually learn your voice and vocabulary.

'Out of the box', the most sophisticated dictation software had pretty poor results by today's standards. To improve accuracy, you were first required to read numerous passages to the software to teach it to recognise your voice (and woe betide anyone whose accent strayed too far from standard English pronunciation) and, over time and use, recognition would slowly improve.

It was also necessary to collect as many of your own drafted documents as possible and set the software the task of importing them into its digital innards in order for it to learn the sort of words you most often used. Go away and make a cup of tea and take a long walk and the software should have had time to ingest the information and update its recognition engine to better understand the typical type of text you create.

All this to gain a level of recognition that would result, on a good day and with the wind in the right direction, in documents with most sentences including only a handful of errors. Throw in a sore throat, some background noise or an ill-positioned microphone, however, and you're back to square 1.

All this considered, the advent of voice recognition was nevertheless a truly empowering one. I was an assessor of assistive technology in the early 1990s and vividly recall training users on those early versions of Dragon (that actually – get this - required the user to pause between each word) and, whilst it was slow and inarguably inaccurate, it was also magical and life-changing for the individuals I was working with. These were people with no use of their arms and who, up until that point, had operated their computer by way of a mouthstick to select letters on the keyboard or nudge the mouse, or else puffed into a tube to laboriously select single keys from an on-screen keyboard.

Technology had certainly thrown open the door to the digital world at that point, but it was only now with voice technology that they could begin to explore it with any sort of speed. And they loved it.

Voice for everyone - and every environment

So, voice tech used to be costly, finicky and pretty hard work. Dictation was primarily the domain of professionals with deadlines or people with disabilities. These groups often overlapped, of course.

Despite these difficulties, the ability to dictate text and even control your computer completely hands-free was a handy choice for some – and again, a literally life-changing option for others. From those very first versions of voice recognition software, AbilityNet has championed its empowering potential to provide choice and opportunity in equal measure.

Today, voice technology is virtually everywhere. From the phones in our pockets to the watches on our wrists – from the tablets on our tables to the speakers on our shelves – the ability to talk to a device and have fast, reliable, results has massively matured from those early incarnations outlined above.

Perfect? No. Practically unrecognisable from even the most sophisticated specialist state-of-the-art software available before the advent of the smartphone? Definitely and in almost every way.

We mentioned above all those aspects that combined to make accurate recognition possible. The voice tech of today needs none of those. Let's look at why.

You don't need expensive tech

Thanks to Moore's Law (https://en.wikipedia.org/wiki/Moore%27s_law), today's hardware doesn't need to be top-of-the-range. The software is no longer a specialist, expensive add-on – and we don't need to worry about a professional-grade microphone in the shape of a carefully chosen and positioned headset.

You get great results out of the box

Thanks to huge improvements in both processing power and machine learning, we no longer need to read lengthy passages to train the system to get great results. Whilst most devices do include recognition engines that improve over time, they give results that already match those historical heights before you've even cleared your throat.

You don't need to be you...

As well as great results without all that training, the system no longer needs to be tied to one person. Far from having to teach the software your particular accent and speech patterns before you're able to get up and running, the voice tech of today is user independent.

So, you can now have numerous people using the same device and it doesn't care a digital fig. There is still the option for recognising individual voices to enhance the user experience, however, and we'll take a quick look at that later.

You don't need to read the manual

Whilst we may still need to know some specific spoken commands to successfully bold or capitalise text, add in a comma or exclamation mark here or there when dictating our emails or What's App group messages (if we even still care about such arcane considerations as punctuation), there's certainly no need to read a user manual to make head or tail of the tech. Advances in understanding natural language commands means we can just have a stab at saying what we want.

You don't need to have a special setup or setting

The voice tech of today is also far more forgiving when it comes to the placement of the microphone and background ambient noise. It's still as essential as ever to have a good quality microphone but, because the quality of built-in mics in today's gadgets have improved in step with its other components (and largely driven by the popularity of voice technology), there's no need to use a separate, specialist microphone – and no need to worry too much about placement (with the possible exception of heavy breathing directly on the mic).

And though background noise can still be a factor that heavily affects recognition accuracy, you no longer need to be in library-like silence to get good results. The software tries to remove general background noises and all other non-verbal sounds.

So, whilst we're a long way from an equal level of accuracy regardless of user behaviour, language, vocabulary, accent or environment, we're well on our way.

And speaking of language, there are many more that are now supported. From a handful of languages to many dozen – the unstoppable march of smartphones across the globe has meant that demand for versatile, voice-driven features has followed.

The rise of the virtual assistant

So, the voice recognition tech of today has come a long way. Accurate recognition engines in most of our devices now means that using our voice is a really viable option. Under most conditions (with the possible exception of a Glaswegian still surrounded by celebrating fans at Ibrox, trying to text his wife to say that he'll probably be home quite late after a particularly good win for Rangers), recognition is accurate enough to make it a powerful option when it comes to creating text and doing a range of really handy tasks on your phone.

And those 'handy tasks' are possible thanks to machine learning extending beyond recognising speech, to actually being able to interpret a wide range of natural language commands that the software can then act upon. Virtual assistants awake!

I know what you're thinking; it's early days yet. And of course, you'd be right. Artificially-intelligent virtual entities aren't about to take over our jobs wholesale (although that process has already begun) and often seem pretty unintelligent in many of their responses, but the progress made since Siri first surfaced on the iPhone (as a standalone app in 2010 and then integrated into the OS in 2011) has been marked.

Today the leading voice-driven assistant on the market is arguably Amazon's Alexa. Inhabiting a range of Echo speakers (with and without screens), Fire tablets and TVs, smartphones and tablets and an eye-opening array of appliances (from clocks to cars, from smart glasses to singing fish), there's no doubting that she's here to stay.

I might be a bit biased – I do host Dot to Dot (https://podcasts.apple.com/gb/podcast/dot-to-dot/id1205291265); a daily podcast showcasing just how much you can do with Amazon's amazing virtual assistant (and at well over 900 episodes at the time of recording there's still no shortage of capabilities still to cover) – but it certainly feels like we are well and truly into a brand new digital age - the age of voice-first computing.

Voice-first computing

Unsurprisingly, in the age of voice-first Conversational interfaces (https://en.wikipedia.org/wiki/Conversational_user_interfaces), technologies such as speech recognition and natural language processing play a pivotal role.

These technologies have been improved, miniaturised and mainstreamed year on year to the extent that they can be included at little cost in most of today's devices – and believe me they are.

In recent months, we've been inundated by a veritable tsunami of inexpensive devices, imbued with the ability to hear what you're saying, process it's meaning, and be able to act upon your intent. It's true that there is almost always a powerful processor, complete with all the necessary neural networks and machine learning APIs, somewhere out there in the cloud providing the true brains behind these smart devices – but, in the age of voice-first computing in which the technology is often all but invisible to the user (a discrete disc on a shelf, a component of your car's dashboard, or an inseparable element of your watch, phone or laptop), the actual hows and wherefores don't matter. The closer we get to a natural interaction with a helpful, human-sounding entity the less it will feel like tech and more like a normal part of everyday life – and as indispensable.

In future, the ability to talk to the air and get an intelligent answer will be taken for granted. We'll probably not even know or care which of the several virtual assistants that have heard our request respond (after winning an instant and invisible negotiation with the others). They'll all be equally smart and plumbed into the same services and devices we need to control.

Today of course, there's no such polite coordination – but it's coming. Just as autonomous vehicles of various manufacturers will weave seamlessly between each other on our future streets, the various voice technologies in our environment will form an unbroken mesh of machine learning that will seamlessly support us – more on this later.

And, on those rare occasions when we're without the ever-present assistance of an array of invisible, ambient digital helpers, we'll feel disabled indeed. We'll feel as at-odds with life as we do today on realising that we've left the house without our phone.

And on the subject of disability, lest you think that those with a speech or hearing impairment will be excluded from a voice-first future, we can turn to Amazon once more as a great example; in this case an example of what inclusive design looks like when it comes to this emerging tech.

Alexa takes accessibility extremely seriously

You may think that there are two obvious impairment groups most likely to be left out of the smartspeaker revolution; those with a hearing or speech impairment. This might so easily have been the case. Accessibility (even more than two decades after becoming a legal requirement) is still so often a fatally-flawed afterthought... or neglected entirely. Well, thanks to the smart work done by those at the Alexa for Everyone team at Amazon (and one woman in particular) that's not the case. Alexa really is for everyone.

Each year the 8th of March marks International Women's Day, celebrated in numerous articles and news stories around the world that highlight the fantastic and often futuristic work women are doing across all sectors - and tech is absolutely no exception. One excellent example is an article that chose to focus on the top seven women behind Amazon Alexa (https:// tamebay.com/2019/03/international-womens-day-women-amazon-alexa. html) - but the one woman from this number that I would personally like to call out for her amazing work in the area of accessibility and inclusive design for the Amazon Echo is Sarah Caplener, senior manager for product management in the Alexa for Everyone team.

Sarah joined Amazon to lead the Alexa for Everyone team; a group that focuses on making every Echo as helpful, inclusive and useful as possible for every user – and especially for those who are older and those with disabilities. In her tenure, the team has made several strides towards ensuring that Alexa isn't excluding those you may think would struggle; those who can't speak or can't hear.

"I am proud of the team we have built and the first features we have released: Tap to Alexa, an accessibility setting on Echo Show and Echo Spot that enables customers to interact with Alexa through touch or text input, and Alexa Captioning, which allows customers to see text on-screen for Alexa responses. Together these features represented the first steps toward making smart speakers accessible to people who are deaf, hard of hearing, and have speech impairments."

- Sarah Caplener, senior manager for product management in the Alexa for Everyone team

There are at present two models of Echo that have a screen; the Echo Show and Echo Spot. Having a screen means that additional information can be displayed such as the weather forecast, lyrics to songs, YouTube videos or steps to a recipe.

Alexa Captioning

Now, thanks to Alexa Captioning, these screens can also be used to display everything that is spoken out by the helpful assistant. Obvious when you think about it, but unique to the Echo to date. Other assistants serve up some information on-screen it's true, but certainly not a transcript of everything that's said. And of course, subtitles are also switched on for all video content whenever available.

Suddenly a stunningly helpful device that centres around speech output is also open to those who are deaf or hard of hearing. And of course, it might also be great for those who need to use the Echo in a noisy environment where her words would otherwise be lost in the hubbub - even if that noise is only temporary with the pans clattering, extractor fan thrumming and the blender buzzing.

Tap to Alexa

Similarly, a simple addition of allowing people to tap out inputs on a touchscreen rather than speaking them out loud means that people with a speech impairment aren't left behind. And once again (as we so often see with inclusive design) those changes to aid accessibility just end up increasing the flexibility and usefulness of the device for others too. Try talking to Alexa in those same noisy conditions mentioned above and you'll almost certainly struggle to be understood - but being able to tap out a command or choose an option with sticky fingers instead might be very welcome. Just remember to wipe the screen down afterwards.

Still further options for vision impaired users

The Echo also includes the ability to change text size and magnify its screen content. If you've no useful vision, no problem. As a blind person I'm able to access all screen content via the built-in screen reading option; VoiceView.

Of course, other smart speakers incorporate many of these features, but it has been the Echo that has lead the way where others follow. Let's hope that manufacturers vie for being in the van when it comes to inclusive design. Smart speakers should be no exception to the inarguable truth that technology, in all its forms, can be the great leveler.

Technology's ability to empower everyone

Let's take a step back for a moment. Actually, a large leap back to the 1980s and the advent of the personal computer. With the PC came options – options for work, communication and play the likes of which had never been seen before. For people with disabilities, however, the change was much more significant because the technology was also incredibly flexible.

The PC – your flexible friend

Even though the typical desktop computer of the day seemed pretty standard - comprising a big box of electronic gubbins, a monitor, keyboard and mouse - all of those (apart from perhaps the computer itself) came in many, many different shapes and sizes.

The charity that I work for, AbilityNet (www.abilitynet.org.uk), was kept extremely busy keeping abreast of the dozens, possibly hundreds, of alternative keyboards and mice (both specialist and mainstream) and how they may best help those with specific disabilities or impairments. Actually, we still are today.

There were (and are) one-handed keyboards that work on a 'chording' principal to produce every one of the 105 keys on a standard keyboard. Ergonomic keyboards for those with RSI – or for those who wanted to avoid it. Mice of all shapes and sizes from trackballs to joysticks, from the adjustable Whale mouse that fitted every hand size to a fin-like vertical affair that avoids the nasty twist of the wrist still dictated by standard devices today. And I haven't even scratched the surface of alternatives that were and are out there to help with every preference and impairment – including, of course, all the software settings and extra utilities you can bring to play to make how you control your computer completely personalised to your needs.

Can't easily see the screen? No problem. Imagine, for the sake of simplicity here, that I've run through the many different options from monitor size, settings, magnification, speech output etc, etc. In fact, to get the full picture, just check out our website.

The point is that the PC was the great enabler – the great leveler. But still, getting to grips with a desktop computer and all its complexities isn't easy and isn't for everyone. Moreover, many of these specialist solutions were pretty pricey.

Enter the smartphone.

With the advent of the smartphone, all the power of the PC was available with you wherever you went. Not only that, but you now had several additional sensors (a camera, compass, accelerometer etc) built-in and able to add a serious amount of additional assistance to those with disabilities.

The vibrant Assistive technology market, serving those with disabilities, now also moved its focus to the smartphone, which soon also had a similar spectrum of options – in both hardware, settings and apps.

Not only was the smartphone smarter and more portable than the PC, it was also considerably easier to use. The smaller screen and myriad of use-cases meant that much greater discipline was needed by both designers and developers to succinctly convey content on this much-reduced canvas. And everyone benefited - but especially, you guessed it, those with disabilities. This is because having a disability (and this may surprise you) generally makes things harder. It's true. And greater simplicity and ease of use really helps - more on that a little later. So, those with disabilities and older users found mobile apps easier to use than their web-based counterparts and a mobile OS less daunting than a desktop.

Thus this second age – the age of the smartphone – represented a real leap in usability and utility for everyone.

The third age of computing – voice-driven technology

Now let's make things even simpler. Let's reduce the complexity still further. Let's distil the user interface down to its very essence. Let's focus on the most natural way of interacting with technology and discard or demote the rest.

Let's bring to market devices that will make using a smartphone look like rocket science or brain surgery – or at least something quite hard compared to just speaking … naturally and without having to give it a second thought. Oh, and let's make them ridiculously cheap.

That's the third age of computing in a nutshell – and that's why smart speakers, and voice-first technologies more generally, are truly democratising computing – making it available to so many more people for whom cost or complexity have excluded them to date – and also why they are very much here to stay.

The most enthusiastic users of tech

Who are the most enthusiastic (and often grateful) users of tech? Considering the thrust of this chapter, the answer will almost certainly be obvious.

Whilst 90% of jobs in the UK today (and I'm sure this is equally true elsewhere) rely on a computer of some shape or form, it is only people with significant disabilities that use – no, need – tech to be fully independent and empowered (not to mention employed). Before the advent of technology, not having the options available to those who are able-bodied, often meant not having options at all.

As an example, being blind I've undoubtedly benefited far beyond the average individual when it comes to the application of modern technology. It has helped me in almost every aspect of my life. A combination of screen reading and Speech software has made access to computers, smartphones and every other modern appliance possible. Voice recognition has made the input of text and commands quicker and easier. Machine learning has helped turn the printed word (found on pulpy wafers of dead tree people still insist on pushing through our letterbox) into easy to access electronic text, and interprets images online, in print and in the real world into handy spoken descriptions. I could go on and on. Suffice to say that tech helps me in almost every aspect of my life in ways you can't begin to appreciate unless you live and breathe it every day yourself.

This enthusiasm and all-round appreciation for tech may explain why I am so willing to embrace new technologies despite the misgivings of many others. I freely admit it. For me, face and voice recognition, artificial intelligence interpreting my every word or action, and autonomous vehicles to give me unlimited freedom of movement are all developments that I embrace, and wish would accelerate to maturity so I can really live in the future. You, as a likely-able-bodied reader, may feel as equally unconcerned - or you may be highly alarmed. Either way, we'll discuss possible further future infringements to our freedoms a little later on - so brace yourselves...

In the same way that I benefit from cutting-edge technology on an almost hourly basis, for others with disabilities, it's likewise the great enabler. As tech becomes smarter, more affordable and easier to use, people with disabilities are at the very forefront of the curve in benefitting from it in their daily lives.

For example, for people with significant motor or mobility impairments (many of whom may be older and not of the new breed of digital natives) the ability to talk to a smart digital assistant without the need to use their hands (or even stir from their chair), read a manual, or know or even care what an 'antivirus program' is, is powerful indeed.

Someone who is without any use of their limbs is now able to fully engage in the digital world. Moreover, they can control their surroundings through a plethora of smart, very affordable devices.

Full out-of-the-box voice control of smartphones and tablets is now also a reality since the built-in voice control abilities of Apple's iOS 13 (https://www.abilitynet.org.uk/news-blogs/apple-does-it-again-%E2%80%93-full-fantastic-life-changing-voice-control-ios-13).

Furthermore, full eye-gaze control is rumoured for the next version of iOS - so enabling someone with only the movement of their eyes to join in the fun. Yet another example of the inexorable march of amazing tech from the expensive, specialist to the mainstream and even mundane. I love it all.

Tangent alert: Because I'm a nerd of the highest order I can't help but give a brief moment to discuss the rise of eye-control while I've got you. Just like voice recognition, object (and ultimately face and even eye) recognition is based upon machine learning algorithms that can be taught to identify objects with more and more accuracy. In iOS 13, for example, we have the ability for the software, in real time, to remap your eyes in a FaceTime call – shifting them ever-so-slightly so that you appear to be looking directly at the person on the other end of the line, rather than a little to the side. If you've ever done a video call, then I'm told (being blind this has to be a second-hand piece of info) that the tendency is to look at the person on the screen whilst talking to them. This is natural but, as you're not looking directly at the camera that is filming you, your eyes are looking slightly to one side (or below, depending upon the orientation of your device). The FaceTime software takes that live video feed of your face and digitally 'cuts and pastes' your irises a millimetre or so to the side in real time – and you're none the wiser. That is simultaneously cool and uncanny in equal measure. Eye-gaze control similarly locks in on the pupils in your irises and calculates, based upon the location of your front-facing camera and the orientation of your device, exactly where (to the millimetre or so) you're looking on-screen. This sort of magic used only to be possible with kit costing many thousands of pounds and painstaking calibration before each use. Isn't tech amazing?

The rise and fall of assistive technology

This may well constitute another tangent but here goes. I'll keep it brief:

Even though I mentioned earlier that the vibrant specialist (assistive) technology market moved to the smartphone, it wasn't without casualties. As technology improved and more and more capabilities came built-in, many assistive technologies became redundant and their providers started looking for ways to remain relevant.

We mentioned Dragon dictation software at the start of this chapter. Whilst it still exists to meet very specific requirements, its £100 ($150) or so price tag is something most voice users will never need to meet.

Similarly, but far more startlingly, is the cost of that specialist eye-tracking tech. In the order of £8,000 ($12,000), as discussed it may sometime soon be supplanted by out-of-the-box capabilities in every mainstream device.

Ditto for specialist systems to control your environment; from an absolute king's ransom to a pauper's purse in a matter of years as my sister can attest (see below). Nice – but not perhaps for those specialist manufacturers.

There will almost certainly continue to be a niche need for extreme sophistication when it comes to assistive technology. So, whilst it's unlikely that the built-in accessibility options will ever meet the needs of every single user, there's no doubt that the rise of mainstreamed inclusion (leading to an inevitable fall in demand for specialist solutions) has seen some companies struggle and others fold altogether.

This tougher and more competitive environment will surely lead to better products. In the previous three or more decades, prices of assistive tech were often arguably inflated and the products themselves sometimes less than outstanding.

Yes, small companies making specialist products had proportionately higher R&D costs they'd need to recoup to stay viable, and perhaps weren't able to update their products as often as bigger companies, but they typically had little or no competition to help push quality and value.

The budgets of disabled individuals at home (and employment rates for people with disabilities is still shockingly low even today - and even with all this fantastic tech) would often not stretch to affording the assistive technology they needed to join in the fun. A blind person, for example, would need to find £700 ($1,000) on top of the price of their PC in order to make their computer talk. Further to that, every few years they'd need another couple of hundred or so to keep the software working with the inevitable updates delivered to their operating system. Now there are a plethora of free options that fully fit the bill. Phew!

End of tangent. Back to voice-first tech.

Voice-enabling your devices

So we've mentioned dictation in mainstream devices - and even full voice-first control in iOS 13. In fact, all modern devices have a range of accessibility options built-in that we can use to be more productive.

To explore the full set of options available in your computer (Mac or Windows), smartphone (Android or iOS) or tablet (Android or iPadOS) please make a visit to AbilityNet's excellent My Computer My Way (www. mycomputermyway.com) online resource that's jam-packed with step-by-step guides to help you unlock the full potential of your tech. So not just voice, this handy website covers all the settings you need to easily see, hear, operate and understand your devices in all environments.

By the way, lest you think that such OS settings (often found grouped under the heading of 'Accessibility' or 'Ease of Access') are just for those with a disability, think again. We're all computing on the edge every single day we use a smartphone. Unless reading this article is the very first thing you've done today, chances are that you've used your smartphone one-handed. When you do you are, in very real terms, motor impaired. For that time, you need exactly the same design considerations that someone with a permanent motor or dexterity impairment needs 24-7. When you use your phone on a sunny day, you temporarily need the same choices of colour and fonts that someone with a vision impairment needs to see the screen under kinder viewing conditions.

Noisy car or café? Welcome to the world of hearing loss. Hailing an Uber after a good night out? Then you'll be wanting the extreme UX required in all apps by someone with a learning difficulty who wants to successfully use their smartphone without assistance.

Whilst we're at the mercy of designers and developers to make the apps and services we use as inclusive as possible, this age of extreme computing we all live in today really demands that we do our bit too. We need to take the customisation of our devices seriously. Those accessibility settings are no longer the sole domain of people with disabilities or impairments. They are undoubtedly for you too.

So that's the thrust of this section; check out the settings on your devices – even those under 'Accessibility' and see how you can improve your own daily tech experience.

And lastly on this topic, let's really bring the mood down here as I acquaint you with the rather morbid term widely used by the disabled community in the US for everyone without a disability; TABs. This stands for 'Temporarily able-bodied'. That's right. It's a rather morose reminder that, with the inexorable passage of time, disability (or at least impairment) will get us all in the end.

On that happy note, why not begin to personalise your devices today and get a head start?!

A voice-driven environment

One aspect we've touched upon, but which deserves diving into in a little more depth here, is the advent (nay, avalanche) of connected devices that can now be controlled by our voices. Whether you have a disability, want to live in the future or are just especially lazy, there are now a myriad of devices that can be connected to our smartphones or smart speakers and controlled by the tap of a button or a simple voice command.

Every week sees more voice-enabled devices come on the market. From lights to alarms, washing machines to microwaves, fridges to TVs, locks to blinds, coffee machines to doorbells, there's an inexpensive option if you want to make your immediate environment smarter and more automated. You can even buy smart plugs that can instantly make dumb devices voice enabled. And I was serious about the singing fish (https://www.theverge. com/circuitbreaker/2018/11/28/18116016/big-mouth-billy-bass-alexa-enabled-buy-preorder-amazon).

Combine these connected devices with the extra abilities provided by their companion smartphone apps (and often by additional abilities for your smart speaker) and we're really cooking. For example, you can schedule actions (at 7:30 every weekday morning wakes me up with my preferred morning-type music and start that coffee machine bubbling) or have them triggered by certain events (such as lock the door when I leave the house or turn the lights on low at sunset and gradually brighten them to accommodate the encroaching dusk).

You also have the ability to chain several actions together into routines ("Alexa, good night" and all the lights turn off, the doors lock, and the alarm is set, for example). Futuristic stuff – available today.

For people with disabilities, however, this plethora of affordable and relatively easy to implement options opens doors (quite literally) that have historically required specialist, eye-wateringly expensive equipment that necessitated painstaking setup – as well as the visit of an engineer every time you wanted to make a change to any aspect of the system. This is no exaggeration. Let's meet my sister.

My sister uses a specialist environmental control system to operate her TV. Every time she wants to make a change to any of its menu options that send commands to her television, someone would need to travel halfway across the country to manually make those changes.

This system costs many thousands of pounds. Many thousands. Translated into US dollars, for example, we're talking well over $10,000. Oh, and it doesn't have voice control. She operates the menus by pressing a button mounted on an adjustable arm next to her head. One press to start speaking through the main menu of items, another to select an item and begin speaking out sub-menu options and so on. This is not a quick way to interact with something even as straightforward as a TV. It can often take her whole minutes to adjust the volume. By the way, it speaks out menus as she, like me, is also blind.

Now she has an Echo, a Harmony Hub (https://www.logitech.com/en-gb/product/harmony-hub) and the world of entertainment and information at her beck and call – quite literally, one might say. Total cost; around £150 ($200).

For someone with arthritis, for example, the ability to control your environment would be equally as empowering. Whether it's your fingers preventing you from switching channels or setting a spin cycle, or your joints complaining when making frequent trips to the front door to admit family, friends or carers, a voice-enabled environment can really come to the rescue. And if you fall and realise with horror that you've forgotten to wear your alarm that morning, the ability to ask a smart speaker to call for help (and let them in when they arrive) could literally be a lifesaver.

Echo's 'Show and tell' feature

We earlier discussed the accessibility features that enable people with a range of disabilities to use the numerous flavours of Amazon Echo. Another recent development in the Echo ecosystem is the ability for the various models of Echo Show to recognise everyday groceries simply by showing them to their camera and saying "Alexa, what's this" or "Alexa, what am I holding?" Alexa will even provide verbal and audio cues to help the customers place the item in front of the device's camera.

Called 'Show and tell', it mimics much of the abilities of several smartphone apps that provide similar object recognition but, of course, driven by voice. Available in the US only at the time of writing, this feature promises to be a real boon for any blind person who doesn't have a smartphone to hand (or has hands sticky with food preparation) or who is less confident with smartphone technology.

There's more about this fantastic feature in my recent article on both the Echo's new 'Show and tell' feature and the most popular equivalent smartphone app 'Seeing AI' (https://www.abilitynet.org.uk/news-blogs/amazon-helping-blind-new-echo-show-and-tell-feature).

Voice technologies –talking to each other

A future where smart assistants will know who you are and can access your own unique services is already here – but we still have a disparate ecosystem where each smart speaker has its own wake word and siloed services. Hopefully, not for much longer.

Many of the big players in technology – Intel, Qualcomm, AMD, Amazon, Microsoft, Logitech, Sony, Salesforce, Spotify, Sonos, Bose, BMW, Baidu and many more, - are coming together to form the Voice Interoperability Initiative (VII) (https://developer.amazon.com/alexa/voice-interoperability). The mission of the VII is:

In a world with multiple voice services each with different capabilities, we believe customers should have the freedom to choose their preferred service for any task. We aim to deliver this experience through multiple, simultaneous voice services on the same product, each with its own 'wake word' or invocation name—enabling customers to talk to the service of their choice in a secure manner by simply saying its name.

If realised, the mission of this important industry initiative will bring about the harmonisation of all smart, voice-first technologies into a holistic system where every available interface will be, quite literally, at your command.

Voiceprint recognition to drive an ever-listening future

Thus, in a voice-first future, it may be that we won't even need to carry our own virtual assistants around with us in our phones, watches or other wearables. The world around us may be as bristling with ever-vigilant virtual ears as our cities are today with CCTV cameras. The world will be listening and able to respond.

What? You don't much like the sound of electronic ears embedded in every suitable receptacle? If that sounds scary, or simply unsettling and unwise, then apologies but (and I hate to be the one to break it to you if this is news) we are already living in a world where surveillance, driven by numberplate and face recognition software, is an everyday reality here in the UK.

Moreover, the advent of 5G with it's furiously fast but woefully weak signal (the frequencies used not being able to penetrate far or through obstacles of any real heft), will mean that we'll have already rolled out little electronic boxes of internet connectivity every few dozen metres. Our every wearable (and we'll have many) will be constantly connected and have the bandwidth to provide instantaneous responses from the cloud. They could be as dumb as today's spectacles, say, that have had the minimal addition of a 5G modem (a system on a chip that adds little to the cost of a product), a microphone and speaker (bone-conduction or focused-beam audio into the ear canal are already two common options in smart glasses) or optionally a modest heads-up display. This modest device would be all that's needed to interface with whatever virtual assistant (or assistants) are available in this speedy 5G future.

In this way we'll no longer be reliant on fully-fledged smart devices (such as current smartphones) to access digital information and services. Our wearables will be able to be cheaper, lower-powered, lighter and less resource-hungry as a result and, because the true smarts are elsewhere, they won't need updating or become obsolete every few years.

One essential aspect required for receiving a personalised experience in an ever-listening world is that the tech on our bodies or embedded in our environment recognises us as individuals. Most virtual assistants are already able to learn our own unique voices and differentiate us from others in our family (if you've got an Echo handy say, "Alexa, learn my voice.")

In this way, your smart speaker can play your preferred music when you ask, list your personal to-dos, appointments or shopping items and allow explicit content to be accessed by adult users only.

But what about someone trying to fool the system to gain access to your personal services or sensitive information? Couldn't they just record my voice? To avoid the simple recording and playing back of someone's voice to satisfy voiceprint authentication, the user may be required to answer a specific question (or perhaps, in more secure cases, a PIN or passphrase) so that stock phrases would not be sufficient. Moreover, the entire interaction from start to finish could be required to be conducted in that person's voice – not just at the initial point of authentication.

This ability to recognise individual voiceprints, combined with industry collaboration such as the VII, will not only help deliver a personalised experience at home (or with your own devices on the go), it opens up the potential for profile databases to be shared (much like banks of known fingerprints and faces are today) and, after authentication, those siloed services accessed - at which point it will no longer matter whether you access information through your own device, one borrowed from a friend, through something secreted in a bus stop, say, or in any public place. Your voice will be recognised and a personal experience delivered.

This much more ubiquitous approach to the delivery of ambient digital services will make every ATM more secure, every locked door opens at your command, every hotel receptionist able to sign you in after only a few syllables and so on and on and on - and I for one welcome our ever-vigilant overlords.

But that's the future. Today, we already have voiceprint capabilities within our smart speakers as previously discussed. In Amazon's Echo, moreover, these voice profiles have recently been expanded to include third-party skills.

This ability allows developers to make skills that are able to remember a user's custom settings and address their preferences. Alexa will send a unique identifier (a string of characters and numbers) to the skill in question and, if the customer has set up a voice profile, every time they use that skill, the same identifier is shared. This identifier doesn't include any personally identifiable information and is different for each voice profile for each skill the customer uses. If the customer doesn't want to use skill personalization - even though they configured a voice profile - they can opt out of the feature in Alexa's settings.

All my health info accessible via voice technology? I'd Echo that!

Let's talk about health. Healthcare records are increasingly becoming digitized. As patients move between different departments, services and systems, their electronic health records must be available, discoverable, and understandable to all those disparate specialist individuals and teams.

In order to be able to support automated clinical decisions and other machine-based processing, the data must also be consistently structured and standardized.

Initiatives such as the 'Fast Healthcare Interoperability Resources' (https://www.hl7.org/fhir/overview.html) (FHIR) Specification provides a consistent, easy to implement and rigorous mechanism for securely exchanging traceable data between healthcare applications.

Whilst the digitising of our health data, and its standardised sharing across teams, all bodes well for benefitting patience, some thought needs to be given to the accessibility of both the documents and the systems used to access them. Many patients will have disabilities - as will many medical practitioners.

Moreover, something as central as communicating with healthcare services (and the NHS here in the UK in particular) can often be inflexible, frustrating and slow for any patient - and again, having a disability can make that process even more challenging.

Giving patient communications a shot in the arm

Many disabled people find communicating with their doctor, dentist and other healthcare professional difficult, frustrating or at times impossible. People have a wide range of different needs when it comes to their preferred format for communication; for some it might be email, chat, text, IM, audio or even Braille. In the past there hasn't always been choice available – not even large print.

Here in the UK, the NHS are endeavouring to give disabled patients the options they need. A recently published NHS Accessible Information Standard (https://www.england.nhs.uk/ourwork/accessibleinfo/) has kick-started an eventual transformation in NHS-patient communications that should enable people to receive information in a format that suits them.

Speaking out for an inclusive healthcare future

Whilst FHIR and similar standards are making a more joined-up and accessible digital healthcare process possible, there's a long way to go before every patient has a holistic and inclusive experience. Apps to access certain aspects of medical info abound, but whether they are accessible and interoperable is far from assured.

Amongst this proliferation of new digital platforms and channels of communication, voice technology most obviously commends itself as being of huge potential benefit to people who want an easy, natural and intuitive way of interacting with the digital world – and what could be more important than accessing one's health information and services? Throw an impairment or disability into the mix and easy and intuitive voice access might make that crucial difference between making or missing appointments, consulting with a doctor or having to wait until help is available for a physical visit to the surgery, or successfully accessing recent records to assist in recovery as opposed to remaining unenlightened and unempowered.

Such sensitive information and services would need to be delivered securely. End-to-end encryption is not yet available on today's smart speakers, but is as achievable as on any other platform. We discussed above how a user's voiceprint can be used to ensure that only they have access to such sensitive information. Again, if needs be, an additional layer of security such as a spoken PIN could also be added – although voiceprint identification should be more than enough to ensure the patient alone is able to access their records.

So, let's aim for a natural and intuitive voice-first option in addition to apps, telephone and paper communications. Unfortunately, we're still a long way from that healthy state of affairs as yet.

Whilst it's possible to keep on top of up-coming dentist or doctor's appointments with the help of a virtual assistant such as Alexa, wouldn't it be infinitely more powerful if you weren't first required to enter those appointments yourself?

In a more digitally-inclusive future, where all my health information is available to me in all my preferred places, my medical info would be ready to be read to me by my preferred virtual assistant, piped directly from my GP surgery. My upcoming appointments with the doctor, dentist or specialist would be automatically entered into the database available to my virtual assistant - and I would always be able to ask her to confirm when those appointments are coming up if I needed reassuring. On the day she would, of course, chime with a timely notification to remind me – ensuring that I never missed a single visit.

Add to this the ability for me to review my records and interact with frontline health practitioners remotely by a natural voice interface and we would be witnessing a revolution in healthcare provision for sure.

For now, let's settle for a health-savvy smart speaker

Our smart speakers and virtual assistants have always been able to furnish responses to medical queries. Drawn from a variety of sources (such as WebMD or the Mayo Clinic), this information has often been invaluable but also inconsistent and incomplete.

Here in the UK, the NHS has long had a computer system that enables helpline staff to readily bring up expert responses to health-related enquiries. Accessed by dialing 111, an NHS employee would be the interface between the caller and this database. If ever there was an application of a voice-first solution crying out to be realised it is this one.

Thankfully, in a recent development, Amazon and the NHS have collaborated to include all of this information into Alexa. Much, if not all, of this information is undoubtedly available online – but the ability to intelligently query your Echo for the information greatly facilitates the process and opens it up too many (often more vulnerable) individuals for whom accessing digital information is less easy or intuitive. Add in those for whom talking to a person might prove embarrassing and you really do start to open up vital medical information to a much larger audience indeed.

Now let's look to the future. Imagine a time when a smarter, AI-driven interface to medical information is available through your voice-first assistant – one which knows your personal medical issues and history, your medications and past and scheduled appointments.

Many such AI bots already exist as the front line service to mental health and broader support charities. Often not much more than an interactive FAQ (but sometimes considerably more sophisticated) these bots can provide vital, scalable services that handle the vast majority of common enquiries.

If the application of such an approach to vital health services sounds like a very dangerous one – one in which a mistake in an algorithm could spell disaster for the individual – be reassured that it would need to be applied to only those domains where machine learning was appropriate and not to those areas where a medical professional's expertise and experience are required (although the ability of artificial intelligence in this area, like all others, will undoubtedly develop in the years to come).

So, as soon as the need for an escalation to a properly qualified human was detected, then the smart speaker (or whatever voice-first technology of the future was being used for the exchange) would immediately make that seamless escalation to the relevant expert – and would also form the perfect interface for the resulting consultation with the nurse, doctor or specialist etc. In a case such as this, an interface with additional screen and camera would prove useful.

OK – so this might be a little further off (although all the technology is here today) but for now let's at least smarten up our communications with those human professionals who have our health at heart.

Several ways that Alexa can help with health

So, whilst having a voice assistant that can offer the full range of expert health advice and services on-tap is some way off, there are many ways that the voice-first technology of today can already help with wellbeing and it's probably a good juncture to mention some of them here. Let's use the Echo, having by far the most third-party features, as the example.

Alexa, help me keep fit

There are quite literally thousands of superb skills that can help you with exercise, from gentle yoga to high intensity training – and we've covered many of them on Dot to Dot, the daily Echo demo podcast (http://usa2day. podbean.com).

For example, try saying, "Alexa, start Easy Yoga," for your personal yoga coach to take you through a range of poses to relax or energise you, "Alexa, open The Body Coach," for an awesome HIIT (high intensity interval training) workout that gets harder day by day, or "Alexa, launch the 100 Pushups Challenge," to build those dream pecs, and so many more. To give you an idea of just how many, at the time of writing there are currently 184 different yoga skills alone... Some workouts may not be suitable for those with certain disabilities or impairments, but there's undoubtedly something for everyone.

Alexa, help me eat well

There are a similarly dazzling number of recipe and food-related skills available through your Echo. Recipedia used to be a separate skill you needed to invoke but now simply say, "Alexa, what recipes do you have for vegan sausage rolls?" or "Alexa, how many calories in a muffin?" (169 calories in one plain muffin, in case you're interested) and the answer may well come from there.

"Alexa, start the BBC Good Food skill," will open a world of great cooking options, categorized by dish, diet, course or cuisine. You can also search by ingredients to help use up what's been lingering in the fridge.

So there's now no excuse for not knowing a good, healthy recipe to make with what's already in your cupboards, and just how many calories are in that slice of cake or chocolate biscuit.

Of course you can also order a dozen cupcakes through Just Eat, or a large pepperoni pizza through the Dominoes skill – so we won't mention either of those here (oops!)

Alexa, help me relax, sleep well and stay focused

OK – if we thought there were a lot of skills in the aforementioned categories, these pale into insignificance when compared to the sheer number of relaxation, meditation, mindfulness, mind-coaching, hypnotherapy, time management or study focus skills that Alexa has to offer.

Just ask, "Alexa, help me sleep/relax/focus/stop smoking etc, etc," and she will suggest a selection for you to try in each category. Alexa is now exceptionally good at offering you skill options related to any question or request you may have.

There are even skills that will help your pets relax. Say, "Alexa, start Relax My Dog," or "Alexa, open Calm My Dog," and so many more. Want to do the complete opposite? Then simply say, "Alexa, meow."

Oh and by the way, you can also ask Alexa to pretend to be a dog to protect your home while you're away ("Alexa, launch Burglar Deterrent.")

Alexa, help me get help – fast!

If you need to ask a friend to come round to help open a jar or pill bottle, have those sharp pains and need to get help fast, or if you just need someone to talk to to help stave off feelings of isolation experienced by so many (particularly if a disability is keeping you indoors or even in bed), then being able to call a friend or family member by voice can be a life-saver.

You have always been able to call other Echo devices using your voice ("Alexa, call Susan,") but now, thanks to a recent feature to come to the UK, you can also call the mobile or landline of everyone in your contacts too – completely free of charge.

If you've had a fall and can't reach the phone, being able to call for help via your Echo could make all the difference. For the full low-down on how it works check out my recent post on hands-free calling using Alexa (https://www.abilitynet.org.uk/news-blogs/finally-full-hands-free-mobile-and-landline-calling-your-echo). Note – current exceptions include premium numbers and, importantly, emergency services so it'll have to be a friend or family member who helps make that crucial visit or emergency call.

Public services and information on the tip of your tongue

Staying well is, of course, hugely important – and we've discussed some of the ways that voice-first technologies can help both today and (hopefully) tomorrow. However, delivery of the much broader range of essential public services via voice-first tech should also be within the purview of a digitally-proactive, progressive government.

Wouldn't it be great if your voice assistant knew as much about government services as it did about celebrities or stock prices? Wouldn't it be great if you could ask your smart speaker how long it takes to get a new passport, how much it would cost to take your driving test or when your child benefit would be paid?

Well, thanks to the GOV.UK team, you can now ask Google Assistant those very questions as well as others along similar public-service lines - on your Google Home smart speaker, on your Android phone or on an iPhone using the Google Search app. This is as a result of them implementing new 'search schemas (https://schema.org)'; a method recommended by Google to surface succinct responses from a website in a form ideal for being quickly read on-screen or spoken by a smart speaker. Similar approaches exist for Siri, Alexa and Cortana (Microsoft's virtual assistant) and the team hope to add such capabilities to these platforms shortly.

You can read all about their advances, along with their future ambitions for ambient computing in the delivery of public sector services, in a recent post published on their website; 'Hey GOV.UK, what are you doing about voice?' (https://gds.blog.gov.uk/2018/08/23/hey-gov-uk-what-are-you-doing-about-voice/). I was fortunate enough to contribute to their on-going research in this area, and they were kind enough to include a link in this post to my article all about how smart speakers are perfect for people with disabilities; 'Alexa vs Google Home vs Cortana: The battle to reach every user intensifies' (https://www.abilitynet.org.uk/news-blogs/alexa-vs-google-home-vs-cortana-battle-reach-every-user-intensifies).

Prepping your content for the voice-first future

So I think we can all agree that voice already plays a significant role in our digital lives. Whether it's occasional (such as a dictated text on your phone), as a regular habit via smart speakers across your home, or as a core part of your professional productivity (perhaps dictating notes whilst looking at tissue samples down a microscope in the path lab), voice technology is already thoroughly embedded in both our digital devices and our daily habits.

As we've seen by the specific examples of the NHS and Gov.UK initiatives above - along with so many others by global, national and local companies alike - the ability to access information and services by voice-first technology is already considered hugely important. Soon it will be essential.

If you or your company are not already considering how best to tailor your content and services for voice (both as a means of accessing content by verbal commands, as well as having it suitably spoken out to the user) then here's the wake-up call. You really should. You really, really should.

In the inevitable voice-first future, the beginnings of which we already see today, creating content that is not voice-friendly will be as unthinkable as having a website that isn't mobile-ready or delivering a service that requires you to exclusively use a telephone. Utterly unthinkable.

Let's think about the millions (probably billions) of website pages already out there waiting to enlighten visitors. There are several considerations with regards ensuring that your website content and functionality works well with voice search and control.

Make it voice accessible

The first and most important aspect of voice-enabling your content harks back to that good old area mentioned above; accessibility. The globally-recognised web Content Accessibility Guidelines (https://www.w3.org/TR/WCAG21/) will ensure that your content both supports speech as a method of control (to meet the very real needs of those with disabilities using voice recognition software such as Dragon Naturally Speaking) and will also speak well (when converted to synthetic speech to help blind users like myself or when spoken out by Siri, the Google Assistant or Alexa).

So, making your website accessible will not only help it compete in a voice-first future, it will also unlock it for the fifth of the world's population with a disability (not to mention the further 10-20% with dyslexia or a language/learning difficulty) and, still further, it will also ensure it's as easy to use as possible for every individual and environment in this age of extreme computing. Win, win, win.

Why is, say, Wikipedia so widely utilised for furnishing voice search responses? Because it's both accessible and consistently formatted. If it wanted to become even more voice-friendly, it could consider adding some additional aspects of code to make it even more expressive. Let's take a look at that option now.

Adding extra voice prompts

Modern speech synthesisers are quite good at providing clear, human-like speech. I am currently listening to what I'm typing using a female voice with an American accent called Ava. One of the Vocalizer Expressive (https://www.nuance.com/en-gb/mobile/mobile-solutions/vocalizer-expressive.html) voices, Ava, is good at sounding relatively natural without any glitchy artefacts that give away her electronic origins, but she is still very limited in being able to convey the meaning of what she is saying in her intonation, pitch or speed – verbal prompts that we're innately programmed to pick up on in the natural human voice.

Whilst she does rise in pitch at the end of a sentence closed by a question mark, and definitely sounds excited when saying any word followed by an exclamation mark, she still falls well short of fooling anyone that she's a real person reading your content.

Enter SSML: Speech Synthesis Markup Language (https://en.wikipedia.org/wiki/Speech_Synthesis_Markup_Language). Just like the accessibility guidelines above, SSML is also a global standard of the World Wide Web Consortium (<W3C>) (https://en.wikipedia.org › wiki › World_Wide_Web_Consortium).

It's used to provide additional prompts to the synthesiser on how to render text to better convey the meaning of the content, for example which of the available speech synthesizer voices to use (often representing different accents, genders and a range of ages and approximate 'personalities'), as well as the speed, pitch, volume, intonation, emphasis and pauses etc. Until computers can comprehend the actual meaning of text, we will need to painstakingly apply such tags to our content to ensure that speech output sufficiently conveys the meaning of what is being spoken.

These tags are invisible and, as a rule, do not alter the text on-screen (although it is possible to use an emphasis tag, say, to both affect speech output and also bold the text) and thus do not affect web pages in any way other than how their content is spoken.

As you can imagine, reviewing text and judiciously adding such tags can be a time-consuming process but does add real meaning to a voice-first users experience. Until machine learning can take over this task, we're stuck with the manual method.

So, whilst implementing these tags across innumerable Wikipedia pages might be a little too much to expect – even though they'd greatly improve Alexa's (and Ava's) spoken summary of each article, making it sound more natural and understandable – it isn't entirely unreasonable for all organisations with an online presence to consider adding them to the usually quite modest amount of flagship content on their websites; content that will undoubtedly be accessed by the millions of smart speaker (and blind) users of today, and the billions of voice-first (and visually impaired) users of tomorrow.

Going all-out on a voice-first interface

If you think that making a few tweaks to your online content makes sense to maximise its impact when accessed by voice-first devices (or by voice-first users like myself), you might want to consider going all-out and make a true, native voice-first experience for those devices.

A quick glance at the Amazon Echo skill store, for example, shows us just how seriously brands take the importance of having a presence on today's devices – devices that will be front and centre in the inevitable voice-first future. From global news names such as the BBC and Guardian, to retail giants such as Unilever and Procter & Gamble, to everyday conveniences such as Dominoes and Uber, companies are realising that it's vital to have a voice in the coming age of ambient computing.

To be really big in voice, you need to create an additional, add-on ability for each of the most popular smart speakers. Like an app for a smartphone, these extra packets of functionality can be easily enabled by the user. These add-on abilities are called Skills (in Amazon Alexa parlance) and Actions (for the Google Home). All the user need do is call them by name ("Alexa, open Just Eat,") and, voila! They are installed.

At the time of writing, Alexa has over 30,000 skills in the UK skillstore and over 50,000 in the US. Anyone can create a skill, and their quality varies from the very basic to the exquisitely crafted, from the entirely inane to the utterly empowering.

As an example use-case, I use my Echo on a daily (possibly hourly basis) for the news and weather, to send messages and set reminders, to hear up-coming appointments and join online meetings, and to get quick calculations and conversions – I could go on and on.

Whilst there are other ways for anyone (even a blind person like me) to complete all those tasks, as alluded to earlier, none are so quick and natural as talking to the air and getting an almost instantaneous response.

Is the response always accurate or appropriate? No. Is it right most of the time - and getting better all the time? Yes. And for those times where she lets you down and you need to revert to keyboard and mouse - or just keyboard in my case - you've wasted seconds at most.

Many of the everyday tasks I use Alexa for are made possible by these additional, third-party skills we touched on above. If they are poorly conceived or executed then I'm loathed to use them more than once, but when done well they add significant utility to an already amazing device. They also add value to that brand and open it up to a whole new potential audience.

Thus, it's important to follow a best-practice approach when devising an effective voice-driven interface. Whether it's a relatively simple automated phone system, or a full-blown smart speaker skill to deliver all your company's products and services via voice, you should start with another official output of the very busy W3C; VoiceXML (https://en.wikipedia.org/wiki/VoiceXML) - The standard application language for voice interfaces - and follow them up with a generous dollop of user testing – making sure, of course, that your users are as diverse as they'll undoubtedly be out there in the vibrant and ever-growing world of ambient computing.

Transforming lives through voice-first technology

We've come a long way. The voice technology of today can already be said to take the idea of the conversational interface – the simplest and most natural method of interacting with both the real and digital worlds - and begin to make it reality; delivering affordable (and for disabled people, nothing less than life-changing) products.

Call it what you will; conversational interfaces, voice-first technology or the age of ambient computing (you'll hear all three terms and many more I'm sure) – this tech is definitely here to stay.

As each neural network is improved, each machine learning algorithm advanced and each free update invisibly delivered, our devices will become ever-more useful and empowering for everyone - but most especially those whose hands don't work, whose eyesight is failing or who just wants technology to be super-simple.

So, here's to the fabulous, inevitable, inclusive future of voice-first technology!

Chapter 11:

An Overview of Voice Technology in Healthcare

Bruce Wallace, PhD

Frank Knoefel, MD

Timon LeDain

Steve Szoczei

Geoff Parker

Ed Sarsfeld

Editor's Note

This group of voice thought leaders and clinicians outlines for us the remarkable opportunities for the use of voice in healthcare. The point of care is shifting from the hospital to the home, and the remote monitoring and treatment of our population is now more effective and less expensive than ever before with voice applications. Additionally, voice skills are also now in use in the following clinical settings: the OR suite, the LDRP, the ED, and the cardio suite, among others. This chapter makes the case for the use of voice technologies being at the forefront of the transformation of healthcare. Even though voice is still in its embryonic stage, it has made a huge impact on healthcare in the clinical setting and in the home.

Voice technology has surpassed the days of acting as your local weatherman, music DJ, or basic voice-to-text transcriber. Voice technology, in just a few years, has progressed to demonstrate value in much more impactful ways – particularly in healthcare.

In this chapter, voice user interface experts from Macadamian Technologies, in collaboration with Dr. Frank Knoefel and Dr. Bruce Wallace from the Bruyère Research Institute, review where voice assistants are set to make the most impact on the delivery and efficiency of healthcare in the near future. Together, they discuss why voice is such a relevant modality in healthcare today, lay out considerations for developing voice-enabled solutions from a regulatory, technical and design perspective and explain how common business challenges innovators face when bringing their solution to market can be addressed.

Why Voice, Why Now?

Voice interfaces are not new in healthcare. Many physicians have used, and continue to use, Dragon Naturally Speaking (DNS) to transcribe their clinical notes. However, digital assistants powered by natural language processing, ambient computing and machine learning are beginning to emerge in healthcare and are changing the landscape of care delivery. They demonstrate promise to improve how physicians work and provide care, and also how patients (or consumers) are able to manage their care independently.

Siri's debut in 2011 sparked a new wave of interest in voice technology and gave the world a glimpse of what it's like to be able to simply talk to our devices – something we previously only knew in science fiction stories. Siri was never meant as a development platform, however, so the momentum of voice interfaces stalled. When Amazon launched Alexa in 2016, it made the natural language interface accessible and created a marketplace for new voice applications, or "skills", allowing developers the freedom to innovate and give voice technology new purpose to the public. People could now use voice to send SMS messages, control lighting, adjust thermostats and more. Subsequently, the Amazon Echo was the first to introduce the experience of Ambient Computing to the public (the concept was first proposed by Mark Weiser of Xerox PARC). Now, consumers could carry out their daily lives with a voice assistant existing silently in the background, waiting to respond to their every command.

This notion of an always available, non-invasive personal assistant is appealing; it's a luxury previously perceived as solely accessible to business executives and those of a higher socioeconomic class who could afford it. Now personal assistants can be secured by consumers at a more affordable price point. The technology has progressed to the point of being able to fulfill the use cases that are deemed valuable, or worth the investment, by consumers. In the early days of voice assistants, when consumers were merely able to request simple things like information on the weather, they were faced with deciding whether the current solution they had in place for finding that information was inconvenient enough to lead them to invest in a new solution. At this point, perhaps the proposed value wasn't worth the investment. Today, however, not only can voice assistants locate and recite relevant information, but they can also be used effectively in more conversational engagements to do things like book dinner reservations, schedule appointments and make online purchases. And of course, speech recognition platforms have now reached an accuracy level that allows for these smart conversations to occur smoothly. Advancement of the technology to better assist us in our daily lives could partially explain why the adoption of voice assistants has taken off in recent years, with worldwide smart speaker shipments increasing from 16.8 million in Q2 2018 to 26.1 million in Q2 2019.

Aside from the technology simply becoming better with time, voice is also an appealing modality because it allows us to interact without needing to see what we're interacting with. In cases where our focused physical attention is required on one task, and we need additional information to assist us during that task, we can still prompt for contextual information or complete a separate task via a digital assistant in the room (or the car for example) without being physically distracted. Voice is also a modality that is accessible to those who are visually impaired or may have a physical impairment that prevents motor skills (ie. Parkinson's tremors that increase the difficulty of typing). Using voice assistants, users can also interact from a distance. When interacting with a mobile device, for example, the user would need to have the device physically on their person to feel a vibration or hear an alert, then look at the screen for the communicated information and type a response if required.

Speech is also one of our most efficient forms of data input. While most people speak around 150 words per minute, the average typing speed is 40 words per minute. This makes speech a great modality for capturing and interpreting complex information. On the flip side, voice interfaces generally, and cloud-based systems especially, introduce additional latency which makes them less suitable input modalities where responsiveness is critical.

With respect to the current population and the healthcare landscape today, voice technology could not be more relevant. The United Nations states that by 2050, one in six people worldwide will be over the age of 65 and the number of people aged 80 years or older is projected to triple, from 143 million in 2019 to 426 million in 2050. The UN refers to the mass growth in the aging population as "poised to become one of the most significant social transformations of the twenty-first century, with implications for nearly all sectors of society as well as family structures and intergenerational ties". This shift affects not only those who are actually aging and are requiring more care, but also those who are taking on the role of a caregiver.

When we reflect on how this particular generation was raised, voice actually appears to be the modality that is most familiar to them in terms of communicating with others. They've lived the majority of their life in a time where cell phones with visual displays did not exist; video conferencing did not exist; texting did not exist. Hard wired phone lines and some early mobile phones were available, as well as radio – all of which rely on the human voice for bi-directional communication. In their research and development of voice-enabled solutions for the aging population at home, Dr. Frank Knoefel and Dr. Bruce Wallace have found that voice is the modality that this demographic prefers. In fact, Dr. Knoefel, Physician at the Bruyère Memory Program at Bruyère Continuing Care, doesn't typically incorporate modern-day mobile phones into the care plans for his elderly patients with cognitive impairments because the feedback he has received from them has indicated that it is a foreign modality that is difficult to learn, but their use is also affected by vision changes (cataracts, glaucoma, etc.) and fine motor changes (arthritis, tremors, etc.). Additionally, mobile phones are more likely to be lost or forgotten by elderly patients experiencing memory deterioration and/or dementia. A single smart speaker, on the other hand, can cover the span of a small apartment or condo, is centrally located and doesn't move.

Another trait generally found amongst the aging population is their desire to minimize the appearance of "needed assistance". Often they refuse to use a cane or a hearing aid even though it's designed to help them because it's noticeable to others and might indicate a sign of aging and/or needing assistance, or it might prompt a question about why they have it and result in feelings of embarrassment. This is particularly undesirable when you're trying to maintain your independence, or at least, the appearance of independence. With most homes having some type of speaker (ie TV, stereo, computer, etc.) and smart speakers, specifically, becoming more commonplace in the home (<u>about 1 in 4 U.S. adults now have access to a smart speaker based voice assistant</u>), using a voice assistant doesn't stand out as something uncommon or as a sign of requiring help.

Improved capability as both a stand-alone modality *and* as an integrated component of multi-modal solutions, convenience, accessibility, as well as being the preferred modality of a large subset of the population that will require increased healthcare resources, all make voice a ripe opportunity to improve the quality and efficiency of care delivery.

Where Will Voice Have the Greatest Impact on the Delivery of Care?

When we examine how voice has progressed within the last five years, and given the advancement of other emerging technologies such as machine learning and cloud computing, there are a few areas where we believe voice-enabled solutions hold the most impact on patient and caregiver experience. Some of these use cases currently exist today and some we believe will take shape and transform care delivery in the near future (within the next five years).

Home Care and Aging in Place

Many new use cases of voice technology in the home have emerged since the introduction of Amazon Alexa including reminder systems, home automation and medical alert response systems. <u>A small trial by the Front Porch Center for Innovation and Wellbeing in California</u> found that by the end of the trial, 100% of participants felt that Alexa overall made their life easier. Although the trial highlighted the limited ability to adjust treble and bass for those with hearing impairments as a challenge of voice interfaces for the elderly, both Amazon and Google have added the ability to adjust bass and treble in their smart speakers since this trial.

Dr. Frank Knoefel, Dr. Bruce Wallace and numerous partners at the Bruyère Research Institute and Carleton University have launched research projects that leverage voice-enabled solutions to help older adults become more independent and healthy at home, as well as minimize the stress placed on caregivers.

One solution addresses the tendency for those suffering from dementia or memory loss to wander in the night. It was observed that many elderly patients with dementia or memory loss would often wake up disoriented in the night, become confused as to where they are, and as a result, leave their home. This tendency puts an elderly person at risk. They could accidentally walk into traffic, they could have left without being dressed appropriately (ie. without shoes) – there have even been fatal cases where nighttime wanderers have left the house in the winter and haven't been able to find their way home. Unanticipated wandering also places anxiety and stress on caregivers. Lack of sleep due to worry is commonly experienced by caregivers who are looking out for elderly loved ones that wander and this impacts their ability to function on a day-to-day basis and remain attentive at work or as they provide daytime care.

The solution they've tested in 12 week trials uses sensors located in key areas of the home to help direct people once they are awake. For example, when a person with dementia wakes up in the night, contextual knowledge would suggest that they are getting up to use the bathroom, and so hall lights and the bathroom light turn on immediately to help prevent confusion and guide them to their destination. By doing this, the person also does not need to struggle with turning on a light or finding their way to the bathroom in the dark. When a sensor indicates the person has returned to bed, the bathroom light shuts off. After using the bathroom, if the person then begins to wander instead of going back to sleep, sensors identify this activity and a pre-recorded message from a familiar voice (ie voice of a relative or close friend) will gently remind them that it's time to go back to bed. The same gentle reminders can also be played to help reassure that the person is safe in a familiar place. Only when the person continues to proceed to open the front door will an alarm go off to alert the sleeping caregiver; this is a last resort. The solution is aimed at protecting the person with dementia, but just as importantly, offloading the caregiver. For example, one trial participant's caregiver, his son, occasionally worked night shifts. To prevent confusion if the participant woke in the night, the participant's son pre-recorded a message using his voice to remind his mother where he was, that she was safe and that he (her son) would be home soon, so to return back to bed. This solution has demonstrated in trials to improve the sleep and stress levels of the caregiver and decrease the risk associated with wandering in those with dementia. A familiar voice is a key element to the success of this wandering detection and diversion solution – one trial participant found so much comfort in the voice assistant, he actually began to refer to it as his son. When the trial ended and the equipment was to be removed, he exclaimed, "please don't take my son away!"

Drs. Knoefel, Wallace and their colleagues are currently trialing a proof of concept that also leverages sensors to help remind those with memory loss or dementia of certain tasks that help them keep up a healthy routine at home and live more independently. Again with sensors placed in key areas of the home, if a sensor has not been triggered by a certain time to indicate a specific activity has been completed, a voice assistant is prompted to remind the person that it's time to take action. For example, a sensor placed in the fridge detects when it is opened and closed. If the fridge hasn't been opened by 11AM to indicate breakfast has been prepared, the voice assistant will suggest to the person that they should have breakfast. Or, if they open the fridge to get breakfast, but forget to close it, they'll receive a voice reminder to shut the fridge so their food doesn't spoil. This sensor-based reminder system can be used to help those with deteriorating memory keep up healthy habits and in turn reduce doctor's visits, hospitalizations and, ultimately, institutionalization. It can be used to help remind people to do things like brush their teeth, take medications, bathe, etc.

Although the sensors' primary role in this proof of concept is to gently remind people to complete certain tasks, they can also be used to collect valuable data on, for example, eating habits of users or how frequently they're using the washroom. This information can then be used by physicians to tailor treatment plans and intervene when concerning changes arise.

As mentioned previously, voice as a modality is suitable for the aging population. Smart speakers remain in place and so can't be lost; physical conditions that commonly affect this population such as arthritis and glaucoma and cataracts do not affect their ability to use a voice assistant; hearing issues can also be resolved by increasing sound volume or equalizer settings. Voice as an integrated component of an overall connected solution demonstrates great potential to support independent living at home amongst the aging population and, as in the examples above, can be designed without the use of cameras to monitor, avoiding the uncomfortable feeling of being "watched".

The Examination Room

Eric Schmidt from Google highlighted this use case of voice assistants in the exam room in his keynote at the HIMSS 2018 conference. For clinicians to have a listening device in the room with your patient has a lot of potential for capturing clinical notes, identifying billing codes, or even providing clinical decision support during the encounter.

One of the banes of EMR adoption is the loss of clinician face time. Now, more often than not, you face the clinician's back as they enter notes on your encounter on their desktop computer as they continue to speak with you about your condition. As a result, a use case often touted for virtual assistants is one that could listen in on the conversation between a clinician and patient, identify the speakers, and capture the interaction in the form of clinical notes to be filed in the EMR, all while the clinician faces and/or interacts with the patient directly.

At HIMSS 2019, Nuance demonstrated their digital assistant that did just that by leveraging a microphone array and camera in a simulated doctor's office. While the doctor was manipulating the patient's knee, the virtual assistant was translating the diagnosis shared with the patient in layman's terms into the appropriate clinical terminology, and bringing up results from previously scheduled tests as the doctor requested them – all while the doctor focused 100% of their attention on the patient during the five minute exam. Supporting information was pushed to a wall mounted LCD that was available for both patient and doctor to look at.

With certain professions such as physical therapy, which demands that the therapist physically manipulate the area of concern, visit notes are often deferred to later in the day when the notes are written down from memory. These professionals would benefit equally from transcription technology that could capture those in real time.

The Operating Room

With operating rooms being sterile environments, a touchless interface such as voice could be particularly useful for surgeons to interact with the medical devices they're working with. The most common concern is whether a surgical mask would impact speech recognition, but to date, this hasn't been problematic. If the environment is sufficient for a surgeon to hear and have a conversation with a colleague across the room, then speech recognition can be expected to work equally as well. If the device is being used in a noisy surgical environment (ie. while drills or other loud devices are being used) techniques like limiting the size of the grammar (recognized words or phrases) to improve recognition accuracy may help, or it may be necessary to wait until noisy activities subside. Some use case examples include checks and validations that all the pre-op tasks have been done, requesting additional information if there are complications during surgery, or simply getting hold of someone (ie anesthetist) who's had to step out of the room.

The Recovery Room

Whether recovering in a hospital room or being discharged to recover at home, voice interfaces present a new opportunity to connect patients into their local environment when they have restricted mobility. Connected voice-enabled solutions can be leveraged to help recovering patients complete simple tasks that might otherwise drain them in their weak state. For example, being able to dim lights, adjust the temperature of a room, order food, or request nursing assistance and the reason for assistance so that nurses can prioritize appropriately. Recovering patients can even use voice technology to request information on their condition and symptoms from trusted sources such as HealthWise and Health Navigator.

Considering the penalties associated with early hospital readmissions, voice-enabled post-operative discharge solutions can instruct patients on the exercises required for successful rehabilitation and answer questions relating to treating symptoms. By proactively engaging the patient and tracking their recovery, it is then capable of escalating care to a nurse practitioner for additional support if recovery is not progressing, thus avoiding an emergency readmission.

Surveys, Feedback, and Clinical Trials

By providing trial participants a voice interface as an option for interactions, we provide another touch point to gather information in a way that is less intrusive and more convenient with regards to participant's daily routines. Participants are more likely to engage and record daily test results in their kitchen while packing a lunch for work, as opposed to having to set time aside specifically to manually record results. Companies like Amgen have started implementing voice interfaces to make it easier for patients to complete their daily journal and Orbita is working with clinical trial data firm ERT to include voice as a component of data collection (ie. complete surveys, verify completion, report health concerns, etc).

Care Management Platforms

Care management platforms monitor users and provide feedback to clinical staff. Reporting data direct from medical devices is one thing, but in the context of a care management platform, augmenting that with a voice interface allows the platform to start a conversation about the context around the user's health data. It could prompt users for information on why, for example, their blood glucose reading has been high for the past few days – a useful prompt for someone who is managing diabetes. When connected systems are able to gather information from multiple devices to identify that a person is not sleeping well and has put on weight, a digital assistant can then inquire about the current events occurring in someone's life that could possibly have contributed. As a result of this inquiry, richer sources of information could be identified that could help with the earlier intervention of worsening symptoms.

Regulatory Considerations

When developing voice-enabled solutions that will exist within a healthcare ecosystem, especially if the solution is considered a medical device, innovators must comply with the various regulatory requirements around privacy, access and permitted use including the Health Insurance Portability and Accountability Act (HIPAA), Europe's General Data Protection Regulation (GDPR) and Personal Information Protection and Electronic Documents Act (PIPEDA), etc.

One of the most notable barriers to adoption of voice assistants in a medical setting is that none of the major voice assistant vendors yet provide a HIPAA compliant platform for their digital assistants, although Amazon is supporting HIPAA compliance in limited trials this year. While this limitation has slowed some organizations down, others are moving forward with the expectation that speech technologies will be compliant by the time their systems are ready to be deployed commercially and at scale. Others are using carefully designed architectures to de-identify the entire speech pipeline and provide patient matching in an alternative HIPAA compliant environment. The alternative is to use HIPAA compliant voice services and develop solutions around them, but this requires significantly more work, including hardware integration if you want an ambient assistant.

While HIPAA and GDPR provide broad coverage with their regulatory influence, other places, have regulatory environments that are more fragmented. In Canada, PIPEDA is a national privacy act, however, provinces can still implement their own privacy regulation, resulting in a patchwork of policies that increase adherence complexity.

While there are no specific requirements for voice applications, it's important to consider the impact of this new modality during your risk assessment and to design your solution accordingly. In particular, consider things like:

- Physical access, especially to the system interface. Will it be used in a public space (such as a waiting room) or in a private environment where a single patient is being discussed.

- The sphere of information exposure is different for voice applications and may extend to an entire room, in contrast to a computer screen that is limited to line of sight.

- Establishing the identity of the user to ensure that all actions are attributable and access to PHI is restricted to the correct user and their role.

- The input source often has an identifier that will travel with the utterance and any transcriptions and thus may need to be considered as a piece of PHI.

Ultimately, like any other healthcare software, good design practices and careful consideration of risks and mitigations is required to develop secure, compliant voice solutions.

Technical Considerations

Interoperability

Voice as a medium can be imprecise, which can be both a benefit and limitation. As with the difficulty in spelling words correctly, voice can sometimes help identify the correct term when the spelling is difficult (ie. alopecia), but it can also result in confusability when two terms sound similar (ie. metatarsal and metacarpal) – even when the user knows the correct spelling. As such, a mechanism to review becomes important to ensure that the information captured is correct.

Ensuring the accuracy of information is especially important for applications that need to exchange information with others, which is increasingly a requirement of medical applications. While interoperability is not specific to voice solutions, utterances need to be converted from natural languages to industry standard terminology (ie. ICD10, SNOMED-CT, etc) so that they can be shared with other Health Information Systems through standard mechanisms like HL7, to FHIR and CCD, etc.

When it comes to voice assistants, their biggest benefits can come from their ability to interact with and control other devices in our environment. Whether that's changing the temperature and closing the blinds, or knowing what our blood pressure reading was on a wearable tracker, all of this connectivity requires integration with different devices. For the moment, these interactions need to be developed on an individual basis.

In heterogeneous environments where devices (be they voice assistants like Alexa, Bixby, Google, etc. or peripherals like Fitbit, Nest, Garmin, Withings, etc.) come from different vendors, creating a smooth interaction is likely to remain a challenge for some time. It's not always possible to standardize on a single platform because skills are not necessarily developed for all platforms yet either. And for the foreseeable future, we can expect differences in features across platforms while vendors continue to test new ideas in the market.

Cross-Platform Considerations

Outside of Asia, Amazon and Google are emerging as the leading vendors of smart speakers and virtual assistant technologies. Developing conversational experiences is different between platforms. Even the naming of applications that run on each platform is different, with Amazon calling them Skills and Google naming them Actions. Some platforms support functionality that isn't supported on the other platform, so developers need to either select a single platform to develop on and dictate that their users select that smart speaker vendor, or develop two separate solutions for each platform if they are looking to target the broader market of all existing smart speaker users. This can double the cost of developing and supporting the different vendors that currently exist and is not dissimilar to supporting iOS and Android versions of your mobile applications today.

Some companies such as Orbita and Voiceflow have platforms that allow developers to design and build voice apps once, then deploy them as both Alexa Skills and Google Actions. These are similar to low-code environments which can simplify the effort to get a voice experience developed, but can limit what can be built versus building the experiences natively on each platform and may not always support the newest capabilities launched on the platforms.

Data Security and Privacy

Data security is just as important to voice applications as any other application, with the same underlying issues:

- how is data communicated securely?

- how is it stored securely and reliably?

- who is accessing the data and how do we know who they are?

Since most voice applications also integrate with other systems, it's important to develop security infrastructure to allow users to cross modalities, as they may start a task using a voice interface, add or review more data using a tablet or screen, then complete a task using voice once more. Being able to track the user identity, and their context of use across platforms to create a seamless experience is ideal.

How to achieve these security and privacy objectives, depends a lot on the context of where the solutions are being used. Different environments such as hospitals or home environments will result in alternative approaches to manage identity, from voice identification to second factor out-of-band or biometric identification.

In the aforementioned connected homecare projects launched by Drs. Knoefel, Wallace and colleagues, their efforts to maintain privacy has been largely aided by the fact that, to date, their systems omit the use of a microphone. Their smart home sensors and motion sensors in various areas of the home collect input, but the collected data is thin and anonymized. However, the solution does assume that the user of the system is a person either living alone, or is under the care of someone who is aware of their condition and is trusted (ie. care partner), in which case information security and privacy is less concerning.

Innovators of voice-enabled solutions that leverage consumer-available voice assistants must be aware of the privacy safeguards that these products already have implemented and how this affects the ability to integrate them within a larger solution. This was a challenge that Dr. Knoefel and Dr. Wallace experienced firsthand when designing their sensor-based reminder system. The privacy and security infrastructures of both the widely popular Amazon and Google voice assistants were designed to avoid interruptions, protecting users from things like unwanted ads, but it meant that the platforms could not be leveraged to initiate a conversation, such as to remind users to complete a task without the user first prompting or "waking" the assistant (ie. saying "Alexa" in Amazon's case). And so, a custom solution needed to be built.

Which Platform to Select?

There are three broad types of voice interaction systems, each with their own pros and cons.

1. Dictation

These interfaces are often invoked using a non-verbal mechanism and are intended to accurately transcribe what the user is saying until they are finished.

2. Command and Control

A command and control interface typically has a limited set of words or phrases that it understands, and it responds by performing the action requested by the user. Examples of this could be "Start", "Stop", "Next Image", "Zoom In" etc. These interfaces are particularly useful when touching the devices is infeasible or undesirable, and can be implemented without cloud support.

3. Natural Language

Natural language interfaces are an attempt to interpret human speech as it would be used in regular conversation. While it may include phrases to control something, there will likely be many different ways to express the same intent. It may also be mixed with dictation activities and search expressions.

Voice assistants are an extension of the different voice interface styles, integrated with an ability to invoke, or complete external tasks. They are most often founded around the use of natural language, but also incorporate elements of Command and Control and dictation to complete tasks as assigned.

When looking at which platform to use, consider which other applications it will need to interact with, and how that will happen, as well as whether the device will have cloud connectivity, or whether it needs to operate independently. These aspects will affect the accuracy and responsiveness of the system.

Managing Loss of Internet Connectivity

It's one thing if a loss of internet connection disables one's ability to check tomorrow's weather via their voice assistant. However, the situation becomes much more critical if it involves a voice-enabled solution that reminds an older adult with dementia to take a series of health-affecting medications. Drs. Knoefel, Wallace and colleagues of the Bruyère Research Institute and Carleton University have explored two solutions to managing the loss of internet connectivity alone, or as a result of loss of power. The hardware used in their voice-enabled solutions is relatively low power, and so have integrated the elements into a box with a UPS for backup power. In trials, they have deployed an LTE smart hub (leveraging cellular technology) to ensure ongoing Internet connectivity. If a solution were to be life critical, integrating a cellular fallback into the solution to support an alternative connectivity fail-over would be considered. Although weather and/or natural disasters have previously disrupted cellular networks, one can anticipate that this will be addressed in the future and that cellular networks are traditionally more reliable.

Virtual Assistant Limitations

One of the things that is lacking in popular smart speakers today is the ability to deliver notifications to users via voice the way our smartphones deliver them to our screens. This drives the need for omnichannel experiences for things like medication reminders where you might deliver the prompt to take a specific medication at breakfast via a smartphone, but allow the user to confirm that they have taken their medication via voice.

Smart speakers are also reactive. To engage them, you have to start the conversation by invoking a wake word. Companies like LifePod are exploring ways for smart speakers to engage the user first via pre-programmed macros or when a user approaches a smart speaker with a proximity sensor that can "wake" the device via physical presence rather than a verbal utterance. Techniques like these and advances in ambient intelligence will enable future devices to be more natural in starting conversations with users as well as in how they respond to them today.

Design Considerations

It's evident that voice offers consumers convenience by simplifying tasks and increasing product usability. We have quickly moved from audio-only hardware like the Amazon Echo and Google Home to having voice user interfaces embedded in many different devices with screens (i.e. mobile, television, vehicle, computer, etc.) and household equipment (i.e. sound systems, thermostats, lighting, security systems, etc.). When designing voice-enabled solutions for healthcare, it's most likely that voice acts as an enabling component within a greater system. For example, as we touched on previously, a voice-enabled medical device used to assist doctors during surgery or a voice-enabled care management platform that helps users manage chronic conditions at home.

The evolution of voice technology to this multimodal experience has resulted in more complex use cases that involve multiple access points, multiple users and increased integration with numerous commercial products. Given the situational complexity of voice interface access today, product teams must design voice-enabled technologies with context of use in mind in order to provide consumers with a personalized user experience that makes the product that much more useful to them. To use the technology to its fullest potential we must evaluate the context of use to understand what the user is requesting and where and how they're requesting it. This understanding allows us to provide a response in the most appropriate manner.

When approaching the development of a voice user interface, we can frame context of use in three ways:

1. The User's Physical Context

Understanding the physical context of the user while accessing a voice-enabled application will help designers identify what the 'right' interaction is for the user in any possible space and time.

If a user is in a public space, they should be able to interact with the application in a private manner (i.e. via a screen) as allowed by the device and then prompt the voice interface when their privacy is returned in order to create a seamless, fluid experience.

Designers should consider if there is ambient noise that could affect speech accuracy. For example, if someone were at a live concert, a voice interface would not be an effective way to access an application to order a cab ride home. In this case, given the noisy environment, a screen interaction would be more effective. On the other hand, if a group of people wanted to order a cab from the confines of their home, voice would be a viable, convenient mode to do so.

One must also identify how many users occupy the environment and will have access to the voice-enabled solution. In multi-user environments, accurate identity recognition of a specific user's voice can be challenging, but is very important in an environment where those using the voice-enabled solution have different roles and varying levels of authority and access to information. For example, it's critical to design your solution to be able to identify patient vs. doctor vs. visitors in a clinical setting, or between family members and caregivers at home so as to not breach information privacy. Currently, identity recognition is established through Alexa or Google Assistant by training the system to recognize a specific voice. In use cases where this is unachievable, additional means of user validation is required such as two-factor authentication (ie speaking a pass-phrase or a single use password that is provided on a companion mobile application), voice biometric authentication, or other simple biometric identifiers like a fingerprint scan. Designers must develop a logic structure within the application for it to understand 'where' it is being used and present the 'right' interface based on the devices available.

2. The Context of the Devices Available

Aside from considering which modalities make sense for the user's interaction within the context of their physical environment, designers of voice-enabled technologies should think about how to present those interactions based on the user's device preference, as well as the other connected devices that are available within the ecosystem. Increased connectivity of devices presents an opportunity to augment and enhance the user's experience with the application by continuing it across various devices, each of which provide unique benefits. For example, being able to initiate the process of booking an online appointment via voice by prompting a voice assistant, then receiving a visual confirmation of details and information on a mobile device or any available connected device with a screen (TV, Echo Show, laptop, tablet, etc.) before completing the booking through the voice assistant. Rather than having all of the user's details repeated to them by the voice assistant, they can quickly skim over their information, confirm it and complete the task faster, enhancing their overall experience. As another example, someone in post-operative recovery at home who is following care instructions (i.e. cleaning and bandaging a wound) through a voice application might have a better experience if they were able to see visuals or videos of what each step of the care instructions looked like and how it's to be done. When they were confident to move onto the next step after visual direction, they could prompt via voice to continue.

Identifying what devices are available to connect at any point in time provides the application information on the user's location and physical context. When an application identifies a connection to a vehicle's system, it becomes clear that the user will now have limited access to their mobile device. When an application connects to a Google Home in a certain room, it should understand that a user is now in a more private environment.

After establishing which devices should be included in augmenting the voice-first user experience, consider how to design for those specific modalities. For example, vibrations or small screen interactions for a smartwatch, large visuals and audio for a TV, or pre-canned responses for in-car experiences (i.e. "I can't answer right now, I'm driving"). This may also lead us to develop voice-only or combined voice and screen experiences that are platform-specific (Amazon's platform versus Google's) in order to deliver similar experiences on different hardware.

With multiple devices accessing various data sources for different uses, there is a challenge to save the right data in the right place, allowing the user to have their actions saved back to the system from the current context. This data should be saved invisibly by the systems without user intervention. Not only should user data be saved automatically across their experience with a voice-enabled application, but it must also be kept secure yet accessible across different platforms. This allows multiple users to perform tasks through different modalities and to be able to switch between modalities seamlessly.

3. The Context of the Conversation

By examining the context of the possible conversations at hand, designers can also identify the user's available attention span and if they're able to engage in longer interactions. This requires clearly defined and suitable responses when prompted to ensure users are given an appropriate level of detail based on their environment and the device they're using. For example, if a user asks their voice assistant what the weather is today, it would be inappropriate, perhaps irritating, to receive a response with weather details for various parts of the city over the course of the entire following week. Within the context of the question, users are likely looking for a quick response that tells them what the current temperature is, what it will be later in the day and whether it will rain/snow etc so that they can prepare. If needed, they could prompt for additional, more specific weather information.

One critical element that cannot be overlooked when designing voice-enabled applications is if the conversation is sensitive in nature. Depending on the nature of the voice conversation, greater attention to security and privacy may be required. When designing, you'll need to be aware of information stored within the application that needs to be kept private or solely accessible to specific users. Interactions within a healthcare environment may require stricter data security to maintain compliance requirements for HIPAA or others we previously mentioned.

Lastly, visual or vibrational cues need to be designed into the conversational architecture to let users know when voice-enabled devices are listening, have stopped listening, when they're ready for a response, or when the task is complete and the conversation is over.

The value of voice-enabled applications can be optimized by developing a thorough understanding of the user's environment at the moment they use the application. Increasingly, artificial intelligence is being used to develop a better understanding of the context of use (AI allows for a system to be cognizant of events, proactive and dynamic), but it's interaction design that plays the critical role in nailing the user's experience on the head. By following the guidelines outlined above and being aware of the challenges of these digital ecosystems, voice-enabled solutions can provide a superior multimodal experience.

Business Challenges

Aside from some of the previously mentioned technical and regulatory challenges that can interfere with user adoption of voice-enabled technologies, there are business focused challenges that make achieving market success difficult.

Set up & Ongoing Support

For use cases outside of a clinical environment, regardless of how much money you invest or how well you design the voice application, if the patient isn't able to get the voice assistant set up, the solution becomes futile. And if you're conducting clinical trials to demonstrate your solution has impact, improper or unsuccessful setup is detrimental. Today, the setup of voice assistants like Amazon's Alexa is not exactly intuitive and straightforward. It could be an overwhelming process for someone who doesn't fair well with technology in general, not just voice assistants specifically. Also as mentioned earlier, technical workarounds that need to be deployed today in order to make some voice-enabled solutions operate as intended required some programming and integration knowledge and can make the setup more complicated to the general public.

Setting up a voice-enabled solution is one thing, but what about ongoing support? What if a user doesn't understand how to complete a task using the device or what if they can't get it to cooperate or understand what they're trying to say? As mentioned earlier, technical workarounds that need to be deployed today in order to make some voice-enabled solutions operate as intended required some programming and integration knowledge which can make the setup more complicated to the general public.

It is possible that someone like a family member or friend who works well with technology and has the required skills could assist the user with this setup process, however, this temporary solution discounts the significant portion of the population who wants to become more independent at home and *do not* have family members close by to assist them with the technology. It also discounts users who do have access to family/friends, but they lack the necessary skills. Putting responsibility on family and friends who act as caregivers also defeats the purpose of reducing the assistance needed from them.

One possible model to address this challenge is to provide a service-based model, similarly to communications service providers and to Best Buy's Geek Squad, where a dedicated support team is available to contact via phone and also is able to make on-site visits if you need direct assistance. Whether companies supported the implementation of this support service internally or partnered with a service provider, a separate party from the caregiver would be responsible for setting up a solution and providing technical support when needed.

Mental Barriers or Preconceived Notions of Tech difficulty

Even if you manage to devise a plan to provide support, there's still the possibility that a subset of users will feel intimidated by voice technology and have a preconceived notion that it is complicated and/or difficult to use. Perhaps they're not tech-savvy and are stuck in their ways as many of us are, being creatures of habit and routine. If this is the case, you'll need to ensure that you are able to communicate the simplicity of voice technology and the core benefits that it will be able to provide. Emphasizing elements such as its ambient nature, convenience, physical accessibility, as well as offering a demonstration of the solution in specific use cases can help a potential user understand how simple and natural voice is as a modality and how it can impact their quality of life.

Gradual introduction of a solution (ie. slow rollout of features) can help ease any learning curve associated with the technology and allow time for users to become accustomed to using it.

Solution Scalability

We've touched briefly on some of the factors that are currently limiting the scalability of innovative voice solutions today:

Language barrier: Voice recognition for different languages is continually increasing, but it is still limited today and impacts scalability amongst the greater population. When a language or dialect is not supported, there is potential to leverage pre-recorded messages as part of the solution. However, this approach is best applied to purpose-built solutions that have a limited list of interactions.

Scalable support: Scalability from a commodity perspective has been addressed; hardware is low cost and can be purchased from a retailer and installed in two hours. However, scalability in regards to making the solution accessible for the aging demographic to install and maintain in a functional state over time still needs to be addressed. This is where implementing a service model may be useful as opposed to a DIY model.

Accessibility: Solutions that can leverage an off-the-shelf voice-enabled product that consumers can purchase at an affordable price point make the care that much more accessible to the greater population. However, because of some of the technical security barriers that big player brands like Amazon and Google currently have in place, innovators have needed to integrate other voice interfaces into customized solutions to create workarounds. Highly customized systems can be more work to set up and could potentially be more costly to acquire.

Proper Research vs Time-to-Market Dilemma

There is a dilemma that innovators in the voice space may come across where they're torn between conducting thorough clinical research that demonstrates their solution is effective and trying to launch the solution before it becomes old news.

Quite often, especially when the solution is meant for a clinical environment, proper research protocol needs to be executed with clinical trial data that proves a solution will improve the quality of care delivered in order for providers to be interested in investing in a new system and investing in employee training. If insurance companies were to cover systems, they too would need to see significant trial data that demonstrates the solution is making people better at home and is reducing the cost of care by preventing the need to receive treatment.

However, clinical research takes time. And with the pace at which voice-technology is advancing, it's quite possible that a new technology release/update or a new regulatory requirement could impact the current state of the solution, and thus the trial. It's also possible that as clinical research is published and made publically available, competitors could use that to their advantage to develop a competing solution and choose to sidestep the research effort in order to get their product to market faster. If this is the case, then the solution you've worked so hard on to validate is no longer novel and the first-to-market advantage is lost. Ethics approval for research alone can take months before any data can be collected; that's months behind a competitor who is developing an application and releasing it without research. Consider the market for applications that track your sleep or provide "brain training" – these are saturated marketplaces, but few have gone through proper clinical research because it might take several years. The business side of things is not going to wait for a five-year trial and the academia side of things isn't going to change research standards and protocols to please business. So innovators are left with a dilemma if they want good evidence to be part of a business model.

If you *have* committed to conducting the proper clinical research (which is worth it from a sales perspective), recruiting participants for trials can also be quite challenging. Here are some tactics that we and the research team at the Bruyère Research Institute have found helpful:

- Advertising and discussing your project on local morning TV and radio news stations,

- Social media ads if you have company pages to leverage

- Putting out a call for participants when speaking at /participating in local conferences & events

- Leveraging crowdsourcing companies, like Applause, that handle recruiting for voice testing

Securing Partner or Investor Buy-In

How do innovators get heard by the partners and investors that can help them get their solution to market? In many cases, it's not business men and women who are developing ground breaking voice-enabled technologies; it's physicians and clinical researchers or entrepreneurs who, based on personal experience, have a deep understanding of the pains and challenges of the user base they're developing for. To advance their solution, someone has to see the value in it and be willing to invest.

When we think about the ideal path to launching successful voice-enabled applications to help improve healthcare, although not always easy to execute, step one is to find a significant player who wants to take on your project/prototype and sees potential in it. A big player doesn't have to mean a market-established healthcare provider, although that would be nice! Often, it is well established companies that are followers, not first movers, and aren't looking to test new and innovative ideas. Finding a significant player means finding someone who has the interest, resources and contacts to advance your product. This could mean getting picked up by a business/ innovation incubator where you could then leverage that ecosystem's business contacts and resources. The next step would be to partner with an academic group that seems equally interested in the space of voice and healthcare (or in a particular area of healthcare like home care) so as to create a holistic academic-business partnership where the business side of the house can facilitate the first installments of the solution and maintain product functionality and technical support. The academic side of the partnership can then handle how the solution is introduced to people and formulate the measurement methods and tools used to understand how people are using the solution. Business and academia together should then aim to conduct a 6 month to 1 year trial and learn how people adopt the solution and make product/strategy revisions based on learnings.

We've Come a Long Way, But We're Not Done

There's been a lot of progress, but there's still much more ground to cover. It's important to remember that voice is still in its early days of development; people need to be aware of this as they're using the modality in conjunction with other technologies/devices that are much more advanced (ie smartphones). You can't expect the same capacity from a technology that has been under development for 4 years as you can from something that's been in development for a couple of decades. Even though, when we use these technologies in conjunction with each other, it's a natural inclination to expect the same kind of experience from them. Put differently, virtual assistants are at the iPhone 1 stage of development. Think of all of the advancements in smartphones within the last 11 iterations!

As we wait patiently for voice technology to advance, product teams should be on the lookout for regulatory curveballs and consider how changes in technology could affect the design of the voice experience and of the overall solution architecture. Your team should also consider conducting clinical research to generate real-world evidence, to validate product-market fit and to help you become noticed by business partners who can take your solution to market, as many will want to see the data that demonstrates the solution has potential to change lives at scale. Once you have an investor on board, local support providers will be more likely to partner with you to execute a service-based business model to help commercialize and scale your solution.

Section 3

Voice Technology and the Provider Experience

Chapter 12:

Mayo Clinic: Patient-Centered, Innovation-Driven

Lee Engfer

Joyce A. Even, M.B.A.

Paula Marlow Limbeck, M.A

Jay Maxwell

Sandhya Pruthi, M.D.

Jennifer Warner, M.A.

Editor's Note

Emerging technologies are bringing new ways for people to connect and manage their health. In this chapter, Mayo Clinic explores voice-first applications to engage with consumer, patients and providers to advance and support the clinic's mission of providing trusted health information and to bring value and efficiency to the clinical setting. One example of consumer engagement and direct –to-consumer voice space was the Mayo Clinic First Aid skill which entailed conversational, voice optimized content that was deployed on Amazon Alexa and Google Assistant. In the voice-based patient experience space, Mayo Clinic describes how patient education can be delivered post-procedure to enhance the patient and provider experience. The ultimate goal in the clinical setting is for voice -activated devices to provide trusted health information, navigate care systems, improve triage and intake procedures, discharge instructions, personalize interactions with patients and reduce provider burnout.

"The glory of medicine is that it is constantly moving forward, that there is always more to learn."

— Dr. William J. Mayo, *The Aims and Ideals of the American Medical Association, 1928*

Founded more than 150 years ago in Rochester, Minnesota, Mayo Clinic is an academic health system known worldwide for its high-quality care of patients, especially those with complex and difficult-to-diagnose conditions. Our nonprofit organization also educates the world's next generation of practicing physicians and conducts basic, translational, clinical and epidemiological research to advance medicine and improve patient care.

Mayo Clinic's mission is to inspire hope and contribute to health and well-being by providing the best care to every patient through integrated clinical practice, education and research. Our primary value is, "The needs of the patient come first."

Mayo Clinic's commitment to existing and emerging technologies stems from this desire to serve patients' needs, both within and outside the walls of the clinical practice. Our medical professionals currently extend their services through digital technologies to reach patients, other providers and consumers globally. This happens in a variety of ways, including telemedicine, remote patient monitoring, e-consults — and in creating some of the world's most trusted health information. Well-informed consumers tend to make for better patients, who make better decisions about their health, which tends to lead to better outcomes (Hibbard).

Mayo Clinic's health information evolution started in the early twentieth century with Dr. Henry S. Plummer's invention of the standardized medical record and the creation of printed health pamphlets to help patients manage their health. A little less than a century later, the World Wide Web introduced an immediate and immense new information age. Anyone with a computer, modem and finger dexterity to manipulate a mouse and keyboard could tap into informational sources around-the-clock and around-the-world.

Mayo Clinic, and other publishers, adapted and optimized health information for internet consumption, first on desktop computers and then on smartphones (Voicify). At the same time, new digital technologies spurred the development of the modern health care delivery framework, with the electronic health care record, patient online services, telemedicine and more. The explosion in computing power and web services also revolutionized medical research.

Our latest innovation in health information technology is the introduction of voice. As with the earlier technologies, Mayo Clinic has invested in voice-first applications that span the three shields of patient care, education and research. These innovations will bring new ways to serve the needs of patients, providers and consumers.

Voice technology: Rapid growth, new opportunities

Today, disruptive forces are changing how people connect with technology to consume information and manage their health and health care. And some analysts say the rapid pace of voice adoption is faster than its forerunners: radio, television, desktop web and mobile web (Activate). Voice technology is widely available in countless devices and used daily within homes, vehicles and offices worldwide.

A distinctive feature of voice tech is that it turns the human voice into a universal remote control. Machine learning allows computers to converse with humans in their native language (at least some of those languages). Suddenly, humans and technology are reversing long-held roles as computers, including smart speakers capable of conversational artificial intelligence, conform to human preferences. Instead of forcing us to point and click or swipe, tap and pinch, voice tech allows us to simply speak a few words to pose a question or issue a basic command.

Speaking comes naturally to most people. By some estimates, people speak three times faster than they type or text (Ruan). Not surprisingly, voice-first searching is on the rise. By early 2019, about 20 percent of online U.S. adults were actively using voice search on a monthly basis (Magic + Co.).

People also want to use voice to interact with their health care. According to a recent survey, 81 percent of millennials and 44 percent of seniors use assistants such as the Google Home and Amazon Echo to monitor health issues (Dietsche).

As part of the larger trend toward using artificial intelligence (AI) to transform health care, voice technology is expected to bring value and efficiency to the clinical setting. Health care providers hope that natural language processing of speech will liberate them from the time-consuming tasks of data entry and synthesis. This would allow them to focus more on personal interactions with patients while still ensuring quality documentation.

Here at Mayo Clinic, we are exploring how voice tech may also help to lower or even remove barriers for patients and consumers. For example, adults who have impairments or need helpful support with lifestyle changes or managing a health condition might find benefit. Voice-activated devices also can provide ready access to trusted health information and make it easier for patients to navigate care systems. Incorporating voice into triage and intake procedures, wayfinding apps, and patient education also are of interest. Research opportunities for voice applications abound as well, especially when paired with AI methods such as machine pattern recognition and predictive analytics.

While pursuing these worthy goals, Mayo Clinic and other health care organizations also need to ensure that voice technologies do not compromise end-user privacy or data security. In 2019, Amazon introduced the first HIPAA-compliant Alexa skills. But emerging technologies often lack regulation and oversight, which may make patients and providers slow to adopt them (Walsh).

Mayo Clinic became an early adopter of voice technologies, and we continue to innovate and evolve voice-first applications. As with other initiatives at Mayo, our voice activities support the clinic's mission of inspiring hope and promoting health.

Voice at Mayo Clinic: Consumers, patients, providers

Today, Mayo Clinic's work in voice reflects our three-shield approach to fulfilling our mission of putting the needs of the patient first. Throughout our history, Mayo Clinic has invested and made advances in our three shields of practice, education and research. Now we use a similar approach to drive our voice strategy as we evolve the way we engage with consumers, patients and providers.

Consumer engagement. In entering the rapidly evolving direct-to-consumer voice space, our primary objective was to think big but start small. In addition, our goals were to:

- Be one of the first major health brands to enter voice markets

- Learn how to optimize health information for new channels

- Invest in innovation and speed

- Apply lessons learned to future processes, roles and technology

With those goals in mind, we explored and delivered several consumer-focused voice tech products.

Mayo Clinic News Network flash briefings. As a natural starting point, we knew we had a large library of dynamic content published daily by the Mayo Clinic News Network. We started there in 2017, with a flash briefing skill for Alexa-enabled devices, making Mayo among the first hospital systems to offer this skill. Five days a week, the briefings provide one-minute audio summaries of the latest information from Mayo Clinic experts on topics such as cancer, heart and brain health, advances in medical research, and healthy living.

Mayo Clinic First Aid skill. As a next step, we wanted to launch something that appealed to the general public and offered valuable answers to common health questions. Following our "think big but start small" approach, we decided to play to our strength by using our trusted health information as a base for our new product, the Mayo Clinic First Aid skill for Alexa. This skill was designed to help in everyday health situations such as a bee sting, minor burn or cut. Voice-enabled technology allowed us to provide quick, actionable advice in an entirely hands-free experience.

For the consumer editorial team at Mayo Clinic, it was a natural evolution of providing trusted health information delivered in innovative ways, when and where people need it most. Our team has provided evidence-based, expert-reviewed content to empower consumers to effectively manage their health for decades, first in print, then on the web and now in voice.

For the new voice skill, we narrowed our scope to about 50 first-aid topics based on existing Mayo Clinic website content. This allowed us to develop the skill quickly, learn from our experience and apply that knowledge to future voice projects. The skill gave us our first opportunity to create content to be heard rather than read. It quickly became clear that we couldn't just cut and paste our website content and expect it to sound conversational.

We recognized that voice optimization of health information required adapting the content to meet the unique needs of the end user. First, we determined that to give an accurate response, we must clearly define the question or request. Does the listener want to know how to identify a bee sting? How to treat it? When to see a doctor for it?

Since we were designing a conversational experience, we also had to pay attention to how users might pose their questions. We needed to consider the different ways the user might ask for help (the utterance), determine the intent of the question and serve back the appropriate answer. For example, one user may ask, "Alexa, I just touched a hot stove with my hand and it's blistering. What should I do now?" Another user might say, "Alexa, I burned my hand. What's the right treatment?" In both cases, the intent of the question is "How do I treat a burn?" but the utterance is different.

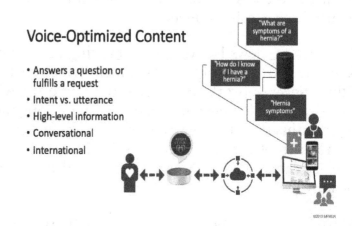

Fig. 1: Key aspects of voice-optimized content and information flow were identified and documented while creating the Mayo Clinic First Aid skill and voice health information library.

In addition to adapting the content to answer specific questions, other key aspects of voice optimization of health information include providing high-level accurate information that avoids confusing medical terminology while being concise and conversational. The context of the user experience and audience also are considerations (see fig.1).

All in all, the Mayo Clinic First Aid skill took us about six months to develop and deploy to Amazon Alexa, with the help of a vendor's proprietary tools. The skill was later deployed on Google Assistant and as a voice and text-based chat feature on Mayo Clinic's website.

First-party health condition content. With those experiences under our belt, by 2018 we were ready to move on to a bigger challenge and expand our voice imprint. Recognizing Mayo Clinic's expertise in providing trusted health information, Amazon approached Mayo Clinic to provide first-party health content for its Alexa-enabled devices.

With first-party content, a voice device responds directly to a user's question, without the need to open a skill. In this case, any time you ask, "Alexa, what are the symptoms of a heart attack?" you get a response directly from the experts at Mayo Clinic: "According to Mayo Clinic, symptoms of a heart attack may include … ." While the first-aid skill involved a small starter set of common first-aid topics, this project's scope was much larger, encompassing thousands of condition, procedure and symptom topics from our online health information library.

Applying the voice-optimization skills we learned in the first-aid project, we tackled the creation of the industry's first large-scale voice-enabled health information library. We scaled up the processes developed in our early efforts and trained additional editorial staff to adapt existing health content for voice delivery. We developed an in-house voice style guide and established best practices based on our rapidly evolving experiences in the voice space as well as industry standards.

Patient experience. Despite the rapid growth of voice skills for consumers and sales of voice-enabled devices, the potential for using voice technology in the clinical practice setting is still developing. Applying our three-shield approach to voice strategy led us to explore whether voice-enabled devices could effectively deliver patient education information. With that objective in mind, our internal Center for Innovation (CFI) team conducted a small study to better understand patient and provider reaction to delivering patient education through voice technology.

The CFI project team set out to understand if patients and providers wanted a voice-based experience for patient education (desirability), and if an effective patient education experience could be built with voice technology (feasibility). A combination of clinical observation, prototype building with the Agile process and experimentation were used to assess the efficacy of voice technology in the clinical setting.

The first step was to find the right type of patient education content. In some clinical areas, providers often present patient education in a highly personalized way that pertains only to that particular patient. This high degree of customization was inappropriate for a voice experience. The team searched for a use case that would use voice to deliver standardized information that needed little to no explanation from providers.

On-call wound care education. For this project, Dermatologic Surgery selected patients who needed post-procedure wound care information as the use case. In this department, nurses consistently deliver the same wound care information to certain types of surgery patients. Using highly trained staff to repeat lengthy instructions was not the most effective use of their time. On an average day, 10 to 20 patients needed that information, making it an easily replicated test case for patient-facing voice content.

Before building the prototype, the designer observed patient and staff experiences. The information technology team also collaborated with voice experience experts and became familiar with a proprietary set of voice experience tools from an external vendor. The developers started building the voice experience using the patient education content typically provided to patients. Agile processes (see fig. 2) were followed for development.

The voice experience was first pretested in-house and improvements were made based on feedback. The main experiment took place in examination

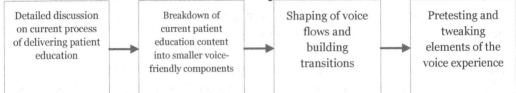

| Detailed discussion on current process of delivering patient education | Breakdown of current patient education content into smaller voice-friendly components | Shaping of voice flows and building transitions | Pretesting and tweaking elements of the voice experience |

Fig. 2: Following an Agile process helped Mayo Clinic's Center for Innovation quickly develop the patient-facing voice technology.

rooms, where an Alexa-enabled Amazon device interacted with patients who had just undergone two specific medical procedures (see fig. 3).

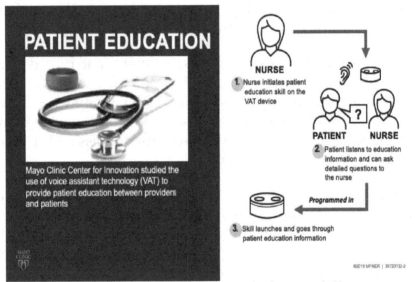

Fig. 3: Mayo Clinic's patient-facing voice assistant technology provided basic post-procedure wound care messages right in the examination room.

After the experience, all patient participants were asked two questions:

- What are your impressions of the patient education experience through the Alexa device?

- Would you use it again in the future?

Impressions from care team members also were collected. The results indicated that voice technology experiences can add value in the health care setting. All in all, providers and patients alike had favorable opinions about the use of voice technology within the examination rooms. In various ways, voice technology enhanced the patient education experience and increased efficiency among the clinical staff.

The experiment also identified aspects of the technology that should be considered to minimize negative impact. Furthermore, our CFI IT team was able to articulate current technical capabilities and limitations for future applications within Mayo Clinic. This work revealed the need for robust security and authentication measures when access to patient data is required. Knowing the capabilities and limitations of the technology allows us to make more informed decisions about where else Mayo Clinic might benefit from voice-based experiences.

Provider partnerships. Before the 1980s it was rare to see a computer in use in a physician's office. That all changed by the turn of the century with the advent of the internet and electronic medical record (EMR), which made physician record keeping far more visible. With these technologies came new capabilities as well as challenges. The internet allowed physicians to easily transfer prescription histories and other medical records and communicate with other medical systems.

But instead of reducing the burden on physicians and increasing job satisfaction, the opposite occurred. Imperfect EMR usability and rising productivity pressures triggered growing dissatisfaction among physicians. More time spent on computer tasks coupled with shorter visits meant physicians spent less and less time interacting with patients, fueling record high levels of burnout (Guo).

Given the cost of health care and the need for new technology to be thoroughly tested, it's a challenge for health care organizations to invest in unproven technologies or rapidly adopt new technologies. However, the use of voice in health care is not new; physicians have been dictating notes for decades. What is new is the growth of voice-enabled digital assistants powered by machine learning, natural language processing and ambient computing (Parker).

As with any novel technology solution, voice must solve a problem. Our approach is to consider the best opportunities to leverage voice in the daily workflow of our health care personnel — providers, nurses, schedulers, and so on. Fitting voice technology within an existing workflow to solve a problem is critical to ensuring efficiency and adoption. Partnering with providers to leverage our expertise in the consumer voice space allows us to better predict how voice technology could be leveraged in examination rooms, surgical suites and other areas.

<u>Giving voice to clinical algorithms</u>. Our experience with voice products such as the Mayo Clinic First Aid skill and our voice-enabled health information library helps inform us on how we can enhance the patient experience and improve care. For example, funneling primary care patients to the right level of care has consistently been a challenge for our practice.

For years, Mayo Clinic has utilized algorithms for telephonic nurse symptom triage to prevent unwarranted visits to the clinic and especially to the emergency room. We've refined the algorithms based on research and clinical knowledge along the way to ensure we are providing the best recommendations to the patient.

We receive nearly 1,000 patient calls a day, and the call center has been very successful in recommending the right level of care for patients based on their symptoms. We are now looking at how those same algorithms could be utilized with voice and chat technology. These technologies could provide the same level of service to the patient using a digital device at home, simultaneously reducing the burden on the call center and supporting personnel.

Interactive care plans. We're currently looking at how we can incorporate voice into Mayo Clinic interactive care plans, which offer digital guidance to patients between visits. These plans are designed to benefit both patients and physicians by using technology to support better patient adherence and outcomes, and reduce the overall total cost of care. The first step is looking at which interactions and conditions are best suited for voice. Currently, the best choices are conditions that could benefit from timely patient education, symptom check-ins and escalations to a higher level of care when needed.

Emergency medicine. Our Department of Emergency Medicine is also exploring the use of voice technology in its patient rooms to enhance the patient experience and increase provider efficiency. By delivering timely and relevant health care information to patients and their families, an in-house emergency department skill could potentially:

- Increase the subjective comfort of patients and families while experiencing care in the emergency department

- Increase access to high-quality, standardized and patient-centered information relevant to the care received in the emergency department

- Increase the efficiency of the health care providers in the emergency department

If successful, the program could be expanded to include clinician-facing skills, such as calling up charts, as well as future use in Mayo Clinic ambulances.

Diagnosis by voice. Voice as a diagnostic tool is an especially exciting area of research at Mayo Clinic and other research institutions that could have huge implications on delivering care at a distance.

Our cardiovascular service line at Mayo Clinic hypothesized that voice characteristics may be an indicator of coronary artery disease (CAD). A study was conducted with 138 patients scheduled to have a coronary angiogram. The patients also had their voices recorded to capture various emotional states. The results showed a potential relationship between voice characteristics (such as intensity and frequency) and the presence of CAD.

The implications are promising in terms of early diagnosis and intervention via a relatively inexpensive, noninvasive means. The results were published in the medical journal *Mayo Clinic Proceedings* and could have tremendous impacts on care at a distance (Maor). At Mayo, voice biomarkers are viewed as additive diagnostic indicators, not the only ones, but helpful tools to include in our arsenal as clinicians.

Because our primary value at Mayo Clinic is, "The needs of the patient come first," voice technology cannot be viewed as a solution in and of itself. It's one in a growing array of tools at our disposal to help us achieve our mission. Our approach to exploring voice technology from consumer, patient and provider perspectives allows us to apply our learnings from one arena to the other and grow our expertise exponentially as a team. Leveraging this tool deliberately and thoughtfully can lead to improved, individualized care.

Mayo Clinic's future voice: From active to aspirational

It's a sparkling fall day in 2030 at the Mayo Clinic campus in Rochester, Minnesota. In the Gonda Building, John is meeting with his surgeon, Dr. Carter, to discuss his surgery the next day to remove a cancerous tumor from his neck. He's nervous, but he appreciates her reassuring tone of voice and smile. As they talk, an ambient voice system captures the clinical notes and updates the medical record with relevant information, including John's anxiety level as indicated by voice biomarkers.

After the surgery, John talks with a nurse in the recovery room at Mayo Clinic Hospital, Saint Marys Campus. He's relieved that the team successfully removed the tumor and cancerous lymph nodes, but there's a lot for him to know in the coming days and weeks. The nurse asks the voice assistant to play the post-procedure instructions. John watches the screen as the device explains how to care for his surgical site, what activity restrictions he'll need to follow, symptoms to watch out for and other important advice. The nurse assures him that he doesn't need to take in all this information now — he'll have access to the same information and more through his voice device at home.

A month later, John is back home in Cincinnati. Recovery hasn't been easy, but he's starting to feel a little bit more like himself. Once a week, his voice assistant checks in with him about how he's feeling. The assistant can also pick up audio cues that can indicate a problem with his breathing and can track key biometrics through his smartwatch. John has used it to help him remember when and how to take the 12 different medications he has and to walk him through his physical therapy exercises. When he runs out of a medication or feeding tube supplies, he simply asks the device to reorder them. The device also prompts him on the amount of protein and calories he needs throughout the day.

The future voice activities summarized above range from ideas to active projects at Mayo Clinic. It's clear that voice technology is a game changer that promises many opportunities in the health care setting, including patient communication, compliance and continuity of care. At Mayo Clinic, the work we have done in creating voice products for consumers will continue to inform our processes as we develop voice-enabled applications that will further develop Mayo's individualized approach to clinical care.

New voice projects are happening within the context of a larger push to embrace artificial intelligence across the clinic. Mayo Clinic views AI as a set of techniques and technologies that serve to augment — not replace — human intelligence. AI is expected to transform health care delivery and outcomes. Mayo Clinic President and CEO Gianrico Farrugia, M.D., notes that AI is a "new set of eyes that allows us to see what humans cannot, making physicians better — not obsolete" ("Standing").

Similarly, voice technology offers a new way to speak for both patients and providers. Advances in the field will allow clinicians to work more effectively and patients to interact more easily with their health care teams (Kinsella). Some near-term improvements in speech recognition include far-field voice recognition, individual voice recognition, whispered utterance recognition, and the ability to read lips or pick up silent reading. Conversational experiences will move beyond pre-scripted responses and information retrieval to more sophisticated natural language generation powered by neural network deep learning.

What might this future in voice look like at Mayo Clinic and other health care organizations? Let's take a look at some of the potential opportunities, whether they're building on our earlier steps or envisioning new ways to improve life for patients, consumers and providers.

Improving the patient experience. Seeking medical care can be a complicated process, and patients don't always know what to expect during a care episode. For patients with complex conditions, seeing multiple providers can be especially confusing and overwhelming. We also know that pre-visit patient education doesn't always happen. Using a voice assistant device is one way to help guide patients through their clinical journey and follow-up care.

Sandhya Pruthi, M.D., is one of many providers at Mayo Clinic who looks forward to integrating voice to enhance the patient experience. "As a clinician, voice-activated devices can deliver information to patients in new ways and make it easier for them to find me," she says. "They can ask about a clinician's location and hours, what types of insurance are accepted, and where the nearest urgent care clinic is. And in the near future, they should be able make an appointment using voice — the logical next step."

Mayo Clinic and other health care organizations hope to improve the patient experience and increase efficiency by incorporating voice into wayfinding apps, intake and triage procedures, and discharge instructions, as we explored in our dermatology clinic pilot. In clinic waiting rooms and hospital rooms, voice offers patients a convenient way to control their environment, especially for those with limited mobility. For example, they could adjust the room temperature, dim the lights, order food or request nursing assistance (Parker). Voice assistants could also have ready answers to frequently asked questions.

Hands-free doctor-patient visits. Research shows that physician burnout is becoming an epidemic (Guo). This can be attributed to clerical burden, especially the time spent on the electronic health record, with its high "click burden" and inefficient workflow (Guo; Shanafelt). The outcome? Less face-to-face time with the patient and more time spent on documentation and billing.

The idea of bringing voice technology into the provider-patient visit — "Alexa in the room" — holds promise for reducing providers' clerical burden. Available AI and machine learning tools for language recognition could elicit discrete information from conversations to improve the efficiency and accuracy of dictations. In addition, a provider could verbally cue the EMR to place orders for radiology tests, blood tests or prescriptions. The goal is to improve efficiency and translate the provider-patient encounter into executable action.

At Mayo Clinic, we've taken the first steps toward hands-free visits by piloting the use of voice assistants in the emergency department. Future goals will be to help patients with convenient and easily accessible education or decision support at the point of care, wherever that happens. New voice technologies may be able to gauge a patient's anxiety when describing symptoms.

Multimodal care plans. Another not-too-distant future use case for voice technology is a truly interactive, individualized multimodal care plan to help patients take care of their health, especially chronic conditions. Interactive care plans contribute to patient activation, defined as the skills and confidence that equips patients to become actively engaged in their health care (Noffs). Activated patients are well informed about their treatment, which makes them more likely to make decisions, adhere to their treatment plan and see better outcomes (Noffs; Taguchi). In turn, this may help reduce the overall total cost of care.

At Mayo Clinic, we're currently looking at which interactions and conditions are best suited for voice within our interactive care plans. For example, a conversational migraine symptom severity check may be more appropriate within a headache interactive care plan than a post-surgical check-in for a thoracic cancer interactive care plan, due to the complexity of the assessment needed.

Combining voice technology with visuals or an avatar can allow patients to access tailored education, report symptoms and complete other tasks. A personalized interactive care plan like this could also improve confidence and trust with the health care system.

Remote care coordination. Remote care coordination can harness voice technology to deliver expert care at a distance and make it more accessible. Voice could help create more efficient processes for medication use, safety and treatment plans. These interactions can be both proactive and reactive. Some examples include:

- *Voice alerts and feedback fueled by real-time data inputs* from wearables and ambient voice information.

- *Medication reminders or a voice-activated medication dispenser*: "Hey Google, what meds do I take today?" "Helen, did you take your two pills today?"

- *Ambient detection of audio cues* indicating an emergent symptom or situation.

- *Voice surveys and data collection*: Use voice to complete surveys or daily journals, verify completion of a task or test, and report health concerns (Parker)

- *Advanced symptom triage* to direct patients to the appropriate level of care and make an appointment if needed.

- *Answers to health and wellness questions* and patient education.

- *Voice guidance for post-procedural education and physical therapy.*

AI would assist in monitoring patient interactions and acting on those interactions. For example, it could analyze, escalate and triage patient education to deliver precisely tailored information at the right time.

Voice as a biomarker for other conditions. In addition to research being conducted at Mayo Clinic into voice as a biomarker for coronary artery disease, other researchers across the world are discovering how voice may serve as a biomarker for a host of other medical conditions. These include dyslexia, ADHD, Parkinson's disease, multiple sclerosis, depression, Alzheimer's disease and sleep disorders (Noffs; Taguchi; Martínez-Sánchez, "Speech"; Zhang; Arora; Ramezani; Martínez-Sánchez, "Prototype"; Tyan).

Natural language processing for data summarization. As noted earlier, Mayo Clinic has an extensive reservoir of health information, including consumer-oriented content on the website and patient education materials that traditionally were delivered in print form. Patients and consumers increasingly will want this information via voice devices, but this requires editing the content to be more concise and conversational — a time-consuming process that isn't fully automated.

As a way to overcome this challenge, researchers at Mayo Clinic are investigating natural language processing techniques that can extract and summarize existing health information to create voice-ready content. This will minimize the need for human curation and editorial effort. Similarly, voice may be used to capture the clinical notes for the EMR, and NLP can then analyze the record to capture diagnostic codes and other key data points, provide relevant decision support, and help providers find the knowledge they need for optimal care.

Getting real about some tough realities. Across the globe, technology companies, health care systems and other stakeholders are dreaming up many other ways to bring voice technology into the health care journey. The possibilities for a hands-free voice interface in the sterile environment of the operating room and voice to support elder care are two areas that are generating excitement (Parker).

Along with sharing this enthusiasm, we recognize the potential pitfalls and barriers to adoption. One of the most important reality checks is the need to protect patient privacy. HIPAA compliance for voice technologies is still in its early stages, and the big tech companies that have pioneered this latest digital tool have had some well-publicized privacy lapses. The attitude among much of the general public remains guarded if not outright suspicious (Lomas).

Another limit to adoption of voice technology is simply its newness. Consumers are still learning how, when and why to use their smart speakers, and not everyone has access to them. As voice interactions increasingly become part of everyday experiences — at home, in our cars, through our phones — people will come to expect conversational interfaces in other locations, such as a clinic or hospital. These interfaces also may be bundled with companion mobile apps or display devices, integrating voice design into already familiar experiences.

To deploy voice effectively, health care organizations likely need to build up their technological infrastructure, but this may be an obstacle. Some may be reluctant to invest in technologies that are still evolving rapidly.

Voice technologies also carry some inherent limits that may slow adoption in health care. For now, the machine can't match the human in terms of a natural-sounding voice, empathetic tone, personality and ability to generate a sustained conversation. In a 2018 study in the *Journal of Medical Internet Research*, researchers found that Alexa, Siri and Google Assistant often could not understand health-related scenarios or gave the user information that could have caused harm.

The study authors noted, "Conversational assistants currently have a minimal ability to process information about discourse (i.e., beyond the level of a single utterance), and no ability to engage in fluid, mixed-initiative conversation the way people do. These were abilities that subjects assumed they had or about which they were confused" (Bickmore).

Amazon and other companies are working on devices that can read human emotions. Another challenge is to create voice systems that can accurately interpret questions and other utterances and provide the most relevant and reliable answers. This will be crucial for patient safety and satisfaction.

Finally, it's important to remember that voice is just the latest in a long line of digital health tools that have been hyped as a way to help patients take ownership of their health. It's true that patients who are well informed, have better personal and digital experiences, and are more engaged in their care are more likely to follow their treatment plan and have better health outcomes (Hibbard; Calvillo). But research also shows that digital tool successes and failures are often tied to what matters most to patients, and patients must show a genuine willingness and ability to take independent actions to manage their health and care. No technology has proved to be a magic wand in increasing patient compliance or adherence to treatment recommendations for chronic conditions (Vallo; Johnson).

For that reason, voice experience designers must identify and target issues that matter to patients to create outside-in, patient-centered solutions. Patient preferences must guide services. Otherwise, the technology will not be used. As researcher Judith Hibbard notes, "Innovative delivery systems ... are including patients as part of the solution, recognizing that high-quality care should help patients gain the skills, confidence, and knowledge they need to manage their health" (Hibbard).

Multimodal, omnichannel, ever more AI. To remain relevant and effective, voice technology will need to be integrated with multiple modes of communication, including face-to-face, phone, real-time chat and virtual visits. Voice may be a patient's best first point of contact, but it won't be the only one.

This means that providers at Mayo Clinic and elsewhere need to consider the best use cases for voice, in the context of a range of potential interaction strategies. Some questions that can guide these decisions are:

- Which experiences would be improved by voice?

- Will voice capture information more quickly and accurately than another means of communication?

- Would patients and providers benefit from a hands-free interface?

- Where are the end users — will environmental or privacy concerns limit the ability to add voice?

- Can content and experiences be redesigned to better suit a conversational interface?

At Mayo Clinic, as at other organizations, voice technology is being developed in tandem with a host of other AI techniques. Hundreds of active AI projects are happening at Mayo Clinic now, and we've created an Office of Artificial Intelligence as a central point of collaboration, guidance and oversight to leverage its potential.

Voice-first, multimodal and AI technologies will continue to follow our primary value of putting the patient's needs first. True to that value, leaders at Mayo have asked all departments to place priority on AI projects that improve patient care and add efficiency.

Shounak Majumder, M.D., a Mayo Clinic gastroenterologist whose research focuses on pancreatic diseases, notes, "The fact that the margin for error in health care is small means that the way in which we integrate [AI] into research and clinical arenas will require careful thinking from a design standpoint and a clear vision of how to use it to improve the lives of our patients" ("Emerging Role").

Mayo Clinic's future: Using digital technology to transform health care

As more and more consumers and patients incorporate voice technology into their daily routines, Mayo Clinic intends to be present to ensure that they have access to trusted health care and information. We've come a long way since the days of static health content and data, advancing to more searchable content via the internet and then to smartphones, which paved the way for customizable, portable, reactive, and self-directed information and data collection (see fig. 4).

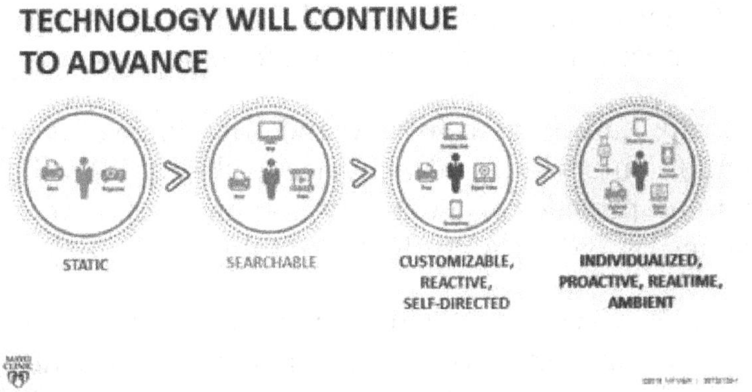

Fig.4: With the help of advancing technologies, Mayo Clinic continues to grow its abilities to meet patient needs.

Voice adds another dimension to the set of digital technologies that extend our reach and impact in health and healing. These tools unlock the insights in data and deliver answers to patients and consumers wherever they are: desktop websites, mobile websites, native apps, printed materials, chatbots, voice-enabled devices, AR/VR, wearables, and other "internet of things" devices. Whatever the device or format, we believe there will continue to be a vital role for trusted health information and an individualized, compassionate approach to clinical care.

Recognizing that the path to innovation includes failures and missteps, we are asking: How do we measure success as we proceed with voice-enabled activities? In the commercial world, it's all about monetization of voice skills, creating a profitable product and driving sales. But health care organizations have different measures of success that merit consideration. These include:

Less paperwork. Deploying voice-enabled FAQs, algorithm-based triage chatbots and other tools can significantly decrease contacts to nurses and providers, speed check-in and discharge, and reduce paperwork.

Increased compliance. Wearable feedback and proactive tools powered by voice can increase compliance for patients with chronic health conditions.

New, more effective diagnostic tools. Continued research into voice biomarkers can lead to new, more effective diagnostic tools.

Individualized medicine. Combining voice technologies with AI allows us to provide more individualized medicine and improve care.

Patient engagement. Voice devices give patients a way to take care of their health needs from their home and on the go, and are more accessible for people with limited hand dexterity or low vision.

Provider efficiency and fulfillment. All of this adds up to increased productivity, effectiveness and satisfaction for clinicians.

"Voice in health care is here to stay and with increased utilization and implementation into clinical care, voice will positively impact patient engagement and provider experience and enhance the overall health care journey," states Dr. Sandhya Pruthi, Mayo Clinic.

For Mayo Clinic, voice technologies are part of a larger digital strategy that allow us to deliver care when, where and how people desire it. Rooted in a legacy of innovation and patient-centered, integrated care, we are reimagining the health care environment for the next generation. As noted by Dr. William Mayo, one of the Mayo Clinic founders, there is always more to learn.

Chapter 13:

Voice First Health Interview: Voice Technology for Behavioral Changes

Matthew P. M. Cybulsky, MA, MBA, MSHA, PhD

Teri Fisher, MSc, MD

Editor's Note

In this chapter, Behavorial Economist, Matt Cybulsky, presents how internal motivation and emotional connectivity can impact health behavior change. Voice first technology can increase connectivity and patient engagement and make healthcare better. The author describes how storytelling can personalize health information, help modify health behaviors, and make the changes needed to improve health.

Hear the complete podcast interview with Matthew Cybulsky at: https://voicefirsthealth.com/9

Teri Fisher:

Dr. Matthew Cybulsky is a behavioral economist. Today we talk about the elements that go into creating a good voice first experience to help someone change their behaviors within the healthcare field. Matt, could you start off by sharing with us a little bit about your background and your take on voice first health?

Matt Cybulsky:

Yeah. My entire career has been unique and a little bit a different, but I think when you pop into the expanding circle of a new technology and how to apply it, it takes unique people to do it, so I'm happy to be involved in the field. I started out my career with too many master's degrees and ended up having three. And then I ended up in healthcare finance with a fantastic company out of Texas, Tenet healthcare. And while I was doing some work for them, I was living in the South Carolina area. They had assumed some extra hospitals there. And all of these folks on Hilton head Island that I was interacting with when they had their healthcare bills, they didn't understand their bills, their EOB, which is in the US the explanation of benefits from the insurance company.

And these were retired executives. And I thought there's gotta be a better way to communicate with them so that they're not dissatisfied. And also we get our money faster. And they don't end up in a credit status where they're in bad debt and getting their credit dinged. So I called the Senior Vice President and said that there's this thing called behavioral economics, I want to get this PhD, I want to use your data and I want to redesign everything that we send to our patients. And before the end of the call, he said, "Go do it!" So I did it and I ended up with some really good experience. I ended up at UAB medical school in Birmingham working with a really good team of open minded patients, very skilled surgeons, and clinicians.

Before I knew it, big four consultancy was knocking on my door and my loans were whispering in my ear and I left the medical school. Yeah, I left the medical school to pursue the business world and sort of leverage my understanding of human influence and persuasion upon multiple healthcare centers across the United States. Eventually, I was tired of doing the data and the PowerPoints and I wanted to really do some work with the patient and the provider. And that's where you find me now. I basically work for myself and several others have joined me as partners. We call ourselves,

IONIA Healthcare Consulting, which is a former Greek warrior state of a scholars and warriors. We focus on everything that has to do with the nexus of patient and provider.

I found myself fascinated by voice tech and voice first technologies and how to apply that and make healthcare better and connect patients 5,000 hours of the year instead of just the few they have in the exam room. And it's been a fascinating journey so far.

Teri Fisher:

I was browsing through your website and you've got this great quote and I wonder if you can maybe explain it a little bit. It says, "We move past the lazy, dangerous ideology of carrots and sticks to strengthen businesses, solve a lot of problems and transform care delivery." What does that mean to you?

Matt Cybulsky:

That's an adaptation from another behavioral economist. And what's unique about that quote is, while I was in doctoral candidacy, it became really clear to me from the research I was reading in behavioral economics and social psychology that people didn't really respond well long term to being punished or given rewards, but they responded more to internal motivation, emotional connectivity, comparisons to others. And I think a lot of health care when it comes to getting people to modify their behavior has had it wrong for a really, really long time! You know, what I call terror management theory when saying to somebody, "If you don't do X, you die," only works for about 24 hours after the threat.

And then you can slide that bowl of M&Ms across to them. Or you can slide that six pack of lager across to them. Or you can say you don't have to work out anymore if you don't want to do anymore physical exercise or anymore hygiene, just be lazy, don't floss, don't brush your teeth! And people will just go back into their habits. So, the point is reframing how we think we take care of people in medicine.

Teri Fisher:

I want to dive into that a little bit more specifically with healthcare. So, how do we change behaviors, whether it be the patient, the care provider, or anybody involved in the healthcare system? What is voice first allowing us to do to create effective behavioral change patterns?

Matt Cybulsky:

Well, the first thing I'll say, and I'll borrow from a literary hero of mine, Malcolm Gladwell, and say that it has nothing to do with just one thing. You know, it's not just like one perfect sauce that we all love for spaghetti. You know, it's the five or six different choices of the spaghetti sauce or booze or pickles that give us true satisfaction and change. The same is true for behavioral modification. There's not just one universal. There's just not one way forward. There's multiple sort of layered interventions we can add towards the way we interact with the patient that gets them into a place that they're able to make the changes they need as well as sustain it by reducing the effort and giving them something to motivate with besides some material reward. It's an internal motivation that we can connect with.

Now for me, my fascination, my hope, my dream, whether I make it doing this or if I end up making this just an interesting merit badge of time and my life, is with voice first. Tech can connect to people all the time. And if we have the right tools, if we have the right platform, we build that in and we can figure out what makes this person tick. If they're diabetic, if they have COPD, if they have CHF, if they have anxiety and depression, we can be with them all the time. What does that do? Well, we are creating a system around them. We're basically taking a mom or a loved one or somebody that thinks they're connected to someone just like them. For example, the movie HER with Joaquin Phoenix, where there was this idea that this guy had sort of a girlfriend and she was with him all the time and it was so convincing.

The same can be said about voice tech. There isn't the one universal, but it is an instrument and a tool that we can place a patient within that basically connects the physician. For example, the MD is with that person more than just being in your office when you say, "Hey, I don't just do this because I can bill you. I do it 'cause I give a crap about you!" And the idea that you have a life and a community of people you're connected to that resonates when they're in your office, but then they leave and when they leave, we lose them. Voice by mobile and voice by smart speaker reduces that distance and increases the connectivity. So, I think that's what's so unique to me about voice first and why it's truly the harbinger of behavioral modification in a sustainable way.

Teri Fisher:

And then when you start imagining these interactions that people are having with their voice devices, I know that you've spoken about the importance of storytelling. What is the deal with that?

Matt Cybulsky:

I imagine the voice technology is a tremendous platform to be able to leverage that, that ability to tell a good story.

Teri Fisher:

Can you comment a little bit more about that and how that impacts health?

Matt Cybulsky:

Yes. I'd love to, and for your listeners sake, I'm going to try and not turn into a Carl Sagan short story moment because I am not Carl Sagan and I can't compare myself to him. But the point is I want to keep this tangible for your audience. So if there are children listening, you might want to put it on mute, but the quote went something like this: birth control doesn't work when it's in the drawer, right? You can have the tool, you can have the drug, you can have the instrument, like the smart speaker or the mobile assistant on the phone. But if the patient isn't using it, it's worthless!

I mean, one of the most scary statistics I heard from a cardiologist went like this: patients upon followup after their initial myocardial infarction, which is a clogged artery in the heart for non clinicians out there, are only 40% in compliance for taking statins and beta blockers and aspirins. After that, when you've had the attack and you've been discharged from the hospital is less than 40% compliance. If you can get people up to a higher level, they succeed. And he did a small experiment using Bluetooth caps on pharmaceuticals and increased compliance to 90% by pinging people through their phones. Well, the same can be said with voice tech. So if I were to say to a patient when they went home, I'm going to give you this

Amazon Echo Dot, I'm going to give you this Google assistant, I'm going to give you this tool from whoever it is, and I just want you to plug it in. When you get home, it's tied into your cell phone and it's going to do some things and you can listen to music on it and do whatever and then you're going to interact with it.

The point being, if we believe, which I do, that internal motivation is what truly makes change in the long term, you have to be able to create a line, a linear narrative where a patient can see him or herself inside of that narrative as a player that's relevant to them, where there's a world around them that can connect to them emotionally. Now, there are many, many steps psychologically that takes me from voice tech to be able to figure out a way to use it for emotional integration that involves a story. The point is, I don't have rigor background to say this is absolutely the case for us with the storytelling, but what I can tell you is there a really more accomplished published authors and Dan Siegel is one of them. There's some other sort of pop psychology folks, but also some real academic psychologists who have sort of talked about this, that integrating someone emotionally into a story, optimizes learning, optimizes retention, can accelerate healing because there's this sense of identity as well as connectivity.

We are pro social animals. And therefore we get a little bit of this regulation. We get a little bit more of this self-control. We get a little bit more of an emotional sort of stability. You know, a secondary diagnosis as you know, Teri to any chronic condition is depression. Also there are some other side effects to diseases that require a lot of maintenance and compliance that reduce our ability to remember or be disciplined or get up on time or go to bed on time or eat the right things and drink less alcohol. The idea that we could create a narrative through a speaker and assistant that's talking to us means I don't ignore it. It means that I interact with it. And for me, the narrative hypothesis I was given about putting a person, a patient into a story was the idea that birth control doesn't stay in the drawer, that the beta blocker gets used, that the alcohol doesn't get purchased.

These are the things that can create real change. So for some it may seem way too liberal on the side of real clinical science. But I think that we can't dissociate the real analytical clinical intervention that we've created through something that is you know, granular as a pharmaceutical to what is the mental state and mental identity and vision of the patient that we're trying to make better. And what's their role in it? It's just not enough to see them as fast as you can, write the scripts and say, don't do this, you'll die. That works for two hours and makes them feel terrible. Very few people respond to that as being like, you know, their rock bottom that they could say totally changed their future and they changed how they took care of themselves and now they're all better.

The point being voice speakers, tech care assistants on mobile phones, the way we choose to design them ought to be inside of that concept of a narrative, right? The call to action I really have is for everyone in this space to think about it differently than what we did with the screen. Even with mobile, it requires us to go towards it with will, right? But we want something more immersive. This is the real opportunity and I think to me it's not the one universal, but it's the one differentiator that voice brings to the tech world that I think can really get us over that hump from will to sort of a internal motivation around the patient, relative to the patient, their financial class, their gender, their race, their sexuality, their religion, their age, everything can be incorporated into that in really intelligent ways if we get the right storytellers designing these tools alongside the programmers and alongside the clinicians.

And let's get the patients in the room. You know, you and I were really fortunate to hear a story at Harvard and the story I told a few times, and it's kind of a tear jerker. The distillation of the story is they wanted to create a tool that helped people in hospice or palliative care. Someone said, hey, at some point we should probably get someone who's got terminal illness to come in here and tell us what they want. And so they were thinking super complex and really deep. Well, no, it was something as simple as "I don't want to die alone and I'm afraid of dying alone. If you could get a playlist playing for me, if I just said 'play my playlist', that meant something that evoked memories of people I loved or moments that mattered to me."

That ripped me to shreds because it was so relevant because I think we've all heard a sound or a smell that brought us back to childhood or to a lover or a spouse or a child or a memory that mattered to you. I think the point of that story that I'm trying to bring up is if we can create something like that alongside the patients with us, and we can say to them what kind of narrative that we have here on a piece of paper, would you respond to and would you say, I want to be the part of Joaquin Phoenix in the movie HER, it was a love that he felt like you couldn't get right. I think that's the extreme version of what I'm getting at.

I think it could be as simple as that. It could be a story of someone else like them and the AI engine says, "Hey, for your activity today, we want you to give this other character in a story with you some direction on how to take care of their problem because they have some exacerbation and we know that you know, how to help them. Can you help them?" Small things like that over time can get someone to stop ignoring and being fatigued or intimidated or turned off or bitter about the system, especially in the United States, and be able to do things through an internal motivation to make themselves healthier and better, which helps everyone and all ships rise. Nothing's more maddening than living in North America, knowing the system we have and seeing people struggle. The truth of the matter is I think that voice tech can really get us to a place where more people can take care of themselves in the home without the exacerbation. But to do that, the narrative tool to me is paramount to success.

Teri Fisher:

You've said a couple things there that I wanted to touch on. One is that I think the voice first technology really lends itself to collaborating with writers. And we haven't really seen that as much in other forms of technology where a creative writer with experience in writing beautiful stories, is working with a programmer. And I think that's one of the really unique things now about voice first. And the other thing that you mentioned is that there's a real emotional connection that can occur when you're talking and listening to a smart speaker.

Now, I'd like to switch gears and talk about something you mentioned to me just before we started recording about the emotional connection that a person can have with their pets, and how this relates to voice first. Can you talk a little about that work that you're doing?

Matt Cybulsky:

Yeah, I don't know what it is about life, Teri, but sometimes you find yourselves in these scenarios and you scratch your head and you think to yourself, ah, is this my life? How did I get here? So I've been focused for a long time on allopathic medicine, human healthcare. I'm fascinated by it. I grew up with it. The community I grew up in, that's all people did, it seemed, was work in healthcare and ancillary industries. And if you think about the GDP of the United States, that's not that so far off. Twenty percent of the GDP is healthcare related work. So that's one in five adults. It makes sense that I would be around it.

But I ended up getting contacted by a group of folks who are doing some work with a publicly traded veterinary company. And they were really curious about how the vet practice of the future affects veterinary care. And so they reached out to me and I've been speaking to them about a few things, but one of the things that comes up a lot is voice first technologies in veterinary care. And one of the advantages of veterinarians is the lack of bureaucracy in comparison to human health care. They can just try anything outside of harm. They can try a whole lot of stuff.

Well, we started talking about what does it mean to be a connected pet owner. And then we started talking even more deeply about veterinarians as this sort of proxy to human health care. By taking care of pets and keeping them around and healthy and well, it is somewhat of a stabilizer for communities and families and with their own health. I mean, think about prescriptions for therapeutic animals. The symbiosis of companion animals throughout the millennia is a real thing. A passive monitoring of patients in the home, reminders to the pet owners about various administrations of drugs or food qualifications, or if they have kidney issues, a fluid restriction. All of those things can be utilized in the home as well as in the practice.

Veterinarians are notorious for, just like physicians, struggling after a heavy debt load of education. But they don't seem to have the same sort of horizon financially. So something like voice first tech can really help them reach more people, more pets and do so at a greater scale. So I have great excitement with the future of veterinary applications of voice tech and I'm super excited about the work they're doing. Imagine what you could do with that as far as wearables in combination with voice tools in the practice as well as in the home itself. It's pretty exciting stuff.

Teri Fisher:

And that just scratches the surface of what you're up to. Thanks so much for coming on the podcast.

Matt Cybulsky:

Well, thank you Teri. The pleasure's all mine.

Chapter 14:

The Laws of Voice

Heather Deixler,
M. Phil., J.D.

Bianca Rose Phillips,
LLB, BComm,
GradDipLP, LLM,
Scholarly Academic

Editor's Note

There are legal and ethical questions that are prudent when building voice user interfaces and applications. If the voice activated device is potentially capable of human-like intelligence and interactivity, should the voice VA device be held to the same standard of care as a healthcare provider? Relevant hypothetical scenarios highlighting legal considerations in the field of digital health and voice technology are described by the authors: pediatric care and consent to record transcripts, duty to inform patients of risks and side effects, genetic testing, cognitive decline, personal health tracking and mental health. The scenarios are followed by provocative questions for voice assistant developers to consider and how the laws should evolve to address these new technologies. The future of law making with the field of digital health is exploding and the laws are yet to be determined.

About the Authors

HEATHER B. DEIXLER

Counsel, Latham & Watkins LLP (United States of America)

HEATHER is a corporate associate in the San Francisco office of Latham & Watkins LLP, where she counsels public and private companies operating in the healthcare and life sciences industries on transactional and regulatory matters. Heather advises clients on innovative healthcare delivery systems, including Medicare Accountable Care Organizations, clinically integrated networks, and IPAs, and other value-based payment programs. She is a Certified Information Privacy Professional (CIPP/US and CIPP/E) with a particular focus on health information privacy and security. Heather is also Chair of the ABA Health Law Section eHealth, Privacy & Security Interest Group, and Vice-Chair of the American Health Lawyers Association (AHLA) Health Information & Technology (HIT) Practice Group's Educational Programs of the HIT - Tech Licensing and Intellectual Property Affinity Group. Heather was a speaker at the Voice of Healthcare Summit 2019 at Harvard Medical School.

BIANCA ROSE PHILLIPS

Lawyer and Officer of the Supreme Court of Victoria, and Adjunct lecturer in Law at Swinburne University of Technology (Australia)

BIANCA is a lawyer examining the domains of digital health and medical law. Her current work investigates issues of law-making, substantive law, and statutory interpretation in those areas. As part of her doctoral program, Bianca has been examining Australian legislative law-making practices in digital health, and has examined a case study to develop a framework for law making. She contends that Australian law-makers should consider the school of thought on law-making developed at Harvard Law School to aid improvements to their law-making practices. Bianca holds a Bachelor of Laws. Bachelor of Commerce. GradDipLP. Master of Laws (Medical Law & Telemedicine. She is an Adjunct Lecturer in Law at Swinburne University of Technology, and engages in legal research projects in the area of health and medical law. Her six-part series entitled "Making the Digital Health

Revolution" was featured in the Medical Journal of Australia, Insight. Bianca was a speaker at the Voice of Healthcare Summit 2019 at Harvard Medical School.

Disclaimer: The information in this chapter is of a general nature. There are a range of compliance requirements that must be considered by any reader. You should always seek legal and compliance advice to address any questions, problems or purported solutions they may have. The information in this Chapter is accurate as of September 2019.

Introduction

Should a voice assistant (VA) be afforded legal personhood status? Should consumers and patients have ownership of information about themselves stored in a VA? These are just two examples of complex legal questions that arise with the emerging use of VA technology in the healthcare space. Those working in the field of Voice may be considering how they can contribute to addressing these questions and to the evolution of applicable laws.

This chapter will present you with a range of hypothetical scenarios incorporating current legal constructs and will ask you to consider how the laws should evolve to address these new technologies, as well as your role in shaping the future of such laws.

Imagine the following Voice scenarios and a law that may be relevant to each.

Using VAs in pre- and post-operative care: Duty to inform patients of remote risks

Introduction

VAs will increasingly provide patients with pre- and post-surgery information. The information may be of a general nature, or the skill could be more personalized. If a potential risk of surgery is so remote that it is rarely seen in practice, and only appears in archaic medical literature, does the VA need to advise of that risk? Imagine the following scenario.

The scenario

A patient, Stacey, is about to undergo cataract surgery. In the pre-op appointment Stacey's surgeon highlights the risks of surgery and, in her concluding remarks, advises Stacey that "you may also consult your VA to learn more about your surgery, and ask questions about the risks and post-op process."

That evening Stacey goes home and says to her VA "[VA name], what are the risks of cataract surgery?". The VA responds "the risks of cataract surgery include: Posterior capsule opacity (PCO), Intraocular lens dislocation,

Eye inflammation, Light sensitivity, Photopsia (perceived flashes of light), Macular edema (swelling of the central retina), Ptosis (droopy eyelid) and Ocular hypertension (elevated eye pressure)."[1] Stacey continues to ask a range of questions about post-operative care and the recovery process.

Surgery seems to have gone well. However, two months after the surgery Stacey advises her doctor of considerable decreased vision in her left eye, which the surgeon determines is sympathetic ophthalmia.[2] The estimated post-operative occurrence is between 0.01%–0.05%. Attempts to treat the sympathetic ophthalmia fail and the patient sustains permanent loss of vision in her left eye. The surgeon failed to inform Stacey of the risk of sympathetic ophthalmia during the pre-op consultation, and Stacey's VA also did not inform her of this risk.

Stacey wants to know whether the surgeon and/or the VA had a duty to inform her of the remote risk.

A legal thought

In order for a physician to obtain informed consent, the physician must notify patients of risks, benefits, and alternatives to treatment. The law generally requires that only "reasonably foreseeable" material risks be disclosed. The law of tort includes a duty for individuals and entities to warn of risks of treatment. If knowledge of the risk could affect the patient's decision to progress with the treatment, then it may be determined that there was a duty to warn the patient.[3] While certain courts rely upon the community disclosure standards (i.e., whether the majority of physicians in a certain community would customarily make such a disclosure), other courts look to whether it would be reasonable under the circumstances to make such disclosure:

> *"Duty to disclose has gained recognition in a large number of American jurisdictions,[37] but more largely on a different rationale. The majority of courts dealing with the problem have made the duty depend on whether it was the custom of physicians practicing in the community to make the particular disclosure to the patient.[38] If so, the physician may be held liable for an unreasonable and injurious failure to divulge, but there can be no recovery unless the omission forsakes a practice prevalent in the profession.[39] We agree that the physician›s noncompliance with a professional custom to*

> *reveal, like any other departure from prevailing medical practice,*[40] *may give rise to liability to the patient. We do not agree that the patient's cause of action is dependent upon the existence and nonperformance of a relevant professional tradition."*[4]

An interesting legal question surrounds the standard of care that will be expected of VA developers and manufacturers. Should the VA and the company that developed it be held to the same standard of care as a physician?

Alternative scenario

What if the VA and surgeon had responded in a more general manner? That is, "the risks of cataract surgery include inflammation, infection, bleeding, swelling, drooping eyelid, dislocation of artificial lens, retinal detachment, glaucoma, secondary cataract and loss of vision."[5]

Loss of vision is now on the list. This is the outcome that the patient in the above scenario experienced. The disclosure now includes a wider range of potential risks, which arguably covers that patient's outcome.

Questions for VA developers

1. What types of disclaimers should the VA include to shield itself from liability?

2. When should the VA refer the patient back to her clinician for more information about risks specific to her circumstances? What triggers should be built into the VA?

3. To what extent is the VA operating independently of the physician versus as an extension of the physician's practice?

4. Could the VA be considered to be engaged in the unauthorized practice of medicine?

5. Should the patient or consumer receive a transcript of the conversation with the VA, or a summary of "advice" that they can maintain? Alternatively, a playback function on their VA?

Timmy is Johnny's eight-year-old brother, and he overheard his parents ask questions to the VA about Johnny. When his parents go upstairs to tend to Johnny before bed, Timmy walks over to the smart speaker and asks questions. He is curious about how Johnny is doing. Because Johnny had been using the VA with parental controls and his voice was recognizable, though difficult to distinguish from his younger brother, the VA now responds to his brother.

In the morning, when the parents wake up, Timmy seems withdrawn. He does not eat his normal breakfast and does not seem like his normal cheery self. Timmy asks them a question about the VA, and the parents realize that he must have interacted with the VA the night before when they were tending to Johnny. The parents are somewhat concerned — what else did Timmy ask the VA and what has he heard? The doctors informed the parents that Johnny's condition may be more serious than they originally thought, and Johnny's parents wanted to shield Johnny and his younger brother from this news. They are worried how Timmy and Johnny will handle the news, believing them both too young to understand the potential severity. They are wondering why the VA did not seek out parental consent as a precautionary measure, and in particular why it could not distinguish between the voices of the children.

A legal thought

From the perspective of the VA company, the parents are obliged to protect the child in this instance, and the parents will have been required to agree to a privacy policy and terms of use prior to accessing the device and skills. If, as here, there were controls in place to prevent children from accessing such information, the terms of use will likely shift the risk to the parents to take the necessary steps to protect the child from accessing the skills by using voice recognition training — for example, placing timers or codes after hours and/or moving the speaker to an area of the house that is not accessible by the child. But, what if the terms of use do not address those obligations? Or what if the VA does not include such controls?

In relation to the responsibility of the VA company, the Children's Online Privacy Protection Act and its associated rules (COPPA) require the company to obtain verifiable parental consent prior to collecting, using, or disclosing personal information about a child under 13 years of age.[9] Under COPPA, personal information is defined to include audio files containing a child's voice, as well as a range of other information sources.[10] COPPA outlines methods for obtaining such verifiable consent:

"Obtaining verifiable consent means making any reasonable effort (taking into consideration available technology) to ensure that before personal information is collected from a child, a parent of the child: (1) Receives notice of the operator's personal information collection, use, and disclosure practices; and (2) Authorizes any collection, use, and/or disclosure of the personal information."[11]

The words "reasonable effort" and "taking into account available technology" are important.

<u>Questions for a Voice developer</u>

- What are the available technologies that could prevent a child in this instance from accessing the VA? Can you foresee your company using biometric sensors to verify a user's identity and age?

- Are you employing the currently available technologies to prevent an occurrence like this?

- Are there sufficient parental controls in place to ensure that only appropriate information is available to children?

- Would these mechanisms protect the privacy of the child whose information is being accessed?

Assisted reproduction: Recording complex processes

<u>Introduction</u>

We will now consider several hypothetical scenarios in which a patient wishes to understand what rights they have to health information maintained on their behalf.

<u>The scenario</u>

Jane had undergone an IVF cycle, and a number of her embryos underwent genetic testing. The testing involved biopsy of trophectoderm cells at day five. The embryologist recorded the steps that he had taken using the VA that sits on his desk in the lab. The VA records a transcript of exactly what the embryologist has said. That information is maintained by the laboratory, but is not integrated into the laboratory's patient portal. The laboratory portal permits each patient to view his or her laboratory test results.

Jane and her husband, Bobby, did not check the laboratory portal prior to their appointment with their IVF specialist to receive the results.

They are sitting nervously in the specialist's office, preparing for the moment they are going to find out whether they have an embryo to implant. The doctor prints out the lab results and hands the sheet of paper to them. They look down to see that the result for one embryo reads "no result" and "no DNA present."

The physician looks at them and says in a serious tone, "the lab messed up." When he calls the lab to demand answers, he speaks with a representative who informs him that although they maintain certain internal notes regarding the genetic testing they perform, those tests are not a part of Jane's medical records and they are only permitted to provide access to laboratory results that inform the patient's medical records.

Jane and Bobby return home and, on reflection, decide that they want more information. They submit a records access form to the lab, and receive only the test results, not the commentary recorded by the VA.

A legal thought

A fascinating legal thought here is who owns the health information and does the patient have a right to know about the particulars of the process the provider followed? In the US, state law generally governs whether medical records belong to patients or their providers. For instance, in Florida, the "records owner" is defined as:

"(i) any healthcare practitioner who generates a medical record after treating a patient; (ii) any healthcare practitioner to whom records are transferred by a previous owner; or (iii) any healthcare practitioner's employer, such as a physician practice."

In New Hampshire, on the other hand, medical information contained in a patient's medical record is deemed to be the property of the patient.

Under the Health Insurance Portability and Accountability Act of 1996, as amended, and all regulations promulgated thereunder (HIPAA), individuals have certain rights with respect to their health information, including the right to access and amend it. An individual's right to access her health information extends beyond the records that a healthcare provider, including a laboratory, maintains about an individual in an EHR or paper medical record, and includes all protected health information included in the "designated record sets" maintained by or for the healthcare provider, whether in electronic or paper form.[12] For purposes of HIPAA, a designated record set is broadly defined to include "a group of records maintained by or for a covered entity that is:

i. The medical records and billing records about individuals maintained by or for a covered health care provider;

ii. The enrollment, payment, claims adjudication, and case or medical management record systems maintained by or for a health plan; or

iii. Used, in whole or in part, by or for the covered entity to make decisions about individuals."[13]

In FAQs listed on the Office for Civil Rights' (OCR's) website, the agency has made clear that an individual has a right under HIPAA to access more than just test results from a clinical laboratory.[14] OCR states that "[t]o the extent an individual requests access to all of her information held by the laboratory, the laboratory is required to provide access to all of the PHI about the individual in its designated record set. This could include, for example, completed test reports and the underlying data used to generate the reports, test orders, ordering provider information, billing information, and insurance information."[15] OCR has also noted that with respect to genomic information, an individual has a right under HIPAA to access genomic information the laboratory has generated about the individual, including "the underlying information generated as part of the test, as well as other information concerning tests a laboratory runs on an individual."[16]

On September 9, 2019, the US Department of Health & Human Services, OCR settled its first case in the HIPAA "Right of Access Initiative." This initiative was announced in 2019, and promised to enforce the rights of patients to receive copies of their medical records promptly and without being overcharged. Bayfront Health St. Petersburg paid US$85,000 to OCR and adopted a corrective action plan to settle a potential violation of the HIPAA Privacy Rule right of access provision, after OCR determined that Bayfront failed to provide a mother timely access to records about her unborn child.[17] In addressing OCR's focus on patients' right to access their health information, OCR Director Roger Severino stated that "We aim to hold the health care industry accountable for ignoring peoples' rights to access their medical records and those of their kids."[18]

This legal area raises a number of interesting questions. What is the extent of the patient's right to access her healthcare information, and where is the line drawn with respect to what will comprise a designated record set for purposes of HIPAA? Does this right of access create an affirmative duty on the part of the IVF company to provide certain particulars to patients like Jane and Bobby?

Questions for a VA developer

• What types of information do you think the clinical laboratory should need to share with the patient?

• To the extent the VA company is acting as a business associate of the clinical laboratory, what obligations does the VA company have to respond to requests from the patient? Do you believe that a VA company should share ownership of information with the patient? What are the benefits and risks to the VA company?

Genetic testing: Uses to claim a pre-existing condition

The scenario

Please read the above scenario on assisted reproduction, as we are going to revisit it in this section. The patient did in fact have a healthy embryo to use, which was then implanted and resulted in a healthy live birth. Can the genetic information about the child be used by an insurance company to argue that the child has a pre-existing condition that was detected in their genes as an embryo?

A legal thought

Under federal US law, patients may restrict disclosure of protected health information to their insurer under certain circumstances. While HIPAA permits a healthcare provider to disclose protected health information to a health insurance company for treatment, payment, or healthcare operations purposes without patient authorization, a patient has the right to request restrictions on the disclosure of protected health information to a health insurance company if the disclosure is for the purpose of payment or healthcare operations, the disclosure is not otherwise required by law, and the patient has paid out-of-pocket (i.e., in full from a source other than the insurance company).

The Affordable Care Act of 2010 includes prohibitions against insurer discrimination on the basis of a pre-existing condition, prohibiting an adjustment to premiums on the basis of a medical condition. Title I of the Genetic Information Nondiscrimination Act of 2008 (GINA) protects against health insurance companies using genetic information to discriminate against patients, however, some forms of insurance are exempt, such as "long-term care insurance, life insurance, or disability insurance."[19] As such, several US states have passed laws to ensure protections against discrimination under these forms of additional insurance.[20]

Question for VA developers

- In addition to the privacy policy and terms, do you think that a VA should repeat via Voice how the data the consumer or patient shares with a VA is protected from third-party access?

- Should the patient be able to opt out of data-sharing with third parties?

- What measures do you have in place to prevent unintended third-party access? How would you ensure that a scenario such as the Cambridge Analytica scandal does not occur again? The Cambridge Analytica scandal involved the Facebook[21] profiles of individuals being used for the purposes of political advertising, without their consent.

Mental health: Grounds to refuse access to record if not in the patient's wellbeing

The scenario

Fred has been drinking excessively for a while and has realized that it is affecting all aspects of his life. He wants to get help, but is not quite sure where to turn. He found an app that pairs an initial consultation with a VA skill and a follow-up consultation with a psychiatrist in the psychiatrist's clinic. Fred decides to give it a try. He registers on the app, clicks the box that he agrees with the privacy policy and terms of service, and starts using the app. In his first session with the VA skill, Fred talks about his drinking problems, and reveals very personal information about himself, his wife, children, work, finances, and prior health challenges. During the session, Fred reveals that he has had some "dark thoughts," but notes that he would never act on them. He does not elaborate further and does not make any specific threat.

Fred leaves the session feeling quite vulnerable, but is comforted knowing that he will have a follow-up session with a face-to-face clinician in a few days.

At the appointment, his psychiatrist informs him that she will access the recordings and transcripts of the VA session. She tells him that she is doing this to "ensure he is being honest about any negative behaviors" and to "ensure that he is taking his recovery seriously for his own protection and that of his family." Fred asks his psychiatrist to provide him with a copy of the transcript from his first session on the app.

A legal thought

Will Fred be able to access the transcripts? This depends on whether the transcript constitutes psychotherapy notes under HIPAA, i.e., notes to which the patient can be denied access. Psychotherapy notes are defined as:

> "...notes recorded (in any medium) by a health care provider who is a mental health professional documenting or analyzing the contents of conversation during a private counseling session or a group, joint, or family counseling session and that are separated from the rest of the individual's medical record. Psychotherapy notes excludes medication prescription and monitoring, counseling session start and

> *stop times, the modalities and frequencies of treatment furnished, results of clinical tests, and any summary of the following items: Diagnosis, functional status, the treatment plan, symptoms, prognosis, and progress to date.*"[22]

In this scenario, would the VA be considered augmented intelligence, acting on behalf of the healthcare provider who is a mental health professional documenting the contents of their conversation with the healthcare professional's patient? If so, the records made by the VA may constitute psychotherapy notes that are collected on behalf of the psychiatrist. Alternatively, the VA could be considered a standalone skill engaging with the patient for purely informational and educational purposes. If the latter applies, the information recorded by the VA may not be deemed psychotherapy notes, and the psychiatrist may be able to share the information with the patient.[23] But what if the VA is a standalone skill that is not augmented by a licensed healthcare provider, and the VA is engaging in the practice of psychiatry, and thereby constituting the unauthorized practice of medicine?

Questions for a VA developer

- Who should have control over the patient's records? Should access to the VA's records be patient-driven? What if the VA is owned by a professional corporation and ultimately the decision-making falls to a licensed professional? Does that change your opinion of how the VA should act?

- Would you think it best for the patient to have a safe place to share information without the ability for others to access it? Or should there always be exceptions to help protect the patient if they pose potential harm to themselves and others?

Personal health tracking – Legality of requests to understand the process of diagnosis

<u>Scenario</u>

As a psychiatrist you have recently diagnosed a patient as having a personality disorder. The diagnosis took several months to be established. You have informed the patient of the diagnosis and he disagrees with you. He advises you that he has independently been tracking his mental health using a VA skill and that nothing has been detected. He accuses you of conspiring against him. You receive a letter from the patient requesting all particulars and notes of any kind that you have to confirm the patient's diagnosis according to the DSM manual criteria for personality disorders. You receive the letter and consider the records that you hold about the individual. You have typed notes and transcripts. You decide to compile the typed notes and send them to the patient as per his request.

The patient calls you stating that he does not just want a copy of the notes but also wants to know the exact process you undertook to reach your diagnosis.

<u>A legal thought</u>

Please see the scenario above entitled "mental health".

This scenario may seem farfetched, however, in 2017 the Victorian Supreme Court in Australia considered a patient's right to information about the process used by a doctor to reach a diagnosis of narcissistic personality disorder. In that case the person requested: "all records and material of any nature, in your possession or control, which you purport to substantiate and or support your expressed 'diagnosis', i.e. those which record the specific (DSM-IV) criteria satisfied to make your personal diagnosis."[24] The court considered whether such access was permissible pursuant to legislation, and found that the purpose for which the information was sought was not allowed under the legislation.

The case demonstrates that patients are potentially willing to make such requests, and this could extend into the realm of Voice. The scope of legal access and ownership of data remains an area to watch with interest.

Questions for a VA developer

- In this hypothetical the patient is using a VA skill as separate healthcare support from the psychiatric assistance he received from a healthcare professional. Should users of these skills be encouraged to use them alongside face-to-face assistance, and how could the data be integrated with that of the professional they see?

- In the future, will AI be as sophisticated as the human brain? If so, will patients or consumers expect to understand the exact AI processes utilized to come to their diagnosis?

- What should be the role of law in drawing "lines" on permissible access to information? Do patients need to be protected from themselves, or should they be permitted to see all relevant data?

Cognitive decline – Capacity to purchase and use a VA

Introduction

Uses of a VA by those with cognitive decline raise concerns regarding their ability to consent to using the VA. This scenario explores the legal issue of capacity.

Scenario

A VA was purchased by the children of a woman, Sally, who suffered from Alzheimer's with moderately severe cognitive decline. The children are excited about the benefits that certain VA skills could offer their mother, including encouraging her to exercise, decreasing loneliness, playing music, and checking on her wellbeing. They see the VA as enabling tracking of her progress to enable timely reporting to her doctor and interventions where necessary.

Sally lives independently, but receives daily visits from a caregiver who helps her with mealtimes and other household tasks, however, she sleeps alone at home. One night, feeling lonely and a bit frightened, Sally starts talking to the VA. The following day her children arrive to take their mother out. She refuses, stating that she would rather talk to her VA. They ask her questions about her conversation with the VA, which she cannot remember. Would removing the VA from her home raise legal concerns?

A legal thought

Capacity to contract is relevant here. In this scenario, it appears that Sally lacks capacity to consent to using the VA, although this would likely need to be verified by a doctor in the circumstances. Her children have entered into a binding contract in their own right and with their own money, purchasing the VA as a gift, and therefore it is now their mother's rightful property. If they act as administrators then they can be privy to making decisions alongside their mother about appropriate care plans.

Removing the VA from the mother's home in these circumstances and without her consent raises a range of legal and ethical concerns, and does not respect her right to autonomy. They may be better suited to finding alternative solutions alongside their mother and other caregivers. Consider how the alternative scenario below could benefit this particular individual and may be a safer method for those with a lack of capacity to consent.

Alternative scenario

Sally has a skill set up on her VA that can detect mental health and cognitive decline such as depression and Alzheimer's. Sally's has a proactive VA that is set up by a team of healthcare providers to allow her to use the VA in a manner that will better support her wellbeing and ensure appropriate follow-up.

Questions for a VA developer:

- Should the family or a doctor be required to sign off on her capacity prior to her use of the VA?

- What do you see as the role of proactive VAs to protect safety and also to ensure that capacity is verified and legal consent obtained?

- What other alternatives would you consider to verifying consent in this instance?

The future of law

The ability to make sound laws to regulate digital health will depend on the willingness of law makers to consider core values and principles that have been, and will continue to remain, an enduring part of our legal system and society at large – Bianca Phillips.

Scenario

Congress seeks to legislate on two key questions: 1) whether a VA can hold personhood status, and 2) whether consumers or patients are the legal owners of health information about them.

Public consultations are under way, and you have the opportunity to write a submission to government.

A legal thought

Here is a framework[25] that may be useful in structuring your submission.

The Constitution, Bill of Rights, and Human Rights

Will the proposed laws advance civil rights and freedoms enshrined in the Constitutional Bill of Rights and International Human Rights?

Clinical benefit

What evidence exists that any particular approach to lawmaking will have clinical benefits? Provide sources in your submission, e.g., recent, high quality, and reputable sources, that provide these clinical benefits.

Societal benefit

How will approaches to lawmaking in these areas benefit society? You could consider moral, ethical, technical, and philosophical factors, for example.

Harm reduction

Is there any foreseeable harm to any people or persons if lawmakers were to take a particular approach on these topics?

Risk reduction

Do the proposed laws mitigate risk? Here you may consider a range of risks, including a) risks to the rule of law, b) legal compliance risks, and c) standards of privacy and security, etc.

Business case

Consider the business case arguments that have been put forth by government to date and whether projections are based on relevant, up-to-date data.

Public consultation

Has the public and stakeholder consultation process been adequate? If not, what solutions do you propose for improving the consultation process?

Accountability for the reasons behind a decision

From what you can tell of publicly available documents, have lawmakers been accountable for the reasons for their decisions, e.g., by providing evidence in support of their decision-making.

<u>Question for a VA developer:</u>

- What has your engagement in the lawmaking process in the field of digital health been to date, if at all?

- What are the benefits of engaging in such processes, and are there any risks to your business in doing so?

Conclusion

The preceding discussion has demonstrated a range of legal considerations in the field of Voice in healthcare. As we enter this new frontier, lawyers and lawmakers will seek your expertise on the future of technology and society. We hope that this chapter has provided some inspiration to participate in discussions of what the law ought to be. Please do not hesitate to contact the authors should you have any questions.

For legal assistance, contact first-named author Heather Deixler, who is a practicing lawyer in the area of digital health law.

For questions on the future of law and law-making contact Bianca Phillips, who is a legal academic examining law-making processes, the values and principles considered by law-makers, and the evidentiary support relied upon by law-makers when they make statements in support or against law-making within the field of digital health.

References

1. Chris A. Knobbe, MD, *Cataract Surgery Complications*, https://www.allaboutvision.com/conditions/cataract-complications.htm.

2. Arevalo JF, Garcia RA, Al-Dhibi HA, Sanchez JG, Suarez-Tata L. Update on sympathetic ophthalmia. *Middle East Afr J Ophthalmol.* 2012;19(1):13–21. doi:10.4103/0974-9233.92111.

3. The High Court of Australia decision in <u>Rogers v Whitaker</u> 175 CLR 479. In this case a patient suffered post-operative sympathetic ophthalmia, and was not advised of this risk. The patient succeeded in a claim for damages. *See also, Canterbury v. Spence*, 464 F.2d 772 (D.C. Cir. 1972)), and the decision of the Supreme Court of Canada in Reibl v. Hughes (<u>(1980) 114 DLR (3d) 1</u>), which held that the "duty to warn" arises from the patient's right to know of material risks, a right which in turn arises from the patient's right to decide for himself or herself whether or not to submit to the medical treatment proposed. For further information see: http://www.ncsl.org/research/health/mental-health-professionals-duty-to-warn.aspx

4. 464 F.2d at 783.

5. Mayo Clinic, *Cataract Surgery*, https://www.mayoclinic.org/tests-procedures/cataract-surgery/about/pac-20384765.

6. Michael Greenberg MD, *Medical malpractice and new devices: defining an elusive standard of care*, Health Matrix Clevel. 2009 Spring;19(2):423-45, p429.

7. Judicial Council of California Civil Jury Instructions (2018), No. 501, *Standard of Care for Health Care Professionals*, available at: https://www.courts.ca.gov/partners/documents/aci_2019_edition.pdf

8. Bathae Y, The artificial intelligence black box and the failure of intent and causation. *Harv J Law Technol.*2018;31(2):889-938. Google Scholar cited in https://journalofethics.ama-assn.org/article/are-current-tort-liability-doctrines-adequate-addressing-injury-caused-ai/2019-02.

9. 15 U.S.C. 6501, *et seq.*, 16 C.F.R. § 312.1 *et seq.*

10. *Id.*

11. 16 C.F.R. § 312.5.

12. *See, e.g.,* OCR FAQ: https://www.hhs.gov/hipaa/for-professionals/faq/2043/does-an-individuals-right-under-hipaa/index.html.

13. 45 C.F.R. § 164.501 (definition of "Designated record set").

14. *See* OCR FAQ: https://www.hhs.gov/hipaa/for-professionals/faq/2049/does-an-individual-have-a-right-under/index.html.

15. *Id.*

16. *See* OCR FAQ: https://www.hhs.gov/hipaa/for-professionals/faq/2066/if-an-individuals-physician-orders-a-test-from/index.html; https://www.hhs.gov/hipaa/for-professionals/faq/2048/does-an-individual-have-a-right-under-hipaa/index.html.

17. *See* OCR Press Release: https://www.hhs.gov/about/news/2019/09/09/ocr-settles-first-case-hipaa-right-access-initiative.html

18. *Id.*

19. Pub.L 110-233 (May 21, 2008).

20. *See*, e.g: California Genetic Information Nondiscrimination Act of 2011, S.B. 559 (Sept 6, 2011).

21. In April of 2018 Facebook CEO Mark Zuckerberg stated before Congress, Link: See 4h:53m "… we didn't take a broad enough view of our responsibility and that was a big mistake. And that was my mistake and I am sorry…. So now we have to go through all of our relationship with people and make sure that we are taking a broad enough view of our responsibility. It's not enough to just connect people we have to make sure that those connections are positive. It's not enough to just give people a voice, we need to ensure that people are not using it to harm other people or to spread misinformation. It's not enough just to give people control over their information, we need to make sure that the developers they share it with protect their information too. Across the board we have a responsibility to not just build tools but to make sure they are used for good…"

22. https://www.hhs.gov/hipaa/for-professionals/privacy/laws-regulations/combined-regulation-text/index.html

23. *See*: hhs.gov/sites/default/files/hipaa-privacy-rule-and-sharing-info-related-to-mental-health.pdf

24. Victorian Supreme Court case of *Kitson v Dennerstein* [2017] VSC 381, https://jade.io/article/535401. Read more: http://hospitalhealth. com.au/content/technology/article/my-health-is-shifting-the-control-paradigm-179464748#ixzz5xxxVgHVH

25. This framework is a component of the doctoral dissertation of Bianca Phillips and was drafted following a review of Australian law-making practices. The headings are not placed in any particular order. Note that additional considerations may be relevant in the USA.

Chapter 15:

Voice First Health Interview: Medical Documentation in the Voice First Era

Harjinder Sandhu, PhD

Teri Fisher, MSc, MD

Editor's Note

Physician burnout has been attributed to the EMR, medical documentation, clerical burden and increasingly more time spent interacting with the medical record. The patient-physician interaction needs to be preserved and patients expect their provider to listen to them and look at them during the medical encounter. It is well known that the EMR is a barrier that can negatively impact the patient-physician interaction. Dr. Harjinder Sandhu is the CEO of SayKara and took speech recognition to the next level and developed an app to capture the patient-physician conversation and insert the documentation into the EMR. Innovation in voice based technology and augmented AI solutions can improve accuracy in medical documentation and potentially transform the clinical encounter.

Hear the complete podcast interview with Harjinder Sandhuat at:
https://voicefirsthealth.com/42

Teri Fisher:

Dr. Harjinder Sandhu is the CEO of SayKara, a company that is tackling the issue of medical documentation. Can I get you to introduce yourself and let the listeners know a little about who you are?

Harjinder Sandhu:

Sure. So, I'm currently the CEO of SayKara, but I've been in the health IT, speech recognition / machine learning space for about 20 years. I started my career as a professor of computer science, taught at York University for a number of years and then co-founded a startup that was doing speech recognition for dictations, which 20 years ago was the predominant way that physicians would capture and document their notes. I sold that company to Nuance and I spent about five years as the VP and CTO for Nuance's Healthcare division. I've done another startup in between which was focused on patient engagement, and SayKara, which I founded about four years ago now has been focused on this problem of physician documentation.

Teri Fisher:

So as a physician, I'm happy that there are people like you that are doing this work because, as I've said a number of times before, I keep referring to being able to address that problem as the "Holy Grail" for physicians. Why do you feel that this is an important problem?

Harjinder Sandhu:

Having spent a lot of years in speech recognition, one of the things that I've been able to do is follow the trajectory of how the technology has evolved and how the user expectations and the user problems themselves have evolved ....and they've definitely evolved. So as I said long ago, physicians used to do dictation and generally they were happy with that. They would see a patient, walk out of the exam room, dictate onto a handheld recorder, and they're done with the documentation. Of course they have to review it later on, but they were generally happy with that process. What happened within the last decade when electronic medical records (EMR) started becoming popular is that physicians were basically being told, well, now you actually have to type directly into the EMR because we need data in the EMR. You can't just dictate, like you were doing before and create a note. You need to actually put the note into the EMR, into the proper places.

You need to put diagnoses in the right places, meds, allergies, orders, everything has to go into the right places in the EMR. And so now what you have is that physicians are spending an inordinate amount of time staring at screens. So there's a lot of studies that say they're spending two hours of screen time for every hour of patient time. And most of the time if you watch physicians these days, if you go and visit a doctor, you'll see a lot of the doctors are staring at the screen while they're trying to talk to patients. So their back or side is to the patient. They're typing, they're trying to listen to the patient and type at the same time. And it's a terrible experience for both the doctor and the patient, but they do what they have to do to get their notes completed.

The ones that aren't doing that during the encounter are spending their evenings doing this documentation and they're the ones that are actually suffering the most burnout because they're spending anywhere from two to four hours every evening closing their charts. And so, as I was watching this speech recognition technology evolve and seeing how the user problem was evolving into capturing just the narrative, which we used to do really well, to actually capturing data that goes into the right place in the EMR. I thought, well, this is, this is a grand problem. This is a really hard challenge. Nobody's figured this out yet and it's worth working on. So that's how I came into this space.

Teri Fisher:

As a clinician, I can really appreciate what you said. I'm certainly guilty of doing that. I recognize it's not the best patient experience when I'm looking at a screen and taking notes while I'm with a patient. But the reality is there's so much documentation that if I don't do that and I have to stay at the office, my family life suffers at home. And so, it's about trying to find that right balance. Can you describe a little bit about how your platform works?

Harjinder Sandhu:

Yeah. So what we started thinking about was to change the equation in terms of how speech recognition works. So the traditional speech recognition, if you use Dragon for example, is that you're looking at a screen and you're basically watching the words appear on the screen. You're pointing and clicking into the right boxes, first of all. And if you're doing any kind of point and click, which is menus or checkboxes and things, the speed recognition doesn't help you at all. So what we started building was a solution that you could sit and face the patient and not actually look at a screen.

So basically, what happens is the SayKara app runs on an iPhone or an iPad. You walk into an encounter, you select a patient, then you just set, you turn it on and you just sit and talk to the patient. And what the app does is it listens in the background. It's capturing the entire conversation. But what we typically tell the physicians is when you're talking to the patient, just make sure that you summarize or recap the important parts of that conversation. And what the system does is it's very good at listening for those little points of narration or summarization that the physicians are doing and it captures those and turns them into the note. If you say an order or you say a diagnosis, that will capture that and put that into the right place in the EMR.

So it's all about just making it a really convenient way for physicians to interact with their patients while the system is capturing the appropriate information, putting it into the right place in the EMR.

Teri Fisher

I'm curious what that looks like. Once the note is captured, does it come out in note form? Does it come out in a paragraph form? When I go to look up that chart note, say the next time that patient comes in, what am I actually seeing in the chart?

Harjinder Sandhu:

So, the note will look a lot like you wrote it yourself, except it'll be written a little differently, of course. But we create notes in narrative form. So we capture information as data, but we translate those into narrative form. So, you wouldn't be able to tell that note from a note written by another doctor.

Teri Fisher:

With this type of technology, it is very important to ensure that it's accurate. Somebody's health is on the line. How do you ensure that the AI is capturing what the physician is saying accurately?

Harjinder Sandhu:

That's a great question. In fact, that is the central question because capturing conversations, conversational information and translating that into the form of a note is a really, really difficult problem. In comparison speech recognition in retrospect seems trivial but back 20 years ago of course, it was a really difficult problem, but speech recognition is just about capturing words without necessarily understanding any meaning. It's just about predicting the next word and making sure that you understand the sounds that were generated and translating those into the appropriate words. What we're doing now is to listen in on a conversation and fully interpret that conversation.

And this is a really hard problem and it's a problem that takes time and a lot of data to actually solve adequately. So what we started putting in place right at the outset, we said, well, we don't have the data today to be able to solve this problem completely. What we need to do is we need to capture that data. The only way to capture that data is to actually create a service that physicians actually use. And so, we created this augmented AI solution. You can liken it to when people were building driverless vehicles. The first autonomous vehicles have people behind the wheel, and the people are making sure that the car is staying on the road, not running anybody over and is following the rules of the road. Over time the system is learning based on the feedback provided. It's adapting and improving - and that's exactly what we have done.

We have drivers behind the wheel effectively that are making sure that the AI does the appropriate interpretation so that the very first time the physician sees this note, the first time they use it, they're going to see an accurate note. It's going to be correct. They're going to see it in their EMR, in the right place, and they'll just sign off on it.

Teri Fisher:

That was actually my next question. When does the physician sign off on that note? Because the platform is listening to what I'm saying. It's being captured and being parsed and then presumably at some point I have to sign off on the note. How does that work?

Harjinder Sandhu:

Yeah, the sign off depends really on the physician and what level of service they signed up for. But you're right, it'll be after the encounter. It's not going to be immediate. They're not going to complete the encounter with the patient and just walk out right within a minute and sign it off because that review process, that human part of that process, is what takes time for us. And so, it'll be some time after that encounter that they'll have it available.

Teri Fisher:

Whenever I hear about this type of technology I get very excited because I can see the potential for freeing up a lot of my time, but also ultimately helping with patient care. Now, I know that you recently there was a press release about new features. Perhaps I can get you to explain what that was all about and why it's so important.

Harjinder Sandhu:

Sure. So, the new release is very much like what I described right now. What our first version did was much closer to the Alexa model, which is that you say a keyword. So if you're using Alexa, you're going to say "Alexa" every time you're going to issue an instruction. Now in our platform, we always understood that physicians needed to do long form interactions, not just simple one sentence kind of interactions. We would capture long form interactions, but we always required them to say a special phrase like "Okay Kara" as a preface to that so that the system knew to listen in on that particular point. And what we found was that when they're interacting with patients, this is very disruptive to that conversation with the patients. So if you are talking to the patient about their history, for example, and every once in a while you have to stop and say "OK Kara" and get it to listen in while you're continuing that conversation - you can do it, but it's disrupted the conversation. We spend a lot of time trying to figure out how to make this interaction, this dialogue, much more natural; listen in to the natural ways that physicians actually interact with patients as opposed to doing this with a disruptive form of listening. And so our new product allows us to capture these more natural interaction points rather than having a special word that we have to train the physicians to use.

Teri Fisher:

I can appreciate that if you're constantly talking to your assistant, that would take away from the patient interaction as well. Can you talk a little bit now about where you're at? Is it in beta now or what's the current status and how are people responding to this?

Harjinder Sandhu:

We've had a phenomenal response to it. We are in a number of large health systems. We've been live commercially for about a year and gradually growing our user base. Our user base has been a combination of physicians and large health systems, as well as small medical groups... entirely within the United States with no Canada deployments yet. The physician response has been phenomenal - and largely what physicians are saying is - particularly the ones that spend a lot of evening time doing their documentation – we take that evening time spent completing charts away entirely. We've had physicians actually tell us how life changing this is for them. In fact we have an Orthopedic Surgeon who said "I read books again for the first time in years because all my evenings before were spent doing documentation - and now I'm finding I have spare time, so I'm actually reading again".

We also hear that doctors who use Kara are spending more time with family and those kinds of things. For physicians that are doing a lot of their documentation during the course of the day we improve their productivity and generally they'll have more time to do other things, such as seeing patients. We have some physicians that choose to see more patients and some that don't want to see more patients but rather spend more time with the patients that they do see. That's entirely up to them. But for the ones that choose to see more patients, we've been able to see a dramatic increase in their patient volumes - for the ones that are motivated to do that.

Teri Fisher:

And what about patient feedback? Have you had a chance to get a sense of what the patients are feeling when their doctors are using this technology?

Harjinder Sandhu:

So, generally we hear anecdotally - as we don't talk to patients directly - from doctors is that their patients love it. And this is actually a point where a lot of physicians are tentative about this initially. They're not sure how their patients are going to react. What they generally find is that there are two things that happen in this process. One is that because our system forces the physicians to think out loud, they have to talk out loud, otherwise the system is not going to capture information. And because they're now talking out loud where they might have either been silently typing or they're kind of writing notes that they're going to type in later, they're actually saying things out loud and the patients love it. Actually, the patient reaction to that based on what the physician tells us is the patients really appreciate it when the physicians are saying things out loud as a recap of their understanding, their thinking process and their proposed next steps and plan of care.

That's one part. The other thing is that we've heard from physicians that they're making fewer mistakes. This was actually a surprise because I did not expect that when we were first thinking about this. But what's happening is because the physicians are saying a lot of their thought process out loud, one physician told me, that she is now getting corrected by a patient at least once a day since she started using Kara. And that's because I'm saying, for example "it sounds like you've been having this foot pain for the last week" and the patient might say, "no, no, I said it's about three weeks ago". And those kinds of corrections would never actually have been done before with the physician silently typing, and the patient never seeing what the doctor is typing in and they don't know if there's a translation issue. This is especially true for the physicians documenting later in the day. You know, your ability to recall is always going to be compromised by the fact that you saw 20 patients that day and you're now mixing up what patient said what.

Teri Fisher:

The whole idea of the patient correcting the physician is interesting. I can think of multiple times when that happens. It's just natural. Even sometimes you can miss a little word here or there. And if you do happen to recap your conversations, it makes a lot of sense. What's the future plan here? What are the next big goals or challenges that you're trying to tackle?

Harjinder Sandhu:

The big innovation for us, and this has been part of our overall mission from the beginning, is to build a system that is not just passively listening and capturing documentation but is a true Clinical Assistant. And what that means for us is that our system, we're teaching it not to just listen, but to actually predict and understand what's going to happen in that encounter. So if you have a patient that comes in for a shoulder injury, for example, our system is now beginning to understand what typically happens in the course of a shoulder injury encounter between a doctor and the patient. What is the information that the doctor wants to know? What is the physical exam, what are the likely assessments, plan, orders and so forth? And what we're now injecting into that process is - aside from this prediction where the system will always already be able to tell you, well we think you might do one of these two orders and if we got it right, go ahead and just say this order and it's done you don't have to relate all the details 'cause we have all the details 'cause we predicted them - but beyond that, injecting clinical guidelines into that process. So, if you're part of a health system that has specific guidelines around when a particular order should be performed or particular screenings that need to be completed, filling in care gaps, for example. So, we're trying to make the system smarter when it comes to clinical pathways and have it become an actual, as I said, Clinical Assistant. So, it's not just a dumb system that's trying to capture information and listen for words, but actually participating in the process and helping to transform the process of care too.

Teri Fisher:

Thanks so much for spending some time here on the podcast.

Harjinder Sandhu:

Thank you very much, Teri.

Chapter 16:

Voice First Health Interview: An Electronic Health Record Voice Assistant

Yaa Kumah-Crystal, MD, MPH

Dan Albert, MS

Teri Fisher, MSc, MD

Editor's Note

Transforming the patient provider experience and reducing physician burnout entails understanding how to leverage the electronic health record to synthesize patient information and make it relevant to the clinical encounter. VEVA, the Vanderbilt EHR Voice Assistant is a tool equipped with the Nuance NLP software and enables providers to launch the assistant in the exam room. The authors describe how this tool has been able to generate useful and focused patient summaries relevant to the clinical question and potentially to impact patient care. Challenges with HIPAA compliance and voice assistants are limitations that will need to be addressed.

Hear the complete podcast interview with Yaa Kumah-Crystal and Dan Albert at: https://voicefirsthealth.com/11

Teri Fisher:

Today we are speaking with Dr. Yaa Kumah-Crystal and Dan Albert, both from Vanderbilt University, about the Vanderbilt EHR Voice Assistant (VEVA). Yaa, could you please take a moment and introduce yourself first?

Yaa Kumah-Crystal:

Absolutely. I am a Pediatric Endocrinologist and a Biomedical Informaticist. I spend about 20% of my time seeing patients in the outpatient clinic and taking call. The remainder of my time is actually spent with the Biomedical Informatics Department and HealthIT, coming up with ways to improve physician workflow primarily through documentation and coming up with innovative strategies to solve problems.

Teri Fisher:

How about yourself, Dan?

Dan Albert:

I'm an associate director for our product development group in HealthIT. We do custom software and service development in partnership with the Department of Biomedical Informatics that Yaa represents. So we work on both operational and innovative efforts here at Vanderbilt.

Teri Fisher:

So let's talk about what you are working on, what it is, and why you decided to do this.

Yaa Kumah-Crystal:

Absolutely. The problem we're trying to solve is something that providers have been complaining about for a long time. This isn't unique to the EHR per se, but finding information and trying to build a patient story in a picture in your mind to help you understand what's important today and how you need to address the patient you're about to see has always been very challenging. I think it gets even more challenging with the EHR because it's so easy to gather and collect and amass information since you're not doing all the writing and using copy forward, etc. So foraging through the EHR to find the relevant components to build a summary in your mind has always been a challenge for me personally. So we were trying to leverage existing tools and things that exist in the consumer domain, like voice assistant to say, what if we could dynamically pull out the relevant parts of the patient's picture and have it spoken back in natural language to the provider to help them understand what's going on for the day?

Teri Fisher:

Now, this is obviously a very complex problem with lots of moving parts. There must be a lot of technology, a lot of natural language processing and understanding going on. Dan, when you first started to tackle this issue, what were the first big challenges that you encountered and how did you deal with them?

Dan Albert:

Yeah, good question. So actually, this is sort of the second phase of the project. The first phase was around just what you're talking about, then looking at the speech to text and text to speech and natural language processing tools that were available and doing some evaluations of tools from Amazon, Google, Microsoft, etc., and realizing that for this effort, partnering with Nuance made a lot of sense. Both because of their experience in the medical domain, the way they were able to deal with medical vocabulary, and most importantly because of their ability to support HIPAA content in a way that was compliant and safe. So that was for the first phase. Then also dealing with EHR integration issues so that once we had a partner that could help us interact with users and understand what they were asking for, we also of course needed to be able to figure out how to fulfill those requests from the EHR and present data in a way that was meaningful to users.

Teri Fisher:

So with where you are right now, how does it work? Can you explain what the the process is? What does a clinician do?

Yaa Kumah-Crystal:

So in order to use the voice assistant - it is named VEVA for the Vanderbilt EHR Voice Assistant - the provider is able to launch the assistant in the context of a patient. We use the Epic EHR at Vanderbilt, but we're actually building this tool out in a way that can eventually be EHR agnostic. But within Epic, within the context of the patient, you launch an interface window that has a simple microphone and a speaker, and a window that can present content back to you. You enable the microphone, and you ask a question such as tell me about this patient, or what was their height, or what was their last A1C? The language is processed through the Nuance NLP software. Then we do the fulfillment on our end to generate what we consider useful summaries for the provider to let them know the information they wanted within the relevant context of the patient. One of the things that we're really trying to make sure we do is make the summaries that come back as concise, yet useful as possible. So, for example, when a provider asks, what's this patient's weight? Certainly, they want to know how much the patient weighs. But what you really want to know is, are they gaining weight, or are they losing weight? Does this mean that they're getting better or worse? Is their weight considered normal for their age or not? And these are the kinds of things we try to pull together to give a summary back to say, Mr. Jone's weight is currently 65 kilograms. He has gained five kilograms since his last encounter with you two months ago. And that just gives you a little more context to understand the bigger picture.

Teri Fisher:

How are you determining what information the assistant should provide to you? How do you make that decision?

Yaa Kumah-Crystal:

What is the useful information that the average clinician wants to know? That is what we're working to figure out right now. So to start off with, in terms of the skills that we're building, we're really just going for the low hanging fruit and things that are already well-structured and well-defined in the EHR. And also by looking at clinical notes that people write and things that people are communicating to each other, we can extrapolate and say, well, someone made an effort to write this in a clinical note, therefore this is something that would be considered useful to communicate to another person. But actually, during the next few months, we're going to be doing usability studies with our providers. We will go through the skills that we've created and the summaries we've generated and have them give us feedback about, how useful is this for you? What's missing here? What's extra here and actually does not provide value to you in your decision making?

Teri Fisher:

That makes sense. One of the issues with voice technology is it's a linear type of interaction. Dan, do you want to comment on that and the challenges that provides in this context?

Dan Albert:

Yeah, that's a great point. We certainly don't anticipate some sort of solution where providers will always want to use voice for every interaction with the EHR. It's an additional modality as an option. So even now with our initial solution in prototype, we've got the ability for example, to say either tell me about this patient, or show about this patient, and 'tell me' means speak the information out loud and displayed on the screen. 'Show me' means just show it on the screen. So you can imagine somebody talking to the system while also navigating through various screens simultaneously. And furthermore, to extend the point Yaa was making, the goal is to be able to have really parsimonious interactions that result in contextually sensitive information that's summarized really well. And that's very rich.

Teri Fisher:

So I'm trying to imagine myself using this voice assistant. And for me the first thing that I would do when I see I've got a particular patient on my schedule is I'd want to go into the chart and have a quick review and refresh my memory of what are the issues, what are the active problems that we need to deal with. And so if I were using the system, what would I do? How would I interact with it, and what's the kind of response that I would get to obtain that first overview when I'm opening the chart?

Yaa Kumah-Crystal:

One of the first components of the things we tried to tackle was a general summary, just exactly as you described, orienting the provider to who this patient is to you and what the problem you're trying to solve for them today might be. So the summary that we have right now pulls general demographics, like Sally is a 12 year old female here for follow up for tonsillitis. All those things we're able to pull directly from the chart. One of the strategies that we're using is whenever we can, we tried to make a reference call so that, again, this information could be more generalizable and is not tied just to the EHR that you have. Then we'll give information about the last visit they had with you at the last visit they had within the system. So you can say, well, they're here for this right now, last time they were here for so-and-so, and then maybe another appointment they have upcoming. Right now the use cases we're building out - because I'm an endocrinologist and I think diabetes is the most important disease in the world - is to satisfy the use case of a patient with diabetes. From that we can generalize to other diseases once we can justify that this workflow actually makes sense. So, it tells you what the patient's A1C is, and we're building skills to tell you what health maintenance they're due for based on how long they've had the condition and what other things have currently been satisfied.

Teri Fisher:

What is the feedback you're getting when people try out this voice assistant?

Yaa Kumah-Crystal:

It's been really positive, actually. And I think it's kind of a running theme with other folks who've used any kind of voice technology. With Siri or Alexa or Google, when it works, it's magical. You're like, wow, I can't believe we're here with technology. This is futuristic! If it doesn't work, it is beyond a fail, you know? And what's interesting about interacting with voice technology is when there's a lag or a lack of a response, it's equivalent to someone giving you a dumb stare when you ask them a question. It's one thing when you're typing something into a computer, and there's that spinning wheel, there's that lag. We already have this expectation with technology we interact with, that it will behave like that sometimes. Because voice is so new and voice is so inherently human and natural and part of what we do, there are just these preset expectations of how something should respond to you when you use voice. So if there's ever a disruption, then people become more than disappointed. So what we're trying to make sure of is that we have the platform as tight as possible so that people are getting the responses they expect.

Teri Fisher:

Now Dan, obviously you've designed this so that you can get information out of the chart. Are there plans to be able to actually control the EHR and for example, do things like I need a requisition printed? Is that in the roadmap or have you done that?

Dan Albert:

Yeah, absolutely. It's in the roadmap. We always want to do things in an iterative fashion here. And so our first iteration is really about getting information from the chart and trying to be really smart about that in a way that actually helps providers and makes their day better. But we want to get good at that and get some experience with that under our belt with significant usage and so forth before we really take the next step into writing orders and doing things that are going to directly change the patient's care.

Teri Fisher:

What's the deal with HIPAA compliance and your voice assistant in it's current state?

Yaa Kumah-Crystal:

I'll start and I'll let Dan speak towards the majority of it. As he mentioned in the beginning, we were evaluating a lot of different platforms and we met with a lot of representatives from these different companies, including IBM and Microsoft and Google and Amazon. So we tried to find out what would make sense and which of these platforms could best support these interactions we were trying to build. Time and again, we found that the biggest limitation was that they didn't have a way to protect PHI, which is obviously a very important thing in the work that we do. But it was always on their "roadmap," and I mean any of these companies will tell you that this is something they're going to try to achieve. But getting to that place certainly takes a lot of work and a lot of bureaucracy. When we had the discussion with Nuance we were very happy to find out that they were actually already building out a platform that could support that infrastructure because again, this is kind of in the body of work they already do, live medical dictations and translations and transcriptions.

Teri Fisher:

Anything to add to that, Dan?

Dan Albert:

Well, yes, that's exactly right. So Nuance is using Azure and they're using a HIPAA compliant instance of Azure for storage. And then, of course, we have our own internal infrastructure that's part of this project as well. And, of course, that's been HIPAA compliant for a long time.

Teri Fisher:

Now, as you said previously, the idea is to eventually build this out to other EHRs. Can you comment a little more on that in terms of the challenges to do that?

Yaa Kumah-Crystal:

Yes. I'll let Dan take the first whack at this. This has definitely been one of the more challenging things we've experienced.

Dan Albert:

Yeah, that's right. So even with a leading vendor like Epic - they've heavily invested in FHIR and so forth - but even they're not everything that we need access to. So we're doing what we can to get information using standards like FHIR. And that gives us a big head start. But the reality is that right now as things mature, there are still data elements that we need to get through custom API calls and so forth. So those kinds of things would have to be tweaked to go to another EHR. But we're getting a big head start using the standards.

Yaa Kumah-Crystal:

Absolutely. And for things like labs, etc. you have to very well define the element that you want to pull out, like within Epic, they have an interface where you can type in the lab you want. And it already has groupings of labs. So if you say sodium, it will show you different kinds of sodiums. But now we have to do the work of identifying every specific LOINC code for every sodium that could possibly exist so that when someone asks for a sodium we don't give them a null response back just because we didn't have that LOINC code in place. So that definitely adds to the complexity because the pre curation has not been done already and we're essentially doing that.

Teri Fisher:

Now that you're building this out and you're trying it out, what do you feel is the biggest impact that this has had on your practice?

Yaa Kumah-Crystal:

I think the biggest impact for me is just being able to have the information summarized back in a way that is useful and in a way that's more natural where I'm not having to put the pieces together myself. I use the prototype when preparing for patients, mostly for the summary, mostly for the weight trends and things like that. Being able to naturally ask for something that you need and getting the information back allows me to do more multitasking at the same time. It takes it to a different level of interaction with the EHR where I'm not just typing all the time to try to find the things I need, but as if I were interacting with another colleague or a student. I could just ask naturally, which is something that we do anyway as people; we asked for the things we need. That's just been a more satisfying experience for me.

Teri Fisher:

I have another follow-up question on that. So when you're using this system in front of a patient, what is the patient's impression of this?

Yaa Kumah-Crystal:

I've shown the prototype to a few of my patients and they get really excited. Specifically, I'll show them the things like the height trend and the weight trend. And they're really like, wow, I didn't know we could do these kinds of things yet - when it works. I had one time where we had kind of a lag but when we were able to get the response fulfilled, then they were very happy with the way it looked. And one of the things that we're really hoping that this interaction provides regarding the patient-provider interaction is to free up the doctor from being tied to the screened computer and allow them to call out things they want, and ask for information they need without having to stare at the screen. You can spend their time and energy engaging with the patient as if you had a scribe in the room and you said, when's their next appointment with me? Cause you're trying to figure out with them when the next time they should come back to get a blood draw or something. You would just want to ask the EHR that and have it look that up for you versus having to go to the computer yourself. And this is an interaction that we hope to be able to fulfill for the providers.

Teri Fisher:

Dan, where do you see the future going in terms of this voice technology, these types of assistants, and the computer science behind this?

Dan Albert:

Great question. So I think that the more we're able to do with really using context in a smart way and predicting what people want, the more useful this will be. And I think that we're just sort of at the beginning of the curve here and the tip of the iceberg in terms of what this kind of interface will provide. So I think it's going to become naturally a larger and larger part of our interactions. And, hopefully, as you said, not only will it allow us to get data but also to place orders and otherwise interact with patients and then in fact also be part of the patient's interaction with their own chart through patient portals and so forth.

Teri Fisher:

Thanks to both of you for spending some time here.

Yaa Kumah-Crystal:

And thank you getting the message out to folks about these new interaction modalities in health and how they really have the potential to impact patient care.

Chapter 17:

The Power of Voice in Western Medical Education

Neel C. Desai, BS, MD

Taylor Brana, DO

Editor's Note

Medicine has a long history of educating the next generation of healthcare providers through the old adage of "see one, do one, teach one." The "teach one" component is most often accomplished by using our voices to explain an idea, concept, or procedure. In fact, using our voices to transfer medical knowledge, "the oral tradition," goes back as long as medicine has been practised to the time of Hippocrates in the 5th century B.C. History seems to have a way of imitating itself, and in this case the transfer of medical knowledge through humans speaking to one another is now being imitated by computers speaking to us. Voice technology is the next frontier in medical education. In this chapter, Drs. Desai and Brana take us on a journey through the history of medical education from the 5th century B.C. to today, and explain why and how voice technology is impacting the next generation of healthcare learners.

In order to understand where medical education is heading, it is important to understand it's foundations. This chapter begins by briefly exploring the historical roots of medical education and then will proceed to discuss current technologies and future implications of voice technology.

Ancient Greece - 5th Century B.C.

Most scholars cite the age of Hippocrates as the most likely origin of western medicine. The Hippocratic Oath, the oath which newly minted physicians take to serve their patients, was named after the Greek physician. Hippocratic medical teaching consisted of the use of observation and reasoning skills to discuss various disease processes. Rational questioning based on observations of patients led to further interpretation, discussion, and learning. "The oral tradition", often referred to in medicine, can find it's origins from the teachings of Hippocrates and his methods during this time period.

Western Medicine - Middle Ages (Starting in the 5th century)

The rise of Christianity during the Middle Ages evolved medical education. Christianity's focus on protection and care of the sick provided a cultural foundation and ethos to impact the larger population. Institutions were being built to not only care for the sick, but further propagate opportunities for physicians to observe, study, discuss, compare, and contrast with colleagues. However, most medical training during this era was done as an apprenticeship. The middle ages provided an environmental training ground for further knowledge and innovation to progress.

Salerno, Italy - 9th-11th Century

The apprenticeship model of medical education continued in Salerno, Italy, but it is here a resemblance of modern day medical schools started to take shape. The systematization of knowledge and a series of health tenets were formulated during this time. A form of registration to practice medicine, approved by the Holy Roman emperor Frederick II, was also created.

The evolution of medicine was not confined to the Christian world. During this time medical education was also thriving in the Muslim world. Cities such as Cairo and Baghdad saw medicine and medical education thrive. This gave rise to universities not just in Italy, but all over Western Europe, from Cracow, to Paris, and to Oxford. This marked a major transition in medical education history, as many teachers of medicine were lured away from hospital life to the status, prestige, and opportunities of university professorships and lectureships. Subsequently, the focus of medical education transitioned from studying sick persons to theories about disease. This could be referred to as the 'sage on a stage' model where practicing physicians were now lecturing to peers and larger audiences in large lecture halls.

London, England - 16th Century

The Royal College of Physicians of London was established in 1518, largely due to the efforts of Thomas Linacre. This system established the need for examination of medical practitioners and elevating the standards and accountability for medical practices.

Concurrently, the discovery of circulation by William Harvey (a future fellow of the Royal College of Physicians) was the impetus for a major change in medical education as well. The circulation concept altered the paradigm of the current medical theories and doctrine of the time which led to even more theoretical work and discovery.

Western Medicine - 17-18th Century

Hospitals were a key element evolving during this period. Hospitals were previously dwelling places of the poor and diseased, maintained by mostly charity. During this time, additional private and public funding transformed the hospital into a well-equipped, well-staffed, efficient facility available to the entire community.

The hospital became the training ground during the 17th and 18th centuries with a focus on clinical education and observation. Students would utilize their senses of sight, hearing, and touch to learn disease processes. European medical education slowly began to evolve into more modern day models whereby natural science, knowledge, and understanding was applied to actual care for patients. Systematic study of basic sciences such as anatomy, botany, chemistry was considered the basis of medicine and emphasized. A key element to recognize during this time is that hospitals mirrored the commonly associated bed-side training seen in modern day times.

Western Medicine - mid-19th Century

During the mid-19th century an ordered pattern of science-oriented teaching was established. This is where the traditional medical curriculum seen in the majority of Western medical schools started. This era marked the standardization of medical education.

The passage of the Medical Act of 1858 in Britain became a landmark event in British medicine, and offered a new direction in medical education. The Medical Act established the General Medical Council, a body controlling admission to the medical register. The General Medical Council also shaped medical education and had a strong influence on medical examinations.

Further interests in medicine during this era were fostered by various medical discoveries. Louis Pasteur's microbiology concepts, Joseph Lister's applications of Pasteur's concepts in surgery, Rudolf Virchow's pathological studies, and Robert Koch's works in cellular pathology and bacteriology can be traced to this era.

United States - late-19th Century

Medical education in late century America was influenced greatly by the 1893 Johns Hopkins Medical School in Baltimore, Maryland. The school only admitted college graduates with a year's training in the natural sciences. The medical school's clinical work excelled due to the partnership with The Johns Hopkins Hospital, founded expressly for teaching and research by medical faculty.

United States - early 20th Century

One of the greatest impacts on American medical education in the 20th Century was from a report published in the Carnegie Foundation for the Advancement of Teaching. It was written by the medical educator Abraham Flexner in 1910. In the report, Flexner argued medical education was a form of education, as opposed to some obscure process of initiation or apprenticeship. To further his view, he promoted the structures of full time working academic staff, each with their own department. Each faculty member was to be dedicated to their subject of specialty, and teaching students their chosen subjects. The Flexner report also called for laboratories, libraries, teaching rooms, as well as ready access to a large hospital. The report urged having a hospital administration to reflect the academic staff's influence. This model formed the basis of the modern day teaching hospital. The execution of concepts laid out in the Flexner report improved medical education between 1913 and 1929, in part through a combination of efforts by the General Education Board, the Rockefeller Foundation, and a large number of private donors.

United States - late 20th Century

As medical education progressed throughout the 20th Century, clear patterns emerged. Medical education integrated a thorough understanding of scientific and theoretical knowledge, combined with clinical experiential knowledge. This gave rise to the four stages of modern day medical education: pre-medical, medical, postgraduate, and continuing medical education.

Premedical education occurs during college and university years, most often involves requisites for medical school admission, as well as standardized testing like the Medical College Admission Test (MCAT). This time is also considered the preclinical years for future physicians.

The second stage of medical education, medical, encompasses the years during medical school. Medical schools in the US involve a four-year curriculum (whereas it is not uncommon to have a five-year curriculum in Britain). The first two years focus on the basic sciences of the human body and include subjects such as gross anatomy, histology, embryology, physiology, biochemistry, and pharmacology. Third and fourth years of medical school generally involve rotating through various core specialties in hospital settings. Core specialties include internal medicine, general surgery, pediatrics, psychiatry, and obstetrics/gynecology. Elective rotations are also integrated into a medical student's clinical training years. The clinical years are a medical student's first exposure to being part of a healthcare team in caring for patients in the hospital setting.

The third and fourth stages of medical education are postgraduate and continued medical education. At this stage a medical student has progressed to internship, residency, and board specialized certification. Upon completing residency, which ranges generally from three to six years (with possible additional fellowship training), the resident must then pass a specialty board examination to become a fully licensed and specialized physician. The completion of this phase leads the physician to ongoing clinical practice with patients and continuing medical education with recertification as necessary.

United States - 21st Century Medical Education

As previously discussed, traditional medical education has revolved around didactic lectures, clinical clerkships, research, and time spent in various labs. This traditionally involved professors lecturing in front of a chalkboard or whiteboard. Students would take notes using pen and paper. They would take standardized tests using a number 2 pencil, filling in multiple choice bubbles on answer sheets. The answer sheets would then be scanned and scored electronically by computers. This was true for the majority of the second half of the 20th Century. Yet with the internet and evolving technology, everything has changed.

The modern day internet and technology of the 21st Century has changed how medical students learn and take exams. It has also changed how medical educators teach students. Today's 21st century classroom still consists of the traditional whiteboard and chalkboard, but there also has been an emergence of various technological tools. Most classrooms are taught in lecture halls with large projector screens and digital presentation slides with access to large internet audio, text, and video databases.

Standardized exams such as the MCAT, USMLE (United States Medical Licensing Exam), and COMLEX (Comprehensive Osteopathic Medical Licensing Examination) today are now computer based, as are routine medical school exams. Accordingly, there has been a proliferation of digital medical education platforms. This wide host of platforms includes digital flash cards, online videos, social media accounts, live streaming lectures, and online question banks. The above tools are taught utilizing screen-first based formats.

The second half of the last decade has also seen a rise in audio content. Podcasts and audiobooks have emerged as a new medium to consume personalized continuing medical education. Students today can now listen to attending physicians, residents, and fellow medical students discuss the latest research on an area of interest while exercising, preparing a meal, driving, and on demand. Podcasts and audiobooks are free passive audio content and allow students to save time. Whereas podcasts are passive content, a new interactive medium is budding in the next iteration of digital medical education formats: Voice.

A New Future: The Power of Voice

In reflecting on the evolution of medicine, there are themes that can be seen throughout the past. Most significantly, the oral tradition which encompasses teaching from trainer to trainee. Utilizing voice has always been at the core of medical education. Voice of teacher to student has been a method of communicating and passing down important generational, experiential, scientific, and clinical knowledge to trainees.

Technology evolving to voice-assistant platforms is taking medical education to the 21st century and beyond. Voice-first as opposed to screen-first technology is part of and will continue to be a part of the emerging future. Current technologies will first be discussed.

Voice-assistants are now one of the central pieces of technology being developed. Companies such as Amazon Alexa, Google Home, Samsung Bixby, etc.., are proliferating throughout the world. These devices can listen to language, understand language, and respond with an appropriate answer. Due to this technology, the landscape of medicine has already begun to shift.

Considering a space where technology will be utilized at its highest capacity, one can imagine a future where voice will be intimately involved. The intimacy of voice can be seen in the earliest moment of every human that is born. The first thing a child hears, even before birth, is their mother's voice. The voice passes on content, familiarity, emotion, indicators of safety, etc.... to tell the baby information and context about the outside world. It is in the same way that one will utilize voice technology to provide important contextual information about current knowledge and emerging knowledge about the landscape of our medical world.

In this new era of technological advance all areas of life will be simplified, connected, interactive, and integrated. Routines and tasks will be simplified to an incredible degree. Simple day morning routines will be highly impacted as one example. Individuals will wake up with the voice, or alarm sound of their preference. They will be able to customize information and data that comes to them in the morning in an order of preference. They can stay in a rested position and begin to assimilate important contextual information about the world. They can learn new innovations, ideas, and commentary about their area of interest without even leaving bed or opening their eyes. Those who would like to learn and grow in this day and age will have the ability to prime their knowledge base at a capacity greater than ever before.

Tasks such as turning on the light, faucet, shower, etc. can and will be controlled with voice. Customizations in the bed room such as mattress angle, light color, water temperature and flow rate, and floor temperature, will be controlled via voice. Learning about one's morning schedule, important tasks, expected weather, travel time, recommended dress, and suggestions for one's day will be provided via voice. The routine system will be advanced enough to know dietary preferences such as a preferred morning beverage, temperature, size of beverage container, and will be prepared prior to entering the kitchen.

Objects at all areas of life will be voice-enabled allowing one to take control of different technologies throughout the day. For example, voice activation of the vehicle will allow the car to turn on, arrive, and have a preferred destination selected prior to leaving the front door. Given a world in which this type of technology exists, education will clearly be impacted and changed.

The future of medical education with voice will be changed in a variety of settings, from the lecture hall to the operating room. In terms of lecture series, medical educators will have the opportunity to record their lessons on multiple platforms including video, audio, and voice. Educators and students alike will be able to create question sets and study tools while utilizing interactive voice question and answer tools. Students will be able to be active outside of the classroom and still test themselves in an interactive way by utilizing voice technology.

Examples of Current Use Cases:

Current software and platforms have already been developed to impact areas such as public health, age-specific health, disease-specific health, pharmacology, general medical information, medical education, and data extraction technology.

Current use cases for general medical education include the WebMD Alexa skill which allows users to ask questions about symptoms, possible treatments, definitions of medical terms, conditions, drugs, nutrition, and side effects. The Mayo Clinic has also produced a skill on Alexa called Mayo Clinic First Aid. This skill allows users to ask questions in regards to any general medical issue.

Some early medical education use cases involve the voice platform providing most of the verbal content and having the user input basic verbal input such as "A" or "1" to answer multiple choice questions. Medical education use cases include the Medical Terminology Quiz Skill, which allows a student to hear a random medical term and the user identifies the correct definition. MedFlashGo is a voice-based interactive flashcard set for USMLE and COMLEX boards examinations. This skill offers multiple choice and short answer questions for medical students to test their knowledge and it offers in-skill purchasing.

An additional layer to voice is in clinical settings. Voice or data extraction software will be a highly sought out and utilized technology, given its implications for patient care efficiency and documentation. One of the most difficult areas of physician and health professional care is documentation as it is an area of excessive time consumption. Documentation across all health professionals takes a significant amount of time and energy away from essential patient care. Voice extraction technology will listen to clinician-patient encounters and intelligently extract important data to be utilized for documentation purposes. The data extraction technology will allow the clinician to perform necessary medical tasks without the additional burden of needing to document all of the information. The opportunity will still be available for clinicians to edit and correct the information as necessary through voice and manual editing.

A use case for this is Suki.ai, a digital assistant which intelligently listens to conversations and extracts vocal data. This technology removes the friction of needing to write documentation while providing patient care. It additionally lets clinicians call up important data such as the problem list and medications. It can even start the process of prescribing medications. This platform utilizes voice extraction while keeping data HIPAA compliant.

Potential Use Cases

In the operating room, surgical teams require check lists in order to maintain surgical safety standards. This includes data such as patient name, type of procedure, location of procedure, medical issues, allergies, etc. Vocal technology will allow the ease of documentation and confirmation in the surgical room. Upon a surgeon or staff member utilizing a tool, an individual will be able to verbally state the tool they are using and technology will document this with a time stamp. Findings can be discussed in real time with a digital assistant, documenting this as it is being seen. Additionally, surgeons may prefer a specific type of song or ambience in the room, which also can be voice controlled. Being able to document findings in the operating room will save critical time and allow surgeons even more additional time for patient and self care. Allowing the surgeon or health professionals to control their environment will also save valuable time.

Post-operative or procedural care is another area that can be impacted by voice technology. After a procedure it can be overwhelming for the patient and family to remember important information for the patient. Specifically, for the patient, it can be difficult to remember post-operative care instructions when they have just undergone anesthesia. Voice education around common questions or information that a patient might require will be helpful days after the procedure when the patient is home. An example of this is with the knee arthroscopy post-op Alexa skill that answers patient's common questions around post-operative care for knee arthroscopies. Having this information readily available days after the procedure can be a powerful learning tool to reduce unnecessary errors in post-op care, while simultaneously saving physicians time from answering common questions.

Discharge summaries and discharge instructions may also be an area impacted by voice in the future. As technology improves to allow for HIPAA compliance, a personalized text and voice set of instructions may improve follow-up care and allow the patient to ask technology questions about discharge care utilizing just their voice.

Scheduling is another important area to consider with voice technology. Calendars can be easily synchronized. A health professional can call up their schedule utilizing their voice. As this technology develops, patients and health professionals will be able to schedule visits with their voice. For example, if a patient is only available on Thursdays, the voice technology will be able to synchronize calendars and assess the next Thursday available on the clinician's schedule. The voice technology will be able to provide the patient with options of times and dates. The patient then can select the one which is most convenient.

Voice will also have an impact on general patient medical education at home. Most patients forget most of the information they hear in the exam room. Voice technology will allow the patient to have access to their treatment plan, medication, list, and care instructions at home. While patients are often handed sheets of paper to be a part of their care, these are often thrown away, misplaced, or unable to be found. Voice technology will allow another layer of centralizing information, by creating HIPAA compliant easily accessible, personalized care whereby the patient has access to it at home. This will save the healthcare team time, energy, and resources. It will also reduce unnecessary phone calls and improve patient care.

Public health is an area that could be impacted by voice. One hypothetical example would be for the CDC to create a flash briefing for public outbreaks. A notification could be sent to a voice device. Information would be read to the public as well as provide common answers to questions a user may have. Examples of current public health information skills are the Mayo Clinic First Aid Skill and Flu Doctor Skill. These skills provide information on common diagnosis, treatment, and basic information about First Aid, the flu, and flu vaccine, respectively. These public health information voice platforms provide the general population with basic education around health topics.

Increased accessibility for those with disabilities is important to consider with the future of voice and medical education. Individuals with disabilities, particularly the blind, cognitively impaired, and physically impaired can have improved education through voice. The blind or visually impaired, who may have more difficulty getting access to their physician or care information, would be able to access scheduling, physician information, medical information, and personal data via voice. Instead of requiring additional assistance, this population may regain their autonomy and ability to access information through voice.

Another area to consider are vocal biomarkers and how this may improve medical education. Information such as cadence, tone, pitch, volume, and other parameters are known as vocal biomarkers. These biomarkers can trace the individual's normal speech patterns versus the speech patterns they are currently exhibiting. This would be of note in voice education as an area of interest as biomarkers may assess an individual's understanding or confidence of educational material when being tested or learning health information. The voice applications in the future may be able to accurately assess if an individual truly understands the information they are learning or if they lack confidence. Clinicians may better be able to assess their teach back methods of important clinical information to see if the patient or student actually understands the information they were given.

Gamification is an important area to consider. Gamification is the practice of taking any form of testing or educational experience and making it entertaining, fun, achievement-based, or competitive for users. In terms of medical education, this can be a powerful incentivizing tool to allow students to learn in a fun and enjoyable way. Medical education of the future may include more opportunities for students and clinicians to gain even more knowledge as voice technology will make the experience of learning more fun. Flashcard sets or testing platforms will have sound effects, digital prizes, and additional feedback to provide extrinsic reward to a field which has traditionally had only intrinsic value.

Gamification can also be an effective tool for patients to be incentivized to follow treatment plans, lose weight, form community, adopt healthier habits and develop new lifestyle formations. Voice education platforms will utilize these achievements with other community members to adopt healthier habits.

One should also consider multiple modality or "multimodal" experiences. Multimodal include the availability of screen and touch into voice platforms. Multimodal experience will allow patients and clinicians to call up important information and data while also having access to buttons on screen, expanding and contracting images, scrolling through different tabs of information, etc. This is important as it provides another layer of creativity and interactivity to programs which will also utilize voice. For example, an application for anatomical landmarks may allow the user to zoom in and out of different anatomy while simultaneously allowing the user to call up a specific anatomical landmark utilizing their voice. This additional interactivity improves the speed of learning and accessing information. This is important to note as saving time allows clinicians, students, and patients more efficient access to important information. Multimodal experiences in and of itself can provide an entirely additional layer of creative platforms to create innovative landscapes for medical education. Multimodal will provide the gateway to the next layer of education and will be a complete immersion virtual and digital training.

Voice will impact medical education as it will be a part of the evolution of digital information in the virtual reality and augmented reality space. A total immersive experience in virtual reality or clinical simulations will require voice responses to provide accurate and important information in scenarios at the correct time, in the correct place. Clinical training includes needing to appropriately assess, interpret, and provide decision making within time constraints. The combination of voice technology with emerging virtual reality and augmented reality concepts will create the medical education of the future. While it is not the scope of this chapter to discuss all the implications and possibilities of this technology it is important to note that voice will be an important aspect of this technology to create an immersive experience.

Benefits of Voice

There are many benefits of utilizing voice technology for medical education. The following is a list of direct benefits that voice can provide to medical education: 1. Increased time 2. Increased knowledge 3. Personalized educational experience 4. Health 5. Confidence 6. Financial

Voice technology saves students time by providing opportunities for students to learn when their hands are busy or when they are completing tasks which do not require deep cognitive processing. Examples of this include walking outside, exercising, driving, doing laundry, etc. At times when one is moving throughout their day, it can be an opportunity for ambient voice technology to be utilized to learn. This then increases the students time, as they may assimilate more information during gaps of time which were not available to be productive.

Voice platforms provide a database of knowledge which can be extracted by the student. Questions, facts, stories, etc., can be uploaded via a database and allows the students to learn that database over time. Utilizing a call and response format, the student is able to test their knowledge and accurately assess if they actually know the information. This will enhance the student's knowledge and improve their ability to perform on exams and clinical situations.

Voice platforms provide an additional tool in a student's arsenal to study. This tool is something that can be applied to a student's schedule in gaps of time when it was not possible before to study. For example, most students will spend time at the library or at home doing work in front of a computer, reading, or taking notes for hours on end because they feel guilty or stressed needing to get through information. With the incorporation of voice technology, students can now add in time to separate their studies into different areas or moments where they can still be productive, but don't necessarily have to be inside the home. The students can better personalize their day and studies to incorporate more events, connections, and activities which include the consumption and study of information.

Students are also provided additional self-directed learning by utilizing voice. They can utilize the study methods that are best for them, as opposed to being required to learn information in a modality that is not their preferred learning style. However, the learning style that is always present in medical education is oral, given that important information and events are often transmitted via health professionals and patient's speaking to one another.

There are numerous health benefits to the incorporation of voice technology for medical education. First, digital fatigue is an issue that arises across many professional careers and industries. The constant use of screen technology causes eye strain and eventually mental fatigue. The use of screens over time causes individuals to drift from screen to screen never having normal face time and connection with individuals. Voice will reduce digital fatigue by providing an educational opportunity which doesn't require the user to focus their eyes on a screen.

Voice allows users to be physically active and on the move while learning information. An interactive question set or content stream alongside physical movement allows individuals to naturally multi-task while taking care of their physical health. Walking, running, etc., can all be done with the utilization of voice and let an individual have a more fluid and natural day of content consumption on the individual's terms. Additionally, consider the postural implications of having individuals have more opportunities to stand, walk, and move as they study which can reduce anatomical inefficiencies, atrophy, and strain on the body which occur with prolonged time in specific positions such as sitting in a chair.

Voice may have the opportunity to connect individuals in new ways as technology continues to develop. Educational platforms may incorporate interactive voice technology to connect students in new ways not thought of previously. Additionally, the decreased need for screen time can allow students to spend more time with each other, friends, and family members.

Students can often feel lack of confidence when it comes to their ability to perform on medical examinations or on clinical rotations. Voice platforms provide an additional benefit of improving student confidence by testing students without the added pressures of the social dynamic and hierarchical components of medical training. "PIMPing" is an often used term on clinical rotation which means "Put In My Place". This has been reduced in many clinical sites, however being able to test oneself in a verbal fashion without the additional social pressure may improve student confidence. As students are able to complete questions and answer them correctly on voice-interactive platforms, they will be better able to trust their knowledge base in clinical rotations and beyond.

Possible financial savings may occur due to the use of voice interactive technology on an individual and population level. If voice platforms are created to enhance studying through a variety of settings, there may be a reduced need to purchase expensive study tools, books, and additional materials. If performance is improved, students will be able to pass the exams on their initial try and not need to take additional coursework or examinations.

On a population level, voice provides another layer of information transfer which can reduce the amount of physical waste needed for educational material. This also implies possible environmental impact as well as voice technology develops and becomes more ubiquitous.

Limitations of Voice

Limitations of current voice technology are also important to note. Limitations include: 1. Credibility 2. Nuances/cultural context 3. Overuse and inappropriate use 4. Distraction 5. Privacy 6. Accessibility 7. Learning curve/education/adoption 8. Internet Connection/Infrastructure issues

Information that is being provided from databases needs to come from reputable or trusted resources and professionals. If information is being learned from sources that are not reputable, this can have deleterious effects on those who are utilizing the information. This is a limitation because not always will it be easy to discern where information is coming from. It will be important for students to check information as they learn it to make sure that the information is accurate. A way to circumvent these issues will be to utilize opportunities such as leaving a review online to either appreciate the resource or let others know that the resource has issues or faults. Providing feedback to the creators will also be beneficial, as it may be possible that the resource is mostly factual with a few minor mistakes. However, with medical education, there is a possibility that the population listening will not have enough knowledge to discern accurate medical information versus inaccurate information. This is an area where medical professionals can aid again by reviewing materials to check that information the population is hearing is accurate.

An area that makes voice difficult in some respects will be how the devices translate the input of the individual asking a question or making a statement. There will be times when the user will make a statement and the device will translate it inaccurately. This will be frustrating for the user who was looking for a specific set of data and receives another. When situations like this occur, it will remove the benefits of this technology.

Additionally, individuals who have heavy accents or speech impediments may have a more difficult time enunciating or speaking words in a way the device can understand. In these scenarios again it will be frustrating to the user. As Voice develops and the technology becomes more accurate, more and more dialects and speech variations will be incorporated. This will limit the mistakes voice technology will make. Additionally, artificial intelligence learning will likely help the devices learn one's personal speech and vocal patterns, which will likely aid in decreasing errors in the technology.

Cultural context will also be important as different terminology may be used in different regions and areas of the world. For example, a medical term commonly used in the United States may not be utilized in a different English speaking region like the United Kingdom. As voice technology spreads globally, region specific considerations will need to be accounted for in order to reduce cultural contextual error.

There is a common expression, "Give a man a hammer, and everything looks like a nail." While voice has many benefits, it may not be the correct data gathering resource for all situations. For example, if a student wants to learn about a particular disease that may be a public taboo, it may be socially embarrassing to use vocal technology. For example, one could imagine how comical or embarrassing it may be for someone to say the word "diarrhea" or "herpes" in public. Additionally, crowded areas where one must make vocal commands may be difficult to do if the surrounding environment is loud. The need for some level of space and quiet will be required. Situational awareness will be paramount.

Voice enables users to multi-task, which can be time efficient, however it can also direct attention to the voice platform and remove critical attention. This is especially important when individuals are operating heavy machinery, driving, exercising (such as bicycling, walking, etc.) and may reduce environmental awareness. This can pose a risk to the users and others around them. A consideration should be taken to utilize voice at times when it is environmental and situational factors are not a concern. For example, it may be more appropriate to use Voice when there is heavy traffic, or a clear highway as opposed to driving in an unknown or unfamiliar area with multiple drivers and distractions. Another consideration is when Voice device wake words are triggered accidentally. During these times the device may speak or provide information which is unnecessary and frustrating to the user. This can also lead to further distraction and reduce valuable time.

Data that the user generates from using voice platforms can be saved and used by the creator of the platform. The user should exercise discretion when speaking to the device and using the platform. There may instances when the user is speaking and unintentionally says a phrase that the device did not intend. For example, an individual may be called on the phone to discuss a personal matter while using a device, and the device captures some of that sensitive information. Platforms may record in text format the received data, and this may be seen by the creators of the platform. This should be specifically addressed in the platforms' privacy policy as to reduce the risk of transmitting unintended data. Security considerations should be accounted for situations when one does not want their data public. For example, if an individual has done questions on a platform, but does not want to let others know the statistics of their performance, it would be helpful for that individual to secure that information. As platforms progress, voice detection software may be able to differentiate who is speaking, and this may mitigate the transfer of secure data.

As voice technology is new, the relative accessibility is variable by region, as well as with culture and socioeconomic status. While platforms can be developed, it is important to consider the availability of the software, and who will actually use the technology. While it may be helpful to design a program to educate a developing country's population, the country will likely not have access to the Internet, which limits voice technology applications in these regions.

Disability will also be an important consideration. Individuals with speech impediments, vocal cord injuries, strokes and/or related neurological disorders, will have an alteration in their ability to speak. This will limit their access to the technology. Additionally, those who are hearing impaired or who have complete hearing loss will not be able to hear responses. Understanding this limitation is important and the use of multimodal experiences which include as many senses as possible will minimize the impact to this population in regards to voice technology. Developmental delay or cognitively impaired individuals may also have difficulty utilizing the technology due to speech or hearing deficits, or inability to understand the technology. These individuals will likely require assistance to perform tasks utilizing voice.

Technology adoption will change over time and will increase as it improves and becomes mainstream. A limitation of educational platforms will be the overall acceptance and use of the culture/region. Overcoming barriers and misconceptions about the technology will help to increase adoption. Creators and students alike will need to be aware of the limits of users on platforms and how this may vary as adoption and trends change over time.

Educating populations on voice will be a useful strategy to amplify voice technology. Methods include online and social media marketing, attending conferences, text materials, podcasting, blogs, and word of mouth discussion about voice. As more and more communities utilize the technology, it will become more ubiquitous and practical.

Another consideration is the traditional learning curve which is a barrier of any technology. It takes time to understand the device and the variety of associated applications it can have. Every user will have a variable amount of time necessary to learn the technology based on their relative experience and comfort level with general technology.

Voice hinges on the ability for the technology to have access to internet and proper wireless connection. In areas where this is not available or the connectivity is poor, the platforms will suffer in performance. While the technology may be useful it may also provide a frustrating or difficult experience if connection is poor. The infrastructure of the community or area is important to consider when marketing or creating a technology where internet connection may not be available or of poor quality.

Considerations for Creators

The goal of creating medical education platforms on voice is to ultimately provide an enriching, delightful, fun, and educational experience to students. While the platform may look and feel different based upon its context and parameters, the following principles will often apply. Please consider the following: 1. Content 2. Engagement and sustainability 3. Gamification 4. Fun and Delightful experiences 5. Freemium model 6. Cost 7. Sonic Branding 8. Marketing 9. Developing Trust 10. Keywords

Content is the most important aspect of any platform. If the content is poorly written, inaccurate, or verbose, users will not use the platform. It is important to generate a database of useful content that students will want to use. If the content is accurate but poorly written, the experience will not be enjoyable and as such there will be no retention of use.

Content must be engaging in order for students to use the technology. When an individual utilizes the technology, that individual is providing their time and energy. If an individual feels that the content is not engaging enough, that individual will not return. Engaging content includes informative content which is delivered in an interesting, entertaining, or delightful way. While strong content may initially attract a student, creating engaging content will create return uses to the platform.

Strong content and engaging content will bring students onto the platform, and create retention. However, gamifying the experience will elevate the platform even higher. Gamification is the simple principle that by applying achievements, points, ranking, competition, etc., to the platform it will feel more like a game rather than an obligation or duty. The gamification of the experience allows the student to feel that the material is fun and provides extrinsic reward to a traditionally solely intrinsic field. This may allow the student to stay on the platform longer and learn greater information over time. The possibility of rankings and playful competition embedded into platforms adds an additional incentive for individuals to learn more and use the technology more.

If the student is having fun while using the voice platform, they are more likely to use it again. Creating an experience that is fun for the student provides positive psychological reinforcement for them to return. Strong content which is fun and engaging will not only retain students but entice them to tell friends to join as well. Word of mouth engagement is a key indicator of the platform being effective, useful, and will be required for more global adoption.

The freemium model suggests that students will utilize a platform if they first are able to receive free content and develop trust with the platform. It is only after the student has utilized the technology over time, that they may be apt to purchase additional features or content from the model. This is important to note as creators will require funding in order to maintain their platforms. If the platform is completely free, creators will need to consider where they will be receiving funding to maintain the platform.

Cost is an important consideration of developing voice platforms. At the current time, there are multiple ways to design voice software online for free. However, the upkeep, maintenance, and continued generation of content will require time. As most individuals do not have unlimited time, it will be important to consider the amount of funds necessary to develop content, and review content and performance of the platform. Prices vary from company to company as to the generation of the initial platform as well as upkeep. Additionally, if the platform will have high levels of mp3 and/or additional media content, there may be an associated data fee charged by the supporting parent voice technology company.

Sonic branding is defined as the overall feeling, emotion, and experience that the sound profile creates on a voice platform. The sound pallet is a distinct set of sounds utilized by the brand in order to create a consistently recognizable experience that students will know. Just as large companies and corporations have a distinct logo a voice platform requires a distinct set of sounds. The importance of consistent and familiar sounds cannot be understated as this helps propagate a voice platform.

Effectively marketing a voice platform will require the use of current marketing channels as well as creative and innovative ways to promote the platform. Current channels includes social media, e-mail, podcasts, blogs, conferences, networking, and word of mouth. Given that the medium of voice is not visible, it is important to create complementary channels to direct attention to the voice ecosystem. Given that voice is in an audio format, the most likely channels that would attract individuals to voice-interactive platforms will likely be podcasts, audiobooks, and flash briefings. The above tools serve as funnels to bring students into the voice ecosystem and platform.

The concept around a user staying for longer periods of time and promoting a brand is through developing trust. If a user has limited awareness, it will take time for them to build trust. A student will first need to develop an awareness around the technology prior to using it, and then it may take more time for them to tell others about the brand. The above marketing channels will need to be used to attract a student onto the voice platform and then bring them further into the platform ecosystem. It is only through the development of trust that one can use voice education platforms to their maximal levels and garner support.

Keywords are very important to utilize properly with the creation of a skill. A voice skills name and keywords must make intuitive sense as the platform is not visible or seen. One must think of the words that a student would use to search for a particular medical topic. The earlier one creates the platform, the better, as there are only a select few ways to ask for a particular idea in voice. Creators should consider their keywords to ensure that the platform is discoverable via voice and other marketing strategies. The name should be memorable, easy, and as simple as possible for effectiveness.

Considerations for Students

Students utilizing voice platforms will become better students if they consider the following: 1. Supplementation 2. Effective use 3. Utilization of additional time 4. Choosing effective sources

Voice platforms are a supplement to medical study and are not a replacement at this time for traditional medical study. Information in the classroom and clinical setting are the primary learning tools to develop an effective and robust understanding of medicine. Voice platforms are a way to supplement gaps of knowledge and reinforce current understanding of medical topics. If the tool is used correctly it can promote retention and improved confidence of medical knowledge. At a future time, the technology may be more immersed in clinical scenarios and in medical schools, however at the given time the knowledge is supplementary.

Voice platforms are used in a way that allow students to save time by studying in areas and times that were unavailable before. This includes what has been previously described, including travel and commute times, as well as being outside or at home, or in a variety of environments. Utilizing the technology to add additional content throughout the day will increase a student's capacity to learn more in less time. Effective use includes developing routines during the morning, after class, and at night. Developing routines to utilize the technology will allow one to increase their knowledge at natural times of the day where one does not normally or could not have normally studied previously. Developing habits around study will maximize the effectiveness of the time-saving effect of this technology.

The implications of increased amount of time to study allows a student to have more free time. It is recommended that students use this time for self-care, exercise, connecting with peers and family members, and rest. Voice has the opportunity to be a novel approach to reduce burnout, depression, and anxiety. However, if students utilize the technology to fill up all of their time, they may experience increased fatigue, and potentially cause deleterious symptoms. Discretion should be utilized in order to maximize the supplementary effects of voice platforms without increasing harm to the student.

As with any source, students should use discretion of which platforms they download and use. Strong tools utilize credible resources and are transparent about what the product is, it's mission, the contributors with the proper credentials, etc. Students should choose resources that are created by professionals and should test the material that is right for them. Some students may prefer a more gamified experience, while others may want direct content without additional sound effects or achievements.

Conclusion

Voice-first technology provides a new and emerging interface that will impact medical education. Students, clinicians, and patients should be aware of the current use cases and possible use cases. The implications of this technology are vast and potentially very powerful. There are many benefits, limitations, and considerations to be aware of in the creation and consumption of voice technology.

Sources:

https://www.theatlantic.com/magazine/archive/1910/06/medical-education-in-america/306088/

https://www.britannica.com/science/medical-education

Chapter 18:

Voice First Health Interview: Voice Technology for Educational Simulations

Michelle Wan

Teri Fisher, MSc, MD

Editor's Note

In the previous chapter, we had the opportunity to learn about the history of medical education and how voice technology is having an impact on educating the next generation of healthcare providers. In this chapter we learn about a specific use case - using an Amazon Alexa skill to help nursing students simulate real-life patient scenarios. This interview with Michelle Wan is about her experience as a student at the British Columbia Institute of Technology, where she created a multimodal Alexa skill to help nursing students practise their clinical skills in the simulation lab. This is a great example of how voice first technology can take medical education to the next level. As you read this chapter, imagine similar educational use cases that can leverage voice technology.

Hear the complete podcast interview with Michelle Wan at:
https://voicefirsthealth.com/18

Teri Fisher:

Michelle Wan is a Computer Systems Technology student at the British Columbia Institute of Technology (BCIT). I had the opportunity to see a demonstration of an Alexa skill that she has been working on in collaboration with the BCIT nursing department to support educational experiences for nursing students in their simulation lab. The idea behind it is the nursing students are able to ask Alexa for pertinent information in about simulated patients.

Michelle, could you start off by telling us a little bit about your background?

Michelle Wan:

Sure thing, Teri. My name is Michelle Wan and I am a Computer Systems Technology student at the British Columbia Institute of technology. I'm in my final year and have a specialty in cloud computing.

Teri Fisher:

Please tell us a little bit about how you got into the voice first space?

Michelle Wan:

Well Teri, I'm currently studying Cloud Computing and my instructor Bill Klug recommended an Alexa skills workshop that was happening. So I went there and learned a lot about Alexa skill development. That was the starting point of me getting into voice first programs with Alexa.

Teri Fisher:

And so what was your impression when you first started learning about Alexa? What did you think of the technology?

Michelle Wan:

I loved how interacting with Alexa was simple and intuitive. Developing Alexa skills required a whole new thinking of how to design programs compared to traditional GUI first applications. I liked learning good design practices so that the Alexa skill I made could be easy for people to interact with.

Teri Fisher:

So then you started talking with Bill Klug, your instructor, and you started working on the skill that we're going to talk about. Before we get into the details of the skill, how did the idea come about?

Michelle Wan:

At BCIT we have nursing students that go through lab scenarios every single day. Each of these lab scenarios contained blood tests and diagnostic reports that would all be stored on paper. The School of Health Sciences wanted a way to manage all the charts in one central space. They also wanted a way for students to access the lab information hands free so they could focus on taking care of their patients during the labs. The Alexa Lab simulation skill that we built allows students to interact with Alexa as if it is a nursing assistant. Students can ask for blood tests or diagnostic results of the patient and use that information to make decisions. Alexa would also display the results on a screen so the students can refer to the visual charts as well.

Teri Fisher:

So if I'm understanding you correctly, this skill is to be used by the nursing students at BCIT in their simulation lab where they're learning nursing skills and they need some way to access data on demand when they're working with simulated patients. Is that correct?

Michelle Wan:

Yes. That helps the students with developing their communication skills. In a real life scenario, another nurse would be in charge of handling the paper charts. So this way, the student has the ability to ask Alexa for particular charts as needed. Usually at school when you sit with a science lab assignment, all the information you need to complete the task is in this piece of paper in your hands. However, by asking Alexa for the charts, this allows students to practice their thought process for when they see patients. For example, a student may think, "I see this patient, what do I need to look at first?". Depending on what they think is most important, they will ask Alexa for the information and the skill will allow them to practice making those decisions.

Teri Fisher:

And this was done in partnership with some faculty in the nursing department as well. Who is it that you're working with from nursing?

Michelle Wan:

Rob Kruger. He is the one who had the idea of bringing this Alexa technology into the nursing simulation lab.

Teri Fisher:

Could you please tell us a little bit about what the skill actually does. How does this work?

Michelle Wan:

So you start up the skill, and you ask Alexa about a particular patient. Alexa would then ask, "Would you like the blood tests or diagnostic reports?" You would tell Alexa your choice, and then Alexa would read out and display the results on the screen.

Teri Fisher:

So I'm trying to imagine this in action. There's a nursing student, they're working in the simulation lab, and they're practicing a scenario on a dummy simulated patient. And at some point they realize, oh, in order to continue on with my simulation or this scenario, I need some lab tests. And that's when they turn to Alexa and they initiate the skill.

Michelle Wan:

Yes, correct.

Teri Fisher:

You mentioned that there are lab tests and diagnostic reports. Can you be a little more specific? What sort of information is included in each of those?

Michelle Wan:

I don't study health sciences, so just a disclaimer. Lab tests contain lists of blood tests for the patient. For example, for hematology, the results would have white blood cell count, hemoglobin values, and more. For the diagnostic reports, Alexa displays radiology images and reports. Alexa shows the x-ray and reads out a summary of the report.

Teri Fisher:

So, for example, if there was an x-ray, you'd see the image on the screen and then there would be written report of what you're seeing in the x-ray as well. Are you aware of any other educational institutions that are using this type of technology right now in their simulation labs for nursing or otherwise for educational purposes?

Michelle Wan:

Not that I'm aware of. This is pretty cutting edge technology.

Teri Fisher:

I know that you had a chance to go and present this information at a number of conferences. Where have you been able to present this?

Michelle Wan:

Yeah. I went to Calgary where I presented this Alexa skill to an audience of critical care nurses. They were really excited when they heard about this. I also did a presentation in Halifax at the Canadian Celebration of Women in Computing conference. This was more of a technical presentation and I spoke about how to develop Alexa skills using the Lab simulation skill as an example.

Teri Fisher:

And what was the response there at that conference?

Michelle Wan:

Both conferences had a different type of audience, but they both really enjoyed the presentations.

Teri Fisher:

Now I understand you've got your Alexa device next to you. Are you able to give us a short little demo of how it would work?

Michelle Wan:

Yeah, sure thing. Alexa, open lab results.

Alexa:

Welcome to the lab results skill. Use this skill to obtain a patient's blood work or diagnostic reports. How can I help you?

Michelle Wan:

Get me patient one.

Alexa:

Thanks. I have found the results for patient number one. Simon from January 22nd, 2018. Is this correct?

Michelle Wan:

Yes.

Alexa:

Would you like a blood test or a diagnostic report?

Michelle Wan:

Diagnostic.

Alexa:

What type of diagnostic tests would you like?

Michelle Wan:

Radiology.

Alexa:

Technically difficult exam done by portable. Good expansion. Normal size heart. Aortic arch and mediastinal structures normal. There is a significant amount of diffuse infiltrates noted. Dx: Pulmonary edema.

Michelle Wan:

So you can't see it, but Alexa displayed a picture of an x-ray along with that summary that she was just explaining.

Teri Fisher:

And for the medical professionals that are listening to this, they'll recognize that that was a description of a chest X-ray. How did you find actually developing the skill? Were there certain things that you found more challenging? Was it an easy thing for you to do as a computer science student?

Michelle Wan:

It was a bit of a learning curve for me. I didn't really have too much background on Alexa development prior to doing this, other than the workshop I attended. So I had to learn how to design the skill with a voice first approach while also making sure the content looked good on the screen. This project was really fun and a nice challenge to tackle.

Teri Fisher:

How long did it take you from the concept to having this at the stage that it is at now?

Michelle Wan:

I worked on this over the summer; 3 months, 15 hours a week.

Teri Fisher:

So if I've done my math right, that's about 180 hours. Michelle, congrats to you. Congrats to to your supervisors, Bill Klug and Rob Kruger and BCIT. Thanks for coming on the podcast.

Michelle Wan:

Well thank you Teri. It was a pleasure being here.

Chapter 19:

Voice Control of Medical Hardware

Ed Chung, MD

Editor's Note

Human help has been the norm in the healthcare environment for many years and has translated to increasing and unsustainable healthcare costs. Consider clinical scenarios where advanced voice - technology solutions encompassing natural language processing (NLP), natural language understanding (NLU) and speech related computing can transform the healthcare environment and how medical hardware has the potential to become voice-capable. The technological advances in voice tools with NLP/ NLU capabilities can in essence unburden the end user and positively impact patient care and provider efficiency and satisfaction.

The hand shortage problem

The use of voice to control medical hardware came about, much like many prior, humbler innovations, primarily because of need. Imagine a surgeon in the operating room, both hands sterile and gloved, actively cutting or tying or otherwise executing their craft. There will come times where the surgeon wants to do more - adjust the electrocautery settings, tweak the position of the bed, even change the music playing overhead - but the surgeon is unable to do so directly. Their hands are as good as locked away, isolated and occupied with more important tasks.

Consider an interventional cardiologist or radiologist mid-procedure. Like the surgeon, they are gloved and gowned. Like the surgeon, they only have two hands to bring to bear. And like the surgeon, the reach of those hands is limited. When it comes to documenting their actions, changing the imaging mode on an ultrasound machine, or silencing an alarming monitor, those hands might as well be in another time zone.

There are countless similar examples in the healthcare environment: the nurse rolling a patient, the medical assistant applying a blood pressure cuff, the ED physician doing a lumbar puncture. In all of these situations, there are two hands dedicated to a task, and none to spare for anything outside of that specific task.

Traditionally, healthcare workers have gotten around these human limitations primarily by enlisting the help of more humans. In this way the clinician extended their will through others, having the circulating nurse dial up the electrocautery settings or asking the anesthesiologist to give the bed a little bit of Trendelenburg. Even the patient themself gets involved at times, holding down a piece of gauze over a phlebotomy site while the phlebotomist unrolls and rips off a piece of tape to cover it.

Compounding this shortage of hands is the increasingly difficult economics of healthcare, especially in the United States. Costs, already high, are increasing unsustainably.1 Hospital care makes up roughly a third of total national health expenditures2, and of this portion, fully half is spent on labor costs.3 So any effort to control costs while preserving revenue will, almost by necessity, affect the count of hands available to a given organization, not to mention the demands on those hands. As a whole, the healthcare system is being asked to do more in less time and with fewer people.

In all of these scenarios, hands equate to the ability to manipulate the environment. Clinicians have long been limited in their ability to manipulate their environments by their complement of hands; all humans are allotted no more than two. And even as medical machines and technology have become more advanced and more powerful, increasing the scope of what's possible, each clinician still has a hard limit of what they can control with two hands.

In fact, it can be argued that advancements in technology have worsened the hand shortage problem. As medical devices have become increasingly capable and complex, so too have the user interfaces that drive them. A modern patient monitor has hundreds of functions and settings spread out over dozens of screens and menus. Accessing one of these commands can mean swiping past multiple screens followed by drilling down a menu or two, and that's if the path to the destination command is known. The command and function hunting that plagues the modern electronic health record is also an issue for today's medical hardware, and just as in EHRs, poor usability leads to more manual manipulation. In the same way that a poorly-designed task turns into a time-sink, medical hardware with poor usability becomes a "hand-sink". Stuck in a UI is, with very few exceptions, not where clinical hands ought to be.

What's more, healthcare economics and healthcare technology advancement have combined to exacerbate the technology usability problem. A prime example exists in echocardiography, where economics and labor force issues have pushed the responsibility of most echocardiogram acquisition to sonographers. Additionally, anesthesiologists have taken up some echocardiography duties in the operating room. As a result, operation of a cardiac ultrasound machine is now open to a larger array of users with a wider range of training backgrounds. At the same time, the expertise of use has been spread out and diluted in commensurate fashion. The net result is that the cardiac ultrasound machine, which is itself increasingly powerful and complex, needs to be usable to a wider range of users with a wider array of training, many of whom who have had less individual exposure to the device than in years past. This has made for some particularly difficult headwinds for UX engineers and designers.

Delving deeper into usability, the concept of memorability has been steadily diffusing from the design world into the healthcare space. A piece of medical technology has good memorability if a user, when returning to the technology after some time away from it, can quickly re-attain their former level of proficiency. The classic example here is the EHR, but this idea applies to all forms of medical hardware, as well. And just like general usability, memorability is also challenged by the modern healthcare environment. Clinicians often work in multiple healthcare institutions, each with its own unique technology environment, or in the common circumstance where mixed technology exists even within a single institution. Remembering how to use one piece of technology is difficult enough, but remembering how to use multiple pieces of the same kind of technology is even more difficult. Can the user remember that a particular function is accessed via this specific series of menus and button presses on one machine, while the same function on another brand of machine is accessed in a completely different place and in a completely different way?

For much of the last twenty years, this situation of advancing technology and worsening usability and memorability has just been something that healthcare workers have dealt with. Throw more people at the problem, or don't. Shift responsibilities, or just add them to an already full plate. Add more training and retraining, or just accept that schedules are already too tight and that training will always take a back seat to other responsibilities. Clinician burnout, once discussed mainly in academic circles, has become part of public discourse, with long treatments in mainstream newspapers and magazines.[4,5] Fortunately, while technology has arguably exacerbated many aspects of burnout, some relatively recent advancements in technology have shown promise in fighting for the good guys.

Now we're talking - the voice solution

Voice technology is one such technology category where enough advancements have been made in recent years to enable its broader use in healthcare. Voice transcription is a relatively mature and ubiquitous technology now, with transcription resources readily available to technology developers via any of a number of cloud computing environments. Within the healthcare environment specifically, products such as M*Modal's Fluency Direct and Nuance's Dragon Medical One allow clinicians to speak directly into a computer microphone and receive near-instant transcripts with a very high degree of accuracy. Even most phone transcription in healthcare, once solely the purview of human transcriptionists listening to cassette tapes, currently takes a first pass through a transcription engine.

Looking beyond the simple transcription use case, other speech-related technologies such as Natural Language Processing (NLP) and Natural Language Understanding (NLU) have also become more capable and more available. With these and other tools, technology developers have the ability to take a freeform utterance from an end user, break it down into speech elements, and extract meaning and intent. Additionally, the power of machine learning algorithms coupled with the massive amounts of computing power made available relatively recently through the cloud have allowed for speech-related computing to become both more robust and more widely available. The pace of development in this area is sure to remain brisk.

In addition to the technological advancements that have been made around voice, there's a simple mechanical advantage, as well. Up until now, voice has been an almost entirely unused resource when it comes to controlling and manipulating medical hardware. A clinician's hands have always had too many things to do, but the clinician's voice has been comparatively free and unencumbered. Simply speaking, hands are saturated, but there is a lot available headroom when it comes to voice.

On an even more mechanical level, command entry by hands is rate-limited by direct access to those commands - you can't click or tap on a command that's hiding in a drop-down menu or on another screen - or by typing speed. Voice actuation of commands has the power to essentially bypass a user interface, making even hidden, nested commands available potentially from any part of the UI. And while average typing speeds hover around 40 words per minute, speaking speeds typically range from 100-150 WPM. Voice presents a much faster and more efficient means of entering commands.

Perhaps most importantly, the addition of NLP/NLU to the mix allows for a uniquely powerful advantage of voice: the ability to infer intent from a freeform utterance. In current state, a hardware operator must determine what they wish to accomplish - their end goal - and then work out the individual steps and commands they must carry out in order to achieve that intent. This is cognitively demanding and requires detailed knowledge of the command library and UI for that particular piece of hardware. A particularly compelling example from the nursing world is illustrated below:[6]

The operator is essentially being forced to translate their intent into a specific machine/command language.

Consider as another example a nurse who wishes to change the upper alarm limit for heart rate on a patient monitor. That nurse has to take that end goal - changing the upper heart rate alarm limit - and then translate it into a series of actions - push this button, find that menu, scroll down to the intended value, confirm, etc. However, with NLP/NLU capabilities, that nurse can instead say, "Raise the upper heart rate limit to 120," and then software does the job of analyzing that utterance, inferring the desired intent, and translating that intent into the appropriate machine/command language. The cognitively burdensome steps are off-loaded from the nurse to a computer, and special machine/command knowledge is no longer needed. This ability to unburden the end user is perhaps the most powerful technical advantage brought to bear with voice control.

Table 1

Required steps for programming an NS infusion within the M/S drug library on the Alaris, Baxter, and Hospira Plum A+ IV smart pumps

Step	Sigma (SW Version v6.02.07)	Alaris (SW Version 9.19)	Plum A+ (SW Version 13.41.00.002)
1	Push "ON" button	Push "ON" button	Push "ON" button
2	New patient? Hit YES	New patient? Hit YES	New patient? Hit YES
3	Brings up library list, use arrow key to choose M/S library	Displays profile used last. Hit NO	Brings up library list, use arrow key to choose M/S library
4	OK	Brings up drug library list, select M/S library	ENTER
5	Enter IV	CONFIRM	Hit Arrow up "A"
6	Use arrow to scroll down to IV Fluids	Asks for patient ID, Hit EXIT	Arrow/Page down to IV Fluids
7	OK	Brings up list of available channels (up to 4), select channel	ENTER
8	Choose PRIMARY or SECONDARY	Chose from Guardrails drugs, Guardrails IV fluids, or basic, Chose IV FLUIDS	Enter RATE
9	OK	Select alphabet range that includes the letter "N"	Hit ARROW DOWN BUTTON
10	Enter RATE	Select the letter "N"	Enter VTBI
11	OK	Select NS	Hit START
12	Enter VTBI	Correct? Hit YES	
13	OK	Hit RATE ARROW KEY	
14	Confirm volume given as 0	Enter rate using keypad	
15	Hit RUN	Hit arrow key to chose VTBI	
16		Enter VTBI	
17		Hit START	

Abbreviations: IV, intravenous; M/S, medical-surgical; NS, normal saline; VTBI, volume to be infused.

The rapid ingress of voice technology into the healthcare space has benefited from the intrinsic advantages of voice technology mentioned above as well as consumer forces external to healthcare. Healthcare as an industry has historically been slow in terms of change and technology uptake. Perhaps because of this, technologies that have become mainstream and trusted, or at least sufficiently convenient, in the consumer space have often been pushed into healthcare by end users as opposed to being pulled in by health system initiatives. An obvious example of this phenomenon is smartphones. Few, if any, healthcare institutions foresaw the tremendous impact of smartphones and proactively set up systems to facilitate their use in healthcare environments. Rather, as personal smartphones caught on quickly in the consumer space and were brought by clinicians into the healthcare arena, healthcare institutions found themselves behind the ball and were forced to move reactively to accommodate, manage, and leverage these devices. The consumer space jumped first, and then healthcare had to move to catch up.

This same order of events is occurring with regards to voice as a control modality. Siri, Cortana, Google Assistant, Alexa - these technologies and others like them are rapidly diffusing into people's homes and everyday lives. With them, people can control their house lights, perform an Internet search, play music, and so much more. As people are discovering the utility of voice as a control modality and becoming more comfortable with it, voice control is quickly evolving from an interesting feature to an expectation. That expectation is now steadily being brought by clinician end users into the healthcare environment. Clinicians now know that their work can be improved through the addition of voice as a control modality. They know because they've done it at home. For better or for worse, the demand for voice control has been imported into the healthcare environment, and now it falls to healthcare-related technology and hardware companies to meet this demand.

The value proposition

The value proposition for voice control in the healthcare environment is potentially a strong and multifaceted one. Unfortunately the relative newness of the technology means that the body of research on specific benefits is essentially nonexistent. Still, the immediate avenues of value are clear.

Probably the lowest-hanging fruit comes in the form of procedural efficiency gains. When clinicians operating a piece of medical hardware no longer have to hunt in nested menus across multiple screens for specific commands, procedure time can go down. When a provider can utter a single phrase that triggers a complex string of commands that would otherwise have to be located and actuated individually and manually, the time savings add up quickly. This leaves more time for documentation, patient contact, or any number of other activities that were previously displaced. A provider can fit more procedures into a day for a direct financial benefit, or if they wish, go home to their families at a more reasonable hour.

The secondary, trickle-down benefits of procedural efficiency are numerous. Nurses can spend more time at the bedside. Providers can reduce their waiting lists. Clinician satisfaction rises, burnout falls. Patients, in addition to being happier with the added attention, also spend less time under anesthesia or getting irradiated. While attribution might get harder to assign the further one goes down the benefit chain, the impacts can be very real and very powerful.

In addition to a reduced time requirement, voice control also offers the potential benefit of requiring fewer people for some procedures. As noted previously, the historic answer to a need for more hands was to throw more people, and hence more hands, at the need. With a cardiologist needing to keep both their hands on a transesophageal ultrasound probe, a sonographer was often called upon to operate the actual ultrasound machine. With voice, however, a cardiologist has the means to control the ultrasound machine even with both hands otherwise occupied, obviating the need for that sonographer. These reduced staffing needs then translate to reduced cost for that organization.

Also along the lines of staffing, the increased ease of use afforded by voice control allows for procedural responsibility to trickle down to less trained and/or less costly staff while preserving quality. Again using the example of cardiac ultrasound, sonographers will be able to take on more imaging responsibilities while still ensuring that the images obtained are still of high quality.

Optimizing image quality or procedural quality presents some amount of cognitive burden to the user. Getting things right naturally requires a certain amount of thought and discernment. As mentioned earlier, the need to translate user intent into machine/command language also represents a significant cognitive burden. What's more, these two cognitive burdens are very distinct; positioning an ultrasound probe to obtain the best image of a 3D anatomical structure is entirely different from getting the ultrasound machine to do what you want it to do, for example. Typical procedural workflows demand, however, jumping back and forth between these two burdensome tasks, oftentimes frequently. This context switching becomes an additional cognitive drain in and of itself. Fortunately, when voice control enters the situation, the latter cognitive burden - that of controlling the machine - is lessened or even disappears completely. This then leads to the additive effect of reducing the cognitive burden of frequent context switching. Image-focused and procedure-focused workflows are then able to emerge, making way for improvements in quality while reducing operator fatigue.

While perhaps not as obvious as cognitive fatigue, physical fatigue can also be a consequence of working with modern medical hardware. Playing off of the earlier concept of poorly designed, highly complex UIs being "hand-sinks", this author proposes "reach" as an objective metric to measure procedural/workflow comfort and efficiency. Reach in this context can be defined as the percent of time during a procedure or workflow where one or more of a user's hands are positioned in unsupported extension while contemplating or manipulating the UI of a piece of medical hardware. High-reach workflows and procedures involve more manual interaction with the UI, which can reflect difficulty in navigation, excessive manual data entry, and/or user focus being pulled away from the core task. Reach correlates directly with operator fatigue and ought to be minimized. Improvements in user experience, whether through enabling voice control or other means, can be tracked by measuring reach before and after UX changes.

Lastly, but certainly not least, voice control is a potential player in the fight to reduce nosocomial infections - those infections that are acquired in a hospital or other healthcare facility. The role of clinicians' hands in the carriage and transmission of pathogens in the healthcare environment is well documented. Also well documented is the undesired role of medical hardware as depositories of pathogens.[7,8] While disinfection strategies - for hands and hardware alike - will always be of high importance in the fight against nosocomial infections, it's also clear that transmission of pathogens between patients, caregivers, and pathogen reservoirs will be reduced by minimizing touches where possible. Voice technology has a strong role to play here, as reducing the need for manual manipulation of a piece of hardware will naturally reduce the opportunity for pathogen contamination and transmission.

Historical and current efforts in voice control

Many of the earliest inroads of voice control into the medical environment have been direct imports of consumer technology and applications. The first example many health system CIOs cite is the presence of Amazon Alexa and similar devices in operating rooms and procedural suites solely for the purpose of playing music. Much like early adopters who integrated their personal smartphones into their clinical workflows, end users have brought consumer voice technology into the medical environment on their own. Many of those same aforementioned CIOs shudder at the security implications of having such devices in clinical areas, but that is a discussion that deserves its own special treatment.

Other examples of medical-hardware-adjacent voice control include the Aiva pilot at Cedars-Sinai[9], in which patients can control their TV and contact their nurses using an Amazon Echo. Northwell Health, based in New York, is taking a similar approach while also adding functionality that allows patients to review their own medical records.10 While these and many similar projects are making the news and demonstrating the level of interest in voice across the healthcare industry, it's important to note that none of these projects have involved the actuation of controls on a piece of medical hardware using voice. Thus far voice has enabled environmental control, communication with staff, and even EHR manipulation in some projects, but at this point in time, voice control of medical hardware has yet to develop to any substantial degree.

Robot-assisted surgery is perhaps the earliest field to have made explorations into voice control. The AESOP voice-controlled robotic endoscope holder, conceived as a way to provide surgeons with an extra hand, was tested in cadaveric sinus surgery in the early 2000s and even used on at least one live patient11, but when evaluated for convenience and time savings, results were mixed.12 Computer Motion, the American robotics company that made AESOP (as well as the ZEUS robotic surgical system) merged with its rival, Intuitive Surgical, in 2003. While AESOP is no longer on the market, Intuitive also performed some investigations into rudimentary voice control of its own da Vinci robotic surgery system as recently as 201113, but this work does not appear to have transitioned into production yet. Even more recently, a 2018 study focused on voice control of the Viky robotic camera positioner and its effect on laparoscopic prostatectomy demonstrated some time savings.14

Mindray, a global medical instrument developer based in Shenzhen, China, already has a point-of-care ultrasound product, the TE7, on the market with their proprietary iVocal voice command feature.15 Now in its second generation, iVocal enables simple voice commands on the machine with the goals of improving user ergonomics, enabling more focus on diagnostic quality, and facilitating use in sterile environments.

These few efforts, along with a noteworthy Alexa hack by Bob Paradiso16, seem to comprise the current state of publicly-known development with regards to voice control of medical hardware. That said, the patent literature is rich with filings in this arena. With end user demands and market forces being what they are, it will likely only be a matter of a couple years before the launch cadence of voice-controlled medical hardware ratchets up significantly.

Future directions and challenges

When looking at trends in voice control technology specifically, there are clear factors pushing development further in the direction of enhancing NLU-esque capabilities. For starters, when an operator is able to utter a freeform phrase expressing a command intent, such as, "Check BP every minute for ten minutes and then plot the results," a couple things happen. One is that the need for an operator to learn and remember a command library basically disappears. Consequently, usability and memorability improve markedly. Second, user interface woes, to a large degree, simply melt away. Instead of figuring out ways to cram a long list of commands into limited screen real estate, UX designers will be able to focus more on guiding and communicating with users. Training gets streamlined and focused on capabilities as opposed to "button-ology". UIs become assistants as opposed to barriers. This scenario is now within reach and is sure to be a focus of development.

Something else interesting happens when medical hardware becomes voice-capable. All of a sudden, all of these pieces of equipment - ultrasound machines, endoscopy towers, patient monitors, infusion pumps, beds, etc. - become versatile entry points for voice data. What's more, these data entry points can quickly outnumber computer terminals, and they also win in terms of proximity to the point of care. Instead of having to hunt for an open computer terminal to document findings or interventions after the fact, caregivers can do so in real time, hands free, using the voice-capable medical hardware that's already right next to them. Voice is an extremely valuable form and source of data, and it is this value that will continue to drive the capture of voice in as many physical spaces and as close to the point of care as possible. By adding voice capabilities to a piece of medical hardware, that hardware suddenly gains strategic value in the data-centric healthcare landscape of the future.

Voice control is not without its challenges, however. Voice commands are powerful and convenient, but how does a piece of medical hardware know from whom a voice command is originating? Having commands be triggered by unintended users would be problematic if not outright hazardous, especially in a healthcare context. To date, various techniques to identify a speaker through their speech have achieved accuracy rates of over 90%, but these rates fall quickly with the addition of background noise.[17] It is also likely impractical to collect and maintain an identification database of voice samples of all potential authorized users of a given piece of medical hardware. Given this, access to voice control will need to be limited for the near future either through physical access control - limiting access to the hardware itself - or a more manual form of user identification, such as a badge swipe.

Closely related to the user identification problem is the user isolation problem. Medical hardware frequently operates in noisy environments with multiple sources of speech in the vicinity. While having a smart speaker play the wrong song because of a noisy environment might be inconvenient and annoying, having a piece of medical hardware execute the wrong command could be dangerous. Microphone choice has an important role to play here, as certain microphone designs offer directionality and/or exhibit higher levels of dropoff with increasing distance. These choices must also be balanced against portability, if the microphone is intended to be carried on the user, or user mobility, if the microphone is intended to be stationary and the user mobile. Once captured, the voice signal can be further tuned with signal processing techniques, and while voice as a form of user identification might not yet be robust enough for clinical use, identifying other voices as being different from the intended command voice and ignoring them is a much more tractable problem. No matter the use case, strong consideration will have to be given to the means of audio capture and processing to ensure user isolation and voice accuracy.

The medical hardware industry exists right now in an interesting moment with regards to voice technology. Voice tools have become very powerful and broadly available. The value of voice data has created a gold rush to capture voice and control those data assets. The consumer market has created pressure on the medical industry to adapt voice capabilities. This heady confluence of factors has made for fertile ground for companies - from giant multinationals all the way down to small startups - to come in and create truly meaningful, even transformative, value. There are challenges, to be sure, and this is still early days, but the excitement around voice control of medical hardware is real for a reason. The near future is sure to be very exciting.

References

1. https://www.cms.gov/Research-Statistics-Data-and-Systems/ Statistics-Trends-and-Reports/NationalHealthExpendData/ Downloads/ForecastSummary.pdf

2. https://www.cms.gov/Research-Statistics-Data-and-Systems/ Statistics-Trends-and-Reports/NationalHealthExpendData/ Downloads/highlights.pdf

3. https://www.beckershospitalreview.com/finance/exposing-hidden-labor-costs-could-save-hospitals-millions-of-dollars-annually. html#close-olyticsmodal

4. https://www.theatlantic.com/health/archive/2018/05/the-burnout-crisis-in-health-care/559880/

5. https://www.newyorker.com/magazine/2018/11/12/why-doctors-hate-their-computers

6. https://www.ccnursing.theclinics.com/article/S0899-5885(18)30006-6/pdf

7. https://onlinelibrary.wiley.com/doi/pdf/10.1111/j.1365-2044.2009.05914.x

8. https://www.ncbi.nlm.nih.gov/pmc/articles/PMC4332272/

9. https://www.cedars-sinai.org/newsroom/cedars-sinai-taps-alexa-for-smart-hospital-room-pilot/

10. https://www.statnews.com/2019/02/06/voice-assistants-at-bedside-patient-care/

11. https://dx.doi.org/10.1055%2Fs-2006-939679

12. https://doi.org/10.1007/s00464-003-9200-z

13. https://pdfs.semanticscholar. org/9f4e/9cbe73a9f8a93955aa0d7b97c15a2fd5d6b5.pdf

14. https://dx.doi.org/10.5173%2Fceju.2018.1800

15. https://www.mindray.com/en/presscenter/iVocal_TE7%27s_ innovative_voice_command_function.html

16. https://bobparadiso.com/2018/03/22/amazon-echo-controlled-hill-rom-hospital-bed-in-hospital/

17. https://doi.org/10.1109/MCAS.2011.941079

Section 4

Voice Technology and the Future of Healthcare

Chapter 20:

Voice First Health Interview: Voice Applications with Dr. David Metcalf of METIL

David Metcalf, PhD

Teri Fisher, MSc, MD

Editor's Note

In this chapter Dr. Fisher interviews Dr. Metcalf on some of the past, present and future voice technology in health work the team is doing at UCF's Mixed Emerging Technology Integration Lab (METIL). We discuss the early work for Microsoft, our long history of designing audio tours, games and experiences for Smart Homes, Connected Vehicles and even recent efforts to create voice-enabled social companion robots (both 3D printed and holographic/Augmented reality versions) for the clinical setting. With a broad set of partners and sponsors, we have been able to explore some of the leading edge use cases and gather evidence on their effectiveness and patient/provider reactions. We end with a view toward the future - how can we combine the power of blockchain for privacy, trust, scale and efficiency with the ease of use and unique biometric signature of voice... stay tuned.

Hear the complete podcast interview with David Metcalf at:
https://voicefirsthealth.com/33

Teri Fisher:

Today I am joined by Dr. David Metcalf, who is the director of the Mixed Emerging Technology Integration Lab (METIL) at the University of Central Florida. He has a lab where they are experimenting, developing, and researching emerging technologies in healthcare, everything from voice to blockchain and we discuss all of this here on the podcast. Without any further ado, let's get right into it. David, let's start off with learning a little bit about you.

David Metcalf:

I run a research lab at the University of Central Florida. It's a technology development lab and it's at the Institute for Simulation & Training. The specific name is the Mixed Emerging Technology Integration Lab or METIL for short. We are involved in a lot of different emerging technology projects, a lot of things within the Internet of Things space, and particularly how you might make some of the interfaces for the public easier like using voice.

Teri Fisher:

How did you get into that? How did you decide to create such a lab?

David Metcalf:

Well, I'd always wanted to have a lab like that and I did for a while at NASA. I had the multimedia lab at Kennedy Space Center that was modeled after some of the labs that I really admired, like MIT's Media Lab and Nicholas Negroponte came and visited and really gave me some good tips and thought maybe we should do the same thing at UCF within that context of emerging technology. So after I spent a few years out in the corporate arena, after spinning off my NASA laboratory, I was able to come back to academia to try and help other young people do what I did early in life to create spinoffs and understand how to take some of this emerging technology and bring it out from the public sector to the private sector.

Teri Fisher:

And I know you've had a lot of success, a lot of great projects that have come out of the lab. Now as you said, we're here to talk about voice and how voice is going to, at least I think, revolutionize healthcare. Can you tell us a little about your thoughts in general about voice and why this is a compelling area at this time?

David Metcalf:

Well, with so many new capabilities of the smart speaker movement and the ability to have voice capabilities integrated into so many of the devices that surround us within the Internet of Things landscape, it's just a no brainer that this is going to make people's lives a little easier and be a more natural interface than some of the things we've asked people to do in the past with keyboards and mice 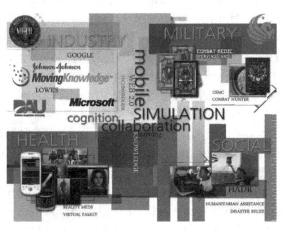 and other technologies. Even some of the wearables and some of the phones are not as easy to use as using your natural voice.

Teri Fisher:

Absolutely. So voice, as far as I'm concerned, is just like you said - the most natural way that we can communicate. So it only seems natural that that's the way the world is going. Now you're deeply involved with voice technology in your lab. I'd love to have you share some of the projects that you are working on and highlight some of those for our listeners.

David Metcalf:

Sure. Well our voice technology experience goes way back to almost the interactive voice response days using some of this technology with Microsoft's sales force to go and build out their whole learning capability. You could just say whatever product you wanted to hear about over the telephone and it would give you back the information that you wanted with natural language. And we've expanded upon that over the years as new technologies like Alexa has come on board and Siri and Cortana so that we have the ability to go in and build these different tool sets and apply them in new and unique ways. Some of the ways we've been able to apply them is in some of the most advanced intelligent homes for health across the world, in particular some of those here in Florida that we've helped build, like Lake Nona Medical City has their Wellness Home Built on Innovation and Technology, or WHIT for short. We did all of the Alexa integration work for that home to be able to go through the home and ask any question over the air and it will tell you about why there are blue lights for antimicrobial, or tell you about the medical devices or the telehealth devices that are found throughout the home, or give you sort of a concierge-based guided tour of the different health features of this unique home, as well as to control some of the things like the lighting or some of the ambient temperature or other environmental health controls that you might have throughout the home and home automation features. We even had one feature that we built in our lab that allows you to also control intelligent vehicles too. So you can have kind of full autonomous control and interactive control of some of the different features for health or for home automation throughout those types of environments.

Teri Fisher:

So the whole home is essentially set up for having this voice concierge?

Image courtesy of Lake Nona Institute

David Metcalf:

Yeah. We did this with a number of really interesting companies too. Of course we had baseline technology from companies like Cisco and GE. Then we also had some of the overlay of health data from Florida Blue and GuideWell, their parent company, our Blue Cross Blue Shield here in Florida and also Johnson & Johnson and Florida Hospital at the time, now AdventHealth, have all participated in this along with a number of other specialized groups like the sleep labs and others too. And this was all done for the Lake Nona Institute, which is a nonprofit that is trying to advance some of the state of the art in these areas.

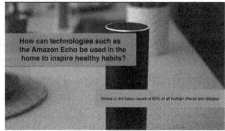

Image courtesy of Lake Nona Institute

We've also been able to do this in other communities like in North of Tampa, in Connected City, along with Florida Hospital, or now AdventHealth and Philips too. So combining some of these technologies has been really fun and interesting too because you get the different ecosystems that use the different standards-based protocols that are emerging like Hue, a network from Philips and some of the other capabilities. So that's been really fun to get to explore, not just one, but multiples of these intelligent homes, including the one at HIMSS that we do every year, which is called the iHome, found in the Intelligent Health Pavilion with Harry Pappas and other people that we know well. So that's been a lot of fun over the years, to do a road show-like tour of some of these advanced technologies and how voice is enabling them.

Teri Fisher:

And how do you think that type of scenario with these homes is going to play out in the general public? Do you think that this is the way our homes are going?

David Metcalf:

Yeah. I think that it doesn't require having a very expensive, intelligent home as a showcase to be able to use this technology. Some of these smart speakers are as low as $25 to $50. So they're, I think you've had the stats before too, they're the fastest growing market right now too, even faster than smartphones for technology enablement. So if you're looking at this, it doesn't have to cost millions of dollars. Some of this capability is even integrated into the smart phones so that you

Image courtesy of Intelligent Health Association

don't have to buy some new unique device. These are things that if you teach people just a few things about the capabilities or free apps that are out there too, like WebMD, to be able to ask questions just over the air and not have to do a complex search or to be able to go in and use HealthTap to get specific answers to questions. Those are some of the examples of easy to use tools that don't cost an arm and a leg and that should be available to everyone. It is very democratized and not something that is just for having an expensive home.

Teri Fisher:

I agree. I think we're starting to see that particularly with some of the elderly population, where it's easier for them to just speak than to have to use a device or a keyboard. I think we're going to be seeing a lot more of this as the months and years go by. Now, you have other projects as well that you've been involved with in your lab. Can you tell us a little bit about those?

David Metcalf:

Sure. Some of the projects we've been involved in have not just been in the home, but also in a clinical setting. We had the privilege of working with some really smart doctors in the cancer ward of Orlando Health, that's the

Orlando Health UF Cancer Center. They had this idea to put in place a social companion robot that would be able to converse with, and answer questions for, some of the people coming into the waiting room and into the exam rooms at their ward of the hospital. So the main use case for this was looking at some of the social history and having a cute little engaging robot, both a physical one that was 3D printed by one of our sister laboratories, and also a virtual one, which was sort of like a hologram of the robot that you could interact with by voice. So you could say, "Hi, Betty" and Betty would start talking to you and maybe tell you a little joke and ask you if you'd like to get some of your forms filled out in advance and ask you a few questions or guide you right into the visual interface of the electronic health record, whichever was most convenient for you. So after some study they saw some of the benefits of using this social companion robot in terms of people feeling more comfortable answering frankly, some delicate questions about past drug use or sexual history or some of those types of things. There's been years of study showing that people are more comfortable telling either a machine, or in this case a robot, about this because there's no judgment. A human you might tell this to and they're going to look at you maybe a little funnier. You'd be nervous that they might think differently about you based on the answers that you give to some of these more delicate questions. So they were finding they were getting better data and maybe in some of those past studies more honest answers that help with determinants of health that are going to be outcomes of having that social history and that data. So those are some other examples of clinical settings of voice that have been interesting to our team.

Teri Fisher:

That's really interesting. The whole idea of a person being more forthcoming with a robot - I find that fascinating. Are there certain strategies that you use in the way that the robot asks the questions to encourage the person to divulge some of this information?

David Metcalf:

Yeah, there was a team of psychologists that really did their homework on what works to engage people and make them feel a little bit more at ease too. So we had a nice, very pleasant female voice that was recorded and expressed a lot of emotion and empathy within the speech patterns and also told little, cutesy jokes to disarm the person a little bit too, so that it was not a threatening situation. So a lot of the things that you would choose to do about the patterns and use of voice and speech are going to be really important to get right. If it was just a mechanized, computerized voice and felt very cold and sterile, that may not have the same effect as something that felt a little bit warmer and engaging.

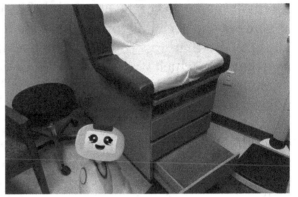

Image courtesy of Consystent AI

Teri Fisher:

And so what's the status with Betty and that type of robot right now? Is that being expanded? Is it being rolled out to hospitals?

David Metcalf:

Yeah, it's being expanded right now. There's a program called the Foundry X at Orlando Health that their foundation has sponsored with a million dollars of support for innovation. And luckily this team of doctors, Dr. Hajdenberg and Dr. Dvorak, won one of those coveted slots for expanded investment from their hospital system. And they're in the process of expanding that right now too. So it will be first expanded at Orlando Health as one of their signature innovations, but of course the plan is to expand that out and have these innovations benefit other hospitals and systems and patients as well.

Image courtesy of Consystent AI

Teri Fisher:

Is the speech recognition behind it your own proprietary technology that was developed in the lab or does that leverage one of the other current big companies that's doing speech?

David Metcalf:

It's interesting because in the version that was 3D printed, we actually used Siri technology because it was an Apple-based platform. But then when we use the Microsoft HoloLens to do this, to emulate that same thing in a hologram of the Betty robot, we actually use Cortana. So we use the exact same recordings, the exact same speech patterns and flow diagrams of that dialogue, but within two systems to see if there are any differences. And so far it seems like there is no significant difference. There's still more study to be done, but that's what our early results show.

Teri Fisher:

I wish we had something like that here that I could just put into my clinic and help to collect some of the information and disarm some of the patients when it gets to sensitive information. Are there any other key projects that you'd like to highlight coming out of your lab?

David Metcalf:

Well, we're very interested right now in what's going on with the ability to tie in voice and games. And that was one of the things that you and I saw at a recent conference, one of the award winners was the X2 games. And I was really intrigued. That was Nolan Bushnell and some of his team too, that it put together some games using voice. And I thought that was really cool. It really was a way to engage people socially. But we've also been looking at ways that we can engage people in their health using these same techniques. So Nolan and I have had a number of discussions and we've been talking with other groups too. So right now we're in the midst of building some of these games that use voice and voice enablement, to engage people in social play that hopefully helps with their health. One of those environments that we're doing this in is the new Center for Health and Wellbeing that's being opened in Winter Park, Florida, just North of downtown Orlando. And it's a large complex and we're looking at ways that we can enable both the voice and motion-based games in this environment too. So stay tuned. That's something that we're releasing shortly. That's one of the areas that we're pretty excited about.

Teri Fisher:

Sometimes I think it takes a little bit of this extrinsic motivation to get people to change one of their behaviors and games are a really great way to do that. I definitely want to stay tuned for developments in that area. Now I know that there's another area that you have been looking at and that is with blockchain and how that can affect healthcare, and how specifically that affects voice in healthcare. Can you comment a little bit about that?

David Metcalf:

Well, you know, there are kind of two trend lines going on right now in healthcare that are really exciting. One is on the front end, and that's the voice technology for the user experience. But behind the scenes right now, some of the most powerful technology for being able to verify records and trust those records between multiple organizations is the use of blockchain. And this goes beyond Bitcoin and cryptocurrencies and just financial transactions to anything that you might need to trust. The problem with some of this technology, with blockchain, is that it's sometimes seen as a little bit harder to use. There are multiple steps and people have to do certain things to be able to use the technology effectively. If we could pair and marry some of the best of the front end technology of voice with the backend power of blockchain, that's going to start to create some new use cases for us.

Like wouldn't it be great just to be able to ask a question or speak something about a technology transaction that you want to make and then have the power of the blockchain to verify that technology across multiple systems? By systems, I might mean that you could just say a transaction that you want to have happen, like you want to have a telehealth session and all of a sudden it would not only automate the process through a smart contract of contacting your provider and automating that through a voice transaction, but also automate the process of your financial transaction or that being paid for by your insurance company, or being able to know what your copay is and automate the process of paying that through their credit card or cryptocurrency, all in one easy transaction. This is the power of combining two technologies, not just blockchain by itself, not just voice by itself, but how could you have the best of the front end with the best of the backend and make that an easier and more holistic healthcare experience for people.

That's what I think might be really interesting too for us. And also keeping track of that through a blockchain transaction over the course of time.

Teri Fisher:

So are you specifically working on projects that are looking at that interaction now in your lab?

David Metcalf:

We are. We're looking at some of the ways that we can do that with defining what some of those standards might be for the Defense Health Agency and the Navy as well, and seeing where we might use that for the large numbers of people that are doing this either in uniform or that are veterans that we may want to be able to help with their healthcare transactions and figure out what the future of that looks like to the space. This may be a few years away, but of course we're a research and development lab so that's what we're supposed to be doing, looking at how some of this technology is going to come in and how we might serve those who have served us so well as some of the first people that have access to some of this technology and some of the standards that will be rolled out to make this possible.

Teri Fisher:

This is quite a unique thing that we haven't really spoken much about on this podcast, the concept of marrying the idea of blockchain and voice-enabled healthcare technologies. And I know that you've been looking into this quite a bit. You actually have a book that recently came out about this and I was wondering if you could share a little bit about that.

David Metcalf:

Yeah, so HIMSS (Health Information Management Systems Society) asked us if we would write a book for release at their global conference. The book is called Blockchain in Healthcare. We had written a number of other books too, called Connected Health and mHealth for HIMSS. So it wasn't a surprise that we'd be able to pull off a book within a year, but it was quite a challenge because there were so many people doing great things in the space too, both thought leaders who had been working in the past who are also working on present cases, and also some futurists who had some big ideas about what can happen in blockchain. We wanted to make it a very realistic book though and have a lot of real world case studies too. So we enlisted a number of people. We had over 50 authors that contributed to the book, either in case studies or thought leadership, and we curated a book of some of the best thinking in blockchain across a number of different areas.

Teri Fisher:

I was able to have a look at that book and hold it in my hands and it's a great book. It covers a lot of information.

David, thank you so much for spending some some time here on the podcast. You are involved in many incredibly exciting areas of healthcare technology innovation. I really appreciate you taking the time and I'm sure the listeners do too.

David Metcalf:

Thank you Teri. Talk to you soon.

Chapter 21:

Voice First Health Interview: Vocal Biomarkers and the Voice Genome Project

Jim Schwoebel

Teri Fisher, MSc, MD

Editor's Note

As we've seen in earlier clinical chapters, measuring voice, vibration and exhaust can be used in diagnosis. Jim Schwoebel provides an expanded view of these measurements for physical and mental health with details on evidence of disease state sensing including psychosis, Alzheimer's, and Parkinson's. His background and skill guides both the current advanced work he describes and points the way to the future of voice for diagnosis. Concluding with relevant examples, Jim hints at the future of voice and deep learning.

Hear the complete podcast interview with
Jim Schwoebel at:
https://voicefirsthealth.com/20

Teri Fisher:

Jim Schwoebel is the CEO of NeuroLex and he is doing work in the area of voice modeling. They're looking at vocal biomarkers and how these can be correlated with various types of illnesses and diseases. Jim, can we start off by learning a little bit about you and your background?

Jim Schwoebel:

Sure. Happy to share it. So I'm a bio engineer by training. I attended Georgia Tech. And right out of school I actually started a venture fund focused in neuroscience. So I got really into investing in early stage technologies and we found that a lot of our fastest growing companies were in the area of machine learning and security. So we actually invested more into that space afterwards and formed a satellite fund called CyberLaunch in that area. And I was the lead partner there for vetting a lot of the machine learning companies. We've vetted over 400 companies over the span of two years, invested in 11, in the areas of machine learning and security. And so I really have a deep background in investing. But all the while, I've always had a deep passion and interest in the area of mental health.

This goes back to my family. My brother had a psychotic episode halfway through my experience in college and it was very deeply personal and so I was always curious about the cause of it, and the imperfections of the medical system and how we as a community come together to improve the process of diagnosing psychosis. In his particular situation, he actually visited the primary care doctor 11 times over the span of around three to five years and he complained about the same symptoms: things like unclear thoughts, headaches, really vague symptoms that the medical system often misses. He actually visited a psychiatrist multiple times, different psychiatrists, and he was misdiagnosed with anxiety disorders and depression all leading up to a psychotic episode while I was in college, a very severe episode.

I was always curious, could you model data of some sort that he had you know, been on the internet, on Facebook? He had been messaging me on my phone and various ways really caught my attention. A lot of his messages and his voicemails he left on my phone were more disordered leading up to his first episode of psychosis. He started speaking in new words. One of the symptoms leading up to a psychotic episode is something called "~word salad' in psychiatry. So I actually modeled a lot of his early voicemails and it looked like there are patterns and anomalies in the syntax and it's particular words. So I was always curious, could you use voicemail data, and specifically voice data to detect psychiatric abnormalities, and in particular psychosis?

So fast forward to about three years ago, there was a paper published out of Columbia university and IBM's research arm that showed in a high risk group for psychosis you could predict with very high accuracy just with a voice sample similar to my brother's voicemail who would or would not develop a psychotic episode. It was like a hundred percent accurate with 35 patients and followed that with a hundred patients and it was about 85% accurate-ish. They were using models very similar to techniques as I was modeling for my brothers. So it really caught my attention at that point. There's a lot of momentum in the field. There are a lot of other publications and other diseases like depression and Alzheimer's and Parkinson's that show their signals in the voice for these conditions in various ways.

So I actually spun off a company from my machine learning venture fund focused purely in the area of vocal biomarkers and vocal diagnostics with the vision that one day you go to the doctor and particularly our primary care doctor and instead of giving a blood sample - in the case of my brother, he had probably 12 blood samples - you'd give a voice sample and just from a voice file like describe this picture in a phone or on a laptop, you can predict a panel of various diseases. So in the same way that serum bilirubin is measured as a blood marker for liver function abnormality, something like the speaking rate could diagnose something like bipolar disorder. Or in the case of my brother in psychosis, something called the Brunette's index. If it's disordered in the text it's often indicative of that feature.

So we're starting there. And then in the future we're building formal diagnostics through FDA in a similar way that other diagnostics are approved, but we're starting very, very simply there. And over the years we've grown the team. That was about two years ago. We found that the biggest problem is just building data sets. And these data sets are small at academic centers and there's a lot of complexity in voice data as opposed to say heart data or other data, with accents as the community knows, accents, ages, genders, ethnicities, dialects, smoking histories, etc, that can overfit models. So we've really worked hard to overcome these issues and launch some of the largest research initiatives in the world focused on enabling health information with voices. So that's a little context. I thought it was better to tell the story and go from there.

Teri Fisher:

The whole idea of vocal biomarkers is fascinating to me. So, can you tell us a little bit more about what it means to collect a voice sample and how it is used?

Jim Schwoebel:

Sure. So we envisioned this as an in-clinic procedure initially. We think there's a lot of issues taking samples at home, particularly with people speaking away from microphones and using the device not as intended or differently than you'd expect. But the idea would be you go to the doctor, they screen out a lot of other things, so they'd probably rule out liver function issues or other issues with other tests. And then the idea would be they would refer you to give a voice sample in a separate room, sort of like the way a blood sample is drawn guided by a nurse or another healthcare professional, to prompt the voice file and just give some instructions. Usually it's a short test. You have a laptop or a phone. And there's a series of tests, sort of like a survey experience, but with voice. So you speak your responses to a survey. There's often an image for example that you can describe and the task is, describe this picture. Another common task is just describe your day from start to finish for that day. So very, very open ended tasks. For some diseases as well it's important to have alternative tasks, like in Parkinson's disease the power matters.

And so we actually have some tasks, like saying "ah" out loud because there's a lot of work in that area just with power analysis. There are also a few other tasks that we've innovated over the years. The baseline Alzheimer's patients, such as counting back from 300 to 285, or just some count back task for working memory. So the idea is you do a panel of these audio voice responses and it's sent to the cloud or locally in the clinic in case of HIPAA compliance, it's often good to have on premise installations. And then you can get a report back just like you would a blood test and the provider can use that information to infer the health of the patient.

So that's where we're starting. And I think over time we'll find more robust models that then can be used more in at home environments, but we think it's better to have control initially in the clinic so that things are consistent, the operation modes the same, and ultimately it's empowering physicians, right? I think we don't want to replace any physicians. I think this is just another tool in the toolkit for others to use, including psychiatrists in the case of inpatient hospitalizations or other things to assess severity of symptoms and chronic care management.

Teri Fisher:

I have a couple of followup questions on that. So if someone goes in to do this, to give the voice sample, how long does that take? What sort of time commitment is there for the healthcare provider that's guiding them through this?

Jim Schwoebel:

It's less than three minutes, three to five minutes. It's faster than any other procedure. One thing that's remarkable to me when I started this company with our team is that I asked what's the ideal length for a voice sample? And the research shows that the ideal length is something around 20 seconds. And if you get two minutes or three minutes or an hour of audio, it makes really no difference to the model accuracy, which is remarkable when you think about it. So that's the idea. You just have a very simple task, very time constrained, and you just output a model in the case of building a diagnostic later.

And things like the Brunettes index or the part of speech tags or the pause length are very correlated with cognitive symptoms that often are missed. And then in the clinician context, things like dysarthria are often hard to detect. And when you start thinking of it like a blood test or another marker it can really add to helping diagnosing. And, I'm a huge fan of pushing it in primary care. I know that's pretty far away from reality, but I just know that's where patients are going for treatment. So I really think it needs to be there. I'm a huge believer of that, but we're very careful not to over-diagnose patients or make too bold of claims right now. This is a long journey. We have other routes for revenue initially. But ultimately I think this is an area that we think can be embedded in primary care, you know, five years down the line with new codes and everything.

Teri Fisher:

So that's how the person would interact with this from the patient's perspective. And what's happening on the back end, because you said a lot of these questions are open ended, so it must be a difficult task to take all of this audio data and model this. Can you explain how that is done?

Jim Schwoebel:

Yeah. So when I first got into this field, I was new to audio featurization modeling voice analysis techniques. A lot of this research has been hidden for years within nuance and Google research and a lot of the tech companies. And I actually found it was quite difficult to learn on your own. And I actually, as a CEO, learned to code. I actually recently wrote a book on Python called Introduction to Voice Computing and Python to really open source a lot of this work so people can learn how to code and model this data. We build a lot of new feature embeddings. A lot of the audio embeddings are typically things like MFCC coefficients, which had been used traditionally in the speech recognition field for identifying phonemes, for ASR models, automatic speech recognition models.

So we've taken a lot of these techniques and applied them to voice labels and we're using a lot for small datasets, 35 to 100 patients, usually small studies. We typically use old school techniques like support vector machine modeling or logistic regression or whatnot. We look at it either as a classification task. Is it a diseased person or not, or within a scale like the PHQ9 is a scale for depression. So we can look at it as a binary problem or we can look at it as a regression problem and actually estimate the scale itself question by question from a voice file, which is pretty cool. So we really honed in and really I think probably built the world's largest laboratory focused on this. Our chief medical officer is at the University of Washington. We have about 20 research assistants just actively publishing on this work. We just got a paper in IEEE on Parkinson's diagnosis for example. And I look at this space kind of like where the human genome was back when it started. I think we need a voice genome project to make it such that we know all the features in the voice that matter. Kind of like all the genetic code that mattered when the human genome project took off. And I think we're on that journey and really learning every day, new features, new traits that are correlated with voice features and text features. We transcribe the audio as well.

Going back to your question, we extract features from the text and we have something called mixed features as well - like a correlating text features with audio features. And so every day we're learning. I think we're engineering new features for diseases as we know clinical mechanisms and we know what to look for. And building new features for diseases, schizophrenia for example, is a good example of what that would be. It'd be really cool to have a million patients across the world at some point in the far future that have schizophrenia labeled versus controls. We just haven't had the data sets and that's where we're really focused now. And we're looking at the launch of the voice genome project soon, very similar to other projects, to do this work at a larger level.

Teri Fisher:

Would you say that's the biggest challenge right now? Coming up with enough data and getting enough samples to move this forward as quickly as you'd like to?

Jim Schwoebel:

Yeah, 100%. And I can tell you that healthcare is a risk averse field. Obviously health plans don't wanna take any liability and overnight we could curate these datasets. And it's frustrating because you know that patients are on health plans, a lot of them would opt in if they knew how they consent to this, to give a voice sample for their health information and maybe an incentive like a Starbucks gift card or something. You know, they can contribute. I've thought about even revenue share models for our company. Like, if you contribute a voice file and an MRI image, for example, you could get a capitated data royalty if it's quality data upon a commercialized model that we build and put through FDA so that you actually are incentivized. And it's just hard. It's just really hard. I think it's just incentivizing patients.

The privacy implications of this field are very unclear from a regulatory perspective. State-By-State recording laws are odd. They're all complex and I think even Apple and Google and Amazon are figuring out what the landscape will be with GDPR provisioning and whatnot. And also the ethics of it, what is ethical and what is not? How do you label data on a server? I think we're very clear in our terms of use how we model data and how we plan to use data and we don't want to be in a situation like other companies where we're selling data without users knowing how we're using data or even how we're manipulating their data. Like if you give a voice sample on our server and you know age, gender, ethnicity and a lot of health traits, well the users should know our policies. And I think with a lot of the larger tech companies, it's very unclear how they manipulate data. I think this is an increasing problem that I think we're going to start seeing regulation around that. We're, I guess, innovating our terms of use and whatnot, but there are a lot of issues. So I think all these issues create complexity, curating data, getting data sets, and we're at the forefront. So I think you always have to self police and be ethical when you're at the edge of something and we're very careful not to overstep our boundaries.

Teri Fisher:

I think it's great that you're looking at these different issues and not blasting full steam ahead without taking into account these things because you're right, there's a lot that's unknown in this space right now. I'm curious, with these challenges that you just described, how are you actually collecting the voice samples? Where do the voice samples come from right now?

Jim Schwoebel:

We get it from a lot of areas. One is through academic collaborations. We have collaborations, the University of Washington, where we have actually a lot of undergrads going into clinics and collecting data from patients across 13 indications. They go in the clinics and often the provider or the physician says, are you interested in consenting to our study? And then the undergrad works with what I was saying before - having a guided session, right? The undergrad works with the patient who consents to give a voice file and in the format that we've discussed. That's been scaled across other universities and systems and we're doing larger studies at other institutions. So that's one way. The other way is we've created this product called SurveyLex where you can create, design, and deploy the voice survey in the cloud, like a survey monkey survey. And so I think we actually are really at the forefront of audio signal processing and even voice survey creation. I think it's really, really hard to know how to deploy an Alexa skill for example, or a Google assistant action without being a developer. And even I struggle now and I think I'm a pretty proficient Python developer "˜cause a lot of it is optimized for JavaScript. And I feel like this creates a lot of issues with the average Joe wanting to do a voice survey. Well, we really optimized it initially for research use in this area and that makes it so we can create N number of surveys across any place and get a lot of data quickly and partner with pharma companies and SAAS contracts or with even health plans or whatnot to create large datasets.

And they pay us as a subscription to curate them and really work with them. A lot of the pharma companies are looking for new diagnostic markers for depression, for example. And they really like the idea of blind data extraction across many entities to create the most robust model. So that's an area where they're willing to do a SAAS subscription through this product, collect data sets with us. And then at a larger scale, we've done nonprofit collaborations and community and the voice genome project is one that's coming up and we're going to be just launching it and really partnering with as many entities out there that really have reach. We've worked with mental health America in the past, for example. They do 1 million depression surveys on their website each year. And so opting in through their website, it's like a little forum, that's pretty cool to get traffic and get a PHQ9 score labeled with a voice file.

So we're doing stuff like that. And our hope is that at some point we can create the most comprehensive dataset in the world of health information with voices. And that spans way beyond your surveys. We think there are things like brain images where we can measure things or actual sizes of parts of the brain from a voice file directly. None of this work has really been done so we're looking at MRI images, physical information of the brain. We're also gonna look hopefully soon at chemical information like serum cortisol levels and voice samples. So you can imagine having a realtime endocrinology estimate of someone's cortisol levels or even hormone levels from a voice. That would be really cool. That'd be so clinically useful if we found a way to build it robust and accurately.

I just think there are things like that that the medical system has never seen before. There's really no way to pay for it. There's no way to get it done, but there has to be some implication long term where this sort of thing can affect patients and improve outcomes. And really my goal as the CEO of this company at some point is to see this work diagnose patients earlier in the disease pathophysiology process so they don't go down the route of having an acute event like a hospitalization. In the case of my brother, if you're headed towards the direction of psychosis, get early intervention and perhaps even be preventative and really save tons of money for the health system, people are healthier. They're not living with huge chronic diseases. There's a huge burden. We're kind of falling in line with a lot of other digital health companies, but I think this is just a very new innovative way to look at it.

Teri Fisher:

The whole idea of the voice genome project is fascinating to me. Can you speak a little bit more about that?

Jim Schwoebel:

We've been planning this for not that long. My chief medical officer and I have come together and thought, how do we engage external collaborators and entities in a more comprehensive way and also like really centralize this work. I think it's really scattered. There's work at Harvard, there's work at MIT, there's work at Stanford, there's work at ECSF, they're all separate, and so we're trying to create a survey using one of our core products, our SurveyLex. We have a lot of surveys that we're gonna do with it. The first step is just getting a lot of survey information tied to voice information. So a lot of self reported health inventories and things like that, labeled with voice files.

So that's something that I feel like you can contribute to in two ways. I think that if you want to donate your voice and be part of the research study and consent process, we'll have a website up. I'd just reach out to me by email and I'm happy to get you on a list early. And then the other one is if you want to partner as a research collaborator, if you want to analyze this data in some way beyond us, we're very cooperative in our lab and co-publish with a lot of entities. If you want to help distribute this link to others to help get more participants, I think this could be an area where you can collaborate in a research way either as a channel to distribute on a mailing list. That's often a great one, or as a researcher and co-publish with us. Whatever the goal is we look at it as a researcher or a participant in the clinical study. And at the end of the study we'll publish the results. We'll publish all the contributors. I think that's a really awesome thing to do and have hopefully a very similar dataset as 23andme has for genetic information and health traits. We'll have a very similar dataset for voice. And my goal ultimately is not necessarily to keep this all within our company.

I really want to get this work out there. I think this is a new space. I think it needs to be open sourced and I think it needs to be done ethically. So we're very open to third parties. We'd love to see more people in this space, find utility as well as commercialize this work. So I think that's our core mission and core focus, at least initially. And we need to show that this space is credible and that people believe the claims we make, and also we need to publish a lot and really show a peer reviewed publication list, that our work is robust and have large scale population health studies.

Teri Fisher:

Being this is the Voice First Health podcast, the question I'd like to finish off with is what does 'voice first health' mean to you?

Jim Schwoebel:

To me, it means something differently probably than a lot of others. But for me it's really looking within the voice and using that information to improve health care through our work. That's what it usually means to me. It's like, hey, I'm hearing somebody's voice and I'm using that as a way to guide care. It's my knee jerk reaction. But I think for a lot of others, I find that they often associate voice first with Alexa because Amazon sponsors every single conference out there at the diamond level. And Amazon is trying to, I guess, put that image in everybody's mind to associate voice first with their products. So if there's one thing I'd like to throw out there it's that I think voice computing is much larger than these at-home devices.

It's a field that spans way more than just a hardware device. And I think voice assistants are just scratching the surface of the potential of deep learning applied to voice data. And, and I think we'll see some of the work like our work or even other work out there. I'm sure there'll be a lot of other amazing work out there and in healthcare with voice outside of us that really shows that voice first means a lot, something much more comprehensive than just the voice assistant. It means any voice data applied to improve the health system in some way.

Teri Fisher:

When I hear you speak about these kinds of ideas and what the technology can do for diagnostics, who knows where we're going? Maybe there will be pathognomonic voice signals, signals contained in what somebody says and the doctor then knows a particular diagnosis. I believe that voice could become a vital sign - a voice vital sign.

Jim Schwoebel:

Totally. And I think even your sleep quality, you know, we get polysomnography tests. It's $3000-$5,000 per test in the clinic to diagnose somebody's sleep disorder. Well, if you can just give a voice sample every morning at 9:00 am, the same time every day, testosterone concentrations are maxed in the morning. So the fundamental frequency, for example, if measured day over day is more variable, just from a high level you could think, oh, well a more variable fundamental frequency and morning probably relates to sleep quality issues and you probably should go to the sleep doctor instead of relying on really vague inventories like the Epworth sleep scale that are useless. So I think this is where we're at in healthcare and I feel like there's so much we can do to incrementally improve it. Obviously these are exponential changes, but I feel like there's increments and I think the increments are in research for us. I think that's where we have to focus.

Teri Fisher:

Well, thanks so much Jim for coming on the podcast.

Jim Schwoebel:

I'm always trying to evangelize this space and if you feel like you can contribute in some way, just reach out. I think we all can do more. I think there's something anyone can do to contribute to this movement. And really I think it's a movement to get this philosophy embedded at least in research so we can prove that what we're doing can really make the changes that we think they can. So, thanks so much for that Teri. We really appreciate you giving us this opportunity to be on the show.

Chapter 22:

Artificial Intelligence and Voice Analysis: Potential for Disease Identification and Monitoring

Suraj Kapa, MD

Editor's Note

Picking up on the hints of the potential for deep learning and voice from Chapter 21, Dr Kapa leverages his clinical background as a top cardiologist and the use of sound in diagnosis, to present compelling evidence of the future of voice technology powered by artificial intelligence. Starting with an overview of voice and breathing patterns for physiologic analysis, he then provides important background in AI and its history in medicine and automated voice processing. Further exploration of voice/AI for detection of disease states, and evidence from cortisol to mood to Parkinson's and even coronary disease, reveals promise based on current, empirical studies. Future uses could even lead to devices like a recent test in our UCF lab of the Lumen metabolic breath analysis device that unlocks new wellness measurements easy and inexpensive enough for patients to use.

Introduction

Changes in voice parameters have long been associated with other physiologic findings, including autonomic tone, blood pressure, and heart rate. The mechanisms by which other physiologic states may impact voice are complex and multifactorial, but are due to a highly integrated physiology that includes elements such as blood flow, vocal cord innervation, and pressure distribution during inhalation and exhalation that relate immediately to breathing patterns. While traditionally these relationships have been only obscurely defined through associative studies, recent developments of complex, non-linear models using machine learning and deep learning approaches has allowed for the development of programs that may allow for automated identification of the presence or status of a variety of disease states from an individual's voice. (Figure 1) Such approaches may allow for scalable health solutions for detection of the risk or presence of diseases through cost-effective mechanisms such as at home voice assistants, smartphones, or other such technology. In this chapter, we will briefly review some of the mechanisms in how voice and other human physiology interact, what artificial intelligence (AI) is and how it works, and recent work in using AI for disease characterization using voice.

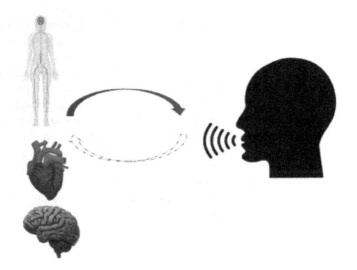

Figure 1. Relationship between physiologic systems and voice. It is well established that abnormalities in a variety of physiologic systems, including the autonomic nervous system, the cardiovascular system, and mood disorders may directly impact vocal characteristics. Evolving data using artificial intelligence approaches supports, in turn, that abnormalities in voice may be used to detect the presence of diseases such as coronary disease, Parkinson's, and depression, likely due to these direct physiological relationships. However, the accuracy of such predictive algorithms remains to be determined.

How do other diseases affect human voice?

A wide variety of vocal features may change over time, including elements of pitch, volume, tone and duration. Pitch is defined as the highness or lowness of sound on a scale; duration is the length of time spoken; tone refers to vocal quality; and volume relates to the degree of loudness. Other specific features such as range and vocal inflections may be derived from voice data. Such information contained within voice may serve as a sort of biometric signature that may differentiate individuals, similar to a fingerprint or retinal scan. [Rogers. Science. 2016] However, even within individuals, voice data may be affected by the presence of other diseases through a variety of mechanisms.

There are well established connections between physiologic state and changes in specific vocal parameters. For example, emotional stress has been associated with increased in the frequency of human voice. [Protopapas, et al. J Acoust Soc Am. 1997; Johannes, et al. Eur J Appl Physiol. 2007] In turn, an increase in voice jitteriness has been associated with the use of the beta-blocker propranolol in a double-blind placebo-controlled study. [Giddens, et al. J Voice. 2010] Similarly, other medications such as levodopa have been associated with changes in vocal parameters. [Pinho, et al. Codas. 2018] These findings and others support the importance of autonomic tone in features of human voice. In turn, many disease processed have been associated with changes in autonomic tone, including coronary disease, blood pressure, arrhythmias, and mood disorders. [Bairey Merz, et al. JACC Heart Fail. 2015]

A recent review summarizes the association between autonomic nervous system function, voice, and dysphonia, suggesting a strong mechanistic association. [Cardoso, et al. J Voice. 2019] Similarly, through a variety of pathophysiologic mechanisms largely mediated through direct effects on the left recurrent laryngeal nerve, cardiopulmonary conditions have been associated with effects on vocal quality. [Mulpuru, et al. Heart, Lung, and Circulation. 2008] This association is known as the cardiovocal syndrome, or Ortner's syndrome, having first been described by Norbert Ortner in 1897 in a patient who exhibited vocal hoarseness associated with mitral stenosis. Other data has supported that features such as heart rate and fluid status may have direct effects on vocal characteristics. [Alvear, et al. Logoped Phoniatr Vocol. 2013; Univer, et al. Ren Fail. 2015] These findings of discrete effects on vocal characteristics through fluctuations in other, seemingly unrelated physiologic parameters, suggests the potential for identifying associations between any of a variety of disease states and vocal findings, though such associations may be highly complex and not easily definable by thresholding for changes in discrete vocal findings alone.

Artificial intelligence in medicine

Artificial intelligence may be broadly defined as the ability of machines to integrate and reason using complex data to arrive at unique insights. In modern parlance, this does not necessarily refer to the ability of a machine to come up with fundamentally unique innovation on its own, but more so the ability to integrate data when paired against a specific outcome to arrive at insights as to how those data may be related. One example of this is recent work in electrocardiography (ECG). While the ECG is well known to reflect cardiac status, in the form of heart rate, heart rhythm, and the presence or absence of certain structural and functional abnormalities, and these states may be easily identifiable by humans with an understanding of ECG interpretation, it is likely that there are subtle features in the ECG reflective of other diseases that may not be so easy for a human interpreter to glean from a standard ECG. However, recent work has suggested that AI methods used on a 10-second, standard clinical ECG, can allow for determination of whether an individual has a low ejection fraction, a risk of future atrial fibrillation, or how old they may be physiologically. [Attia, et al. Nature Medicine 2019; Attia, et al. Lancet 2019; Attia, et al. Circ Arrhythm Electrophysiol. 2019] These are all disease states that would make physiologic sense to impact the ECG in some way, but that do so in such complex, multifactorial ways that it would not be reasonable for a human interpreter to glean those insights while reviewing the ECG during standard interpretation. However, this is where modern approaches such as AI may carry particular benefits in arriving at complex insights in a rapid, automated manner.

What is artificial intelligence and how does it work?

Artificial intelligence techniques can be broadly subdivided into machine learning and deep learning. Machine learning generally engages some amount of human supervision of the data, within which humans may identify features to extract from data for complex statistical models to be derived from. Subsequently, these features are compared against a given outcome. Deep learning is another form of AI that relies on a computer "learning" the relationship between a set of input data and an output, independent of human description of features for the machine to focus on. The theory lies in that after a certain amount of repetitive exposure to a set of input data paired against a given output, if any relationship exists, the computer will learn it and with subsequent exposures to an input, will reliably identify the output. An example of this is differentiating cats and dogs via image analysis. In machine learning, a human reviewer may identify specific features that differentiate a cat versus a dog (the anatomy of the snout of the animal, characterization of teeth, etc) and provide these features to a computer to derive complex statistical relationships that will allow the computer to identify a cat or a dog. In deep learning, one would start with a data set of images of cats and dogs and feed those to a computer paired against information of which images reflect cats versus dogs. Eventually, with enough exposure, accepting that, in general, cats and dogs should be able to be differentiated from images alone, the computer would be able to identify a cat or a dog. On one hand, one may require larger amount of data for the computer to arrive at a robust algorithm to discriminate cats versus dogs using deep learning. On the other hand, particularly in situations where the features that tie an input to a given output are multifactorial and related in complex, non-linear ways, deep learning may be more accurate than machine learning in accurately pairing some input data with a related outcome. There are a multitude of approaches to machine and deep learning with reviews summarizing these approaches for clinicians interested in using them in research. [Johnson, et al. J Am Coll Cardiol. 2018]

History of AI in medicine

The use of AI in medicine is not novel. Neural networks – one of the earliest examples of deep learning – have actually been researched in medicine since the 1980s. Review articles in the 1990s have demonstrated the potential utility of such approaches over standard of care in improving disease identification. [Itchhaporia, et al. J Am Coll Cardiol. 1996] However, these algorithms were not implemented in routine care. There are several reasons for this. The most critical were two elements: 1) integration of computers into medical practice was not as widespread in the form of electronic health records and integrated smart-phone and other such devices; and 2) the computational power of computers was such that training deep learning algorithms using complex data (eg, audio or visual data), would take long periods of time and running developed algorithms in real time would be impractical or impossible. However, the last several years have seen an exponential improvement in computational power, partially through the development of novel integrated circuits, materials to allow for miniaturization of critical computing components, and innovations in the programming and design of computers. These developments have been responsible for the explosion of interest in, development of, and implementation of AI algorithms in medicine. The FDA has recently approved several such algorithms for routine clinical care. In turn, these algorithms are praised for their potential to improve scalability of healthcare delivery, such as in the form of automated interpretation of radiology. However, consideration of the precise ways in which such algorithms should be regulated, vetted and implemented is still evolving. [Parikh, et al. Science. 2019]

Use of AI for automated voice interpretation

The main impediment to integrating AI to recognize the presence of disease-specific characteristics reflected through human voice is the lack of large, well-characterized libraries of voice data from normal and disease-affected humans. Specifically, in order to develop an algorithm, a researcher would require a library of voice data from both individuals without a specific disease and individuals with that disease. Alternatively, if one is trying to study how disease progression may be reflected through vocal changes, a library of auditory data from multiple individuals' voices paired over time against the state of their disease would be required. For example, if one wants to detect blood pressure from voice, one would require multiple examples within specific individuals and across different individuals over time pairing blood pressure against auditory examples of voice. Compared with other examples of using AI in medicine, such as radiology data for automated interpretation, or using the ECG to automatically determine presence of a low ejection fraction, there are no such large repositories of patient voice data in existing health records. As a result, development of such algorithms would require prospective data acquisition and thus be much more resource intensive in both construction and validation.

Current state of use of AI to detect identification of disease states from voice

While the use of AI in voice is in its early stages, there are promising data to suggest the ability to identify presence or absence of various diseases through voice data alone. Areas of specific focus where implementing an AI algorithm to detect presence or absence of disease or in the monitoring of a disease state may include mood disorders such as depression, anxiety, or stress evaluation, or the evaluation of more subtle physiologic data such as the presence or absence of cardiovascular disease. In the former example, recent data has suggested that several features of voice may correlate with measurement of stress. However, while complex machine learning approaches have suggested direct associations, these vocal indices of stress have not been well validated against biomarkers of stress such as circulating cortisol or cytokines. [Slavich, et al. Stress. 2019] Similarly, while specific vocal parameters have been associated with other mood disorders such as depression or anxiety, there are limited data on whether AI algorithms may be able to reliably and automatically determine the presence of acute depression or anxiety from voice alone reliably. [Tasnim, et al. Canadian Conference on Artificial Intelligence. 2019]

In addition to evaluation of states of mood, recent data has suggested that vocal characteristics may be used to discriminate the presence of autistic disorders with an accuracy of 86%, coughing due to pertussis versus other cause with an accuracy of 90%, and the presence of Parkinson's with an accuracy of 91%. [Bonneh, et al. Front Hum Neurosci. 2011; Parker, et al. PLoS One. 2013; Benba, et al. 2015 International Conference on Electrical and Information Technologies. 2015] However, all these studies were done in relatively small patient samples. In turn, recent data has suggested a similar relationship between vocal characteristics and the ability to detect the presence of coronary disease. [Maor, et al. Mayo Clinic Proceedings. 2018] In addition to these studies, recently presented data suggests that there may be an association between vocal parameters and pulmonary pressures, suggesting the potential to track pulmonary arterial pressure using voice data alone. [Sara, et al. Circulation. 2019]

Despite these data, to date, there are no AI systems approved for research or clinical use to automatically determine the presence or absence of disease on the basis of voice alone. Next steps will require the validation of algorithms on larger, diverse populations prior to any consideration of integration into practice. Furthermore, their value needs to be balanced against the risk of both false positives and false negatives. Thus, rigorous research will be required prior to adoption of such algorithms for common use, in particular in ambulatory settings.

How may such algorithms be used?

Ideally, automated voice detection algorithms that allow for the detection or monitoring of disease may be used in non-hospital, ambulatory settings to facilitate cost-effective care. The largest limitations to broad use of such algorithms historically would have included cost-effective systems to record voice and advanced enough computational power to drive algorithms in real-time to interpret vocal data. Modern smart-phones and at home voice assistants provide both an effective means by which to record voice data in real-time as well as to run real-time algorithms on such data either through embedded or cloud-based algorithms.

However, while there is feasibility of such algorithms to be deployed in a scalable, population-wide manner, the potential public health benefits need to be balanced against both perceived and actual risks. Actual risks include those of inaccurate representation regarding disease state. For example, a false negative may lead to excessive comfort regarding the absence of a condition on the part of a patient who may thus not seek medical care. In turn, a false positive may lead to otherwise unnecessary testing. When most such algorithms are developed, they are done in a clinical setting which may not necessarily reflect the prevalence of disease in the general population. Thus, rigorous clinical validation in a hospital setting may not be sufficient to support population-wide implementation.

In addition to the practical implications of false positives and false negatives, one must also consider the social implications of voice-enabled AI at a population level. First, a consumer should be comfortable with such technologies embedded in their home setting. Second, there are reasonable considerations of privacy when recording voice. Finally, if home-based, consumer-facing electronics are being used for disease identification, mechanisms of facilitating referral to appropriate clinicians to address positive findings need to be considered, lest individuals be left with fear of presence of a disease without access to validate the findings.

Thus, while there is much promise in using AI-enabled algorithms to assess presence or absence of disease based on voice alone to offer scalable health solutions, this promise needs to be balanced against practicality of implementation in light of impacts of inaccurate diagnoses, privacy considerations, and implementation issues in terms of healthcare access. Future research will need to focus on many of these social determinants alongside standard measures as to the utility of such algorithms.

Conclusion

Voice is a powerful tool because any human with the capacity to speak does so on a daily basis, tools that can record and that are able to run complex interpretation algorithms off of voice data have become ubiquitous, and newer data are starting to validate the assumptions that disease states may be identifiable through voice information. Such algorithms may allow for scalable technology for the identification of the presence of disease or for tracking the progression of disease. However, population-level validation is still required and acceptability of implementing such products into commonly used products such as smartphones or at-home voice assistants needs to be considered before broad implementation may be considered feasible.

References

Alvear RM, Baron-Lopez FJ, Alguacil MD, Dawid-Milner MS. Interactions between voice fundamental frequency and cardiovascular parameters. Preliminary results and physiological mechanisms. Logoped Phoniatr Vocol. 2013; 38; 52-58.

Attia ZI, Friedman PA, Noseworthy PA, Lopez-Jimenez F, Ladewig DJ, Satam G, Pellikka PA, Munger TM, Asirvatham SJ, Scott CG, Carter RE, Kapa S. Age and sex estimation using artificial intelligence from standard 12-lead ECGs. Circ Arrhythm Electrophysiol. 2019; 12: e007284.

Attia ZI, Kapa S, Lopez-Jimenez F, McKie PM, Ladewig DJ, Satam G, Pellikka PA, Enriquez-Sarano M, Noseworthy PA, Munger TM, Asirvatham SJ, Scott CG, Carter RE, Friedman PA. Screening for cardiac contractile dysfunction using an artificial intelligence-enabled electrocardiogram. Nature Medicine. 2019; 25: 70-74.

Attia ZI, Noseworthy PA, Lopez-Jimenez F, Asirvatham SJ, Deshmukh AJ, Gersh BJ, Carter RE, Yao X, Rabinstein AA, Erickson BJ, Kapa S, Friedman PA. An artificial intelligence-enabled ECG algorithm for the identification of patients with atrial fibrillation during sinus rhythm: a retrospective analysis of outcome prediction. Lancet. 2019; 394: 861-867.

Bairey Merz CN, Elboudwarej O, Mehta P. The autonomic nervous system and cardiovascular health and disase: a complex balancing act. JACC Heart Fail. 2015; 3: 383-385.

Benba A, Jilbab A, Hammouch A, Sandabad S. Voiceprints anal-ysis using MFCC and SVM for detecting patients with Parkin-son's disease. In:2015 International Conference on Electricaland Information Technologies (ICEIT)2015:300-304. Marrakech,Morocco; March 25-27, 2015.

Bonneh YS, Levanon Y, Dean-Pardo O, Lossos L, Adini Y.Abnormal speech spectrum and increased pitch variability inyoung autistic children.Front Hum Neurosci. 2011;4:237.

Cordoso R, Lumini-Oliveira J, Meneses RF. Associations between autonomic nervous system function, voice, and dysphonia: A systematic review. J Voice. 2019. [Epub ahead of print]

Giddens CL, Barron KW, Clark KF, Warde WD. Beta-adren-ergic blockade and voice: a double-blind, placebo-controlledtrial.J Voice. 2010;24(4):477-489.

Itchhaporia D, Snow PB, Almassy RJ, Oetgen WJ. Artificial neural networks: current status in cardiovascular medicine. J Am Coll Cardiol. 1996; 28: 515-521.

Johannes B, Wittels P, Enne R, et al. Non-linear function modelof voice pitch dependency on physical and mental load.Eur JAppl Physiol. 2007;101(3):267-276.

Johnson KW, Torres Soto J, Glicksberg BS, Shammer K, Miotto R, Ali M, Ashley E, Dudley JT. Artificial intelligence in cardiology. J Am Coll Cardiol. 2018; 71; 2668-2679.

Maor E, Sara JD, Orbelo DM, Lerman LO, Levanon Y, Lerman A. Voice signal characteristics are independently associated with coronary artery disease. Mayo Clinic Proceedings. 2018; 93: 840-847.

Mulpuru SK, Vasavada BC, Punukollu GK, Patel AG. Cardiovocal syndrome: A systematic review. Heart, Lung, and Circulation. 2008; 17: 1-4.

Parikh RB, Obermeyer Z, Navathe AS. Regulation of predictive analytics in medicine. Science. 2019; 363: 810-812.

Parker D, Picone J, Harati A, Lu S, Jenkyns MH,Polgreen PM. Detecting paroxysmal coughing from pertussiscases using voice recognition technology.PLoS One. 2013;8(12):e82971.

Pinho P, Monteiro L, Soares MFP, Tourinho L, Melo A, Nobrega AC. Impact of levodopa treatment in the voice pattern of Parkinson's disease patients: a systematic review and meta-analysis. Codas. 2018; 30: e20170200.

Protopapas A, Lieberman P. Fundamental frequency of phona-tion and perceived emotional stress.J Acoust Soc Am. 1997;101(4):2267-2277.

Rogers N. Whose voice is that? Science. 2016; 351: 1140.

Sara JD, Maor E, Borlaug BA, Orbelo D, Lerman LO, Lerman A. Non-invasive vocal biomarker is associated with pulmonary hypertension. Circulation. 2019; 140(Supplement). [Abstract]

Slavich GM, Taylor S, Picard RW. Stress measurement using speech: Recent advancements, validation issues, and ethical and privacy considerations. Stress. 2019; 22: 408-13.

Tasnim M., Stroulia E. (2019) Detecting Depression from Voice. In: Meurs MJ., Rudzicz F. (eds) Advances in Artificial Intelligence. Canadian AI 2019. Lecture Notes in Computer Science. 472-479.

Unvers S, Hardal U, Esertas K, Sezen A, Celikbilek F, Altundag A. Objective analysis of voice changes in a hemodialysis session and its correlation with ultrafiltration. Ren Fail. 2015; 37: 268-272.

Chapter 23:

Roundtable Discussion with David Metcalf, Teri Fisher, and Sandhya Pruthi

David Metcalf, PhD

Teri Fisher, MSc, MD

Sandhya Pruthi, MD

Editor's Note

Wow, you made it! We leverage our lead author/ editor team to unpack the critical themes and "a ha" moments throughout the book. We hope this helps guide your own study and ad-vancement of the science of voice technology for healthcare. Whether you are an academic, in industry, government or nonprofit healthcare, we hope you have found useful details and examples throughout the book. In this concluding discussion, we summarize the common themes throughout the book, including voice as an "operating system" and as a biomarker, the security/ privacy challenges and the future of diagnosis through genomics and AI. Thank you to all of our authors and contributors for their incredible efforts to bring Voice Technology in Healthcare to life for our readers. Enjoy our final thoughts and summaries. Hear the podcast version on Voice First Health and join in the dialog that extends beyond the book. Become part of the voice with #VoiceFirstHealth.

David Metcalf:

Well, welcome everybody. I've really been looking forward to recording this particular chapter as a roundtable for us as authors to come and do a roundup of what we learned through the process of creating this book and some of the key highlights and some of them may be future trends that we foresee to round up and roll up the book as we complete that too. So I'd love to hear from you guys and look at some of the favorite ideas or some of the 'aha' moments that you had as you were reading over, editing, reviewing and writing some of the components of the book too. And I guess maybe I'll start with a few things that were of interest to me. We're looking at a couple of the ideas and concepts that you had, Teri, like voice as the next operating system. I thought of it more as the next user interface or sort of the human centered design aspects of it. But that was really interesting, Teri, when you talked about the voice acronym too and I was wondering if you might share a little bit on that as well too.

Teri Fisher:

Sure. Well, that's a really interesting observation and question, David - is voice a new interface or a new operating system? As I described, I view the different technological changes that we've seen over the years as each being a new paradigm shift, a new operating system. I talked about a text operating system with MS-DOS, to a graphical operating system with MS-Windows, and then a mobile operating system in iOS, and now voice is the next leap forward. What makes it a new operating system in my mind is the fact that specific voice dialogs and use cases will be built on top of the basic voice functionality, similar to how mobile apps were built on top of the iOS operating system. For iOS, the interface is the mobile phone. For voice, the interface in the smart speaker/microphone, and the operating system is the act of speaking. After giving this a lot of thought, I came up with the **V-O-I-C-E** acronym that I think does well to summarize why I think this is a completely new paradigm - the vOS.

The **V** in voice stand for versatile. You can do virtually anything while you're talking to someone. We all know you can talk to somebody, you can have a conversation, while you're driving a car. Those other operating systems, DOS, Windows, iOS - you can't do that. And this is the first time that we're seeing that in an operating system.

O stands for the omnipresent voices around you. We're talking to each other right now. I could be looking one way and yet having a conversation with someone behind me. And for that reason, this is again a completely different set of rules that we're playing by.

I is for innate. As I talked about, we're born knowing how to converse using our voices. And that is very, very different than any other type of OS that we have seen where we had to learn skills, how to use a computer, how to use a mouse, how to use a touchscreen.

C is for contextual. We can pick out very subtle changes, nuances in our voice depending on how we're feeling and depending on our physical conditions at the time. And again, that's not something that can be picked up necessarily when you are typing to someone.

And finally, **E** is for efficient. Speaking is way more efficient than any other type of operating system that we have seen. And when you take those all together, that's what really excites me about voice. I think it's a completely new system that we are living through and it's going to expand from here. I think it's really, really exciting and it's a really fun part for me to talk about.

David Metcalf:

Yeah. And in some of the other chapters from other authors, we really start to see information that touches on that and extends that to almost a science of voice design. And there's been years of data and history and doing this even from the old interactive voice response systems. But that carries into a whole new level of digital interaction and human to human interaction using voice for purposes of health. One of the things that I marvel at too is looking at some of the teams that have stepped forward and the real-world examples where there's actual data from groups like Boston Children's, and of course Mayo and Vanderbilt, the Commonwealth Care Alliance, some of the cases that we have throughout the chapter. And one of those that of course is represented by Sandhya with your work too is really your team at Mayo Clinic. And what you guys have been able to achieve too is really quite remarkable. And I was wondering if you might say a few words about that and the team.

Sandhya Pruthi:

Well, thank you David. It certainly is a real pleasure to be able to work with such a congenial group of colleagues at Mayo Clinic who are committed to our primary value which is to meet the needs of the patient. With emerging technologies, and omni-channel delivery options, we explored the delivery of Mayo Clinic health information and knowledge using voice-first applications. And what was even more exciting was how the team came together across the Mayo Clinic three shields: education, clinical practice, and research, to implement voice-first applications within our institution. The integrated team approach was instrumental in preparing and planning the different projects. And these collaborations needed to come together to make these projects successful and sustainable. And it is evident that the team approach makes a difference.

David Metcalf:

That's great. So are there other 'aha' moments or things that you saw as you were looking at some of the other chapters and authors that really stood out for either of you?

Sandhya Pruthi:

Yeah. There were several "aha' moments that sparked my interest. The first one was the chapter on the laws of voice. It really made me wonder as a clinician if voice activated devices were potentially capable of behaving like humans and having human-like intelligence, should they be held to the same standards to that of a healthcare provider? And the authors presented some intriguing scenarios around voice implementations in genetic testing, pediatric patients, mental health and cognitive decline issues. And so I think we need to be more aware about the integration of voice technology in these categories and the future of the laws and legal implications that we will need to create around the different voice applications.

David Metcalf:

Yeah. I remember meeting Bianca and hearing Bianca Phillips and hearing some of her views on this as she finishes her doctorate on this very topic. And it seems like not just in her chapter, but throughout the whole book, there is an underlying theme of looking at voice and the legality, but also the privacy and the standards that we are going to need to have. Let's face it, it's early days right now and to continue that and look at the, whether it's HIPAA or other laws and regulations that we might need to conform to, and think about as we take all of the promise of voice, but also be very realistic about the potential liabilities or risks within that too. So I think that's a great point you make.

Sandhya Pruthi:

David, another 'aha' moment has to do with the electronic health record and impact on physician burnout. The electronic health record has become almost a barrier and obstacle in my ability to continue to preserve the physician-patient face to face interaction. Here is where I think the chapters on voice technology and advancements using natural language processing and cloud computing can really enhance the clinical interaction and help to reduce the clerical burden so that I can be more attentive to the needs of my patients.

Teri Fisher:

Yeah. And Sandhya, I echo that too. As a clinician, I'm sure we have many of the same feelings in that regard. You know, the whole control of the EHR and the extension of not only that, but also having a voice assistant essentially be the transcriptionist for clinicians - I keep referring to that as the 'Holy grail' for physicians because that's a major pain point. And if we could have AI taking care of those issues for us, we could focus more on our patients. And I think ultimately a lot of physicians wouldn't feel as burned out as they do. So I totally agree with you on that.

David Metcalf:

It's been great to have both of you as clinicians too and into the teamwork. I know Harry and I were talking about more of the business and technology side of this, but to have that well-balanced view, especially as we have a whole section on the clinical enterprise and how voice technology is changing in those particular areas. And I'm so grateful that you guys were able to review those sections and contribute so heavily in those particular areas. Teri, are there other areas that you had 'aha' moments or thoughts about?

Teri Fisher:

Absolutely. The first thing I'll say is that almost every single chapter provided me with an 'aha' moment because each of the contributing authors are such experts in their particular areas and there's so much to learn from each one of them. Myself, being a futurist, I love to look to the future, the innovation, and where we're going in the coming years is so exciting to me. And one of the things that kept striking me as being very interesting is the whole idea of Jim Schwoebel's Voiceome Project, similar to the way we have the human genome project and we've sequenced the human genome and can look for patterns and how that can help us clinically.

This gets into an area, another area that I know you're interested in as well, David, about the whole idea of vocal biomarkers and how we can potentially have a database of voice recordings that could then be analyzed through the AI to look for patterns that may indicate that there's something going on in terms of our health. That is fascinating to me because of the implications that has in terms of voice becoming a vital sign. And as far as I'm concerned, voice could become the least invasive and most easily accessible vital sign, and it can be obtained from a distance. Right now doctor's use blood pressure, temperature and so on as vital signs. But for those vital signs, you have to be in the presence of the person. You have to have a blood pressure cuff on a person, you have to use a thermometer. But just imagine if you had a smart microphone somewhere in your home and it listened to what you were saying. And in real time it was analyzing this vital sign. I think that's extremely powerful and I think it holds a lot of promise for the future.

Sandhya Pruthi:

Teri, I really like the concept of voice as another vital sign. But we do need to be cognizant of the concern around authentication and especially if we aim to prescribe management or treatment options taking into account changes in voice as a vital sign. There are several wonderful chapters in the book around HIPAA and security. I think these are some of the challenges that we're going to encounter with voice-first applications and I'm excited about how some companies are presenting new strategies to overcome these challenges and voice technology will be reliable and trustworthy.

Teri Fisher:

Absolutely. Well said.

David Metcalf:

Yeah. The term voiceprint comes up a few times and instead of fingerprint or a retinal scan and it might also be that voice print with another form, a factor of authentication, multifactor authentication is what is gonna rule the day. Some of the patents that we've seen from Apple, from Amazon, from other companies to start to get into how that multifactor authentication and using voice as one of those means. But you guys both took us, right into the next segment of our questions too with starting to already think about the last section of our book and really even just some of our own thoughts too on the future of voice technology in healthcare too. And I'd love to have us continue some of this conversation on some of the topics that are of interest to us.

I know for me, picking up on what you guys were saying, this detection, there were a few things that I was kind of bummed because I really wanted them in the book, but we couldn't quite get the permissions in time and things like that. Like I got to experience firsthand from some of the leaders at Roche and in Switzerland, some of their early Parkinson's detection apps. And they had things like a two finger tap test on the screen. They had a gait analysis test with the phone in your pocket and they had a tremor test where you held the phone out in front of your hand and if you saw a tremor, but there was one other test and it was a vocal tremor test. If you call the "ahhhhhhhh" test, if you say period, the digital sensors really, if you think about it, they're listening to that stream and can bring you into digital, could actually detect some elements of early signs of Parkinson that may not even be perceptible to the human ear.

So this whole concept of hearables and even what the next generation of a hearing aid might do, or a wearable, like a watch that almost Dick Tracy style of watch that that gives us this ability to one of them that we have in our lab at the University of Central Florida even will allow you to talk to Siri or Alexa. So you don't have to choose which operating system you're on and which voice interaction or which apps that you might have for voice too. Those are all things that are starting to be pretty exciting. And there was a whole chapter on wearables and hearables and voice technology too. There was really forward-leaning and some of these types of topics too.

Sandhya Pruthi:

So when you talk about wearables, David, I know for a fact that many people after awhile get tired of the wearable and are not able to engage with the wearable over the long term. I think what we are looking for is how voice can become a personable and empathic tool and is able to better know me. I would want the voice activated device to know my patient. So that you don't want the voice device to be reactive but rather proactive. Here is where I think artificial intelligence can help personalize voice. For example, could the voice activated device say, "Hey Annie, last week you were describing symptoms where you were feeling down. How do you feel this week?" I think of the voice device as becoming a personalized care team member.

David Metcalf:

Yeah. I have to say something about, one of the things that in my chapter that we went into in a little bit of detail is the Betty robot at Orlando Health. And some of the docs, they're doctors, Julio Hajdenberg and Tomas Dvorak. The robotic interface even comes up to you and tells you a joke and has an animated character looking face to it too. So it's warm and it greets you, but at the same time it starts the actual clinical intake process by linking to your actual record.

Image courtesy of Consystent AI

Once you've identified yourself and starting a distress screening in this case. And for those that know distress screening, if you're a doctor or a nurse, your patient might be a little bashful about sharing details of past abuse or sex or sexual abuse or drug use or things like that. But to a robot that's not going to judge them, they give vocal input that you can actually capture the voice. So you know, whether they're nervous about it or whether they're okay with it. And you start to get some of that emotive power of voice too. But in a nonjudgmental way that's already showing some clinical results of being able to get some better data that then leads to hopefully better diagnosis and outcomes for that patient too. By having this voice-enabled robot in the clinical environment and they've done some actual data-driven studies in their own clinic to prove these concepts out before they take it to the next level and have something that could be integrated into multiple electronic health records systems and maybe make the first part of the experience a little more, at least novel, if not enjoyable for some of the patients that might be coming in.

This is the Orlando Health, UF Health Cancer Center, so you can think about the people's reaction when they're coming in. They might be scared and nervous there. They're wondering if they do have cancer, they're going to be diagnosed or things too, so maybe this helps set them at ease a little bit too. That's one of the examples that we have of that too, that might take that a little bit further than even just a chat bot or some voice interface because it's embodied inside of a robotic system in this case.

Teri Fisher:

That's great. And you know, when I hear you talk about that, I also think of how these voice assistants can not only be leveraged in the clinic to gain information from a patient but also in the home. And one of the things that really excites me is how having these assistants - as they continue to get more and more advanced - will actually begin to take pressure off of the healthcare workers. As a Canadian, one of our biggest issues is overcrowded facilities, overworked healthcare workers. And what really excites me is that I see this as an opportunity to relieve some of that pressure. Because, like I said, as these devices become more advanced and more intelligent, perhaps they can actually start to act as a tour guide to the healthcare system and allocate resources appropriately based on what the person is saying to the voice assistant.

And in such a way, I think they actually can bring health home. The voice assistants will decentralize the healthcare to a certain degree and allow for people to manage their healthcare in their homes. And another thing is, because these voice assistants are relatively so inexpensive compared to other technologies that are out there, what does this mean for people that have trouble accessing healthcare due to cost? Will this be a less expensive way for them to at least start to access healthcare in their homes? And I think that's really interesting as well.

David Metcalf:

The whole area of our book that is on home health and wellness talks about that too. And the idea that you could have this voice companion that does simple use cases like a pill reminder, even some of the ones that we've talked to and seen in the past, like the Pillo, a HIPAA compliance system that you not only can speak to and it gives you reminders, but it can even dispense the pills in a 30 day pill pack that's locked into the back of the device too. So you

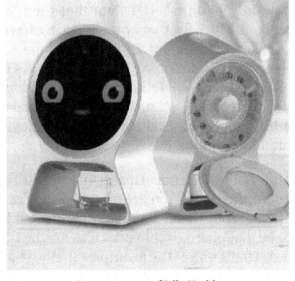

Image courtesy of Pillo Health

start to have more than just the voice and it's the digital linking to the real world and whether that's other forms of measurement or whether that's pill dispensing or things like that, we're seeing the voice interface used in some very unique and novel ways.

Sandhya Pruthi:

Yeah. I really liked this concept of care at a distance. Especially with the voice biomarker space and being able to detect disease when somebody is at home and provide the timely alerts and triage to guide the individual when and where to seek help. I think voice activated devices could really make a difference to improve timely access and revolutionize healthcare opportunities for those at home.

Teri Fisher:

Yes, and as I said in my chapter, I see the voice system evolving to the point where it essentially is a triage nurse. And so you can talk to your device at home, it'll ask you some questions and it'll help you to determine the level of urgency of your concern and where is the appropriate place to go. Or maybe you don't have to go anywhere. Who knows? Maybe eventually the voice assistant opens up a line directly to a healthcare provider and you have that dialogue right through your speaker. The possibilities here really are endless. I love thinking about where we're going in the future.

David Metcalf:

Yeah. Well I think that it's the triage nurse for the home, but also it's how to have the point of physician burnout and helping you guys in the clinical setting too. Some of the examples that we've seen use things like voice within augmented and virtual reality for even something as simple as being able to have a checklist in the corner of your eye on an augmented or virtual reality system, like a Microsoft HoloLens or Magic Leap or one of those, but maybe even more so. One of the most advanced samples we saw, my friends and I actually decided to invest in it, and when we saw it in Israel is the Holoscope. It's actually a hologram surgical pre-planner that you can do for things like interventional cardiology where you have the Holoscope and you don't even have to put on goggles.

You just have a C-clamp that pulls down. You can see through and see the heart and you can actually see it functioning and have all that planning. But you can talk to it. You can say "Holoscope, turn the heart 127 degrees" and it does it. So if your hands are busy because you're doing things either in surgery or surgical pre-planning, you have yet another way to interact with the systems that are around you and do almost some of the same things that your other staff that are in the OR might be doing for or with. So it's going to change the clinic as well as the home, don't you think?

Teri Fisher:

Oh, absolutely. Whenever I speak about voice technology to a group of health care providers, I literally ask, "What specialty are you and what does your workplace look like?" And we can start brainstorming ways that voice technology is going to disrupt everything that everybody is doing. And it's really only limited by our imaginations at this point. I liken this era to when the mobile phone first came out and people were coming up with all these interesting ideas and there was essentially a gold rush to create the next app. Well, I think that we are essentially entering that era now with voice, where people are starting to realize the power of it and for those that are creative and can start to think of ways that this can impact their care, we're going to really see over the next couple of years an explosion of health-related voice skills or actions or whatever you want to call them. That is, getting back to what Sandhya was saying, as long as we can deal with the very critical issues of privacy, security, authentication, the ethics behind it, and all of those issues which are so critically important. But it's tremendously exciting.

The other thing I'll say is that another part of the book that I find fascinating is the idea of designing for voice. We had a couple of chapters that looked at how you craft dialogues so that you can develop the rapport with a patient and to keep them engaged. How do you ask a question so that patients aren't meant to feel embarrassed, but at the same time brings them along some type of dialogue that is efficient and has an ultimate goal to help them with their care? So there was that element from Ilana and also the whole element of bringing in audio, not only voice, but sound from Audrey's chapter on how sound can be such an important part of the voice and audio healthcare experience. And I know that, David, you were interested in her ideas about vibrations from sounds and how that can impact people.

David Metcalf:

Yeah. I found that to be an exciting part of this too because there are so many things that you can do with that, with potential analysis. And it's just opening up a whole new world for us. I think too, as long as we use it correctly. So those are some of the things that we've got to look at, the positive aspects of the future that we want to point towards. And also be very mindful of the negative aspects of the future too that we want to steer clear of too. I think you've pointed out a few of those as well. Sandhya, how about you? Are there other things that struck you?

Sandhya Pruthi:

Yeah, in terms of the future, I think of voice applications as a way to free up my hands so I can focus on face to face care during the clinical encounter and utilize voice to help with documentation and ordering tests or even medication prescriptions. Voice technology and natural language processing can transcribe my clinical assessment into the electronic record. But now imagine you're in an operating room and you are operating using robotics, and how the voice application can help to organize and coordinate the different processes within the operating room and in essence be part of the operating system so that things could be done more efficiently, utilize less resources and potentially even reduce the cost of care.

David Metcalf:

I love that you brought up the cost of care and some of the things that voice holds some promise and maybe some perils to in value based medicine and some of the other future trends that aren't necessarily technology trends, better practice trends, the Quadruple Aim. How do we look at better, faster, cheaper care that doesn't burn out physicians? And it's very, it keeps a very humane view of how we care for you. The clinicians and healthcare workers too. I think that there's some areas that voice could help it in those domains too. Don't you guys?

Teri Fisher:

David, those are great points and I think a lot of what we have spoken about really addresses what you were just speaking of - the fact that we can create personalized medicine through these voice assistance as they begin to authenticate our voices more and more accurately, the fact that they are relatively inexpensive, the fact that they are the next operating system, the fact that they can be so beneficial in the home, in the clinic, in the operating room, in the ER, all over the place. Obviously I'm a big proponent for voice and we've tried our best to cover in this book a cross section of what is happening today, and where we're going in the future with voice. And I think this is just the beginning and it's extremely exciting when you consider all of these different factors that we've talked about.

Sandhya Pruthi:

And you know, let's not forget what is most important around voice and healthcare and that we always want to come back to the patient and the patient-physician interaction. Voice applications will be able to preserve that interaction and reduce physician burnout by enhancing documentation in the electronic medical record or reminding patients about discharge instructions or even helping to address anxiety when the patient is at home. The voice assistant can be a trusted part of your care team and can get the right information at the time when they need it.

David Metcalf:

Yeah, that's great. And then the way that this will affect the business, that Quadruple Aim that I was mentioning to value based medicine and looking at some of those outcomes. I think it'll be great in the future as we start to look at how some of those outcomes are achieved in the clinical setting too. And maybe in the business of healthcare too. So those are some things that we'll continue to dialog on too. And I think see some good examples over the course of time. The last example that I had thought of too, again, that we didn't really get a chance to get all the permissions on, but there was a real highlight of the Amazon Alexa conference that we all were at in the early part of the year, was looking at how Nolan Bushnell had created an award-winning game that includes voice as the primary game master, a driver to that and some discussions that we all had with, with Nolan as a strong futurist founder of and gave Steve Jobs his first job had to someone like that who really thinks about the future is thinking about these crossroads of games and the interaction and the patient engagement it could create and health and artificial intelligence.

And then we had Brian Roemmele, another noted futurist talking about that. And even looking at the quantum aspects of this and how you can really create next generation solutions. Hearing from people like that really sets a course for the future and can have all of us, even if we're somewhat skeptical about voice, believe that there is some interesting interactions that are going to be present in the future when you start to combine things as far as biomarkers and wearables and games and artificial intelligence, the medical Internet of Things, as Harry Pappas often says too, that you would have all coming together in really unique ways. So that was probably the one from a future perspective when I saw those guys talking, just riffing about the potential for this, it really got me excited about the promise that we have in this area. And I've been so thankful to work with all of you who have such strong ideas on this too, as coauthors as we put this this unique book together to.

Teri Fisher:

Well, thank you. And I just want to echo that and say here publicly that it's been a real treat writing this book with all of you. And I hope that the reader, the listener, has got a little taste of where we think health is going with the added aspects of voice.

David Metcalf:

That's great. And just from that standpoint almost to end where we began, a couple of notes about this book too, we're not only doing a hardcover edition for the shelves at HIMSS and to be sold online, but also there's the online version of the book and the ebook version that's available through Amazon and available through Google books and through Apple iBooks, but also an audio book version and a interactive version that's planned as well too. And I just want to say a thank you to you, Teri, in particular for being so gracious to include some of the Voice First Health podcast interviews that you've had from notable industry experts and even where we've transcribed those into the hardcover and electronic versions of the book too. It's so nice to be able to have that warmth and passion that comes through in either the spoken or the printed word while it's interspersed with chapters that are written with scientific evidence and case studies. Hopefully that gives the reader and the listener a good balance of those different styles and even uses orality along with literacy to convey some of the meaning.

We don't want to be hypocritical to not do a voice-based version of his book or have voice elements to this type of book on this particular topic too. And it's been so fun to work with you guys in that capacity too and to mix these different variations of human interaction and data and science together too.

Sandhya Pruthi:

Oh, I would love to end with how much I've enjoyed working with you David, Teri, and Harry on this incredible book. Our collaboration exemplifies that it definitely takes a village.

David Metcalf:

Well, that's a great way to end that too. And again, thank you all, live from Warsaw and from Vancouver and Mayo Clinic in Minnesota. We've got three countries represented too, so another example of the power of coming together across the globe. Thanks so much, you guys.

Index

A

C

D

E

F

G

H

I

M

P

R

S

T

U

V

X

Y